Institutions and Politics

Edited by Peter Nedergaard
and John L. Campbell

Institutions and Politics

Festschrift in honour of Ove K. Pedersen

DJØF Publishing Copenhagen
2008

Institutions and Politics
Festschrift in honour of Ove K. Pedersen

First edition 2008

DJØF Publishing is a company of the
Association of Danish Lawyers and Economists

Cover Design: Morten Højmark
Cover painting by Jens Birkmose: Painting with no name (250x210 cm)
i the meeting room of Center for Business and Politics,
Copenhagen Business School. Reproduced with permission.
Print: Narayana Press, Gylling
Binding: Damm's Forlagsbogbinderi, Randers

Printed in Denmark 2008
ISBN 978-87-574-1814-9

DJØF Publishing
17 Lyngbyvej
P.O.B. 2702
DK-2100 Copenhagen Ø
Denmark

Telephone: +45 3913 5500
Telefax: +45 3913 5555
E-mail: fl@djoef.dk
Internet: www.djoef-forlag.dk

Table of Contents

SECTION 2: Politics and Ideas

SECTION 3. Politics and Business

Contributors

Susana Borrás is Associate Professor at the International Centre for Business and Politics, Copenhagen Business School, Denmark. Her research interests are centered on two main overlapping areas, namely, the governance of innovation and EU governance. Recent publications focus on the design and rationales for innovation policy, the theories and patterns of innovation systems, regional and cluster policies, and new modes of governance in the EU

Anker Brink Lund is professor of Media Management at CBS International Center for Business and Politics, Copenhagen Business School, and former chair of Journalism at the University of Southern Denmark. Current research primarily in varieties of journalism and institutional competitiveness in regional media markets

John L. Campbell is the Class of 1925 Professor in the Department of Sociology at Dartmouth College. He is also Professor of Political Economy at the International Center for Business and Politics, Copenhagen Business School, and Adjunct Professor of Political Science at the University of Copenhagen. His research interests include comparative political economy, globalization, and institutional theory. His recent work includes *The Rise of Neoliberalism and Institutional Analysis* (Princeton University Press, 2001), *Institutional Change and Globalization* (Princeton University Press, 2004), and *National Identity and the Varieties of Capitalism: The Danish Experience* (McGill-Queen's University Press, 2006).

Francesco Duina is Visiting Professor at the International Center for Business and Politics at the Copenhagen Business School (Denmark) and Associate Professor of Sociology at Bates College (USA). His most recent publications include *The Social Construction of Free Trade: The EU, NAFTA, and Mercosur* (Princeton University Press 2006) and articles in the *Journal of European Public Policy, Comparative European Politics, European Law Journal,* and *Economy and Society.*

Eric Gleave is a sociology graduate student at the University of Washington. His other research projects include developing dynamic social network methods, the bases for early modern revolts, simulation studies of cooperation and corruption, and discerning social roles in online discussion spaces.

Carsten Greve is Professor with special responsibilities in public management and public-private co-operation at the International Center for Business and Politics, Copenhagen Business School. He has previously been at the University of Copenhagen and Aalborg University in Denmark. His main research interests include public management reform, governance, privatization, contracting, and regulatory reform. His most recent books include The Challenge of Public-Private Partnerships. Learning from International Experience (co-edited with Graeme Hodge, Edward Elgar 2005) and Contracting for Public Services (Routledge 2007).

John A. Hall is James McGill Professor of Sociology at McGill University, and Visiting Professor at the University of Copenhagen – in both Political Science and Sociology. He is the author of many books, and is currently completing a biography of Ernest Gellner.

Henning Jørgensen is Professor of Political Science at Aalborg University, Denmark. He is former director of the ETUI (European Trade Union Institute) in Brussels (2003-2006) and former director of CARMA (Centre for Labour Market Studies at Aalborg University). His main fields of interest are policy analysis, neo-institutional analysis, European and Nordic labour market and social policies and welfare reforms. Recent publications include: Flexicurity and Beyond – Finding a new agenda for the

European Social Model, 2007 (edited together with Per Kongshøj Madsen), and Consensus, Cooperation and Conflict – The Policy Making Process in Denmark, 2002.

Lars Bo Kaspersen is Professor of Political Sociology and Comparative Politics, at the International Center for Business and Politics, Copenhagen Business School. He specializes in comparative historical sociology, political sociology, and social theory including state formation, globalization, associative democracy, warfare, and the origin of the welfare state. Among his recent publications are »Globalization and Institutional Competitiveness« (Co-authored with Martin Marcussen, University of Copenhagen). *Regulation and Governance*, vol. 1, No. 3, September, 2007, and »The Formation of the Danish Welfare State: Decisions in the State of Exception« in John A. Hall, John L. Campell & Ove Kaj Pedersen: *National Identity and the Varieties of Capitalism*. McGill University Press, Montreal, 2006.

Edgar Kiser, Professor of Sociology and Political Science at the University of Washington, has published papers in sociology, political science, economics, and history journals on topics including the bureaucratization of states, the development of voting institutions, the bureaucratization and centralization of tax administration, and the methodology of historical sociology.

Peter Kjær (Ph.D., Stockholm University, 1996) is Associate Professor in the Department of Organization at the Copenhagen Business School. His research interests include: business journalism, management knowledge and institutions, public organization, and strategic communication. He has published on these topics in Journal of Economic Issues, Scandinavian Journal of Management, and Business History. His most recent publication is »Mediating Business. The Expansion of Business Journalism« (CBS Press 2007), which he co-edited with Tore Slaatta. Currently he is Director of the Center for Health Management at the Copenhagen Business School.

Per Lægreid, Professor at the Department of Administration and Organization Theory, University of Bergen. He has published extensively on central government, public sector reform, administrative policy and institutional change in a domestic, Scandinavian and international comparative perspective.

Cathie Jo Martin is professor of Political Science at Boston University. She is the author of Stuck in Neutral: Business and the Politics of Human Capital Investment Policy (Princeton University Press, 2000), and Aktivering af arbejdsgiverne: Arbejdsmarkedets svage i Danmark og Storbritannien (Activating Employers), Aarhus, Denmark: Aarhus University Press (2004). She has written articles appearing in journals such as the American Political Science Review, World Politics, the British Journal of Political Science, Comparative Political Studies, Governance, and Politics and Society. Her research interests covers politics, business, and institutionalist theory.

Peter Nedergaard, M.Sc. in political science, University of Aarhus 1985. Ph.D. in political science, University of Aarhus 1990. Ph.D. in business administration, Copenhagen business School 1990. Professor in European Regulation and Politics at the International Center for Business and Politics, Copenhagen Business School. Peter Nedergaard's key research interest is the political economy of European integration. Among his recent publications are »Blocking Minorities. Networks and Meaning in the Opposition Against the Proposal for a Directive on Temporary Work in the Council of Ministers of the European Union«, in Journal of Common Market Studies 2007 and »Which Countries Learn from Which? A Comparative Analysis of the Direction of Mutual Learning Processes within the Open Method of Coordination Committees of the European Union and among the Nordic Countries«, in Cooperation and Conflict 2006.

Ulrich Schmidt-Hansen is special advisor at the Danish Ministry of Finance. Previously he has held positions at the University of Copenhagen, the Danish Ministry of Economic and Business Affairs and the Danish Tourist Board. He holds a Master Degree in Political Science, Aarhus University. He specializes in public mangement, governance, organizational theory and the welfare state. Among his publications are »Distributive conflict and the fate of corporatism in Denmark and Sweden« (forthcoming, co-authored with Mette Anthonsen and Johannes Lindvall), »*The* *fight for autonomy – public management in Denmark*« (Co-authored with Søren Aalund) Jurist- og Økonomforbundets Forlag (2005) and »The modern state under pressure« in Lars Bo Kaspersen (edt.) »*Globalization on the wrong side*« Frydenlunds *Forlag* (2005).

Leonard Seabrooke is Associate Professor in the International Center for Business and Politics, Copenhagen Business School, and Adjunct Senior Fellow, Department of International Relations, RSPAS, The Australian National University. His book publications comprise *US Power in International Finance* (Palgrave, 2001), *The Social Sources of Financial Power* (Cornell UP, 2006), and *Everyday Politics of the World Economy* (co-edited with John M. Hobson, Cambridge UP, 2007). Len Seabrooke's research interests are in political economy, economic sociology, and institutional theory.

Sven Steinmo holds a chair in Public Policy and Political Economy at the at the European University Institute (EUI) in Florence, Italy. His most recent books include: »Growing Apart? America, Canada and Europe in the 21st Century« (co-edited with Jeffrey Kopstein) and »Restructuring the Welfare State« (co-edited with Bo Rothstein). He is currently finishing a major project that examines the political, social and economic consequences of economic integration or »globalization« in Japan, Sweden, Germany and the United States titled, The Evolution of the Modern State.

Runolfur Smari Steinthorsson, Professor and Chairman at the Department of Business Administration, University of Iceland. He has some publications on central government, but his main work has been on organization and strategy, both domestically and in a Nordic comparative perspective.

Baldur Thorhallsson is Professor of Political Science and Chair of the Institute of International Affairs and Centre for Small State Studies at the University of Iceland. His research focuses particularly on small-state studies and European integration. He has published a number of articles and books on small states in Europe, European integration and Iceland's foreign policy.

Preface

A festschrift is a celebration and commemoration of an individual's professional achievements. In this case, the honoree is Ove K. Pedersen, Professor of Comparative Political Economy and Director of the International Center for Business and Politics at the Copenhagen Business School.

This festschrift is divided into three sections. Each one addresses some of the most important themes that have concerned Ove in his research over the years. These are institutionalization and institutional competitiveness, politics and ideas, and politics and business. We have made only minor editorial changes to the papers in this volume. Hence, American and British spellings are kept intact.

We would like to thank all of the contributors to this volume. They have all benefited over the years in various ways from their associations with Ove. Their contributions and the volume as a whole symbolize their gratitude to him. We would also like to thank Mette Skovbjerg Jensen for the index of the book, Wilfried Roloff from DJOEF Publishing for intensive collaboration concerning the publication of the book, and Jens Birkemose for allowing us to use one of his pictures on the front page.

Peter Nedergaard and *John L. Campbell*
Frederiksberg and Hanover, October 2007

Introduction

John L. Campbell and Peter Nedergaard
Professor, Dartmouth College, USA and Professor, Copenhagen Business School, Denmark

Ove K. Pedersen's oeuvre covers an impressive range of fields in which he has developed considerable intellectual expertise. These include political and state theory, institutional analysis, discourse analysis, European integration, Danish political economy, comparative political economy, philosophy of science, political philosophy, public administration, institutional history, and more. We cannot review all of these here, especially since his career, we suspect and very much hope, is far from over. But it is well worth noting some of his more important contributions to at least some of these fields.

To begin with, his work on institutional analysis and comparative political economy has had considerable impact on social science in Scandinavia and beyond. For instance, he is largely responsible for making the intricacies and peculiarities of the Danish »negotiated economy« model of politics and political economy known to scholars and students outside of Scandinavia. Ove revealed to many how virtually all aspects of political and business decision making in Denmark during the post-Second World War era involved close consultation and consensus-oriented interaction among representatives from the state, organized labor, business associations, and often other groups in society. This was more than just the centralized corporatism for which other countries, such as Germany and Sweden, were well known. This was a set of increasingly inclusive practices that had been institutionalized since the 1970s in response to the problems of stagflation, and that were transformed and decentralized since the early 1990s in response to the challenges of economic globalization and European integration. Perhaps most notably in this regard is his early work in the late 1980s specifically on how the Danish political economy was organized as set of institutionalized negotiation, campaigning, policy-making, and discursive processes, which he described as a negotiated economy (e.g., Nielsen and Pedersen 1989, 1990; Pedersen 2006b). But a keen interest in these matters is also evident in some of his more recent work on the rise of neoliberalism, for example, and how it affected the Danish political economy (Kjær and Pedersen 2001). It is also present in some of his latest work on the sources of Denmark's institutional competitiveness in the global economy (e.g., Pedersen 2006a, 2006b).

Behind much of this work lies an interest in institutions, how they constrain political-economic decision making, and how they change. Some of this work has been theoretical, such as his writing on neoliberalism's effect on national political economies (e.g., Campbell and Pedersen 2001). Some of it has been more empirical, including his work on the transformation of national systems of public administration in the Nordic countries as a result of European integration (e.g., Pedersen et al. 2004) and his research on the development of labor markets in post-communist Europe (Pedersen et al. 1995).

Although Ove has paid close attention to how the formal aspects of institutions operate and change over time, he has also argued adamantly that an important part of understanding how institutions function requires us to attend to their discursive aspects – that is, how taken-for-granted meaning systems, linguistic codes, and styles of interpretation affect how actors respond to the world around them.[1] Indeed, in a particularly perceptive essay he challenged proponents of institutional analysis with nine questions designed to force them to acknowledge and then incorporate into their work critical thinking about the role of discourse in understanding how institutions, especially states, were organized and operated (Pedersen 1991). Among other things, he argued that an analysis of discourse is necessary in order to understand what institutions really are, how they change, how they can be differentiated from organizations and networks (and how states can be distinguished from

1. Undoubtedly, studying with Louis Althusser in Paris was influential in the development of Ove's interest in discourse. After all, Althusser was much concerned with the ideological apparatuses of the state and the power that they exuded, not to mention the ideological underpinnings of political and economic institutions in general. His reading of Paul Riccour, John Searle, and others has also been influential here.

economies), how actors create meaning and are constituted as subjects, and how institutional rationality is socially constructed. In many ways, this essay, which was published in 1991, foreshadowed many of the key debates that are in vogue today among political scientists and sociologists regarding the nature of institutional change and the role of ideas, broadly construed, in all of this.

The emphasis on institutions, discourse, and the like is evident throughout Ove's career. Some of his earliest work was about the development of Danish state and political institutions. It was conceived in part in terms of the evolution of political discourse. Notably, he conducted very detailed empirical studies on the development of Danish labor market institutions, how individuals were constituted through discourse as individual market actors with certain rights, and how such markets were conceived in the first place. This work was necessarily historical and covered a period of Danish history that stretched back to the beginning of the absolutist period several hundred years ago. In the same vein, he has written about Danish constitutional issues both in historical and contemporary terms.

Perhaps his most obvious contribution to an understanding of discourse is his work on political communication. This is not surprising insofar as he worked as a journalist in Denmark and as a foreign correspondent prior to becoming a professional academic. He also studied political communication for a while in the United States. This led to a keen interest in the discourse of politics, the institutions that shape political and public discourse, and, more specifically, the relationship between the media and politics. All of this culminated in a major study of political journalism in which he argued that the media in Denmark had become detached from the political party system during the 1970s and 1980s; had become more autonomous and competitive; and, thus, had started to cultivate a new relationship to politics. Rather than *reflecting* the agendas of the political parties with which it was associated, the media took on a more important role in *setting* the political agenda and, therefore, in a sense regulating politics. It also began to serve as a vehicle for identifying and publicizing more immediate political problems and scandals of various sorts (Pedersen et al. 2000). Importantly, he viewed agenda setting as a kind of collective accomplishment of a number of media and political actors engaged in mutual interactions.

Ove has also conducted studies and written much about the philosophy of science, political theory, and more. Some of this has been for the general public rather than a narrower academic audience. For instance, perhaps his most well known writing among the general public has been on the nature and problems of democracy in Denmark during the post-Second World War era (Pedersen et al. 1996). Here he revisited Danish political history and refocused it on key institutions. In particular, he showed how an integral part of this history involved the articulation of a kind of socio-economic ideal, which had become very much a part of Danish national identity. This ideal had come to permeate central institutions (e.g., the parliamentary system of governance, the constitution, etc.) but also less obvious ones, such as formal and informal local political orders – institutions of great importance politically due to the fact that Denmark has long been a decentralized society compared to other Scandinavian countries. Institutions of the European Union were also important. The point here was that the challenge for politicians in the 1990s and beyond would be to manage and coordinate these multi-level constitutions, orders, and institutional logics much as a juggler needs to keep many balls up in the air simultaneously.

It should be obvious from all of this that Ove's intellectual interests are both broad and deep. His publications are voluminous. And over the course of his career he has trained and worked with a small army of graduate students who have since gone on to successful careers in academia, politics, business, and public administration. Indeed, his contributions to scholarship – as well as his contributions to the training of a young generation of leaders and scholars in Denmark – are truly impressive. He is especially well-known and popular as a lecturer in the classical style – presenting the big, sweeping, historical picture but arriving at statements about the modern challenges of things like Europeanization, public management, or governance today.

Ove's career trajectory and professional accomplishments aside from scholarship per se are equally trenchant as he has been an initiator and founder to several innovative research networks like Center for Public Governance (Center for Offentlig Styring; COS) at Copenhagen Business School as well as the present International Center for Business and Politics at Copenhagen Business School in 2004. He is also one of the founders of Forum Europe and Forum Competitiveness where academics, politicians, trade unionists, and business executives meet on a regular basis and exchange views.

Finally, Ove has been one of the scholars most engaged and quoted in the public debate in the Danish media. This has also led to literarily hundreds of public speeches all over the country to labor unions, business executives, politicians, journalists, and others. In this regard, he is truly a public intellectual.

References

Campbell, J.L. and O.K. Pedersen 2001, 'The Second Movement in Institutional Analysis', in J.L. Campbell and O.K. Pedersen (eds.), *The Rise of Neoliberalism and Institutional Analysis*, Princeton University Press, Princeton.

Kjær, P. and O.K. Pedersen 2001, 'Translating Liberalization: Neoliberalism in the Danish Negotiated Economy', in J.L. Campbell and O.K. Pedersen (eds.), *The Rise of Neoliberalism and Institutional Analysis*, Princeton University Press, Princeton.

Nielsen, K. and O.K. Pedersen 1989, 'Fra blandingsøkonomi til forhandlingsøkonomi. Mod et nyt paradigme?', in K.K. Klausen and T.H. Nielsen (eds.), *Stat og Marked. Fra Leviathan og usynlig hånd til forhandlingsøkonomi*, Jurist- og Økonomforbundets Forlag, Copenhagen.

Nielsen, K. and O.K. Pedersen 1990, 'From the Mixed to the Negotiated Economy: The Scandinavian Countries', in R.M. Coughlin (ed.), *Socio-Economic Perspectives*, M.E. Sharpe, Armonk, NY.

Pedersen, O.K. 1991, 'Nine Questions to a Neo-Institutional Theory in Political Science', in *Scandinavian Political Studies*, 14(2), pp. 125-148.

Pedersen, O.K. 2006a, 'Negotiated Economy: Corporatism and Beyond', in J.L. Campbell, J.A. Hall and O.K. Pedersen (eds.), *National Identity and Varieties of Capitalism: The Danish Experience*, McGill-Queen's University Press, Montreal.

Pedersen, O.K. 2006b, 'Denmark – An Ongoing Experiment', in J.L. Campbell, J.A. Hall and O.K. Pedersen (eds.), *National Identity and Varieties of Capitalism: The Danish Experience*, McGill-Queen's University Press, Montreal.

Pedersen, O.K., B. Jacobsson and P. Lægreid 2004, *Europeanization and Transnational States: Comparing Central Nordic Governments*, Routledge, London.

Pedersen, O.K., et al. 1996, *Demokratiets Lette Tilstand*, Spektrum Paperback, Copenhagen, (paperback edition of publication 1994).

Pedersen, O.K., J. Hausner, and K. Ronit (eds.) 1995, *Evolution of Interest Representation and Development of the Labour Market in Post-Socialist Countries*, Cracow Academy of Economies and Friedrich Ebert Stiftung, Cracow.

Pedersen, O.K., P. Kjær, A. Esmark, M. Horst and E.M. Carlsen 2000, in *Politisk Journalistik*, Forlaget Ajour, Århus.

SECTION 1

Institutionalization and Institutional Competitiveness

CHAPTER 1

Institutional Competitiveness and its Analytical Foundation – In the writing of Ove K. Pedersen

Henning Jørgensen

Professor, Aalborg University, Denmark

Time Consciousness and Political Strategies

Political role models shift quickly (Scharpf and Schmidt 2000; Schmidt 2002). So do dominant political strategies and world views. In this respect, time is like a harmonica: the nearest can sometimes become remote and the remote can feel very close and appealing. In times of rapid change, a year or a decade may seem to belong to the past before it is even over. This is the way many people seem to feel. But the lack of a sense of history and of a historical perspective on new developments entail the danger of narrow-mindedness. Distance in time is required as a guide in helping to sift the important from the unimportant events and developments, and to devise clear criteria for assessment. This is also the case for political discourses and strategies. Times are changing in our ways of describing reality and in our political and professional ways of influencing developments.

It was Michel Foucault who, in his book on the birth and development of the human and social sciences (*Les mots et les choses*, Paris, 1966; published in English as *The Order of Things*), spoke of the nineteenth century as an age characterised by *the consciousness of scarcity*. It was the age of

Adam Smith (at least in terms of posthumous influence), Malthus and Ricardo – not to mention Karl Marx – an age full of hope in the wealth of nations but also fear of overcrowding, of greed for nature and the idea of diminishing returns. The concept of *work* came into being, and the dominant opinion was that work and (limits to) the wealth of nations were closely interrelated.

The last hundred years, and especially the last half-century or so, have been characterised by a very different economic and social environment, with less severe problems and new political ideas, the development of social protection systems and strong public intervention designed to balance adverse developments. Welfare states embedded and ameliorated the development of competitive economies. Now, *employment* became the principal integration mechanism in society, and political developments ensured that social risks were socialised to a considerable extent. Social citizenship was to be realised also by combating unemployment and giving people social rights and income replacement at an adequate level.

During the recent decades of militant neo-liberalism and neo-conservatism, however, faced with new and severe labour market and social problems, we have been living in an age of *scarcity of consciousness,* marked by the emergence of information-gathering and processing problems – and of marked ignorance about the fundamental needs of working people. For the most part, this ignorance is attributable to central decision-makers and employers at both EU and national levels: those responsible for keeping the economy competitive and for securing welfare in society (Sabel and Zeitlin 1997).

However, some layers of the working population seem to share this scarcity of consciousness, celebrating opportunities for choice and individualist strategies and preferring exit possibilities to collective voice. The same applies to many social scientists, and perhaps particularly economists. Knowledge producers are trying to describe and consolidate a moral and social order with the help of concepts and strategies borrowed from the business world alone (corporate governance, flexibility, benchmarking, and so on), thereby also de-politicising social issues.

This should be of concern to most people. But, increasingly, social risks are being individualised: now *'employability'* is a catchword and the central policy concern. The lack of jobs is no longer the main focus; rather, it is the individual's prospects for bringing him or herself back onto the open labour market, and this is often seen as a matter of morality and goodwill. 'Make work pay' policies are designed to penalise failure to take one's own responsibility for being unemployed (Serrano Pascual and Magnusson 2007). A new definition of full employment is being offered: facilitated access to work for all (also single mothers, part-timers, students, disabled workers, people on social assistance). We are witnessing the de-socialisation of problems like unemployment and poverty. At the time of writing. about 16 million people in Europe are still officially registered as unemployed. This is the reality: the 16 million wage earners have, to express it colloquially, 'been given the finger' by the invisible hand of the market. *The language of the market* – its clichés and ways of thinking – is now creeping into every pore of society and setting all human relations into a pattern of egocentric behaviour. 'Only your own preferences and resources count.' The social ties binding people together on the basis of mutual recognition are not necessarily equivalent or compatible with concepts such as contract, rational choice and maximisation of utility.

Looking at the *current political strategies* being followed at EU level and at the national level in most European countries, it is difficult to find more than a few places where social security, social investment and social understanding in general are awarded a central place. Social policy has to give an economic account of itself. Greater social inequalities are even being talked about as increasing the dynamism of society, thereby creating a road to better competitiveness and economic growth! This can be seen as another aspect of the scarcity of consciousness today. The central political message is that the economy has to be revived before we can even think about social progress and social cohesion. The EU Commission, headed by Mr Barosso, appeared to share this false understanding and flawed strategy when re-launching the Lisbon Strategy in 2005: it seems ironic that the richer society becomes, the less, we are told, we can afford socially! Inequalities are welcomed on this basis. However, in these terms one might wonder why the economy is not performing better now, given that during recent decades social deregulation has taken place, neoliberal discourses and policies have mushroomed, and inequalities have grown. This ought – according to conventional wisdom – to have resulted in the better performance of the European economies. The most obvious result, however, is huge redistribution from wages to profits.

The wage share, calculated as the share of wages relative to profit earnings, has been steadily falling for the last 25 years, as figure 1 shows (calculations based on Eurostat data):

Figure 1. Development of adjusted wage share EU 15 1960-2005 (%)

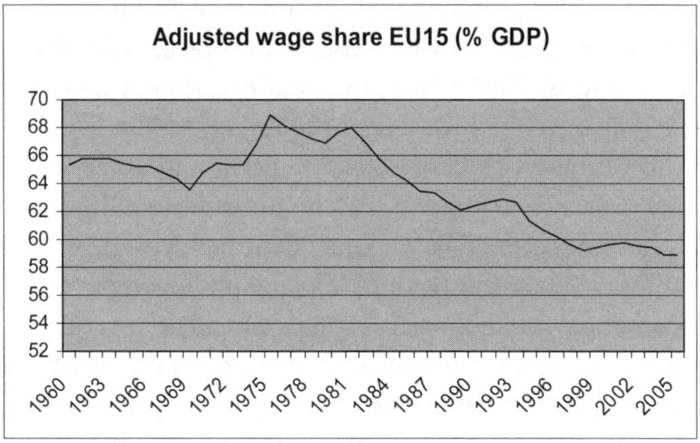

A decrease of 10 percent points of GDP in wages relative to profits since the beginning of the 1980s indicates redistribution from wage earners to owners of capital. We have been witnessing a rapid decline in wage earners' share of the wealth of nations. Seldom before have profit increases been so high. Never before have European societies been so rich. Non-liberals will say that never before have the greed and hunger for more profits been stronger – and more uncontested. This is an amazing change in consciousness. There are few political objections to such rapid profit growth, despite the fact that millions of people are without a job and adequate welfare is unavailable to large parts of the population in Europe. This, indeed, reflects a different climate of political consciousness – or a lack of social consciousness and justice. Equity no longer stands at the centre of policy aims and obligations. However, inequality is not to be measured on a vertical scale alone – that is, in relation to economic standards – but also on various horizontal and more qualitative scales, in terms of social strains, lack of recognition, loss of self-esteem, embarrassment and so on. Authorities and public opinion seem to be ignoring these new challenges or even to be circumventing them by means of a moralistic discourse which questions the individual's economic morale and willingness to participate in the labour market, for example, by referring to the unemployed and those who lack money and 'social capital' as 'problem groups'. Only the micro features of the labour market on the supply side are looked at. If people are not active themselves, they must be motivated by strong incentives and punishments, according to this policy advice. The focus is on institutional rigidities in the labour market and obstacles to further profit creation. Social systems must be »modernized« – preferably with the help of New Public Management reforms – and the size of the public sector reduced.

Increasing numbers of people are perhaps forgetting the conditions under which we can live together in a just and decent way. Many people across Europe have cumulative experiences of bad jobs, poor pay, discrimination, unemployment, social exclusion and even poverty. Part-time work and temporary and low-paid jobs – as well as precarious employment relationships – are increasing in number, especially in Southern Europe and the UK. And in the new EU member states the situation in the labour market is often just as problematic. Atypical employment is not only an insecure relationship, but it also provides few or no career prospects or opportunities for vocational training, and it can disqualify workers from social benefits because of the eligibility criterion of permanent employment. In the case of low wages or part-time jobs, net incomes are often smaller than unemployment benefits. A large part of the workforce is having great difficulty participating actively in the labour market or doing so in a socially inclusive way. At the same time, sluggish growth in the economy and a lack of progress in productivity compared to the figures stipulated in the EU's Lisbon Strategy make it clear that most European countries are not performing very well. The situation was very severe during the years 2001-2005, but even over the last two years of slowly rising prosperity and growth, the situation has not changed that dramatically. Economic growth and welfare are still problems in most parts of Europe. The »structural competitiveness« is often being questioned by neo-liberals and neo-conservatives. More reforms and public cuts are needed according to this position.

But this unsatisfactory situation is not the case in the Scandinavian countries. On the contrary, the economic crisis of the late 1980s in Denmark and the even deeper ones during the first part of the 1990s in Sweden and Finland have been conquered, and now the Scandinavian countries have won reputations as true success stories. A few years ago, those countries were portrayed as rigid, sclerotic and non-sustainable (Olson 1990; Wilensky 1985) in times of globalization and Europeanization. But now they are once again regarded as best performers when it comes to combining economic growth and stability with generous welfare, equity and high employment. Wage earners seem to be employable, and the political strategies adopted are not purely market-oriented. Poverty is practically unknown in these systems, precarious employment relationships hardly exist, and people are enjoying rising welfare transfers and services. Taxes reach world records and people still seem to be happy. Even neo-corporatist arrangements are being re-activated. And the wage share has not fallen as is the case in the rest of the EU 15.

This looks like a paradox to neo-liberal economists, politicians and commentators. How can such countries with institutional rigidities, »over-regulated« labour markets, high taxes, comprehensive public sectors and corporatist structures be competitive at all?

To those who share the concerns expressed in the introduction to this research note, an explanation now seems to be found in the concept of »*institutional competitiveness*«, as developed by Ove K. Pedersen and colleagues (Campbell, Hall and Pedersen 2006; Campbell and Pedersen 2005, 2001; Pedersen 1993; Pedersen and Campbell 2007, 2006, 2005). Institutional competitiveness stresses processes in »the negotiated economy«, and by using the Danish case, it is demonstrated how good results are produced. The formal definition of institutional competitiveness sounds like this: a system's »capacity to achieve socioeconomic success as a result of its political and economic institutions« (Campbell and Pedersen 2005: 4). The concept seems to represent an alternative understanding to the economic orthodoxy of the day, offering a social and institutional interpretation of political strategy and lending credibility to a social consciousness and innovative and welfare-friendly policies. The concept calls in remonstrances to the language of the market. »Institutional competitiveness« might not offer an alternative pathway to the future, but it reduces many of the concerns about a »race to the bottom« in terms of labour, environment and social standards, and points to the importance of social investment in public policies. Social consciousness is included. The concept is attractive not only because it promises an alternative evaluation standard for policies (and not having politics reduced to »business«), but also because it highlights how welfare is embedded in frames (institutions) and content of policies (competitiveness in a broad understanding).

»Institutional competitiveness« is an impressive construction, unfolded in intellectually informed and creative analysis, and capable of attracting much interest and support in discussions about political strategies and the performance of »models« (EU versus the US, and the Scandinavian countries versus the rest of Europe). It also tries to contribute to the »Varieties of Capitalism« debate (see Crouch 2005; Hall and Soskice 2001; Pierson 2001; Schmidt 2002). The *normative* potential of the concept is beyond doubt great. And the timing of publications has been splendid as well. The time is right for the renewal of concepts and outlooks; people are looking for alternatives to the bankrupt neo-liberal view of welfare states and labour markets which dominated the debate over the last two decades.

But what about the *analytical* consistency of »international competitiveness«? Does it stand the test of critical examination of construction principles, internal coherence, and operational usability? I will start considering some of these questions in this article in order to pay tribute to the works of Ove K. Pedersen. It is only one of the progressive elements in his many scientific contributions – often balancing theoretical and empirical analyses – but it is considered to be an innovative, complex and path-breaking concept, clearly with more than professional appeal.

Concept, Analysis and Construction Principles

The initial question for the development of the concept of »institutional competitiveness« was this: what makes nations successful under circumstances in which neo-liberal solutions do not seem to be accepted any longer or able to produce the positive results promised? What are the hidden secrets behind the success of, for example, Denmark in coping with common problems in a globalized economy and in a European context in which countries try to compete with each other? Can a special DNA pattern for competitiveness be found? The answer is, according to Ove K. Pedersen, yes; and by pointing to the institutional arrangements governing the economy, including traditions in public policy coordination, the most decisive elements have been found. The neo-liberal ideas and strategies have not been transferred to every European system and especially not the Scandinavian ones. Denmark is a splendid example of a strong competitive system, with its »flexicurity« system in labour market arrangements (Jørgensen and Madsen 2007; Madsen 2005, 2006) in which neo-liberal elements have never dominated. This will document that more kinds of capitalism exist and that developments are path-dependent.

Ove K. Pedersen is not only describing elements in the Danish negotiated economy and the successful operations of the system, but is claiming to explain the ways in which institutional competitiveness is produced. He joins the new institutional wave in social science research (Guy Peters 1998) but stresses the coordination mechanisms built into the systems strongly. Denmark is treated as a deviant case in dominant political strategies and system developments in Europe. Denmark is also compared to the US system, stressing social policies in the first case as opposed to market oriented solutions in the US (Campbell and Pedersen 2005). In particular, institutions that coordinate labour markets, vocational training and skill formation, and industrial policy in Denmark are highlighted in relation to the operational functioning of this learning system. Institutions develop similar capacities in neighbouring policy fields. The long history of a system has a profound influence on the short history. Structural conditions have been created over many decades which give guidance and restrictions to present actor choices. These conditions can be of an institutional, organizational, and discoursive nature. The coordination system in Denmark brings comparative advantages to the small country. But Ove K. Pedersen is not simply confirming that history and experience matters. He is eager to explain that every economic system also comprises an element of »gambling« (Pedersen 2006b: 456). This has also been a Danish speciality to operate. As the country was changing and evolving into a small and homogenous state, its geopolitical and economic policies became adaptive, and at the same time social cohesion became a dominant political project. Later on, the institutionalization of policies paved the way for the independent development of competitiveness.

The central explanatory variables used by Ove K. Pedersen in his analysis of the genealogy of the negotiated economy relate to processes and compromise structures: specifically, he uses the three processes »learning«, »leading« and »linking« (Pedersen 2006a and b).

Learning is all about interpretation and monitoring by leading social and political actors. In Denmark a socioeconomic framework of meaning to which all actors refer has been developed, but this has happened slowly, allowing collective actors to find their own interpretations and positions. The knowledge gained is cumulative and, consequently, experiences are stored in the collective memory, in macroeconomic and microeconomic databases, always updated and accessible. This is collective – not private – knowledge which is at stake. Actors learn how to be influential and accountable at the same time.

Leading addresses the question of how knowledge is disseminated and utilized. Here, leadership is all important, as to Ove K. Pedersen the array of special interests must be united in one common expression. Secondly, leadership is important because of the need to be adaptive in a small economy; at the same time, considerable gambling on the part of the leaders must be carried out. The decision-making activities of the leaders are future-oriented and all-encompassing – but still tricky.

Finally, *linking* encompasses the coordination activities of actors and institutions, bringing policies to work together with the help of negotiation games and combined programming at different levels. Social pacts and daily negotiation activities comprise the same kind of linking procedures. As Denmark is a strongly decentralized society, many of these linking activities involve local and regional actors, but it is strategies for national action that count when talking about institutional competitiveness.

Negotiation systems have been developed and knowledge helps to link and coordinate policies »in order to improve Denmark's comparative advantages by devising and taking advantage of various institutional complementarities« (Pedersen 2006b: 464). He finds that the Danish negotiated economy has been developed »for the purpose of institutionalizing and organizing institutional complementarities« (*ibid.*: 465). Talking about the purpose of a system without specifying actors expressing these purposes brings a certain danger of functionalist bias into the analysis. The quotations might indicate that I find some of the analysis of Ove K. Pedersen to be a bit functionalist in nature; and, surprisingly, he even postulates that the negotiated societal model of Denmark has been created in order to follow this very purpose of developing institutional complementarities. Then, a teleological type of explanation might be signalled here. It is not always clear whether the epistemological basis of Pedersen's analysis is consistent; is he using causal, genetic, functionalist or teleological explanations, or how are those different types of explanations brought together in different kinds of investigations and for which purposes?

In defining the complementarities mentioned he follows Hall and Soskice in their definition: »Two institutions can be said to be complementary if the presence (or efficiency) of one increases the returns from (or efficiency of) the other« (Hall and Soskice 2001: 17). This win-win situation is surely a possibility, but to presuppose that this is all there is to it in Denmark and that only complementarities are to be found is another thing. Conflicts and contradictions build into the political processes and the policies seem to be marginal and normally impossible if we follow Ove K. Pedersen's formulations strictly. He is much too wise not to know that this is the case. Often he is keen on analyzing conflict ridden processes and decision situations in his commentaries on the politics of the day. Actually, he knows more about power relationships and power asymmetries than most political scientists in Denmark. But the explicit formulations in his scientific writings do suffer a little from functionalist ways of thinking as indicated above. This is not to say that this will damage the concepts proposed and used in concrete analysis. We need to take these concepts very seriously, and I will try to present some critical but, hopefully, solid comments on them in the next section.

First, we have to scrutinize Ove K. Pedersen's concept of »institutional competitiveness« by looking at the construction principles and the use of these in the analysis. He is in fact using three kinds of elements in his construction of the concept. These are:

a) *the entrepreneur or the experimental actor*: heroic efforts of actors – most often leaders – to take the decisions and responsibilities needed in order to secure adaptation and development of competitive advantages. Leading is the key to learning and linking. Lack of competence of the ordinary people in doing this must be presupposed. Why? What kind of documentation exists that demonstrates that »the people« are unable to understand and react adequately in complex decision-making situations? It is relevant to point to the role of ideas and choice in bringing change to a system, and Pedersen has done this, but is it only the privilege of the leaders, the elite, to do this? I seriously doubt that this elite orientation by Ove K. Pedersen denotes a strong mistrust in the competence and judgement of ordinary people, but perhaps his »elitist« training in 1968 Paris and the Marxist-Leninist readings during the 1970s are reminiscent here of »cadre« thinking? It is presumably a serious effort to explain the crucial role of the most significant political actors, and they need to be daring and vigorous. It could, however, look as if there is a problem with conceptualization of »the entrepreneur«, partly removing him, her or them from relationships of power, influence and path-dependent actor strategies. The relationship to the practice of deliberative democracy and consensual decision-making does not seem to be established in an unquestionable, precise manner. Danish decision-makers have seldom been »heroic« in nature; rather, they have typically acted in pragmatic and non-ideological ways. Most historical analyses tell us that there has never been much room for manoeuvre for individual actors and entrepreneurs in Denmark, as common decision-making is mediated through alliance formations and compromises (Christiansen et al. 2006; Jørgensen 2002). You could claim that it is precisely the collective wisdom of social groups and social partners that have produced most of the relevant decisions and multi-faceted arrangements which now count as the »institutional complementarities« in Denmark. Again, this has very seldom happened without the involvement of vested interests and conflict-ridden processes.

b) *the return of classical politics*: partisan politics, party systems, and renewed coalition formation comprise a central explanatory axis in Ove K. Pedersen's work. This is, however, not only a question of reinventing parliamentary democracy; it is also a return to neo-corporatism, social pacts, and common discussions on power and influence. Although he believes in both an »explosion« of traditional politics, having almost all types of questions politicised, he also thinks that a kind of »implosion« of politics has taken place, giving traditional political actors the chance of regaining power and influence in the national system. In reality, the analysis shows that more channels of influence are being used: the numerical, representative government channel, the formal corporatist channel, and informal channels with lobbyism, media exposure, segmentation, and coalition formation as elements. This gives the system a lack of transparency, but it also allows easy access to all kinds of actors to influence politics in different arenas. *Low power distances in Danish society* count for much of the democratic mood and practices. But during recent years politicians have been trying to regain power by recentralizing policies and restrengthening formal political decision-making at state, county and municipality level. Parliamentary democracy and deliberative democracy exist peacefully together in the analysis of Ove K. Pedersen. The historical analysis talks of a change in the socio-economic discourse of the 1980s and the 1990s towards an open economy and fighting low »structural competitiveness«. He thinks a new policy understanding has been developed, together with new policy instruments giving systematic aspects of the negotiated economy new policy traits. »Structural policy« – cross-border coordination efforts, negotiations, and policy flexibility – is also being developed in order to strengthen politics and reunite official decision-makers. The 1980s and the 1990s are, to Ove K. Pedersen, a period of formulation of new strategic policies and formation of new, politically monitored implementation processes.

c) *the public sector as the most important societal arrangement*: According to Ove K. Pedersen, the public sector has gained a new meaning and importance in recent years: a situation in which only marginal utility understanding of public activities (expenditures) were common has changed into a new way of seeing »complementarities« in market mechanisms. This creates the comparative advantages mentioned for countries and is allowing the enterprises favourable conditions to operate in. This is fostering competition for three reasons or functional elements: firstly, income structure and taxes; secondly, the organizational structure; and thirdly, the expenditure structures. All are functional to the enterprises as they do not have to bear the burden of high social expenditure, rigid organizations, or unfavourable public expenditure. For example, investments in child care facilities are most functional to the participation of women in the labour market and to the family structure, facilitating effective resource allocation and productivity. It is argued that a new understanding of public expenditure as social investment is evolving. And here the Scandinavian countries with a huge public sector represent an alternative to the dual model found in Central Europe or to the German model (with the private sector growing in size and importance). Social innovations are regarded as institutional traits of progressive economic systems, Ove K. Pedersen tells us. Change and innovation seem to be equivalents in his conceptualization, and the public sector is in a pivotal position in terms of fostering productivity and »competitiveness«.

But is competitiveness, understood as complementarities, just another way of expressing the positive functions public policies – decided upon by heroic leaders and confirmed by social actors – can have in the economic system and especially on the competitiveness of enterprises? This is to be clarified. Are the decisive societal indicators here not productivity and efficiency, leading correspondingly to profitability? Is it possible to find more kinds of construction principles behind the concept of institutional competitiveness? And in case, what is the possible understanding of productivity and efficiency? Again more interpretations are possible. And, in my opinion, all bring some kind of ambiguity or even conflict to Ove K. Pedersen's concept of institutional competitiveness, as I shall argue below.

Before turning to this crucial question, I will address *institutional coordination and learning,* which are central to Ove K. Pedersen's conceptual framework. His description of the processes within the negotiated economy is often highly sophisticated and always well informed, but his explanation concentrates on the question of knowledge, learning and linking. One can follow him in pointing to the fact that information, knowledge and cognition are crucial, because without some common understanding and sharing of a cognitive ideal, it will be impossible to unite actors and make decisions. Learning is always at stake and leading is involved too because information and knowledge never disseminate themselves and because different propositions and signals must be united into more common messages. Leadership has always had two important functions to perform, namely accountability and coordination. Different conditions as to accountability prevail in the private and public sectors, but coordination is a common function which has to be carried out in ways suitable for the individual organization and policy field at stake.

This does not imply that you have to coordinate in a highly hierarchical way; it can also be done on a more horizontal basis. But someone needs to take action and leadership is vital. The coordination mechanisms built into the system have been assessed as the most important factors in explaining why Denmark has not had a neo-liberal revolution in recent years and why the negotiated economy is performing so well at present.

However, in conducting this analysis, I think that Ove K. Pedersen omits the most important and most difficult element: *cooperation*. Is his scarcity of consciousness as to mutually binding collaboration pronounced? To some extent, yes. Cognition and coordination can more easily be brought to share a common denominator; it is much more difficult with cooperation because here you need actors to develop and choose strategies that are not competitive and do not lead to confrontation. Competition must be abandoned and cooperative strategies implemented (Axelrod 1984, 1997; Rothstein 2003). And this again requires mutual trust by the actors. If social capital, mutual trust, is not developed to a high degree, it will probably not be possible to enter into cooperation games: actors will be gambling alone. The development of collective intelligence will be blocked. Opportunism will mushroom and damage the efforts of cooperation.

Collective decision problems are embedded in those processes. The difficulties stem from the fact that *social traps* can easily develop even if all actors agree from the start that there will be added value by cooperating. The mechanisms at work can be described like this: initially, all actors agree that cooperation will create a win-win situation, bringing added value to everyone. Problems will arise then if all the other actors or institutions involved cannot be trusted to enter into the cooperation game in an honest manner, for it would make no sense for you to do so yourself: the assessment of the interaction might then – on a rational basis – be that now you had better just take care of your own interests. And the result will be that no comprehensive and mutually binding cooperation can be established. Everyone will suffer because of the lack of trust in each other. Everyone needs to choose to cooperate if a solution is to be found. Otherwise, a social trap will emerge.

Rationality rests on institutional conditions and collective actor strategies. Ove K. Pedersen's analysis ought to have had the concept of cooperation brought into play in connection with the assessment of the well performing negotiated economy. Here it is precisely the (Danish or Scandinavian) ways of overcoming social traps in political and professional processes characterised by generalised trust and cooperative strategies that have brought common solutions and consensus to innovation. Coordination mechanisms are not enough because they just synchronize understandings and actions in ongoing decision processes, and they do not unite actors in attaining the development of »*Strategiefähigkeit*« (Scharpf 1997) in the system. It is cooperative adaptation – not coordinated adaptation – that has accounted for the successful development of the Danish negotiated economy over the last 15 years (Jørgensen 2002; Magnusson, Jørgensen and Dølvik 2007), and this is a much more ambitious and more difficult task than simply developing knowledge sharing and having learning implemented. This, in my opinion, is one of the secrets of innovative decision-making and implementation of public policies in the transformation of the Danish system from crisis in the 1980s to the present prosperity and well-balanced environment. The Danish negotiated economy is illustrative of a common prerequisite of cooperative arrangements leading to common and consensual solutions. Cooperation games are part of establishing and developing what Goethe called »*Wahlverwandschaften*«, attractive choices of collaboration partners (Crouch 2005: 55). They form complementary institutions, expressing the paradoxical mix of contrast and similarity. Rituals and relationships should be familiar to actors as they seek difference in the established order and try to act in innovative ways. Future collaboration is anticipated in the calculations and choices made.

Institutional Competitiveness and its Analytical Foundation

Innovation, in the understanding of Ove K. Pedersen, is determined to be contextualized and is always connected to change. Reforms and reform programmes are for him embedded in the relationship between social innovation and output of policies, but these relationships can be of many different kinds. Working within the tradition of Hall and Soskice's Varieties of Capitalism paradigm, Ove K. Pedersen sees liberal and coordinated capitalism programmes as combinations, and he understands these as hybridisation of strategies. The institutional complementarities in explaining costs and benefits of the different combinations are decisive. More sophisticated concepts can be brought into the analysis, but fundamentally the central idea is that a centre working with »building blocks« (business and knowledge regimes, regulation and policy regimes, and a competitive public sector) will bring competitive advantages to the system. National competitiveness is defined by the way in which economic, political and cultural institutions cope with change and challenges, and how they do this in a better or worse way than other nations. Institutional competitiveness is – as the Danish case shows – an economy in which negotiation processes and knowledge sharing (learning, leading and linking) foster productive conditions for growth and welfare.

The central concepts are competitiveness and institutional. Of these, the first of these might seem to be the most unambiguous one, but this is actually not the case. Competitiveness can have quite different meanings as soon as you go beyond the neo-classical way of interpreting it in traditional economics. Although constantly invoked, the meaning of the word competitiveness is unclear. Let us consider some of these possible interpretations of the content of the concept.

a) Competitiveness = a competitive firm

Normally, you will understand by this a firm which secures its market share or expands through sales and profitability. Unproductive firms will simply be forced to leave the market through the adjustment and clearing processes. The market works efficiently and effectively. There might be more ways of competing: through improvement of productivity, low wages and poor working conditions, through entrance barriers or by enjoying dominant positions within the market. Reactions and actions as to prices and quantities steer adjustment processes that will restore balance and develop competitiveness. We all know of this textbook interpretation and there is no reason to go into further detail. The approach is consistent and non-contradictory on its own premises.

b) Competitiveness = the whole economy

In analogy with a firm, an economy can be considered competitive if it maintains its share in world markets, or if it »pays its own way« in the world. This is the central thought of Ove K. Pedersen, and he also offers an explanation for this: institutional arrangements and knowledge sharing within the economy. But this is a problematic analogy because countries are not like firms: they are not managed like them, they do not behave like them, and the consequences of policies are quite unlike market clearance processes. It is an intuitive understanding of competitiveness and having, politically, positive connotations connected. Denmark is performing better now than most other European countries and the EU is performing better than the US in trade surpluses, so – intuitively – it must be because of the institutional competitiveness. Countries might try to »compete« with each other with the help of better quality products, low wages, poor working conditions and entrance barriers or by commanding dominant positions within the world market. But: »unproductive« economies are NOT forced out of the market. Countries continue to exist; they perform well or not so well. They solve problems and do this in different ways and more or less successfully. There is no market working.

There are quite *fundamental differences between a firm and an economy:* Firstly, *firms are in competition with each other, dependent on the size of the economy, sector etc. but an »unproductive« economy cannot be killed off by market competition. You might have a reservation as to foreign exchange quotations, but this does not fundamentally change the argument.* Not all economies can show export surpluses at the same time (and even the meaning of the concept "excess of exports" might be a bit unclear too, being dependent on relative strength of demand). Secondly, unlike firms, *countries benefit from the success of their »competitors«:* the more economic prosperity grows in Germany, Sweden, the US, the UK and other countries with which Denmark has important export and import relationships, the more Denmark and Danish firms benefit from such situations. For countries, it is not a zero-sum game at all. And thirdly, *the role of multinationals* ought to be brought into the picture as well if we are going to discuss how real competition takes place. Who owns companies in different countries? This question is closely related to the one about the political opportunities for controlling and regulating the activities of global enterprises. These differences between firms and the economy as a whole should make it clear that no analogy can be justified. Therefore, the concept of »institutional competitiveness« as a macro concept of the economy has some severe or unsolved problems.

c) Competitiveness = market competition

Competitiveness can, alternatively, be understood as the amount of *market competition*. This seems in fact to be what much of the EU's Lisbon Strategy is about, especially since its revision in 2005. But such an approach or interpretation amounts to linguistic »sleight of hand«: whether more competition will lead to more economic success or »welfare« for a negotiated economy is a matter of faith. This understanding implies that the negotiated economy (or socio-economic model) which comes closest to the model of full competition in the textbooks is also the most competitive. In the Lisbon Strategy this is seen as a way of improving competition, realizing the internal market, liberalizing industries, reducing state subsidies, and reforming the public sector (Ferrera 2005). You could say that the means are changed into goals, all depending on your belief in a liberal socio-economic model. There is a danger of granting an unfair advantage to neo-liberal points of views. But, clearly, this has not been Ove K. Pedersen's intention.

d) Competitiveness = productivity

So, finally, we could take the concept of competitiveness as an alternative word for *productivity*. Normally, higher productivity makes it possible to produce goods and services more cost effectively. Goods and services will be cheaper the more you improve production per working hour, implying that a higher output per head will result. On a national scale, however, there is no clear connection to competitiveness understood as trade performance. Unit labour cost can be compared, wage trends and exchange rates taken into consideration as well, but no direct and undisturbed connection to national performance, economic growth and welfare can be identified. Productivity and improved employment might also be substitutes. The translation of competitiveness into productivity must be regarded as quite unclear and dangerous when seen from an analytical point of view. The relationship to living standards and general welfare is much more important in the present case.

The analytical meaning of Ove K. Pedersen's »institutional competitiveness« rests – in my opinion – on a problematic or false analogy of macro relationships with private companies operating in a market place. Competitiveness is transformed to a macro concept, covering aspects of market competition, improved productivity and efficiency and welfare. Differences between firms operating in decentralized and autonomous markets and nations operating in international surroundings are so fundamental and far-reaching that it does not make sense, analytically, to accept the construction principles of the concept without reservations. Societies or negotiated economies do not have a goal or aims. Actors might try to impose such on them; but there is no clear indicator of »survival success« of systems or national economies.

The *institutional* part of the competitiveness is a success formula, based on institutionalized participation rights for actors and social partners and on public policy results functional to economic and social change. Institutions must be understood as patterns of relationships and actions that persist and reproduce themselves over time without being dependent on the people taking the concrete decisions and implementing policies. Ove K. Pedersen does not reduce the operations of a system to biological individuals and their performance. He places the institutional traits and analyses the complementarities in the system as a whole. The negotiated economy is characterized by good institutions; we are told it works very well. In particular, the way in which a comprehensive and interventionist public sector functions is treated as an orchestration of a well performing welfare society. It might be tempting to see this just as a convenient name for »the good society«. Or, as the Americans put it, *»motherhood and apple pie«*, i.e. everything we want from our society: general economic growth and prosperity combined with low unemployment, high employment and a well functioning labour market within the negotiated economy; generous social security schemes, public services (for example child care facilities, care for the elderly and publicly financed education) and equity in public policies. This seems to be a warm and healthy goal. But such an understanding is also vague because there are no clear standards of evaluation, no precise measures of success. It is parallel to the benchmarking language in which you find firms, organizations and nations to be »more or less competitive«. The approach is too imprecise to be satisfactory analytically.

Good macro-economic performance together with high welfare standards and comprehensive public services do look like a societal model that brings growth and security to all citizens. This is also a popular understanding of the situation in the Danish economy at the moment, and the EU institutions are now labelling Danish »flexicurity« a role model for Europe (Expert Group 2007; Jørgensen and Madsen 2007). Ove K. Pedersen uses Danish »flexicurity« as the most prominent example of the institutional competitiveness of the Danish system. The institutional traits of the system seem to bring synergy to the economy, and the labour market is functioning in a way that brings prosperity to the country. This realizes the thoughts of a welfare society with welfare policies as institutional complementarities bridging economic growth and political aims, including redistributing income and life chances and securing sustainable developments. It is considered and presented as a successful experiment in the institutional construction of competitiveness. The negotiated economy seems to bring »Wohlstand für Alle«, as Ludwig Ehrhardt once put it, and good macro-economic performance. No consciousness of scarcity seems to be at work! Besides the fact that Danish collective actors (»the heroic entrepreneurs«) have presumably never considered themselves to be laboratory technicians or experimentalists for a new competition system, the impression given of this productive economy is exactly that of »motherhood and apple pie«! This is simply too imprecise and ambiguous a construction. Factors capable of explaining growth and welfare in one period might not be the same ones which can be used to evaluate the reasons behind systems performing badly at other times. And it is not sufficient to have institutions that are good at coordination: it is just and impartial public institutions that count (Rothstein 1998). Hopefully, it has been indicated or demonstrated that more specifications are required. We need more clarification as to the internal consistency of the concept of institutional competitiveness; we need to know more about the principles underlying the construction, and about evaluation criteria relevant to the performance of a system. The nature of institutions is also crucial.

To conclude: analytically, Ove K. Pedersen might still owe us an explanation as to the causal relationships behind his construction of »institutional competitiveness«, and to convince us as to successful formulas for evaluating the performance of systems. It is unclear what is covered (only economic circumstances?) and what the concept is balanced against: it seems still to be referring to some hidden neo-classical theory foundation. Remember, he defines it as »the capacity to reach economic prosperity as a result of the political, economic and cultural institutions« (Pedersen 2006: 3). One could sharpen the arguments a little bit more. Analytically, the concept could be seen as

unclear and ambiguous (having no clear indicator for success)
potentially misleading (building on false analogies with the competitiveness of a private firm and writing off welfare elements), and
perhaps an ideological »Trojan horse« (in reality serving as a cover for a mixture of »social democratic« and neo-liberal policy agendas: the first according the warm institutionalized welfare and the second keen market competition and strong economic performance).

I am a bit unsure as to the last part of the judgement, but I do think that »institutional competitiveness« needs more elaboration, avoiding analogies between the operations and conditions of private companies and those of countries. Or it may be argued that an extrapolation from micro to macro economy is not a satisfactory exercise, especially not when more than economic relationships are at stake. At the macro level it is not possible to talk of zero-sum games; unproductive economies are not killed by competition but continue to exist. We just end up with relative winners and relative losers.

Ove K. Pedersen has shown intellectual suppleness in his theoretical and methodological foundations of institutional analysis, and he has contributed in significant ways to the development of the concept. His own work on »discoursive institutionalism« (Campbell and Pedersen 2001) should be regarded as one of these innovative interventions. Without his previous analysis of different forms of institutions within the negotiated economy, we would not have known the difference between, for example, campaign institutions, negotiation institutions, and arbitration institutions, and we would be without understanding of the way policy agreements, polity agreements, and negotiation games in Denmark have emerged from historical compromises and have been involved in the development of both the public sector and market mechanisms. The genealogy of the negotiated economy has been analyzed as solidly built on institutional factors. But: the concept of institutional competitiveness rests on construction principles and analogies which do not seem consistent and analytically fruitful in every respect. More scientific work needs to be done. The message to Ove K. Pedersen is not to give up on the concept but to accord it a more robust analytical foundation.

Competitiveness and Institutional Variety

Ove K. Pedersen considers his analyses to be contributions to the »Varieties of Capitalism« literature – and rightly so. The main contention from the beginning has been that there is no single form of capitalism. Hall and Soskice (2001) postulated that there were two similar types: liberal and coordinated systems, dressed in national clothes. And once a country had established a particular set of institutions, there was every chance that changes in economic capacities and adopted policies were unlikely to occur. These paths were signposted roads with clear directions. Ove K. Pedersen is critical of this position, as mixed types of the two types of capitalism are to be found, and he believes that path-shaping developments are the most important factors for all kinds of neo-institutionalists to scrutinize as globalization grows and international integration proceeds (Pedersen and Campbell 2005, 2006, 2007). He also emphasises the actions and choices of rational or »heroic« actors, yet follows the neo-institutionalist view of path-dependent developments, e.g. routines, rules and norms governing economic and political behaviour. Diverse practices and power relationships are to be found, and change and its timing must be accounted for as well. However, Ove K. Pedersen is not developing this soft critique of Hall and Soskice into an alternative typology of varieties of capitalism; nor does he engage himself deeply in the broad discussions now focussing around these questions. He should.

We do not have coherent economic-political systems that can easily be bundled into two or three models. In the academic debate we have now gone beyond dichotomies to typologies with three, four, five, or six types of systems represented (see Bonoli 1997; Crouch 2005; Esping-Andersen 1990; Ferrera, Hemerijck, Rhodes 2000; Streeck and Thelen 2005). This looks promising, in that it might be possible eventually to overcome the inbuilt polemic or marriage between neo-liberalism and social democracy and, hopefully, also to dispense with the confusion between ideal types and national cases. Often the latter are being treated as concrete examples of the former, rather than the former being used as guiding principles for historical and empirical analysis of the latter. But we still lack strong theoretical propositions and hypothesis. Given Ove K. Pedersen's strong practice of combining theoretical and empirical work, and his experience in analyzing both internal and external relationships and threats to the negotiated economy, it would be interesting to have his thoughts about the »Varieties of Capitalism« developed more.

The perspective must be international, only using national cases as starting points and elements for the construction of broader typologies and theories. Globalization and Europeanization have not produced convergence, even if all countries have experienced common discourses and changed their economic and social policies and practices. Different results are to be seen even though more market-oriented policies have been developed in all the systems. Loss of national autonomy and control are evident. But new answers to threats and demands have been found. Exogeneity and endogeneity must now be regarded more as a continuum than as opposites. This opinion has repercussions as to the theoretical treatment of institutions and Wahlverwandschaften. Boundaries of nations are not necessarily the boundaries of institutions.

The Scandinavian countries have chosen their own »high road« to growth and welfare; other choices have been made elsewhere. But capitalism remains nationally based and different »models« or families of nations are to be found. They were formed long ago and keep on changing. The various policy responses to external and internal pressures suggest that systems will continue to work and respond in their own way. The configuration of system elements and economic interrelationships might have altered, but business has not become »stateless«, although it has become more autonomous and more international in scope. The ties between business and politics have changed, with fewer direct interventions from the state, but business and the economy as a whole have been more dependent on public welfare policies and on governance systems and regulatory practices. National traditions, values and culture count too. And it is precisely the adjustment processes and adaptation practices of each country that are decisive. Greater problem-solving capacities are not developed just by copying other countries' choices or by simply improving coordination structures.

The appropriateness of political strategies rests on *interactive* variables just as much as it does on *structural* variables. The question of how to enable policy actors, social partners and business representatives in multilevel systems to reach agreements on innovative policy programmes presupposes answers to cognitive, coordinative *and* cooperative problems. Ove K. Pedersen should note that the coordination problems are the most difficult and decisive ones, and here social science – and especially political science – needs to develop its contribution to better understandings and explanations and to produce adequate policy recommendations as well.

»*Good governance*« is perhaps a more dynamic and open concept than »institutional competitiveness« of the crucial questions. By governance one should understand those mechanisms and processes by which the behavioural regulations constituting institutions are maintained and enforced. Good governance is characterized by systems in which cooperative games by collective actors and successful adaptation are to be found. This might be a fair description of the situation in Denmark and the other Scandinavian countries since the beginning of the 1990s (Magnusson, Jørgensen and Dølvik 2007), helping the citizens and decision-makers in those countries to overcome the scarcity of consciousness and the ignorance of the needs of ordinary people which has been distinctive in most European countries over the last two decades. Good governance is a question of generalizing and legitimizing changes in policies and practices in ways which are not contradictory to national traditions, values and discourses, while continuing to enhance growth and welfare simultaneously.

Ove K. Pedersen might not disagree. But he needs to be a little bit self-critical, both in relation to his conceptual framework and to his analyses of the successful performance of the negotiated economy. One should invite him to make an intervention in the »Varieties of Capitalism« discussion too. This research note is such an invitation, along with some concomitant critical points of view in relation to the many stimulating analyses of Ove K. Pedersen. Without his contributions these remarks and comments could not have been written.

References

Axelrod, R. 1997, *The Complexity of Cooperation – Agent-Based Models of Competition and Collaboration*, Princeton University Press: Princeton.

Axelrod, R. 1984, *The Evolution of Cooperation*, Basic Books, New York.

Bonoli, G. 1997, 'Classifying welfare states: a two dimension approach', in Journal of Social Policy, 26 (3), pp. 351-372.

Campbell, J.L. 2004, Institutional Change and Globalization, Princeton University Press, Princeton.

Campbell, J.L., J.A. Hall and O.K. Pedersen 2006, *National Identity and the Varieties of Capitalism – The Danish Experience*, DFØF Publishing, Copenhagen.

Campbell J.L. and O.K. Pedersen 2005, *Institutional Competitiveness in the Global Economy: Denmark and the United States*, Working Paper No. 21, Copenhagen Business School, Copenhagen.

Campbell, J.L. and O.K. Pedersen (eds.) 2001, *The Rise of Neoliberalism and Institutional Analysis*, Princeton University Press, Princeton.

Christiansen, N.F. et al. (ed.) 2006, *The Nordic Model of Welfare – A Historical Reappraisal*, Museum Tusculanum Press, University of Copenhagen, Copenhagen.

Crouch C. 2005, *Capitalist Diversity and Change – Recombinant Governance and Institutional Entrepreneurs*, Oxford University Press, Oxford.

Crouch C. and W. Streeck (eds.) 1997, *Political Economy of Modern Capitalism: Mapping Convergence and Diversity*, Sage, London.

Esping-Andersen, G. 1990, *The Three Worlds of Welfare Capitalism*, Cambridge University Press, Cambridge.

Esping-Andersen, G. and M. Regini (eds.) 2000, *Why Deregulate Labour Markets?*, Oxford University Press, Oxford.

Expert Group on Flexicurity (EU). *Flexicurity Pathways*, Interim report, Brussels, April 2007.

Ferrera, M., 2005, *The Boundaries of Welfare – European Integration and the New Spatial Politics of Social Protection*, Oxford University Press, Oxford.

Ferrera, M., A. Hemerijck and M. Rhodes 2000, *The Future of Social Europe: Recasting Work and Welfare in the New Economy*, Presidency Report, Lisbon, 2000.

Hall, P.A. and D. Soskice (eds.) 2001, *Varieties of Capitalism: The Institutional Foundations of Comparative Advantage*, Oxford University Press, New York.

Jørgensen, H. 2002, *Consensus, Cooperation and Conflict. The Policy Making Process in Denmark*, Edward Elgar, Cheltenham.

Jørgensen, H., and P.K. Madsen (eds.) 2007, *Flexicurity and Beyond – Finding a new agenda for the European Social Model*, DJØF Forlaget, Copenhagen.

Madsen, P.K., 2006, 'How can it possibly fly? The paradox of a dynamic labour market in a Scandinavian welfare state', in J.L. Campbell, J. Hall, and O.K. Pedersen (eds.), *National Identity and the Varieties of Capitalism – The Danish Experience*, DJØF Forlaget, Copenhagen, pp. 321-355.

Madsen, P.K., 2005, 'The Danish Road to »Flexicurity« Where are we? And how did we get there?', in Bredgaard and Larsen (eds.), *Employment Policy from Different Angles*, DJØF, Copenhagen, pp. 269-290.

Magnusson, L., H. Jørgensen and J.E. Dølvik 2007, *The Nordic Approach to Growth and Welfare – European Lessons to be Learned?*, ETUI-REHS, (under publication), Brussels.

Olson, M., 1965, *The Logic of Collective Action. Public Goods and the Theory of Groups*, Harvard University Press, Cambridge.

Olson, M., 1990, *How Bright are the Nothern Light? Some Questions About Sweden*, Lund University Press, Lund.

Ostrom, E. 1990, *Governing the Commons: The Evolution of Institutions of Collective Action*, Cambridge University Press, Cambridge.

Pascual, A.S. and L. Magnusson (eds.) 2007, *Reshaping Welfare States and Activation Regimes in Europe*, Peter Lang, Brussels.

Pedersen, O.K., 2006a, 'Corporatism and Beyond: The Negotiated Economy', in J.L. Campbell, J.A. Hall and O.K. Pedersen (eds.), National *Identity and the Varieties of Capitalism: The Danish Experience*, DJØF Publishing, Copenhagen, pp. 245-270.

Pedersen, O.K. 2006b, 'Denmark: An Ongoing Experiment', in J.L. Campbell, J.A. Hall and O.K. Pedersen (eds.), *National Identity and the Varieties of Capitalism: The Danish Experience*, DJØF Publishing, Copenhagen, pp. 453-469.

Pedersen, O.K., 1993, 'The Institutional History of the Danish Polity: From a Market and Mixed Economy to a Negotiated Economy', in S.E. Sjöstrand (ed.), *Institutional Change: Theory and Empirical Findings*, M.E. Sharpe, New York, pp. 277-3000.

Pedersen, O.K. and J.L. Campbell 2007, 'Institutional Competitiveness in the global economy: Denmark, the United States, and the Varieties of Capitalism', in *Regulation and Governance*, (3), pp. 230-246.

Pedersen, O.K. and J.L. Campbell 2006, 'Danmarks Institutionelle Konkurrenceevne', *Økonomi og Politik*, 79 (1), pp. 3-18.

Pedersen, O.K. and J.L. Campbell 2005, *Dansk institutionel konkurrenceevne i den globale økonomi*, Rapport udarbejdet for FTF, København.

Pedersen, O.K., N.Å. Andersen, P.K. and J. Elberg 1992, *Privat Politik: Projekt Forhandlingsøkonomi*, Samfundslitteratur, Copenhagen.

Peters, B.G. 1998, *Institutional Theory in Political Science – the »New Institutionalism«*, Pinter, London.

Pierson P. (ed.) 2001, *The New Politics of the Welfare State*, Oxford University Press, Oxford.

Rhodes, R. 1997, *Understanding Governance*, Open University Press, Buckingham.

Rothstein, B. 2003, *Sociale fällor och tillitens problem*, SNS Förlag, Kristianstad.

Rothstein, B. 1998, *Just Institutions Matter: The Moral and Political Logic of the Universal Welfare State*, Cambridge University Press, New York.

Sabel, C. and J. Zeitlin (eds.) 1997, *World of Possibilities: Flexibility and Mass Production in Western Industrialization*, Cambridge University Press, Cambridge.

Scharpf, F.W., *Games Real Actors Play*, Westview, Boulder.

Scharpf, F.W. and V. Schmidt (eds.) 2000, *Welfare and Work in the Open Economy*, I-II, Oxford University Press, Oxford.

Schmidt, V.A. 2002, *The Futures of European Capitalism*, Oxford University Press, Oxford.

Streeck W. and K. Thelen (eds.) 2005, Beyond *Continuity: Institutional Change in Advanced Political Economies*, Oxford University Press, Oxford.

Wilensky, H.L. 1985, *The Welfare State and Equality*, University of California Press, Berkeley.

Zeitlin, J. and D. Trubek (eds.) 2003, *Governing Work and Welfare in a New Economy: European and American Experiments*, Oxford University Press, Oxford.

CHAPTER 2

Innovation Policy and Institutional Competitiveness in Europe and Denmark

Susana Borrás

Associate professor, Copenhagen Business School Denmark

Introduction

In response to the rapidly changing global context, most national governments in Europe have recently been developing novel ways of approaching the issues of science, technology and innovation. National governments have typically embraced a wider perspective on innovation policy than before, have introduced new and experimental policy instruments in this field, and have mobilised new sets of actors in pursuing governmental policy goals. Parallel to these changes, the European Union launched in 2000 a series of important political initiatives in the same direction, the most important of which are the Lisbon Strategy and the European Research Area, aiming respectively at coordinating national economic policies and at creating cross-border dynamics in the field of research and innovation. Taken together, these initiatives represent a renewed policy approach to innovation in Europe, in a continuous effort to improve competitiveness and economic growth.

Notwithstanding these policy efforts and novelties, the extent to which these initiatives have been able to influence the dynamics and nature of national innovation systems along the goals defined by these policy initiatives is still unclear. National systems of innovation are crucial for understanding national competitiveness and national competitive advantage. They are largely the fruit of historical processes, and tend to evolve in relation to specific institutional and industrial dynamics. Naturally, innovation policy is part of the complex interactions that form the system. But the extent to which policy is a driving force for change within the system is a matter that needs to be studied carefully. This question relates to an important theoretical issue: the role of agency in the evolution of systems of innovation and other complex economic systems. The literature in the areas of comparative political economy, evolutionary economics and innovation studies has tended to partly disregard this issue. For that reason, important questions about the role of policy and public action remain largely unexplored in the institutionalist and system-oriented literature. In particular, the extensive work on 'systems of innovation' has typically addressed policy in the set of general 'policy recommendations' at the end of economic analysis of innovation performance. There are, of course, exceptions to this, which will be examined in the next sections. But for the main part, policy is almost invariably treated as an additional, exogenous element of the process of innovation in these studies. For its part, the extensive literature on varieties of capitalism, which operates at a higher level of abstraction and also has a systemic approach, has tended to consider the firm as the main agent of change. The positive aspect of both strands of literature is that they see the innovation process as a process deeply embedded in a specific (national or regional) institutional context. The problem, however, is that even if policy becomes part of the equation, it is rarely analysed.

This chapter argues that there is one main reason as to why this neglect is analytically problematic when trying to explain historical transformations in systems of innovation. Namely, the objectives of policy and public action are directed towards creating, maintaining, transforming and improving the formal institutional set-up of the innovation system. When, how and why this is taking place in a way that affects the entire innovation system is a matter that needs further attention and refers to the effectiveness of policy and to the performance of the system. In order words, the institutional set-up that forms part of the innovation system might change spontaneously or in relation to purposeful public action. When the latter is the case, we need to explain how and why.

With this purpose in mind, the chapter proceeds as follows. The first section sets the scene by summarising the most relevant changes and novelties introduced in innovation policies in Europe, with a focus on the national and European levels. The following section presents and develops an analytical framework about institutions, politics and agency in the context of the governance of systems of innovation. This theoretical framework is related to Ove Kaj Pedersen's theoretical research on institutionalism and competitiveness in the context of comparative political economy. The next section discusses the notion of institutional competitiveness in the context of the system of innovation approach. After that, the chapter delves into the changes in innovation policy paradigm, contents and modes of governance in Europe over the last decade. This prepares the ground for the preliminary and very succinct analysis of the Danish innovation policy changes undertaken in the section after that. The chapter argues that Danish innovation policy has been an important element in the positive innovation performance of the Danish economy over the last decade. The reason for this is that the pro-active and experimental innovation policy of the different Danish governments has been able to enhance the institutional competitiveness of the national system of innovation over time. Consequently, Danish companies have supportive institutions which allow them to enhance their capabilities and adapt to the globalised economy.

Systems of Innovation and Institutional Competitiveness

Developed by economists in the early 1990s, the 'national system of innovation' is a concept that tries to grasp the complexities of the innovation process generated within and across firms in a specific national and territorial context. Following the latest definition by Edquist, a (national) system of innovation refers to »the determinants of innovation process, and is formed by all important economic, social, political, organizational, institutional, and other factors that influence the development, diffusion, and use of innovations«. Innovation refers to the creation of new products and production processes, and is essentially an economic phenomenon that uses important elements of new knowledge and has remarkable organizational implications. The notion 'system' aims at capturing the context in which companies, entrepreneurs and innovators operate, on the understanding that innovation does not take place in a vacuum but is the fruit of complex actors' interactions within a specific institutional set-up of formal and informal character. »Institutions are sets of common habits, norms, routines, established practices, rules or laws that regulate the relations and interactions between individual, groups, and organizations« (Edquist and Johnson 1997: 46).

Therefore, to a large extent, a system of innovation can be seen to be formed by two types of elements: companies and organizations on the one side, and an institutional set-up on the other (with formal and informal institutions). The interaction between formal and informal institutions and between the institutional set-up and firms and organizations is based on complex forms of selection and adaptation processes (Borrás 2004). Figure 1 below visualizes these elements and interactions.

Figure 1.

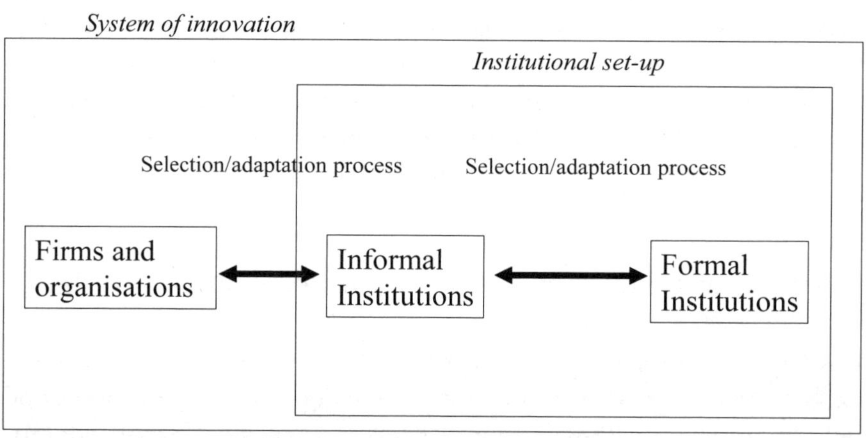

Source: Transformed from Borrás 2004.

Formal institutions refer here to the explicitly formulated rules of the game that define the 'official' definition of the role undertaken by firms and organizations in relation to the production, appropriation, distribution and consumption of new knowledge in the economy. Informal institutions by contrast, refer to the set of customary practices, unspoken rules, routines, and world-views that characterize the activities of all innovation-oriented firms and organizations in the system. Evolutionary and institutional economists have generally understood the change in the innovation system to be a co-evolutionary process of transformation in the institutions and in the knowledge produced and used by firms and organizations (Nelson 1994). National and regional innovation systems are heavily related to the specific dynamics of the industrial sectors in which an economy is specialized, but also to the type of formal and informal institutional set-up that forms that system.

Since the end of the Second World War, most industrialised countries have developed different models of innovation systems (Nelson 1993). There are today a large number of studies about specific national and regional systems of innovation, either in the form of single case studies or in comparative ones. However, surprisingly enough, there have been relatively few attempts to classify these national systems into larger analytical typologies. One of the earliest studies was conducted by French scholars from the 'regulation' economic school (Amable, Barré, Boyer 1997). These authors identify four different types of 'social systems of innovation' following an empirical analysis based on indicators in different areas. These four types are the 'market-based model' (i.e. US, UK, Canada), the 'social-democratic model' (Sweden, Denmark, Norway, Finland), the 'meso-corporatist model' (only Japan), and the 'public-institutions-based model' (Germany, France, The Netherlands, Italy). These four models follow previous model-analysis of state structure in line with comparative welfare capitalism.

Another interesting classification is the one recently defined by Whitley. Largely inspired by the firm-oriented perspective of the institutionalist tradition in the varieties of capitalism literature, Whitley suggests six different types of innovation systems: »autarkic« (i.e. UK), »artisanal« (Denmark and the 3rd Italy), »technological teams« (US), »state-led« (France), »group-based« (Japan) and »highly collaborative« (Germany and Sweden). His typology is based on the institutional conditions defined by the different types of state, and in particular, in a set of eight variables: »state science and technology policy«, »strength of independent business associations«, »strength of independent labour unions«, »financial system«, »scope and strength of collaborative public training system«, »strength of prestige hierarchy of universities and research organization«, »competitive and pluralist public science system«, »segmentation of research organizations and careers« (Whitley 2006). The most interesting aspect of these two typologies is their effort to identify similarities and to compare the nature of different systems of innovation by looking at the diversity of national institutional frameworks. As such, both typologies can provide interesting insights as to what exactly differs across systems of innovation. However, one of the most problematic aspects of these typologies is that they tend to be rather static in their account of innovative structures. In both cases, these models are presented in rather general terms, disregarding in large part the temporal dimension of the study, which is crucial if one wants to examine in-depth the factors that explain change, and in particular, change that is related to innovative performance.

A central tenet in the literature about systems of innovation is the emphasis on the fact that there is no optimal model of institutional and industrial organization. Instead, different forms and degrees of innovative and economic performance are based on a wide variation of institutional set-ups with different and changing features. This, however, does not hinder institutional economists working on innovation studies from pointing to successful and less successful institutional frameworks, and to specific institutional bottlenecks for innovative performance. One prominent example of less successful institutional performance is the current problem surrounding the issue of intellectual property rights which is faced in different regimes, particularly in the US and in Europe (Guellec and van Pottelsberghe 2007; Jaffe and Lerner 2004).

Different institutional performance links to the issue of institutional competitiveness as defined by Ove Kaj Pedersen and John L. Campbell in several of their works (Campbell and Pedersen 2006; Campbell and Pedersen 2007a). Institutional competitiveness, which is defined as »the capacity of a country to achieve socioeconomic success due to its institutions« (2007a: 232) puts emphasis on the role of formal and informal institutions in economic performance. This approach shares two very important issues with the systems of innovation school. Firstly, it shares the view that there is no single optimal model of institutional set-up or of innovation process. Instead, different models and types of capitalism and innovation have institutional features that have advantages and disadvantages when it comes to economic and innovative performance. This is a crucial point when dealing with the economic rationales of innovation policy, avoiding 'one-size fits all' policy solutions based in wrong assumptions of universal optimality (Borrás, Chaminade, Edquist 2007). Secondly, and perhaps most importantly from the analytical perspective of this chapter, is the fact that both schools see institutional performance itself as a crucial aspect in explaining innovative and economic performance, which is ultimately generated by companies embedded in complex webs of interactions with their environment.

Institutional competitiveness is based on the complementarity of the institutions in terms of a certain degree of homogeneity (creating a coherent institutional framework) and of heterogeneity (when institutions are able to cover each others' deficiencies) (Campbell and Pedersen 2007a). Institutional competitiveness is highly related to the adaptability of firms and of innovators to new and ever-changing circumstances. An institutional set-up is competitive if it is able to ensure that the environment where firms operate is well-tuned to the changing needs of firms in the globalised economy. Flexibility and the rapid upgrading and redefinition of firms' capabilities and competences are crucial in this respect. In other words, institutional competitiveness refers to an institutional set-up that is able to enhance the adaptability, flexibility and constant learning of firms and organizations in the system.

Whereas institutional performance is a crucial aspect in the different models and performance of national systems of innovation, there is another aspect that deserves analytical attention: the role of policy in the innovation system. This relates to the issue of policy as an agent of change. Figure 1 depicts the institutional set-up formed by formal and informal institutions. Admittedly, the definition of what is 'formal' and 'informal' is relatively blurred in the real world. However, in analytical terms this distinction is central to understanding that changes in the institutional-set up might be initiated purposefully or spontaneously in the process of adaptation and selection that takes place constantly between formal and informal modes of institutions. Institutional competitiveness can be seen largely as the outcome of these interactions. The analytical question is, whether public policy can generate dynamics of change in the institutional set-up so that this set-up becomes/remains competitive. In fact, the key matter in this sense is whether policy can act as a bridge between formal and informal institutions, so that when the purposive action of public action transforms formal institutions (laws, regulations, obligatory frameworks), it is also able to induce change in informal institutions. The changing nature of public action during the past few decades might in fact be addressing this.

There is currently a growing literature about the transition from a top-down form of governmental public action towards a more 'network-based' form of governance where the borderline between public and private actors becomes increasingly blurred. This is to say that, in advanced capitalist societies, public policy is increasingly being designed, framed and unfolded through thick networks of stakeholders, civil society organizations and civil servants. In the current era of governance, public action is no longer only the action of governments, but one which results from these complex forms of interaction that aim at solving specific problems. An emblematic case at stake is the labour market regulation in Denmark, which is based on highly decentralised forms of interaction and negotiation among stakeholders, the so-called negotiated economy (Pedersen 2006a). This model of heterarchical interaction and co-production of collective goods has the potential of developing a much higher degree of ownership among stakeholders than in traditional 'top-down' governmental steering. The next section examines the changes in the content and forms of governance of innovation policy in Europe since the 1990s.

Changing the Cognitive Paradigm, the Contents, and the Governance Forms in Innovation Policy

It is now generally acknowledged that in the most advanced industrialised countries there has been a gradual transformation in the cognitive paradigm in this policy area. In the 1940s-60s the focus was on science and knowledge production (science policy); in the 1970s-1980s it was on technology and development (technology policy); and since the early and mid-1990s there has been a focus on innovation policy (Lundvall and Borrás 2005). Although very schematic, this three-step historical change grasps the general paradigmatic transformations of the contents and rationales behind policy initiatives. Innovation policy encompasses the previous two, as it builds on the understanding of a knowledge-based and learning economy.

From the perspective of this chapter, the important aspect to consider is that the 'innovation policy paradigm' is largely related to two parallel cognitive transformations in academia and policy-makers respectively in the early 1990s (Andersson 1998). Starting with the first, the advancement of the institutionalist and evolutionary school in economics had a major impact in the formulation of this new paradigm. This school proposed a new way of understanding the innovation process as being essentially a non-lineal social process deeply embedded in specific social, political and economic institutions. The above contrasts with the conventional model of the innovation process proposed by neo-classical scholars, for whom the creation of new knowledge invariably precedes other steps in the innovative process, and its optimal results are largely associated with universally valid market conditions and knowledge appropriation conditions. In other words, neo-classical economics of technical change are based on notions of Pareto optimality and equilibrium between supply and demand of new knowledge. In contrast to this, for institutional and evolutionary scholars there is no ultimate notion of optimality in the innovation process (Metcalfe 1995). The conditions for knowledge creation and utilization are not associated to perfect market conditions or appropriation regimes, but are largely dependent on specific formal and informal institutions in the specific national economic system. Furthermore, countries seem to exhibit patterns of path dependency when it comes to innovation performance (as a result of these embedded institutions). All in all the innovation policy paradigm focuses more on competence building and on the wide notion of competitiveness, in contrast to the equilibrium and market failure perspective of previous economic rationales for policy.

But the cognitive parameters of policy-makers changed as well in the early 1990s, mainly because they looked for alternative approaches to previous policy failures. The technology policies of the 1980s, which had been mainly focusing on supporting high-tech strategic sectors, technology transfer bridging institutions and national strategic alliances for technological development, proved insufficient to cope with the challenges of the emerging globalization trends. In particular, the failure of 'national champions' to redress the loss of competitive positions of some sectors vis-à-vis the emerging South East Asia economies proved to be a decisive concern of most western countries. Policy-makers understood the need to experiment with new types of policy instruments, to have a wider focus on the innovation process (not only on knowledge production and diffusion but also on wider social and organizational dimensions of the innovation process), and to interact with innovators.

In Europe, these changes towards innovation policy have been made step by step. A study of a sample of 10 countries showed that in the early 2000s there were three identifiable groups of countries. Denmark, Finland and the Netherlands seemed to have fully embraced the 'innovation policy paradigm', whereas France, the UK, Italy and Austria could be seen as 'late comers', indicating interesting moves towards that paradigm but no fully-fledge endorsement; and a third group of 'discursive reformers' formed by Malta, Slovenia and Hungary, where these policy changes are related to considerable political and administrative reform and where real effects are yet to be seen (Biegelbauer and Borrás 2003). Likewise, the European Commission was an early mover in this area, endorsing the innovation policy paradigm explicitly in a series of official documents and semi-official publications (European Commission 1995).

Along the lines of the new policy paradigm, most European governments have been changing the contents and areas of public action in the field of innovation. Three specific areas seem to be of particular interest in this context. The first one is the role of universities in the innovation system. The advancement of normative notions about the need to stimulate European universities to follow models of the »entrepreneurial university« (Etzkowitz and Leydesdorff 1997) has had tremendous effects on the formal institutions regulating and defining the universities' role in the system of innovation. The second area where changes have been very visible is in the intellectual property rights' (IPR) regulations, patents in particular. The scope and form of patent systems in Europe have been rapidly evolving since the mid-1990s. In formal terms, the widening of the subject matter (or the type of knowledge that is amenable to be patented) has been substantially expanded de jure and de facto. This has important but indeterminate consequences for innovation, due to the 'patent paradox'. On the one hand, empirical evidence shows that innovative firms use patents only as a secondary way of securing knowledge appropriation (Dosi et al. 2006); on the other, however, the number of patent applications to patent agencies has been soaring dramatically in the past decade (Guellec and van Pottelsbergher 2007). This indicates, perhaps, that there are important transformations in the way firms use patents (the informal institution of routines and practices) which is partly a selection of changes in the regulatory regime (formal institutions). The third area where there have been substantial changes in the content of innovation policy is in the role of research councils. During the 1990s, most European national governments and at EU-level alike started an important process of delegation towards independent agencies. Governments have delegated significant executive powers relating to research and innovation policy to some independent agencies, either with regulatory or advisory capacities (Braun 2003). Many European research councils have changed their roles significantly over the past two decades, gaining relatively more independence (Lepori et al. 2007). This is partly the result of governments' willingness to allocate more resources on a competitive basis, and relatively less on an organizational basis (direct support to universities and public research centres).

Changes in the contents of the innovation policy system also relate to the creation of new arenas for public action at the sub-national and supranational levels. At the sub-national level, regional and local governments have been actively involved in innovation and entrepreneurship-oriented policy initiatives. European regions and local governments have engaged in cluster policies and industrial district policies, giving an important territorial dimension to governmental efforts towards fostering competitiveness and growth (Andersson et al. 2004; Asheim et al. 2003). Something similar can be said about the supra-national and international arenas in innovation policy. With initiatives in the areas of education, standardization, research funding, mobility of researchers, employment conditions for researchers, regulatory regimes for science and technology-related production sectors, bioethics, and »science in society« programmes, the European Union has been substantially expanding the scope of action in this policy field (Borrás 2003).

As mentioned above, the third dimension of change has been in the forms of governance and the role of governments. The expansion of the domain of innovation policy as compared to the previous approaches of science and technology policy has induced a growing number of actors involved in the policy-making process, particularly civil society and 'boundary organizations' (Sujatha 2005). Some of these civil society groups (such as patient groups, green groups, groups concerned with ethical aspects of research and innovation) have strong political opinions regarding issues of innovation policy. The wider mobilization of these groups around innovation policy-making has been combined with the more participatory character of policy-making, particularly in areas like technology forecasting and technology-related risk assessment (Callon 2003). Furthermore, policy-makers have been making extensive use of new policy instruments, also known as new modes of governance. Examples of these include public-private partnerships, codes of conduct, voluntary agreements and voluntary standards, all of them extensively used in the field of innovation policy. These are very diversified types of instruments, but they all share two important features: their voluntary nature (as opposed to the traditional obligatory nature of laws and regulations), and the fact that to varying degrees they are all based on network-like types of interactions between the state and private actors.

A Preliminary Analysis of Change: Denmark as a Case Study

Denmark has experienced very important changes in the way it approaches innovation policy over recent decades. These have taken place within the three dimensions identified earlier, namely, a very early endorsement of the innovation policy paradigm in the mid-1980s, substantial changes in the contents of innovation policy, and last but not least important changes in the mode of public actors to relate with innovation stakeholders and the wider society. This chapter argues that these changes seem to have strengthened the institutional competitiveness of the Danish system of innovation. Nevertheless, the extent to which these policy changes are transforming some fundamental aspects of the Danish system of innovation is still an open question. This section takes these points one by one.

Regarding the policy paradigm, Denmark is a country that had already endorsed the 'innovation policy paradigm' in the late 1980s and early 1990s. The economic problems faced in the second half of the 1980s forced the Danish government to reconsider some of the policy strategies developed until then, and to unfold a new viewpoint on the innovation process which was then mainly based on developing systemic competences (Lindgaard Christensen 2003). It might also be noted that some of the most influential scholars in the field of institutional and evolutionary economics in Europe are Danish. This means that the intellectual efforts geared towards developing new rationales and understanding of the innovation process as a social process embedded in a system took place in the context of parallel efforts from the Danish government to design a new and more systemic-based policy approach. The openness of the Danish economy and its small size make it especially vulnerable to changes in international markets. For that reason, strategies for improving the competitive position of Danish firms in the global economy became the main motto of industrial policy in Denmark as early as the late 1980s. Innovation has been at the core of governmental strategy since then.

There have been many important novelties in the contents of Danish innovation policy since the early 1990s. This section focuses very succinctly on three of the most recent of them which took place in the first decade of the 2000s: the reform in the university and research systems, the renewed emphasis on technology transfer, and the launch of the first innovation plan in Denmark. Starting with the first, Denmark has recently undergone a profound change in the university and public research system. The legal framework for university reform launched in 2003 has generated deep-reaching reforms in the leadership, research, teaching and institutional framework of the universities. The new law aims at strengthening the leadership of these institutions in two ways: by introducing externally-dominated university boards, and by enhancing the internal leadership capacity of their governing bodies. The disappearance of the traditional democratic rule of universities has been based on the logic of strengthening internal organizational control of universities and their external linkage with the social and industrial environment. Furthermore, state endowments to research conducted at universities have increasingly been made conditional upon a set of objectives and criteria, which are partly negotiated individually with each university (the 'development contracts') and partly collectively with the influential national university association. The very recent efforts to merge universities and public research centres are also very important. This process started in 2006 and is not entirely finished at the time of writing. The 12 original universities and 15 public research centres have already undergone a first round of mergers, resulting in three large universities and four smaller (regional) ones. Basically, most public research centres have become part of universities.

The recent emphasis on technology transfer is the second important change of innovation policy content to be examined here. There have long been worries about the patterns of technology transfer in Denmark. The Danish innovation system suffers from a paradox that is common for most European countries, namely, that in spite of the good quality of scientific and technological research, the level of collaboration between firms and universities, and the level of utilization of that knowledge is regarded as continuously insufficient. In Denmark this is aggravated by the large number of small and medium-size enterprises and by its specialization in a wide variety of industrial sectors, some of them of low and medium-tech sectors (Edquist and Lundvall, 1993; Maskell, 2004). This results in the fact that for the most part in Denmark, the innovation process tends to be of a mainly gradual and incremental – rather than radical – nature. (Jensen et al. 2007). Efforts to improve technology transfer have focused on two dimensions: the organizational and the legal. As to the first, the Danish government has been enhancing and improving networks of technology institutes, created schemes for innovation incubators, more tax incentives to companies using knowledge, and an ambitious industrial Ph.D. program. As to the legal dimension, the Danish parliament has passed a series of laws that allow universities to create firms, and to own and manage their own patents. University patents are, however, controversial in Denmark, particularly since Finland and Sweden have decided not to follow this path and yet enjoy some success in technology transfer from universities. One criticism which may be offered is that it is by no means certain that exploitation of knowledge produced at universities in Denmark will improve by stimulating the use of patents, basically because they are expensive to obtain, to manage, and to commercialize for SMEs. Open science and more emphasis on spin-off from universities might be more effective in terms of achieving the objectives of technology transfer, given the patterns of incremental innovation in the Danish system.

Finally, the third change in policy contents refers to the launch of the first innovation plan in Denmark. In spite of many years of endorsing the innovation policy paradigm, most policy initiatives towards innovation (and not just research and technological development) were launched in a relatively unstructured way. The new innovation plan for 2007-2010 gathers existing initiatives together and creates new ones. The plan is interesting because it is based on what innovation policy experts call 'horizontal policy measures', which typically cut across several industrial and scientific fields, aim at complementing other existing, measures, and focus on enhancing some specific dynamics within the whole system. Compared to other European countries, Denmark is relatively late when it comes to the design of such all-encompassing innovation plans, but this effort will mostly be seen as an attempt to order and enhance the political visibility of already existing policy initiatives.

The focus of the Danish government on issues of competitiveness since the mid-1980s were accompanied by an important change in the role of the Ministry of Industry and by the increasing involvement of stakeholders in the design of policy instruments and initiatives in the fields of industrial policy and innovation policy (Campbell and Pedersen 2007b). The Ministry of Science, Technology and Innovation was created in 1993, and was initially quite ineffective. The evaluation of the OECD of the Danish innovation system in 1994-95 helped placing the issues of science, technology and innovation at the core of the competitiveness strategy of the Danish government. However, it was not until 2001 that this ministry gained real political power vis-à-vis other ministries in the design and management of innovation policy. Traditionally, the flexible nature of public administration in Denmark is behind the extensive use of new modes of governance in the field of innovation. The creation of networks of innovators, the use of semi-voluntary 'development contracts' and the extensive utilization of benchmarks and other output-oriented instruments are evidence of that. However, the major reformative trust since

2001 has also made extensive use of traditional instruments of regulation and of economic incentives. Widespread political agreements across most Danish political parties forged at the national parliament have been behind these major reforms, particularly the university and public research system reform.

Are these fundamental changes generating competitive institutions in the Danish system of innovation? In some respects it is too early to say, but in others it is not. It is too soon to assess whether the sweeping reforms of the university and public research systems will yield the expected dynamism and improved innovation. The merger of universities into three large and four small institutions might have achieved the necessary critical mass to internationalize even further the Danish research and higher education systems. However, this might be at the expense of open competition for the best Danish students and researchers within the country, since it is likely that the three largest universities will be the most attractive. Something similar can be said about the creation of 'university patents' in the attempt to enhance technology transfer. The success of this measure in terms of generating institutional competitiveness is still unclear, particularly given the incremental nature of innovation in Denmark and the large number of SMEs. However, university patents might in the long run generate the necessary organizational processes and transparency needed to exploit more effectively the rich pool of knowledge.

On the other hand, these changes might well add up to previous initiatives focusing on improving the institutional competitiveness in the Danish system of innovation. In a recent study commissioned by the EU, Denmark is considered to be one of the »innovation leaders« of EU27, along with Sweden, Germany and Finland (MERIT and JRC, 2007). This is according to two variables, namely the performance of the innovation index in 2006, and the average growth over the last ten years. Denmark is well above the average in both indicators, demonstrating a very strong and sustainable innovation performance. These output indicators show that the institutional set-up in Denmark seems to be adequately tuned to support firms in the globalised economy. And perhaps most importantly, that it seems to be doing so on a continuous basis. This is largely due to the fact that Denmark endorsed the innovation policy paradigm very early, and consequently had already introduced important institutional reforms by the end of the 1980s. This momentum has not been lost along the way. On the contrary, important innovations were introduced in the mid-1990sand in the early 2000s, keeping up with institutional renewal. This means that above all, the institutional set-up of the Danish system of innovation seems to be highly adaptive, both for formal and for informal institutions. And it is not controversial to argue that the experimental nature of innovation policy is largely behind this adaptability. This is why, in many respects, 'Denmark is an ongoing experiment' (Pedersen 2006b).

References

Amable, B., R. Barré and R. Boyer 1997, 'Diversity, Coherence and Transformations of Innovation Systems', in R. Barré et al. (eds), *Science in Tomorrow's Europe*, Economica International, Paris.

Amable, B. 2000, 'Institutional complementarities and diversity of social systems of innovation and production', in *Review of International Political Economy*, 7 (4), pp. 645-687.

Andersson, T. 1998, 'Managing a systems approach to technology and innovation policy', in STI – *Science Technology Industry Review*, 22, pp. 9-29.

Andersson, T., S. Schwaag Serger, J. Sörvik, and E.W. Hansson 2004, *The Cluster Policies Whitebook*, IKED, Malmö.

Asheim, B.T., A. Isaksen, C. Nauwelaers and F. Tödling 2003, *Regional innovation policy for Small-medium enterprises*, Edward Elgar Publishers, Chelthenham.

Biegelbauer, P. and S. Borrás 2003, 'Conclusion: Policy Changes, Actors, Institutions and Learning', in P. Biegelbauer and S. Borrás (eds), *Innovation Policies in Europe and the US. The new agenda*, Aldershot, Ashgate.

Borrás, S. 2003, *The Innovation Policy of the European Union. From Government to Governance*, Edward Elgar Publishers, Chelthenham.

Borrás, S. 2004, 'System of innovation theory and the European Union', in *Science and Public Policy*, 31 (6), 1 December, pp. 425-433.

Borrás, S., C. Chaminade and C. Edquist 2007, (forthcoming), in Göran Marklund (ed.), *'The Challenges of Globalization: Strategic Choices for Innovation Policy'*, Vinnova, Stockholm.

Braun, D. 2003, 'Lasting tensions in research policy-making – a delegation problem', *Science and Public Policy*, 30 (5), 1 October, pp. 309-321.

Callon, M. 2003, 'The increasing involvement of concerned groups in R&D policies: What lessons for public powers?', in Geuna, A., A.J. Salter and E.W. Steinmueller (eds), *Science and Innovation. Rethinking the Rationales for Funding Governance.* Edward Elgar Publishers, Cheltenham.

Campbell, J.L. and O.K. Pedersen 2006, 'Danmarks Institutionelle Konkurrenceevne', *Økonomi & Politik*, 79 (1), pp. 3-18.

Campbell, J.L. and O.K. Pedersen 2007a, 'Institutional Competitiveness in the Global Economy: Denmark, the United States, and the Varieties of Capitalism', in *Regulation & Governance*, 1, pp. 230-246.

Campbell, J.L. and O.K. Pedersen 2007b, 'The Varieties of Capitalism and Hybrid Success: Denmark in the Global Economy', *Comparative Political Studies*, 40, pp. 307-332.

Dosi, G, F. Malerba, G.B. Ramello and F. Silva 2006, 'Information, appropriability, and the generation of innovative knowledge four decades after Arrow and Nelson: an introduction', in *Industrial and Corporate Change*, 15 (6), pp. 891-901.

Edquist, C. and B.-Å. Lundvall 1993, 'Comparing the Danish and Swedish Systems of Innovation', in R.R. Nelson (ed.), *National Innovation Systems: A Comparative Analysis*, Oxford University Press, Oxford.

European Commission 1995, *Green Paper on Innovation*, Com 95 (688) final.

Etzkowitz, H. and L. Leydesdorff 1997, 'Introduction: Universities in the global knowledge economy', in H. Etzkowitz and L. Leydesdorff (eds.), *Universities and the global knowledge economy: A triple helix of university-industry-government relations*, Pinter, London, pp. 1-18.

Freeman, C. (1992): *The Economics of Hope: Essays on Technical Change, Economic Growth and the Environment*, (New York: Pinter Publishers).

Guellec, D. and B. van Pottelsberghe de la Potterie 2007, *The economics of the European Patent System: IP Policy for Innovation and Growth*, Oxford University Press, Oxford.

Jaffe, A. and J. Lerner 2004, *Innovation and Its Discontents: How Our Broken Patent System is Endangering Innovation and Progress, and What to Do About it*, Princeton University Press, N.J. Princeton.

Jensen, M.B., B. Johnson, E. Lorenz and B.-Å. Lundvall 2007, 'Forms of knowledge and modes of innovation', in *Research Policy*, 36, pp. 680-693.

Lepori, B., P. van den Besselaar, M. Dinges, B. Potí, E. Reale, S. Slipersaeter, J. Theves and B. van der Meulen 2007, 'Convergence versus national specificities in research policies. An empirical study on public project funding', forthcoming in *Science and Public Policy*.

Lindgaard Christensen, J. 2003, 'Changes in Danish Innovation policy – Responses to the challenges of a dynamic business environment' in S. Borrás and P. Biegelbauer (eds), *Innovation Policies in Europe and the US. The new agenda*, Aldershot: Ashgate.

Lundvall, B.-Å. and S. Borrás 2005, 'Science, Technology and Innovation Policy', in *The Oxford Handbook of Innovation*, Oxford University Press, Oxford, pp. 599-631.

Maskell, P. 2004, 'Learning in the village economy of Denmark', in P. Cooke, M. Heidenreich and H.-J. Braczyk (eds), *Regional innovation systems. The role of governance in a globalized world*, (2nd edition), Routledge, London.

MERIT and JRC 2007, *European Innovation Scoreboard 2006*, from http://www.proinno-europe.eu/doc/EIS2006_final.pdf

Metcalfe, S. 1995, 'The Economic Foundations of Technology Policy: Equilibrium and Evolutionary Perspectives', in P. Stoneman (ed.), *Handbook of the Economics of Innovation and Technological Change*, Oxford University Press, Oxford, pp. 409-512.

Nelson, R.R. 1994, 'The Co-evolution of Technology, Industrial Structure, and Supporting Institutions', *Industrial and Corporate Change*, 3 (1), pp. 47-63.

Nelson, R.R. (ed.) 1993, *National Innovation Systems: A Comparative Analysis*, Oxford University Press, Oxford.

Pedersen, O.K. 2006a, 'Corporatism and Beyond: The Negotiated Economy', in J. L. Campbell, J.A. Hall and O.K. Pedersen (eds.), *National Identity and Varieties of Capitalism: The Danish Experience*, Montreal and Copenhagen: McGill-Queens University Press and Jurist- og Økonomforbundets Forlag, Montreal and Copenhagen, pp. 245-270.

Pedersen, O.K. 2006b, 'Denmark: An Ongoing Experiment', in J.L. Campbell, J.A. Hall and O.K. Pedersen (eds.), *National Identity and Varieties of Capitalism: The*

Danish Experience, McGill-Queens University Press and Jurist- og Økonomforbundets Forlag, Montreal and Copenhagen, pp. 453-469.

Sujatha, R. 2005, *Introduction: Institutional perspectives on science-policy boundaries, in Science and Public Policy*, 32 (6), 1 December, pp. 418-422.

Whitley, R. 2006, 'Innovation systems and institutional regimes: The construction of different types of national, sectoral and transnational innovation systems', in E. Lorenz and B.-Å. Lundvall (eds.), *How Europe's economies learn: Coordinating competing models*, Chapter 14, Oxford University Press, Oxford, pp. 343–380.

CHAPTER 3

Institutions of Current Affairs: Comparative Research in Varieties of Journalism

Anker Brink Lund

Professor, Copenhagen Business School, Denmark

Introduction

Until recently, institutional approaches to research in media and journalism have been eclipsed by crude empiricism (Miller & Gandy 1991) and competing grand theory perspectives (Peters 1989). Current trends towards comparative research design, however, invite the renewal of this kind of study in a political economy context, especially in order to balance normative claims and dubious generalizations of media convergence based on globalisation theory and of public sphere analysis.

Empirical media research documents that the public sphere, in the classical sense hailed by Dewey (1927) and other social critics of the so-called Progressive Era, is a mere phantom of democratic idealism, as Lippmann (1930) pessimistically argued. On the other hand, it is also convincingly demonstrated that political action continues to take place under human conditions of opinionated plurality, uncertainty and irreversibility. Under these circumstances, journalists still perform the political task of framing public debate among fellow citizens as more or less critical observers, i.e. presenting current affairs to phantom public spheres on behalf of more or less informed citizens (Schudson 1999).

Journalistic choice of newsworthy sources and dramatic narratives constitute institutional conditions for mediated politics. News media share this power of definition with political parties, representative bodies and administrative agencies acting in the political and economic context. From an institutional point of view, the central focus of public sphere analysis is on path dependencies and gradual changes in norms. These aspects, however, are frequently obscured by media scholars preoccupied with normative decline of the public sphere as an utopian arena for communicative deliberation.

I shall argue that as long as traditional public service values are accepted by journalists and mediated elites, they become part of an institutional practice – functioning both as means of legitimacy and vehicles for critical debate. Consequently, I have suggested that researchers substitute the fluffy term »public spheres« with the more fitting concept *Institutions of Current Affairs* (Lund 2004 and 2006).

In order to argue my point, this chapter falls into three parts. First I present the traditional public sphere framework employed by media scholars, primarily inspired by John Dewey and Jürgen Habermas. Secondly I discuss institutional approaches as alternatives (or rather necessary supplements) to normative public sphere thinking – especially focusing on political economy aspects of media and journalism studies. Finally I illustrate the premises and promises of the ICA-framework with research projects currently taking place at the CBS International Center for Business and Politics under the mutual heading *Varieties of Journalism* (Meyer and Lund 2007).

Public Sphere Approaches

In routine coverage, business and politics is typically mass mediated as power games and collective bargaining observed by non-partisan journalists acting as proxy citizens and neutral referees. Such communicative frameworks may constitute foundations for political distrust (Iyenger 1991). Current versions of these collusions employ concepts such as »democratic deficit«, »elitism« and »spin doctoring«, with the suspicion of conspiracy and systematic manipulation of public opinion (Curran, 2005).

Such concerns, however, are by no means a novel phenomenon (Bybee 1999); since the early 1960s European media research has been carrying out critical studies of these phenomena inspired by Jürgen Habermas´ conception of *Bürgerlichen Öffentlichkeit*. Building upon a long tradition of German legal thinking, this normative framework of public participation of ordinary citizens has spread within the heterogeneous field of media scholarship, gaining many followers and strong opponents.

The key feature of Habermas' impressive work on the rise and fall of public man (Sennett 1977) is a normative quest for rationality in political affairs. Habermas (1962) views news media historically as vehicles for public debate and political coordination. In contrast to arcane government, the public sphere offers representative participation in political decision-making processes. According to Habermas, this authoritative allocation of values for rationalization of human actions has been gradually transformed into systemic institutions of legal regulations with little room for communicative action. This, in turn, may cause representative government to lose credibility and turn political decision making into crises of legitimacy.

In his later works, Habermas has downplayed the sociological aspects of public sphere analysis in favour of philosophical aspects of discourse ethics of communicative action. Consequently, we are left with little theoretical assistance when it comes to understanding *how* representative democracy manages concurrent crises of legitimacy (Habermas 1973). In the 1990s, Jürgen Habermas explicitly distanced himself from the institutional aspects of his public sphere analyses published in 1962 and 1973. The main reason stated was lack of research-based updates on the transformation of the news media in late modernity. Habermas had neither the time nor the inclination to provide the empirical data for such a task, and preferred to re-evaluate some theoretical aspects of his public sphere theses, e.g. reflecting upon the potential of transnational citizenship (Habermas 1992).

To complicate matters further, Habermas' 1962 book was not translated into English until 1989. Consequently, the academic reception of the public sphere analysis was strongly influenced by Anglo-American readings of his later thesis on communicative action (1981), where the institutional aspects of public action was put into the shade by normative claims of universal pragmatics. In short, the current use of the concept »public sphere« outside German-speaking contexts is quite ambiguous and differs quite a bit from Habermas' original conceptualization.

In the basic sense of prescriptive *Ideologiekritik*, »public sphere« conceptualises the utopia of informed citizens transforming individual opinion into situational consensus based on rational exchanges of news and views. Habermas and his followers do admit that opinion forming of this kind is exceptional in *Realpolitik*, where public spheres function primarily as arenas of conflicting interests. From a constitutional point of view, the concept serves as an ideological framework legitimizing a parliamentary chain of agenda setting constituting what (inspired by Pedersen et al. 2000) I shall call »the mass audience«. It is expected that adherence to participatory ideals of mass involvement in political debate helps political institutions to perform in a more democratic and credible fashion. But usually neither the audience nor the mass media carrying out such debates are regarded as political institutions in their own right.

The historically deliberative ideal for political debate in European nation states has been translated into legal terms placing public opinion at the centre stage of civil society, separating private interests of markets and household from state interests represented by government agencies. The separation of powers also generates a chain of command connecting government to private citizens, not as private individuals, but as collective associations gathered by deliberation on issues of mutual concern.

This image of democratic rationality invites free men (and somewhat later women too) to step out of the role of consumer and *homo economicus*, leaving their private interests at home in order to act occasionally in the role of responsible and informed citizens debating matters of public relevance. In this transformation process, political associations and cultural congregations are formed, gradually maturing into political parties in order to appoint representatives for public office. Deliberation of this kind, however, frequently turns into bargaining, resulting in compromises and representation of interests in elected bodies negotiating for government and administration of public affairs. This may in turn weaken the legitimacy of mass participation as a constitutional ideal of free speech and equal access to public office.

The role of the media in the idealised conception of public sphere representation is rarely made explicit in European constitutions. By informal precedent, however, the freedom of the press has been deducted from the freedom of speech, granting producers of current affairs privileges as controllers of agencies of power and informers of the mass audience. The news media are expected to provide public coordination of political action, i.e. journalism becomes an important primer and framer of political and financial issues of relevance for representative government.

Two institutional changes, however, primarily developing after Habermas published his sociological interpretation of public sphere analysis in *Legitimationsprobleme im Spätkapitalismus* (1973), must be taken into consideration if we are to evaluate the role of the mass media in a realistic fashion: First, the emergence of professional mediators detached from political associations spinning public debate and, secondly, international co-operation among states defining premises of transnational politics without any kind of (not even phantom) public sphere of informed citizens.

In marked contrast to professional spin, the dominating ideal of political participation in public affairs is still one of amateurism. The deliberative forming of public opinion, however, is increasingly being invaded by economists, political scientists, journalists and other experts presenting themselves as communicators independent of state and private business. These professionals act as an elite audience (in contrast to the mass audience idealised by public sphere theory) representing specialised expertise in public. They also play key roles in mass mediated commentary and in the so-called »quangos«: quasi-autonomous non-governmental organizations (Deacon 2004).

The second problem confronting traditional public sphere theory is that the sovereignty of nation states is increasingly being challenged by international development forming transnational bodies of political correction of domestic action, e.g. OECD and the EU, plus a number of international NGOs. John B. Thompson (1995) has theorised these trends, pointing out the growing importance of visibility and scandal in current affairs. He proposes a framework of institutional change based upon the public sphere concept combining Habermas with sociological concepts inspired by political economy approaches to media and society.

Amending public sphere analyses in this way supplement the ideals of communicative action with strategic considerations and critical evaluation of conflicting power relations. This, in turn, illuminates an important political function of non-aligned journalism: public correction of elite action, i.e. mass mediated news and views not only co-ordinate, but also discipline political institutions. When interventions do not satisfy expectations, ways and means can be publicly criticised. Elected amateurs are held constitutionally responsible and may thereby lose credibility which, in turn, further increases the demand for professional advisers, quangos, and »spin doctors«.

The political and economic rationality of these gradual changes have usually been ignored by media researchers performing public sphere analysis. In late modernity, however, public opinion is influenced by factors unforeseen by national constitutions and normative ideals of representative democracy. Simply put, the prerogatives of mass participation have been supplemented by elite mediated public debate with journalists and expert sources assuming institutional roles of spin doctors and niche nurses (Lund 2004). This is not necessarily a sign of democratic decline, but certainly a symptom of institutional change in the classical ideals of public deliberation.

Institutional Approaches

John B. Thompson (1995) offers nothing short of »A Social Theory of the Media«. His central argument is that the core of Habermasian public sphere thinking is still valuable and normatively useful in times of late modernity. But being historically bound to a national framework, the original concept of public sphere lacks global perspective and a realistic grasp of political action taking place outside domestic institutions. Consequently, Thompson places news media as gatekeepers not only situated on the borderline between the private and the public spheres, but also facilitating (or hindering) rational interaction in transnational business and politics.

In the tradition of *Ideologiekritik,* mediated politics of this kind may be viewed as symptoms of decline of communicative action and national coordination of current affairs. Alternatively, based on Thompson´s revisionism, the mediated response to distant power games may be regarded as a functional transformation of public participation enabling the domestication of current affairs in national institutions of political action and collectively producing »a mediated here-and-now«.

Put bluntly, we may regard institutions of current affairs of late modernity as substitutes for specific arenas of political mass participation. In spite of the changes relating to the role of public opinion in business and politics, deliberative values still produce normative expectations for political and financial institutions. Some scholars take this argument a step further by viewing the news media as a political institution in its own right (Cook 1998, Sparrow 1999, Robinson 2001). The argument behind this kind of media-institutional scholarship is that journalists may regard themselves as autonomous civil society servants, but for all practical reasons they work in pools and packs within a professional framework of informal norms of conduct.

Professional pack journalism fulfils an institutionalised role in political bargaining between the constitutional branches of government (executive, legislative, and judiciary) and private corporations, organizations and tax payers. As an integrated part of this Institution of Current Affairs (dominated by journalists, expert sources, and official spokespersons) news media co-ordinate and correct collective action. Both mass and elite audiences present themselves as promoters of public interests, and both of them depend strongly on mass media to give them reputation and legitimacy, i.e. they are not elected nor selected through the constitutional chain of parliamentary command.

Habermas and his followers warn against this colonization of the public sphere, but the public sphere approaches have little to say about the political responses to the transformation. We may mitigate his sociological omission be applying elements from Mazzoleni and Schultz (1999:247) regarding political mediatisation as an historical development whereby »political institutions increasingly become dependent on and shaped by mass media but nevertheless remain in control of political processes and functions.« The institutional claim is that as long as public sphere norms are accepted by networks of professional journalists, experts and decision-makers, they function ideologically as sources of legitimacy and vehicles for political debate. Even if the public sphere in its classical sense may be regarded as an illusion representing citizenship by proxy.

Consequently, we may regard the public sphere as a normative framework for political action offering common sense and visibility, not only to journalists, but also to any political actor able to present his/her views as reasonable and prudent. Therefore, public sphere analysis ought to focus upon the path dependence and gradual shift in mediated democracy rather than on the speculative decline of communicative action. This can be achieved by critically reviewing classical notions of public reasoning and dialectics of enlightenment in order to observe the extent to which modern journalism lives up to its professional norms as non-partisan framers of business and politics (Lund 2004).

Notably, news media do not exercise the powers of framing in splendid isolation. Organised interests casting themselves as spokesmen for the public good also influence the framing process. These bargaining processes usually take place behind closed doors forming arcane arenas of conflict resolution with restricted access and little public scrutiny. Alliances of elite audiences criss-cross frontiers of private and public spheres, state and civil society. Consequently, expertise acting in concert with interest organizations from the private sector, public administration and the news media become an institutional factor by continuously producing premises for current affairs and collective action.

Typically, journalists and other professional communicators legitimise their framing on behalf of »informational« (but not necessarily informed) citizens. This line of reasoning may be traced to American political thought from the beginning of the 20th century (Schudson 1995: 66). From the American progressives, modern journalism have inherited norms such as objectivism, separating views from news, and non-partisanship in interviews as the favoured format for professional reporting. These ideas spread to the rest of the world, but this did not happen overnight. The gradual change in journalism was slow and institutionally embedded, allowing for different varieties to develop – especially in European democracies (Meyer and Lund 2007)

Over time visibility and mediated legitimacy become essential to political parties and social institutions competing for influence within a framework of ICA-norms. Stakeholders unable to present their interests as reasonable and newsworthy may easily be barred, not only from the front page, but also from the floor of parliament. Realising this, most political actors engage professional journalists for strategic purposes. From a Habermasian point of view, media management of this kind may be condemned as a systemic colonisation of public space. From an institutional perspective, however, strategic framing processes are inevitable in mediated politics. In a political environment of ambiguity and choice, journalists routinely distinguish between stakeholders who command rational and legitimate arguments and those who do not. Political and business actors who are perceived as partisan are subjected to far more critical scrutiny than those representing *vox pops* as a mediated stand-in for mass audience participation in political decision-making.

More specifically, in mediated struggles over political priorities, a key element of success is the strategic capacity of political elites to speak on behalf of ordinary citizens, providing news media with authentic cases to document the prudence of their particular views on current affairs. Simply put, the parliamentary prerogatives have been supplemented by journalists and expert sources assuming the institutional role as gatekeepers and watchdogs claiming adherence to rational choice. The framing of mediated public opinion is influenced by factors unforeseen by national constitutions and normative ideals of representative democracy. This is not necessarily a sign of democratic decline, but most certainly a symptom of institutional change calling for the closer analysis of the development of ICAs in comparative research.

From an institutional point of view, it makes little sense to talk about *the* public sphere, defined as a singular phenomenon inherent to all democratic media systems. In terms of journalism and politics, we must define public opinion forming in terms of ICAs (in plural) – with professional journalists acting as critical gatekeepers and mediators. For most practical purposes, journalism substitutes the voice of common sense in public debates. In the short run, powerful elites may gain marked influence by effectively spinning and priming professional journalists. In the long run, however, the only efficient way to maintain public opinion-driven democracy is to gain legitimacy and authority in the ICA of the system in question.

To sum up, ICAs as substitute public spheres have no stable power structure or constitutional sovereignty. According to Thompson (1995) no political actor aiming to maximise visibility and influence can afford to ignore the norms and forms of news media. In so doing, elite players risk mediated scandal. On the other hand, journalists acting as proxy public opinion depend upon the authority of institutional sources providing raw material for current affairs.

In terms of comparative research, this calls for institutional amendments to the traditional public sphere approaches in three interrelated ways: (1) Changes in the political framework of public opinion forming should not automatically be regarded as a process of decline, but rather as path dependent institutional changes in ICAs, open for empirical evaluation; (2) Journalism should not be regarded as one uniform and global kind of professional practice, but rather as a set of professional norms prone to specific influences of historical development of (political) culture; (3) Mediated politics, typically researched by way of content analysis, should be generalised to political opinion without informed use of other research methods documenting specific impacts on public knowledge, attitudes and collective action – both in relation to elite and mass audiences.

Testing of the ICA-Concept on Varieties of Journalism

In the previous paragraphs I have argued that separating the institutional elements from the utopian ones may provide a better framework for empirical research in media and journalism. The conceptual mess of public sphere analysis, however, is not an adequate reason to abandon the approach altogether. Rather, it should inspire concept hygiene and empirical efforts in order to make the normative framework operational for practical research purposes. I shall illustrate the usefulness of this kind of work guided by the ICA concept with three ongoing research projects conducted by the media management unit at the CBS International Center for Business and Politics.

All three projects seek to trace the political economy of media markets in line with Peter A. Hall (1986: 20), i.e. »formal rules, compliance procedures and standard operating practices that structure relationships between individuals in various units of the polity«. We do so by placing mediated action at the centre of inquiry within this institutional framework of competitive power games involving both political and business players. We place Institutions of Current Affairs at the crossroads of commercial and public service communication by focusing on comparative case studies of competitive (dis)advantages, matching the Danish ICA with similar operating practices in regional and global media markets. This line of research informs and critically evaluates generalization within an illustrative triangle of typical media systems proposed by Daniel C. Hallin and Paolo Mancini (2004: 70).

Figure 1

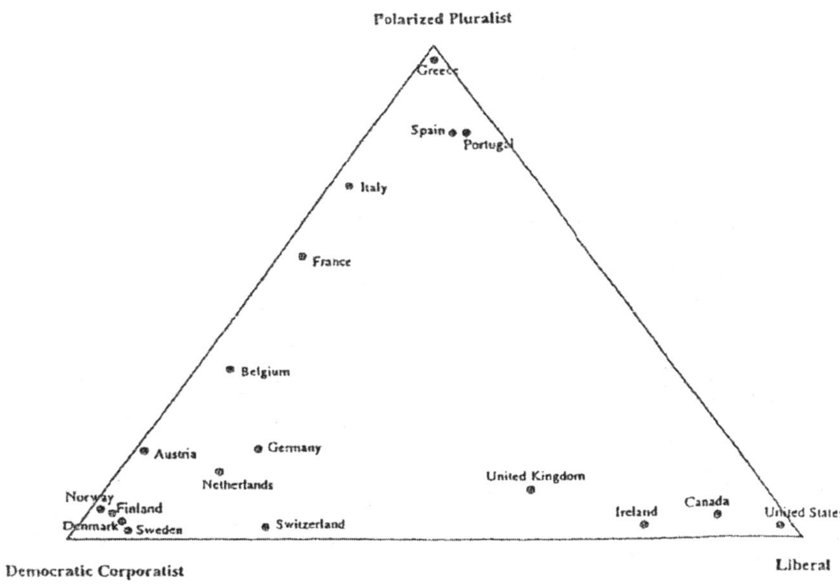

The major aim of Hallin and Mancini is to find interrelationships between media structures and political systems around the world, arguing that there is a diversity of media markets – not one single model of mediated public spheres. Media convergence in the technological and financial sense is not regarded as a one-way street in world wide communications. There is, no doubt, a mutual trend towards liberal norms and commercial business models in current journalism and media management. But divergence in mediated politics still prevails in domestic institutions of current affairs.

By contrasting the so-called »Liberal Model« with a »Democratic Corporatist« and a »Polarised Pluralist« it is clearly demonstrated that, especially within a European context, we detect important varieties of journalism and differences in ICAs. At one extreme we find the USA, Canada, Ireland and the UK as prototypes of the liberal media systems. The Southern European nations are placed at another extreme with pluralistic and polarised party-politics dominating media systems. The rest of the European media systems are located more closely to the »Democratic Corporatist«-pole of the model with the Scandinavian ICAs as prototypes.

Hallin and Mancini primarily base their typological generalizations on institutional structures and legal frameworks. They do not, however, include comprehensive content analyses and case studies of regional convergence and divergence. Their tentative model, I shall argue, calls for research combining the business and technological convergence perspectives with comparative approaches to institutional competitiveness in politics and journalism.

At CBS International Center for Business and Politics one of our ongoing projects addresses this challenge by combining content analysis and representative surveys in order to test the differences between democratic-corporatist and liberal ICAs. The project is conducted by the author in collaboration with colleagues from Stanford University, Goldsmiths College of London and the University of Helsinki. It focuses on comparative samples of news media from the US, UK, Finland and Denmark. In so doing, we measure both how much attention the four ICAs give to different topics and areas of news, and how much citizens of these countries know in relation to these.

It is clearly demonstrated that the actions of elite audiences have an impact on mass audiences, measuring the amount of media attention given in these countries to different topics and geographical locations. For each nation, we have compiled two summary-level indicators of the relative distribution of international and domestic news, and of 'hard' versus 'soft' news. We then proceed to investigate the influence of divergent patterns of reporting on public knowledge with polling evidence showing that Europeans were very much better informed about world events than Americans.

The American ICAs' relative neglect of public affairs and events outside America has long been an object of concern. Subsequent studies concluded that American mass opinion is relatively uninformed and, at times, badly misinformed. American media coverage of public affairs – already low – is declining still further in response to increased competition and deregulation. 'Soft news' grew at the expense of 'hard news' on American network television during the 1980s and 1990s. Indeed, according to one estimate, the time devoted to entertainment, disasters and accidents more than doubled in network television newscasts between 1990 and 1998 (Bennett 2003: 14). The US media's coverage of foreign affairs also declined sharply during the post Cold War period as did its investment in foreign news gathering (Shanor 2003). We do not suggest, however, that the varieties of journalism and differences in ICAs account for all these differences. Furthermore, in conducting the study we have also become aware of marked differences not only within the liberal ICAs (represented by the UK and USA) but also within the democratic-corporate tradition (i.e. Denmark and Finland).

Such inner-type differences are the main object of the second ICA-project taking place at the CBS International Center for Business and Politics, a pan-Scandinavian research project on Public Service on Multi Platform Media Markets applying organizational and regulation data to media systems in Denmark, Norway and Sweden. This research – conducted by the author in collaboration with colleagues from the University of Mid Sweden and the University College of Volda – calls for caution when generalizing trends from ideal type to specific nation states. The Scandinavian ICAs share mutual elements related to welfare state development. But no single common regional media regime dominates. This is clearly shown when we compare state regulation and public service legislation in the three markets. No uniform Scandinavian media model exists in spite of the fact that Denmark, Norway and Sweden share many common traits, e.g. self-regulated journalism and politically regulated media markets based on political compromises (Lund 2007).

The Scandinavian media markets also invite comparative research of institutional competitiveness because their historical developments share many common features with a long tradition in the democratic regulation of radio and television. Recent research, however, has also revealed significant institutional differences. For example, the Norwegian study of democracy and power (Østerud et al. 2003) was considerably more pessimistic about the future of democratic governance than a similar study in Denmark (Togeby et al. 2003). Supplementing these findings with research in the field of media management, we highlight three conditions that are essential to the understanding of the degree of public opinion forming by democratic-corporatist media systems:

- Relatively high newspaper circulation in niche markets
- Competitive, professional and self-regulating news production
- Market conditions regulated through parliamentary compromises

The central research questions are *how* these conditions converge and diverge in Denmark, Norway and Sweden, and *how* regional players compete internationally under changing institutional conditions. For institutional researchers, the lesson is not only to look for convergence, but also divergence, i.e. regional varieties of journalism. The comparisons demonstrate *how* local players in global games administer institutional conditions quite differently. Scandinavian press, radio and television have emerged from a provincial tradition institutionalised by means of politically regulated market conditions. This makes Denmark, Norway and Sweden fundamentally different from most other European countries and even more different from the American media market that usually dominates the research agenda. Interventions of the past did not encourage international expansion and competitive vigour. Consequently, the domestic media industry can probably only preserve its relative autonomy under increasing world competition and EU-harmonization if systematic knowledge of the institutional impact on national competitiveness is available. Political economy analysis may assist in this process.

The third project illustrating the potential of the ICA concept for comparative research in media studies not only includes liberal and democratic-corporatist ICAs, but also polarised pluralist ones. The research, primarily focused on content analysis of material used in formalised journalism education, is conducted by Gitte Meyer in collaboration with Per Øhrgaard and the author with the key focus on the conceptual level, claiming that the term 'journalism' is much too vague for institutional generalizations in a comparative framework. Within Europe, the trend towards increasing standardization of journalism – and, indeed, the perception that professionalism is linked to increased emphasis on techniques – appears to be marked in particular in the UK and in the Nordic countries, but less so in countries such as Germany and France. We intend to find out how and why this is so, and what impact these cultural differences may have on political decision making and public opinion forming.

As of today, journalism is still widely regarded simply as a profession concerned with news and other elements of current affairs taking place in the media. Trends of increasing standardization can, indeed, be traced in course books on journalism, springing from an educational emphasis on the transmittance of technical know-how and objectivist norms of non-partisanship. But, particularly in the polarised-pluralist corner of the Hallin and Mancini model, partisanship and »views« rather than »news« are still playing an important part in ICAs. Furthermore, in liberal systems, markedly the US, opinion-based commentary and openly biased civic journalism is on the rise.

Using these paradoxical developments as a normative turning point for inquiry and reflection, the three research projects in concert identify foundations and barriers for ICA-diversity. They are all concerned with comparative aspects of varieties of journalism, based on the assumption that the lack of an institutional framework and fluffy notions of the public sphere are obstacles to the intellectual and practical understanding of mediated action within a politicized and commercial media market context. In short: without grounded concepts in this area of inquiry, media scholars can hardly expect to develop research into other political economy areas of study.

Conclusions

Mass audiences constitute media markets by delivering »eyeballs« to advertisers. Mass media, however, also play political roles in all systems calling themselves democratic. Public opinion provides legitimacy for representative politics in an institutional fashion: »The medium for this (is) people's public use of their reason,« states one of the prominent protagonists of public sphere analysis (Habermas 1962/1989: 27). It is hard to disagree with such a grand generalization. But in the chapter at hand, it has been argued that the medium for public use of reason may change institutionally – both in terms of time and place.

According to Habermas, critical audiences »of private people come together as a public« ought to be the subjects of political reasoning discussing questions of relevance for democratic governance. When Habermas' original thesis was translated into English, the academic reception was strongly influenced by American debates regarding »the phantom public sphere« originating in the early 20th century. By amending public sphere analysis with institutional approaches, it has been argued that these conceptual ambiguities can be mitigated in order to inform empirical research on mediated action and varieties of journalism.

In line with Habermas, we may view journalism as an integrated part of public opinion forming, i.e. as a vehicle for collective action. In contrast to arcane government, the key feature of public sphere thinking is the liberal quest for communicative legitimacy, rationality and meaning as based on informed citizenship. Habermas warns about the commercial mass media transforming the reading public into an audience of passive spectators. According to his 1962 book, public reasoning may easily decline into strategic power games, leaving little room for communicative action. In turn, this may undermine the legitimacy of representative government and produce crises of political legitimacy.

In this chapter, however, I have challenged the inherent pessimism in critical public sphere analysis. Negative consequences of institutional change in political decision-making (detected by Habermas and his followers as the decline of the public sphere), need not have a damaging impact on the utopia of the public sphere as a constitutional foundation of representative government as long as the model serves ideologically as a common denominator of political expectations and co-ordination of collective action. The news media acting as Institutions of Current Affairs (ICAs) may no longer be legitimated directly in political associations of informed citizens, but as long as journalists and other ICA commentators are accepted by a majority as credible stand-ins located outside the parliamentarian chain of command, the public sphere framework still works for practical political purposes.

Furthermore, mediated action is commonly expected to work on public service conditions rather than commercial business considerations. Consequently, neither constitutional legacies nor market logic are adequate to comprehend the complex webs of norms and interests mediated by ICAs in modern democracies. The aim of comparative research in this field of study should not only be to describe institutional similarities. I have argued for more ambitious designs in comparative research on political communication, aiming at a better understanding of transnational divergence and confluence. Empirical work in business and politics demonstrates how this is a promising way to revitalise »the public sphere« as a contested concept by embedding it in an institutional context as a productive framework for analyses of current affairs and varieties of journalism in democratic media systems.

In order to strengthen this line of research, we must create more transparency in the ICAs around the world. Media scholars in Scandinavia have an institutional advantage at this point because we do have better access to relevant media data than in many other parts of the world. But the base data at hand from the different countries are rarely fully compatible. We also lack specific comparisons of media management and unintended side-effects of political regulation. These inputs are necessary to clarify the political economy foundations of ICAs in order to understand not only institutional convergence, but also cultural diversity in terms of journalism and political action.

References

Bennett, W. 2003, *News: The Politics of Illusion*, Longman, New York.
Bybee, C. 1999, 'Can Democracy Survive in the Post-Factual Age?: A Return to the Lippmann-Dewey Debate About the Politics of News', *Journalism Communication Monographs*, 1, pp. 53-111.
Cook, T.E. 1998, *Governing with the News: The News Media as a Political Institution*, The University of Chicago Press, Chicago.
Curran J. 2005, 'Mediations of democracy', in J. Curran and M. Gurevitch (eds.), *Mass Media and Democracy*, Arnold, London.
Deacon, D. 2004, 'Journalists and Quasi-Government in the UK: Conflict, Cooperation or Co-option?', *Journalism Studies*, 5, pp. 339-352.
Dewey, J. 1927, *The Public and its Problems*, Holt, New York.
Habermas, J. 1962/1990, *Strukturwandel der Öffentlichkeit*, Herman Luchterland Verlag/Suhrkamp, Frankfurt am Main.
Habermas, J. 1973, *Legitimationsprobleme im Spätkapitalismus*, Suhrkamp, Frankfurt am Main.
Habermas, J. 1981, *Theorie des kommunikativen Handelns*, Suhrkamp, Frankfurt am Main.
Habermas J. 1989, *The Structural Transformation of the Public Sphere*, The MIT Press, Cambridge.
Habermas J. 1992, *Facticität und Geltung*, Suhrkamp, Frankfurt am Main.
Hallin, D.C. and P. Mancini 2004, *Comparing Media Systems. Three Models of Media and Politics*, Cambridge University Press, Cambridge.
Iyenger, S. 1991, *Is Anyone Responsible? How television Frames Political Issues*, University of Chicago Press, Chicago.
Lippmann, W. 1930, *The Phantom Public*, Macmillan, New York.
Lund, A.B. 2004, *Niche Nursing Political Networks: Priming and Framing before Spinning*, University of Copenhagen, Modinet.
Lund, A.B. 2006, 'Institutions of Current Affairs – Framework for Comparative Research in European Public Spheres', in F. Marcinkowski et al. (eds.), *Media and Democracy. Experiences from Europe*, Haupt Verlag, Vienna, pp. 145-159.
Lund, A.B. 2007, 'Media Markets in Scandinavia – Political Economy Aspects of Convergence and Divergence', *Nordicom Review*, 28, pp. 121-134.
Mazzoleni, G. and W. Schulz 1999, 'Mediatization' of Politics: A Challenge for Democracy', *Political Communication*,16, pp. 247-261.
Meyer, G. And A.B. Lund 2007, 'Making Room for Pluralism by Re-Defining Journalism: An Essay on Practical Reasoning', *The International Journal of Communication Ethics*, 3, pp. 51-59.
Miller, K.M. and O.H. Gandy 1991, 'Paradigmatic Shift: A Bibliographic Review of the Spread of Economic Analysis in the Litterature of Communication', *Journalism Quarterly*, 68, pp. 663-671.
Pedersen, O.K., P. Kjær, A. Esmark, M. Horst and E.M. Carlsen 2000, *Politisk journalistik*, Ajour, Aarhus.
Peters, J. 1989, 'Democracy and American Mass Communication: Dewey, Lippmann, Lazarsfeld', *Communication*, 11, pp. 199-220.

Robinson, P. 2001, 'Theorizing the Influence of Media on World Politics', *European Journal of Communication*, 16, pp. 523-544.
Schudson, M. 1995, *The Power of News*, Harvard University Press, Cambridge.
Schudson, M. 1999, *The Good Citizen*, Harvard University Press, Cambridge.
Sennett, R. 1977, *The Fall of Public* Man, Knopf, New York.
Shanor, D. 2003, *News from Abroad*, Columbia University Preess, New York.
Sparrow, H.B. 1999, *Uncertain Guardians – The News Media as a Political Institution*, Johns Hopkins University Press, New York.
Thompson J.B. 1995, *The Media and Modernity: A Social Theory of the Media*, Polity Press, Cambridge.
Togeby, L. et al. 2003, *Magt og demokrati I Danmark – hovedresultater fra Magtudredninge*, Aarhus Universitetsforlag, Aarhus.
Østerud, Ø. et al. 2003, *Makten og demokratiet. En slutbok fra Makt- og demokratiudredningen*, Gyldendal, Oslo.

CHAPTER 4

The Institutionalization of Market Mechanisms in Public Service Delivery

Carsten Greve

Professor, Copenhagen Business School, Denmark

Introduction

According to legend, one of the founding fathers of the United States, Benjamin Franklin, was asked by a lady at a dinner party, shortly after the Constitutional Convention has agreed upon a constitution for the United States, what the result was the members of the Constitutional Convention had created. »A republic, mam, if you can keep it« was the answer. By that Franklin meant that establishing a republic was not just done by designing a constitution on a piece of paper, but was about implementation and continuing effort. An analogy can be drawn to the modern-day effort of changing the way public services are delivered: from a publicly based system to a more market-based system. Market-based governance (Donahue and Nye 2002) has been a preferred idea for many governments of how to deliver public services (Hodge ed. 2006). Privatizing public assets (Parker 2006), contracting for public service delivery with private organizations (Greve 2007), issuing vouchers that provide consumer choice (Fountain 2001), and establishing public-private partnerships (PPPs) (Hodge and Greve eds. 2005) are current institutional practices in many countries. One thing is generating the idea and the design of a market-based public service delivery system. Another thing is to turning the idea into institutions in different countries. »A market, if you can keep it« to paraphrase Franklin. The institutionalization of market mechanisms in many countries is perhaps much more difficult than anticipated and demonstrated by the »founding privatization fathers« in Britain and the U.S. in the late 1970s and 1980s. The aim of this chapter is to show how institutionalization of market mechanisms is a slow-moving process that depends on different forms of institutional change mechanisms and different types of market mechanisms. Besides countries like Britain and New Zealand (liberal market economies), where very special institutional conditions at the time made the marketization journey comparatively easy, institutionalization of market mechanisms takes time, and demands continuous commitment to the system. This chapter shows how challenging institutionalizing market mechanisms is in a so-called »coordinated market economy« or negotiated economy (Nielsen and Pedersen 1989; Campbell, Hall and Pedersen eds. 2006) in Denmark.

Institutionalization

In historical institutional theory the concept »path dependency« has enjoyed prominence in analysis of institutional development (Steinmo, Thelen and Longstreth eds. 1992). Paths begin in certain situations called »critical junctures«. The role of »the critical juncture« in historical institutionalism has played the same role as »the policy window« in theories of the policy process. As Pierson (2004: 44) has described it: »under a set of initial conditions conductive to positive feedback, a range of outcomes is generally possible« A path sets forth a specific developmental course of action that cannot easily be change. Path dependency has been defined as »social processes that exhibit positive feedback and thus generate branching patterns of historical development (Pierson 2004: 21). Pierson also speaks of »relatively small events, if occurring at the moment, can have large and enduring consequences«. Determining which event can be called »small« or »big« is, of course, a challenging question, and can only be settled by careful empirical analysis.

The widespread acceptance of path dependency in historical institutionalism has been challenged recently (Thelen 1999). Institutions are both formal and informal rules that guide and constrain behaviour (North 1991). Researchers have begun to think about more nuanced ways of institutional change. Campbell (2004) uses the concept of »bricolage« to describe institutional change processes. Governments cannot give a hundred percent directions on how organizations should behave. The leeway for actors comes from the situation that the institutional guidelines (the formal rules) are not always complete or consistent. Rule makers cannot produce tight rules that cover all contingencies. In fact, the rules may even be contradictory. This means that service providers (rule takers or agents) have some possibility for independent action in the areas where the rules do not apply or are inconsistent. There will always be room for interpretation. Streeck and Thelen (2005) compare the situation with a court case where they may be general or specific rules, but where an attorney will always have the possibility to make a specific interpretation when dealing with an individual case, and a court (and the judge) will always have to make a specific judgement concerning the specific case if there is no obvious precedence. Recent research in historical institutionalism has therefore focussed attention on more gradual and dynamic change processes that allows for strategic action.

> »Political institutions are not only periodically contested; they are the object of ongoing skirmishing as actors try to achieve advantage by interpreting or redirecting institutions in pursuit of their goals, or by subverting or circumventing rules that clash with their interests. Instead of separating institutional development into periods where agency matters more than structure or the other way around, the aim must be to understand (...). the way actors cultivate change from within the context of existing opportunities and constraints – working around elements they cannot change while attempting to harness and utilize others in novel ways« (Streeck and Thelen 2005: 19).

Streeck and Thelen (2005) point to five strategies for change process that »go beyond continuity«: »Displacement«, »layering«, »drift«, »conversion« and »exhaustion«. Change processes must be understood in their historical context, and by examining the dynamic processes change occurs within. »Displacement« concerns when rules are gradually displaced by other rules in time. This process will mean that some rules more active and is slowly replacing previous rules. »Layering« means that new rules are laid on top on previous rules. Older rules lose their meaning. »Drift« means that rules gradually fades away and stop becoming important. »Conversion« means that older institutions are reworked to new apply to new conditions and thereby get a new life or identity. »Exhaustion« means that rules become inapplicable, either because they cannot handle the amount of activity going on, or they might not »have run their course« in relation to the problem they were first meant to address.

It is possible to find discussions that are like some of Streeck and Thelen's five categories. Campbell (2004) sees »bricolage« as a process where new institutional solutions emerge after a combination of existing elements in an innovative process. Genschel (1997) has examined »patching up« and »transposition« as two categories of institutional change in his study on telecommunication and health care. »Patching up« is similar to »layering«, and »transposition« is similar to »conversion«. Norwegian scholar Kjell Arne Røvik (1998) has been writing about »institutional standards« for a long time, and has demonstrated how institutional change occurs through incorporation or rejection of new »institutional standards« into an existing institutionalized setting.

There are bound to more examples like those in the literature on institutional theory. These brief examples offered here will help us be cautious towards using the Streeck and Thelen typology as the only approach to a more nuanced institutional change understanding. But for the purpose of the present chapter, the Streeck and Thelen typology serves as an inspirational framework that will help structure the discussion in the later part of the chapter on the institutionalization of market mechanisms in public service delivery.

One issue that emerges as important is how ready a given institutional setting is for change? Pierson (2004) has noted how focus should be both on change and resilience. One particular area of focus – how »tight« or how »loose« institutions are coupled may give a signal as to the readiness of change (Pierson 2004: 162-164). We would therefore need to look at the tightness of an institutional coupling in a particular setting before we could say anything about the prospects for the five categories of institutional change proposed by Streeck and Thelen.

Market Mechanisms

The second part is concerned with market-mechanisms. They include various principles such as choice, competition between entities, individualism and rivalry (Hood 1998). Competition keeps public service organizations awake (Peters 1996). Markets for public services seldom functions the way markets in perfect competition functions. The most appropriate way to characterize the market mechanisms are as quasi-markets (LeGrand and Bartlett 1993). A number of factors influence why markets for public services are not perfect that include both supply-side imperfections and demand-side imperfections (Kettl 1993: 31-35). If there is not competition, a competitive environment can be constructed. To build a market is a political process. As most governments and scholars have recognized, markets cannot stand alone. Competition is always institutionalized (Fliegstein 2001). Market building is institutionalization process that must address property rights, governance structures, exchange rights, and conceptions of control (Fligstein 2001: 32). Dominant market players (»incumbents«) are challenged by emerging firms (»challengers«), and analyzing that game is an important aspect in understanding the competitive process. The aim is to make a level playing field where both public and private providers compete.

Customer orientation is vital in competitive public service delivery. It is supposed that citizens can make distinctions between roles as citizens, voters, users and customers. Citizens are being given a »free choice«, they are issued with vouchers, and encouraged to »vote with their feet« and choose alternative service providers. Customers need service information. Customers are supposed to be rational actors at the outset who are capable of understand the information in the marketplace. Governments can try to empower citizens to act as customers in public services. Customer orientation has only recently begun to achieve serious scholarly attention in the literature on public management (Fountain 2001; Aberbach and Christensen 2005). The »customerization« of the public service is partly encouraged by governments to put pressure on public service providers »from below«. The implications of customer-orientation are not thought through in public service delivery (Fountain 2001). For example, can public service providers differentiate between customers? Can providers defy

»unsuitable« customers«? Can providers reward »loyal« customers (like the airlines' bonus systems)? Can providers customize their services to a particular »customer segment«? A recent empirical investigation in the UK found that despite much talk on customers' rights and customer focus, people still felt a difference between using a public service and private consume: »It's not like shopping«, was one comment that the research project reported as a general statement from the empirical investigations (Clarke, Newman, Smith, Vidler and Westmarland 2007).

Globalized organizations are also looking across borders to provide public services in other countries than their homeland. Recently, a part of the administration of the East Riding local government in the UK was taken over by a German daughter-company of the Bertelsmann business empire in Germany (Der Spiegel nr. 34, 2006). Researchers have referred to global public service production or »transborder network service delivery systems« (Roberts 2004). Companies are preparing more standardized services that can be delivered in many geographical locations. Public service delivery organizations are therefore not confined to specific and localized »markets«, but try to sell their goods and services where they can. The global service providers develop concepts that travel easily and if they are allowed into national markets, they can benefit from productions of scale. The global company Group4Securicor has been mentioned as one example of this. Other types of companies include »facility management services«, and here companies that act as sub-providers in public-private partnerships in Britain may serve as examples. Consultancy firms are also examples of global service providers that collect and disseminate knowledge on good public management practices.

Generally, there are four principal institutional forms of market mechanisms that have been employed in public service delivery in OECD countries (OECD 2005):

- Privatization of public assets (sale of shares)
- Contracting out
- Consumer choice
- Public-private partnerships

Privatization involves the sale of shares in state owned companies. Privatization was led by Britain in the 1980s, but other countries have followed suit all over the world since. Contracting out involves the provision of public services by private providers through contractual arrangements. Contracting out has been one of the preferred use of market mechanisms by governments around the world (Greve 2007). Consumer choice, or the issuing of vouchers, has been a third market mechanism that has proved popular with governments. Issuing a voucher or extending consumer choice to public services focuses on the »customer orientation«. The empirical knowledge of customers of public services is still relatively limited (Fountain 2001). Recent research has shown that although customer orientation is more widespread than before, people don't see themselves solely as customers when they use public services (Clarke, Newman, Smith, Vidler and Westmarland 2007). Public-private partnerships are the latest addition to the »privatization familiy«, although public-private cooperation has been known for decades and centuries. Public-private partnerships, in their modern carnation, is concerned with infrastructure projects, joint ventures between firms and public organizations, new agreements between voluntary organizations and the public sector, and a host of other institutional arrangements that fly under the partnership banner.

In the public management literature and in the broader governance and regulation literature, the emergence of a new regulatory state as a response to marketization has been recognized and is now considered standard knowledge in many areas. As we have seen, the movement, »this paradoxical combination of deregulation and re-regulation is what is usually meant be regulatory reform« (Majone 1994), has led a number of researchers to talk about a new regulatory state. So-called »free markets« meant that more rules were produced (Vogel 1996). The characterization of the regulatory state has been neatly explained in the literature (Braithwaite 2006; Jordana and Levi-Faur eds. 2004; Christensen and Lægreid 2006).

We will include a number of forms of »monitoring and enforcing compliance« that has gained prominence as part of the regulatory effort, including evaluation (Dahler Larsen 2005), auditing (Power 1994), standardization, accreditation, benchmarking (Van Helden and Tillema 2005), and best or »smart« practice identification (Bardach 1998).

Regulatory agencies could be organizations within the state such as the National Audit Office or a government department. In recent years there has been a trend towards delegating authority to independent regulatory agencies (Thatcher 2005). In accordance with the dis????? above, regulators may come in the form of independent regulatory agencies, evaluators, audit organizations, including audit and accountancy firm, standardization organizations, best practice clearing houses and courts

A specific kind of regulatory agency is international associations or organizations that issue standards that are followed by delivery organizations and seen as authoritative. Organizations include the International Tele Union for telecommunication and standardization councils in each country. Performance data on public service delivery is increasingly being collected by international organizations, and compared through sophisticated benchmarking practices. A well-known example is the OECD PISA report on the level of learning in primary school systems in OECD countries. Suddenly, schools in Denmark are compared to schools in Japan and France. Benchmarking is becoming an integral part of the way public service organizations are assessed.

Institutionalization of Market-Mechanisms: The Case of Denmark

How have market mechanisms for public service delivery been introduced over time? In this section we illustrate the process of institutionalization of market mechanisms by examining the case of Denmark. Britain was the forerunner in the privatization movement (Parker 2006). The movement itself is now global in reach and perspective (Hodge 2006). Other OECD countries followed more gradual steps. Denmark was one of many countries where market ideas were praised in the early 1980s, but where implementation of market mechanisms was slow. The chapter examines Denmark's development with market mechanisms, using Streeck and Thelen's five categories of institutional change: »Displacement«, »layering«, »drift«, »conversion« and »exhaustion«. The examples mentioned below are illustrative examples only. More room is needed for an elaborate version of the institutional development of market mechanisms in the Danish context.

Displacement took place in turning public enterprises into private law corporations, many of which were later privatized (government sold shares in the corporations). Public enterprises in Denmark had been regulated by a special paragraph in the public budget (§ 2). They were therefore called § 2-companies. They were publicly owned and the rules for the enterprises were determined by the government. A director was employed, but referred directly to a government minister, who was, in fact, the head of the enterprise. In the early 1990s, the situation changed. A reform (although it was not called that at the time) turned the public enterprises under public law into corporations under the limited companies act. Some companies, like DONG (Danish Oil and Natural Gas) was already established as a limited company, but with the government as the sole shareholder. Other enterprises were changed into limited companies: Copenhagen Airport, GiroBank, State's Army Clothes Factory and other companies. The telecommunication company was created as a limited company from a number of regional telecommunication companies. Many of the companies were later privatized. This is an example of displacement of one set of rules (public enterprises) with another set of rules (limited company). The shift towards the limited company form allowed the enterprises to change almost overnight. Salaries' for directors and for employees went up. New types of employees were hired at more competitive salaries. Focus was on financial performance and developing new products instead of more routine production. The long term consequences of corporatization and privatization have yet to be examined. But recent evidence shows that companies were transformed into »market players« as opposed to public enterprises that acted on political directives.

Layering has taken place for contracting out measures. Rules for ordinary public service delivery exist within the local government legislation and many policy areas. Rules on contracting out have been added to the existing rules for public service delivery. Especially EU-rules for competitive tendering is influencing the way government contracts for service delivery. If government contracts for above a certain sum of money, the tendering process has to follow EU rules for competitive tendering. Not all public services are eligible for EU-tendering (many social services are not, for example). But if government decides to contract out, then the EU-rules have to be obeyed. Proponents of contracting out encourage government to attempt to expose more services to competitive tendering processes. EU rules are thereby »layered« on top of existing rules. If more services are delivered through this set of rules, then EU-tendering will gradually become the chief rules to observe for public service delivery. A second example concerns rules for consumer choice that have also been introduced gradually over time, another sign of »layering«. Rules on consumer choice do not replace the existing rules, but they are added as another layer that guides public service delivery. Rules on consumer choice allow consumers to choose between different service providers. Local governments are obliged to make sure that there are enough providers to choose from. Local governments can either contract out the service to a number of private providers, or acknowledge the private provider as a provider if certain criteria are met. The EU-rules themselves change over time as well. The most recent addition to the rule set is that EU allows for a so-called »competitive dialogue« between purchasers and providers. A third example of layering may be the continuing addition of new regulatory and evaluation bodies. In connection with the Structural Reform (where 271 local governments were reduced to 98 local governments and 13 county councils transformed to 5 regions), a new Local and Regional Evaluation Institute (Kommunalt og Regional Evalueringsinstitut) was established. The purpose of the Evaluation Institute is to collect and compare data on public service delivery performance by the main providers (local governments and regions). Benchmarking and »best practice« guidelines are the leading tools of the new institute. The institute did not replace any other evaluation body, but were established as another layer on the already dense population of evaluation bodies and organizations in the Danish public sector.

Drift can be observed in choice of service providers. More citizens are choosing private health providers (like the well-known example of private pensions, see Hacker 2005). Companies pay for private health insurance schemes for their employees in greater numbers than before. The nature of the public sector health system is gradually losing its appeal if more citizens choose private hospitals and private clinics for their essential treatments. The importance of the extended public health system in Denmark is being challenged by private sector health provision. Drift can be observed through a longer time frame in this area.

Conversion is a phenomenon in the area of the Competition Authority and the application of competition policy to the public services. The Competition Authority has been preoccupied with the private sector and with competition of private companies. As services are being competitively tendered, and new services are being added, the Competition Authority must turn some of its attention to the relationship between public providers and private providers. A new task is to ensure fair competition among public and private providers. Competition policy and competition law is more frequently applied to public service delivery organizations from the public sector. A »conversion«, or »redirection of purpose«, has taken place within the well-known institution of the Competition Authority.

Exhaustion can be observed in a number of areas. The now defunct State Regulatory Councils »Tilsynsråd«, regional regulatory bodies set up by the Ministry of Interior to watch over local governments, were severely tested in the late 1990s when the local government of Farum experimented with a variety of market mechanisms for public service delivery, including a comprehensive contracting out scheme and a new scheme of public-private partnerships. The State Regulatory Council for Frederiksborg County was not sufficiently staffed or resourced to control the behaviour of the local government effectively. Farum local governments many new schemes and practices were not adequately regulated by the State Regulatory Council. When the regulatory council issued warnings and directions to the local government, the local government either ignored them or challenged them openly. And the regulatory council did not have sufficient sanctions or other means to change the direction of the local government of Farum. The design for the regulatory council was drawn up in another age when local governments were not as challenging, and the council's tasks had been exhausted.

Summing up, successive Danish governments did not try to introduce market mechanisms over night in one big reform effort. Instead, market mechanisms have been introduced in a variety of institutional rule sets during the last decades. Institutional change has concerned the way public enterprises operate, the EU-induced rules guiding contracting out, the possibility for citizens and employees to choose private providers over public providers in the health sector, the purposes and applicability of the competition rules, and the operations and the rules guiding specific regulatory agencies.

The Politics of Market-Mechanisms: Tight or Loose Institutional Coupling?

If we are to understand the institutionalization of market mechanisms over time, we must also try to understand how market mechanisms fit into the existing institutional framework. In Denmark, market mechanisms were not used systematically in public service delivery until the early 1980s. Before that, the use of market mechanisms in public service delivery was predominantly uncoordinated or fragmented. When the modernization programme of the Conservative-led government from 1983 was introduced, market mechanisms were accorded a special place in the broader, systematic modernization effort.

Pierson writes about tight coupling among distinct institutions that »The existence of complementarities among institutions would carry a number of significant implications for patterns of institutional development. Where such complementarities are substantial, we should expect to observe distinct clusterings of institutional arrangements. If institution X is present, we will be more likely to see institution Y, all other things being equal« (Pierson 2004: 162).

The institutionalization of market mechanisms could be said to confront the tight institutional couplings of the Danish welfare state where use of market mechanisms was not a tradition. Seen in this light, the institutionalization of market mechanism is an up hill struggle with very limited prospects of eventual success. The resilience of the existing institutions will defy the challenge of using market mechanisms more systematically.

As we have seen, central policymakers and other types of policymakers have carried on their effort to introduce market mechanisms over a period of more than 20 years. That is why we can use Streeck and Thelen's typology as an inspiration: Market mechanisms are introduced gradually; in different sectors (the health sector is one example), in different institutional settings (central government, regional government, local government) and in a variety of institutional forms (privatization as in sale of assets, contracting out, consumer choice and public-private partnerships to name the most predominant ones).

Some forms of market mechanisms have been more »successful« than others in terms of implementation. Most of eligible public enterprises are now transformed into companies and in many of the companies have been privatized partly or wholly. The next big privatizations are the state owned commercial television station (TV2) and the natural gas and oil company (DONG). The telecommunication company was sold off more than ten years ago and is today owned by a capital fond. Contracting out has been less successful in terms of implementation. Around 12-13 percent of services are contracted to private providers in local government, and this figure has been stable for years, despite many policy initiatives to change the figure in an upward direction. Consumer choice can be seen as more successful in some ways: National legislation has meant that consumer choice is now something that local governments are responsible for arranging. However, not many citizens use their consumer rights. In elderly care and child care, only 5-10 percent of the citizens make use of their consumer choice option in choosing a private provider over a public provider. Although the number of »consumers« is rising, it is still far from the expectations of the present government in Denmark. Public-private partnerships, at least in their »PFI-infrastructure« version, has had a tough time getting off the ground in Denmark. Whereas the UK can boast of more than 500 current PPP-projects in the infrastructure sector, Denmark only has a handful of PPP projects, and only two official PPP projects working in local government and central government.

What does the implementation of market mechanisms tell us about institutional change? We may want to return to the tight/loose coupling argument from above. One hypothesis could be that the most successful types of market mechanisms in terms of their implementation that are introduced in the Danish public sector, are the types of market mechanisms that fit the tight institutional coupling of the established Danish welfare state/political economy identified by Pedersen and others (Campbell, Hall and Pedersen eds. 2006). Let me try to elaborate this point below.

Privatization of public enterprises could happen because it fitted the tight institutional coupling of the Danish political economy. Ownership of public enterprises in Denmark was never ever an integral part of the state's identity. Whereas other countries like Britain and France have had huge public enterprise sectors, Denmark has never had a strong public enterprise identity. Some companies are of a newer breed (DONG from the 1970s) while other was organized regionally (telecommunication companies). Danish State Railways and Post Denmark has been the enterprises closest to the state, and they only began their privatization talks late. Another aspect is that the Danish government early in the 1990s foresaw that the companies would not be able to compete on internationalized and globalized markets on their own. They would have to go into mergers or be bought up eventually. In other words, privatizing public assets have been a strategy for the government that would enable an efficient economy without sacrificing any state identity or key part of the economy. »Load shedding« was a wise and strategic decision by the Danish government in this perspective, and a decision that did not alter the »tight coupling« of the political economy, but strengthened it.

Contracting out has not had the same strategic position in the Danish government and local governments, and it is a much more difficult (Pallesen and Christensen (2002) from University of Aarhus has also argued this point forcefully). When contracting out a public service, local governments employees are facing a shift in work conditions. Any »burdens« will be borne immediately by the citizens if services are poor. Contracting out can be an up hill struggle. Extensive contracting out will challenge the tight corporatist coupling and may therefore be more difficult to introduce politically.

Introducing consumer choice is a long process in a developed welfare state. Citizens are used to receiving reasonably good public services, and they are not always used to choose among a number of providers. Introducing this market mechanism is therefore going to take time. The first step is to add layers of rules on choice option on to the existing rule sets. Consumer choice does not challenge the tight coupling directly, when it is seen as harmless, and in the long run, consumer choice can help regulate the behaviour of providers, both public and private. Therefore consumer choice must be seen in the long perspective, and could therefore be incorporated slowly in the institutional setting of the welfare state.

Public-private partnerships have also been introduced gradually in the Danish welfare state. PPPs do not present a direct threat to the tight institutional coupling. Because of the ambiguity of the concept and the practice of PPPs, PPPs can be incorporated into the tight coupling of the welfare state over time. The aim of the PPPs in some versions is to strengthen the relationship between the public sector and the private sector, and to provide synergy in solutions in public service delivery, so PPPs may find their »natural place« in the institutional ecology over time.

The four forms (privatization, contracting out, consumer choice and public-private partnerships) described here shows how »market mechanisms« are introduced in public service delivery. The relationship between these forms could be explored more, and the existence of an underlying »marketization discourse« could also be examined in more detail, but for now the purpose have been to discuss the different forms and the different pace that the institutionalization of market mechanisms take.

Conclusion

This chapter is focussed on how the institutionalization of market mechanisms takes place in the Danish political economy. The concept of institutionalization was discussed first, and Streeck and Thelen's typology of five categories of institutional change was presented as a supplement to the established path dependency concept. A discussion followed on market mechanisms, and four types of market mechanisms were singled out for attention: privatization (sale of public assets), contracting out, consumer choice and public-private partnerships. Their regulatory context and the »rise of the regulatory state« were also emphasized. After that followed a discussion of the institutionalization of market mechanisms using Streeck and Thelen's typology as a framework. The discussion revealed how market mechanisms for public service delivery, and their accompanying regulatory framework, has not happened in one overriding reform effort, but has been the product on a continuing effort by governments over a period spanning several decades.

Many different institutional change mechanisms have been used by the central policymakers in the Danish government to institutionalize market mechanisms: displacement (company law instead of public enterprise rules), layering (adding contracting out rules to existing rules for public service delivery), drift (allowing for more private health care payments), conversion (redirecting existing organizations' attention towards competition for public service delivery) and exhaustion (ending some forms of traditional oversight and control functions for public service delivery). We are not yet in a position in the research where the specific dynamics between these institutional change mechanisms have been explored and revealed. That remains an area for further research.

In the end, the chapter has reflected upon the importance of the established institutions of the Danish political economy for the success of the various market mechanisms forms. The Danish political economy is often described as being tightly coupled institutionally. Therefore, institutionalization of market mechanisms may be seen as difficult, and if any market mechanisms have succeeded, then that would require an explanation. It was noted how privatization of state owned enterprises have been the most successful types of market mechanisms, while the actual implementation of contracting out, consumer choice and public-private partnerships are still relatively modest. We hypothesized that one possible explanation for this may be that privatization of public assets did not challenge the tight institutional coupling in the same way as contracting out, consumer choice do (while the ambiguous character of public-private partnerships makes it open as to whether it is a threat or a supplement to the existing institutional setting). Contracting out and consumer choice, if carried out differents, might alter the way the Danish political economy, and the Danish public institutions work, while privatization of public assets was never such a threat because Denmark did not have a high profile public enterprise sector to begin with, and selling shares actually helped make the Danish state more competitive.

References

Aberbach, J. and T. Christensen 2005, 'Citizens and Consumers. An NPM Dilemma', *Public Management Review*, 7 (2), pp. 225-245.

Bardach, E. 1998, *Getting Agencies to Work Together*, Brookings, Washington D.C.

Braithwaite, J. 2006, 'The Regulatory State?, in R.A.W. Rhodes, S. Binder and B. Rockman (eds.), *The Oxford Handbook of Political Institutions*, Oxford University Press, Oxford.

Campbell, J. 2004, *Institutional Change and Globalization*, Princeton University Press, Princeton.

Campbell, J., J. Hall and O.K. Pedersen (eds.) 2006, *National Identity and a Variety of Capitalism: The Danish Experience*, Jurist og Økonomforbundets forlag/McGill Univerisity Press, Montreal and Copenhagen.

Christensen, T. and P. Lægreid (eds.) 2006, *Autonomy and Regulation*, Edward Elgar Publishers, Chelthenham.

Christensen, J.G. and Pallesen, T. 2002. "The Political Benefits of Corporazation and Privatization" Journal of Public Policy Vol. 21, pp. 283-309.

Clarke, J., J. Newman, N. Smith, E. Vidler, and L. Westmarland 2007, *Creating Citizen-Consumers. Changing Public and Changing Public Services*, Sage, London.

Dahler-Larsen, P. 2005, 'Evaluation and Public Management', in E. Ferlie, L. Lynn and C. Pollitt, *The Oxford Handbook of Public Management*, Oxford, pp. 615-642.

Donahue, J. and J.S. jr. Nye (eds.) 2002, *Market-Based Governance*, Brookings, Washington D.C.

Fligstein, N. 2001, *The Architecture of Markets*, Princeton University Press, Princeton.

Fountain, J. 2001, 'Paradoxes of Public Service Customer Services', in *Governance*, 14 (1), pp. 55-73.

Genschell, P. 1997, 'The Dynamics of Intertia. Institutional Persistence and Change in Telecommunication and Health Care', in *Governance*, 10 (1), pp. 43-66.

Globaliseringsrådet [Globalization Council, Denmark] 2006, *Danmark i den globale økonomi*. [Denmark in the Global Economy], Danish Government, Copenhagen.

Greve, C. 2006, 'Public Management Reform in Denmark', in *Public Management Review*, 8 (1), pp. 161-167.

Greve, C. 2007, *Contracting for Public Services*, Routledge, London.

Hodge, G. (ed.) 2006, *Privatization and Market Development. Global Movements in Public Policy Ideas*, Edward Elgar, Chelthenham.

Hodge, G. and C. Greve (eds.) 2005, *The Challenge of Public-Private Partnerships. Learning from International Experience*, Edward Elgar, Chelthenham.

Hood, C. 1998, *The Art of the State*, Clarendon, Oxford.

Jordana, J. and D. Levi-Faur (eds.) 2004, *The Politics of Regulation*, Edward Elgar, Chelthenham.

Kettl, D.F. 1993, *Sharing Power. Public Governance of Private Markets*, Brookings, Washington D.C.

LeGrand, J. and W. Bartlett (eds.) 1993, *Quasi-Markets and Social Policy*, MacMillan, London.

Majone, G. 1994, 'The Rise of the Regulatory State in Europe', in *West European Politics*, 17, reprinted in R. Baldwin, C. Scott and C. Hood (eds.) 1998, *Regulation – A Reader*, Oxford University Press, Oxford, pp. 77-101.

Newman, J. 2001, *Modernising Governance. New Labour, Policy and Society*, Sage, London.

Nielsen, K. and O.K. Pedersen 1989, 'Fra blandingsøkonomi til forhandlingsøkonomi: mod et nyt paradigme?', in K.K. Klausen and T.H. Nielsen (eds.), *Stat og marked*, DJØF Publishing, Copenhagen, pp. 171-226.

North, D. 1991, 'Institutions', in *Journal of Economic Perspectives*, 5, pp. 97-112.

OECD 2005, *Modernising Government*, OECD, Paris.

Parker, D. 2006, 'Enterprise Sales. Thatcher Leads the Charge', in G. Hodge (ed.) 2006, *Privatization and Market Development. Global Movements in Public Policy Ideas*, Edward Elgar, Chelthenham, pp. 9-35.

Peters, B.G. 1996, *The Future of Governing. Four Emergent Models*, University Press of Kansas, Kansas.

Pierson, P. 2004, *Politics in Time*, Princeton University Press, Princeton.

Power, M. 1994, *The Audit Explosion*, Demos, London.

Roberts, A. 2004, *Transborder Service Systems: Pathways to Innovation or Threats to Accountability?*, The IBM Center for the Business of Government.

Røvik, K.A. 1998, *Moderne organisasjoner*, Fakbokforlaget, Bergen.

Sahlin-Andersson, K. 2001, 'National, International and Transnational Constructions of New Public Management', in Christensen and Lægreid (eds.), *New Public Management*, Ashgate, Aldershot.

Spiegel, Der 2006, *Der private staat*, 34, 21.08.2006, pp. 40-42.

Steimo, S., K. Thelen and F. Longstreth (eds.) 1992, *Structuring Politics*, Cambridge University Press, Cambridge.

Streeck, W. and K. Thelen 2005, 'Introduction: Institutional Change in Advanced Political Economies', in W. Streeck and K. Thelen (eds.) 2005, *Beyond Continuity. Institutional Change in Advanced Political Economies*. Oxford University Press, Oxford, pp. 1-39.

Streeck, W. and K. Thelen (eds.) 2005, *Beyond Continuity. Institutional Change in Advanced Political Economies*, Oxford University Press, Oxford.

Thatcher, M. 2005, 'The Third Force? Independent Regulatory Agencies and Elected Politicians in Europe', in *Governance*, 18 (3), pp. 347-373.

Thelen, K. 1999, 'Historical Institutionalism in Comparative Politics', *Annual Review of Political Science*, 2, pp. 369-404.

Van Helden, G.J. and S. Tillema 2005, 'In Search of a Benchmarking Theory for the Public Sector', in *Financial Accountability and Management*, 21 (3), pp. 337-361.

Vogel, S. 1996, *Freer Markets, More Rules*, Cornell University Press, Itacha.

CHAPTER 5

Institutional History

Peter Kjær

Associate professor, Copenhagen Business School, Denmark

Introduction

The following is a presentation and elaboration of key elements in the analytical approach of Institutional History. The Institutional History approach was developed by a network of researchers at Roskilde University, the University of Copenhagen and Copenhagen Business School from the mid-1980s until the early 2000s. Institutional History has many commonalities with other approaches to institutional analysis, but it also constitutes a particular and productive way of addressing the problems of institutional analysis. While there is hardly a 'school' of Institutional History in Denmark today, some of the basic questions and issues of the approach continue to inform the research of several scholars both in Denmark and elsewhere.[1]

1. An earlier version of the present chapter appeared in A. Esmark, C.B. Laustsen and N. Åkerstrøm Andersen (eds.): Socialkonstruktivistiske Analysestrategier (2005) which was an edited volume presenting a series of analytical strategies within a broad constructivist paradigm. I benefited greatly from editorial comments by Anders Esmark on that early version. Parts of the present argument also draws heavily on an earlier working paper by Niels Åkerstrøm Andersen and myself (1996).

Institutional History[2] is an analytical strategy developed for the study of institutionalization and institutional change. The analytical strategy is first and foremost rooted in neo-institutionalism but also draws on discourse analysis among other things. Institutional History is concerned with the fundamental issue of constitution; that is the formation and transformation of social order. The purpose of Institutional History is to develop principles and guidelines for conducting concrete analyses of the constitution of social order – without being captured by the dominant logics of the social orders that we are part of and without imposing our own taken-for-granted world-views on the processes of constitution and change that we are observing.

In this context Institutional History offers a dual analytical strategy: one that analyzes the construction of contexts of meaning and their stabilization into spaces of action (institutionalization analysis), and one that observes ruptures in spaces of action and forms of governance (change analysis).

In the following I shall outline Institutional History by first describing some of its sources of inspiration, especially in neo-institutional analysis, then outlining some of the fundamental issues of constitutional analysis, and finally presenting the key analytical steps in the dual strategy that offers a response to these issues.

The Challenge of Neo-Institutionalism: Description, Exposé and Constitutional Analysis

I will present Institutional History as an attempt to deal with the challenges emerging with the development of *neo-institutionalism* in the social

2. The term 'Institutional History' came from a 1985 publication by Ove K. Pedersen and was the term originally used by the research network. I use the term in the present article although it will almost certainly entail some confusion for an English speaking audience having grown accustomed to the term 'Historical institutionalism' that designates a somewhat different approach to institutional analysis especially in political science. Partly for that reason, Institutional History was renamed 'Discursive Institutionalism' in Kjær and Pedersen (2001).

sciences, although initially Institutional History was also deeply inspired by debates in epistemology, structural Marxism and discourse analysis (Pedersen 1985, Andersen 1994).

Neo-institutionalism is a generic term for a series of theoretical positions within political science (March and Olsen 1989; Peters 2001); organization studies (Powell and DiMaggio 1991; Scott 1995) and economics (Williamson 1975; North 1990). The only shared property of these quite varied contributions is the concept of institution and a common interest in studying how behavior is regulated in the broadest sense of the term. The concept of institution marks a common ambition to shift the analytical focus from the level of behavior and decision-making or from macro structures of society to the more intermediary conditions for action. At the same time it also entails an ambition of being able to observe conditions for action as constructed endogenously and not given exogenously. In other word, *the institutional* is something beyond the individual actor, but also something that is created and changed in concrete contexts.

An additional but more recent common feature of institutionalism within political science and organization studies is an interest in cognitive regulation. Whereas neo-institutionalism within economics rediscovered formal organization, political science and organization studies discovered the importance of common systems of knowledge and meaning.

Neo-institutionalism is 'new' compared to at least two forms of 'old' institutionalism: an early institutional tradition within the social sciences established at the end of the 19th century (Scott 1995: 1 cont.) – and a somewhat later school, especially related to the sociology of organizations in the 1950s (Scott 1995: 17 cont.; Powell and DiMaggio 1991; 12 cont.). I will briefly elaborate the two to highlight some of the key differences between the 'old' and the 'new'.

'Old' institutionalism – first edition: Political science and historical political economy as practiced at the beginning of the 20th century were in many ways institutional approaches. They were first and foremost historical and descriptive, and typically lacked a strong theoretical foundation. Instead there was a shared empirical focus on societal institutions: political constitutions, cultural forms, forms of economic organization, etc. The function of a given institutional arrangement was best understood by describing its present manifestations and mapping out its ori-

gins: the early predecessors, the debate prior to its institution, variations over time, etc. A couple of decades into the 20th century this type of social analysis was replaced by approaches that were either constructed around axiomatic models for rational decision-making, as in economic science, or rooted in behavioral systems models focusing on social psychological models of human behavior, as in sociology and political science (Manicas 1987; Wagner, Wittrock and Whitley 1991).

'Old' institutionalism – second edition: Within the field of organizational sociology an institutional school developed in America in the 1950s that attempted to reintroduce the 'institutional'. With what Charles Perrow has described as the basic figure of *exposé* the approach demonstrated that 'things are not as they seem' (Perrow 1986: 159). A number of empirical analyses illustrated how the gradual adaptation of organizations to the interests and values of members and to the environment displaced formally defined goals and structures. Organizations became institutions when governed by participants' 'commitments' to a social community rather than by formal structures and objectives (Selznick 1992: 234 cont.). Empirical analyses also showed how institutionalization – and thus goal displacement and structural adaptation – took place through both spontaneous adaptation and local power struggles. Compared to the understanding of early institutionalism of institutions as social phenomena immediately observable, institutions were now understood as something underlying and explaining concrete empirical phenomena. Partially in contrast e.g. to the legal understanding of institutions of political science, a sociological understanding is added that ascribes decisive importance to shared norms and values. This sociological institutionalism never assumed a dominant position, but became an important point of reference for later attempts to develop institutional perspectives on social organizing. The basic figure of exposé was continued, but gradually with a focus on how institutionalization should have been understood as a process through which the institution is captured, not by local interests and values, but by broader conceptions and norms that are institutionalized at the level of society or sector.

The new institutional schools that developed from the mid-1970s and especially during the 1980s differed from the previous ones in two ways.

They focused on the question of change and they expanded the concept of institutions to also include cognitive aspects.

The issue of *change* was first and foremost raised as an issue of the institutional conditions for change. This implied challenging both a rational and a deterministic understanding of change (March and Olsen 1989: 6 cont.). In challenging an understanding of change that emphasized planning and calculation, and challenging an understanding that attached central importance to economic, technological or class structures, neo-institutionalism operated with an intermediate layer of institutional variables. Political choices, organizational decisions and economic strategies are developed in an institutional context that defines the 'menu' of potential avenues of action. Theoretically the analysis of change turned into a question of identifying the institutional structures, dynamics, trajectories, etc., that define but also establish avenues of action in various contexts. Key notions in this context became concepts such as learning, path dependency, and institutional isomorphism (Hall 1993; North 1990: 94 cont.; DiMaggio and Powell 1991 [1983]: 67 cont.).

The *understanding of institutions* developed. Common to almost all contributions was that they saw institutions as the underlying explanation challenging both materialist or functional explanations and the rationalizations given by individuals, organizations and institutions to justify behaviors. Within economics one (re)discovered the importance of formal regulations (legislation, contracts, etc.) for economic transactions, leading to the development of an economic theory of organization focusing on what Scott calls 'regulative' aspects of institutions (Scott 1994). Within political science and political sociology the state was re-discovered and thus also the importance of formal organizational frameworks, but focus was even directed toward informal aspects such as norms, routines, and rules of the thumb that were reminiscent of the debates of the 1950s.

Within organization studies and certain areas of political science there was, however, also a new interest in cognitive aspects of institutions (Meyer and Rowan 1991 [1977]: 42). The cognitive approach drew inspiration, in particular, from phenomenological positions within ethnomethodology (Garfinkel) and the sociology of knowledge (Berger and Luckmann) and implied a focus on how social actors always operate in a layer of institutionally produced 'taken-for-granted' everyday understandings of the world. Here rationality was seen as a retrospective contextualization in which actions could be described in legitimizing and normalizing terms. The distance to a theory of language and discourse was short, and institutional theory oriented toward cognition also became interested in systems of knowledge and structures of meaning carried by language, as signaled by concepts such as 'accounts', typifications', myths', and 'scripts'.

The neo-institutional debate did not give rise to one shared concept of institution. There have been a number of proposals for synthesis that have attempted to bridge the gap between debates within economics, political science, and organization sociology. The American organization sociologist Richard W. Scott understands institutions to be composed of 'cultural-cognitive, normative, and regulative elements that together with associated activities and resources, provide stability and meaning to social life' (Scott 1995: 48; Scott 1994). In continuation of this, Scott has attempted to develop an aggregate theoretical model for institutional analysis. The general tendency is not, however, pointing toward a synthesis (but see Campbell 2004), but rather toward continued philosophical and epistemological dispute between a cognitively and language oriented institutional theory and institutional theories working from more conventional epistemological and ontological premises.

The cognitive orientation implies that certain parts of institutional theory have moved towards *constitutional analysis*. When institutions cease to be viewed simply as stable regulatory arrangements sanctioned by law or custom, but are seen as naturalized ideas drawing strength from their being taken-for-granted in certain contexts and systems of knowledge, then institutional analysis potentially takes on a new function. It thus comes to suggests that entities such as 'organization', 'individual' and 'state' can no longer be subject to theorizing and empirical analysis in a straight-forward manner. Rather their very constitution as social entities in institutionalized systems of meaning must be subject to analysis (Meyer, Boli and Thomas 1987: 26). Organizations and other social entities are thus seen as symbolic and institutional constructions whose formation must be studied if we are to be in a position to challenge their status as almost natural-given entities and consider their effects on concrete contexts of action.

Constitutional analysis thus perceived is a broad field that encompasses a number of sociological and philosophical contributions. However, the particular contribution of neo-institutionalism to constitutional analysis has been to place two key issues on the agenda. On the one hand a *temporal* issue of change. In the jumble of reforms and organizational changes during the 1980s and the 1990s, institutional theory offered an understanding of change that challenged the curious mixture of given exogenous demands for change and strong ideals about autonomous rational decision-making. The contribution has been to demonstrate that the very idea of »change« (and its corrolaries) is a historical construct and that it is related to particular institutional arrangements that supply both expectations of change (e.g. reform models) and standardized stories (rationalized myths) about rational action (Brunsson and Olsen 1993). At the same time, the neo-institutional approach to constitutional analysis was delimited in important ways since institutions – in concrete analysis – were often seen as given and relatively stable formations that were ascribed certain effects that could be verified empirically. The core message of neo-institutionalism is not that institutions exist (hardly anybody doubts it), but that they vary and thus make a difference. In practice, however, institutional analyses have typically directed empirical attention toward institutional effects (at the organizational level), while the institution itself, as a naturalized system of meaning, is taken for granted. This becomes one area where Institutional History attempts to make a distinct contribution.

On the other hand, neo-institutional theory has raised the issue of how *spaces* for social action are ordered and how they change. Here the analytical interest is displaced from formal or normative conditions for action toward naturalized/cognitive conditions for action. The key question is thus how particular types of knowledge and meaning that become institutionalized gain a structuring force and organize a space for action. Within organizational analysis focus has been on identifying different types of causal mechanisms which link institution and the organization or the individual: formal organizing of the environment, the drive for legitimization at the organizational level, resource dependencies, and institutional 'pressures' for isomorphism. While this focus has been productive in identifying concrete objects of empirical analysis, it has also tended to maintain or reproduce a theory of organization and action that still distinguishes between core and surface and between organization and environment. In the classic article 'Institutionalized Organizations: Formal Structure as Myth and Ceremony' Meyer and Rowan conclude:

> Organizational structures are created and made more elaborate with the rise of institutionalized myths, and, in highly institutionalized contexts, organizational action must support these myths. But an organization must also attend to practical activity. The two requirements are at odds. A stable solution is to maintain the organization in a loosely coupled state. (Meyer and Rowan 1991 [1977]: 60).

The difference between demands from the institutional context and practical activity points back to the distinction of classic organization theory between core activity and institutional requirements as discussed in structural functionalism (cf. Scott 1992: 71; Thompson 1967). Under the surface of the 'talkative' and institutionalized organization, there remains an authentic organizational level, threatened by institutionalization.

Constitutional analysis in neo-institutionalism has thus implied criticism of exaggerated notions of rationality and formal structure, while paying less attention to the nature of social entities such as organization, individual, and group, probably because the analysis has often been embedded in a theory of organizations and their environments (Pedersen 1991; Andersen and Kjær 1996).

Historical Constitutional Analysis

Neo-institutionalism thus evolves from institutional 'description' and 'exposé' to 'constitutional analysis'. The ambition of Institutional History is here to radicalize constitutional analysis, in part by giving priority to the historical 'diachronic' dimension of institutional analysis emphasizing the creation of institutions over time. And in part by opening up for empirical analysis the question of how fundamental social entities and boundaries are constituted and how constitutions change.

There have other been efforts in this direction, for example, within organizational analysis and political sociology, making Institutional History only one of several attempts to deal with the limitations of conventional analytical approaches within neo-institutionalism. The debate about the creation of organizational fields thus reflects attempts to analyze institutionalization processes over time (see e.g. Fligstein 1990; Scott and Christensen eds. 1995). We find this ambition in, among others, Paul DiMaggio's (1991) call for analyses of the creation of organizational fields. DiMaggio stresses that the concept of organizational field and similar concepts are extremely important to institutional analyses as the very embeddedness of institutions in certain fields explains the diffusion of certain forms of organizations. Nevertheless the dominant focus on diffusion processes [and institutional effects, pk] has, according to DiMaggio, made us blind to the genesis and structuring of fields:

> The neglect (...) provides a one-sided vision of institutional change that emphasizes taken-for-granted, nondirected, nonconflictual evolution at the expense of intentional (if boundedly rational), directive, and conflict-laden processes that define fields and set them upon trajectories that eventually appear as 'natural' developments to participants and observers alike (DiMaggio 1991: 268).

At least two issues are at stake here: On the one hand, DiMaggio wants to introduce actors into institutional analysis and discourage the lurking tendency toward structural-determinism in institutional analysis. On the other hand, the historical analysis holds the possibility of capturing a context of meaning before it has become entirely natural: before we become blind to it.

A parallel attempt to break with implicit assumptions about the constitution of social entities is found in the introduction of the concept of 'translation' (from actor-network theory) into institutional analysis. In an attempt to challenge the focus of diffusion research on the diffusion of certain organizational models and thus the tendency to begin the analysis 'top-down' with given institutional standards, Scandinavian organization researchers, such as Barbara Czarniawska, Kjell Arne Røvik, and Kerstin Sahlin-Andersson, have attempted to escape the diffusion metaphor and have focused attention on the local creation and selection of meaning and context related to certain models (see Czarniawska and Sevon eds. 1996).

Against this backdrop, Institutional History can be seen as entailing a stronger emphasis on historical processes of institutional construction of knowledge and meaning and a strong emphasis, not on local translations, but on the transformation of social orders observed primarily at the meso-level of analysis.

In concrete terms Institutional History consists of two separate but interlocking analytical problems: On the one hand, the problem of capturing the special movement toward 'sedimentation', that is, from the controversial and problematic to the uncontroversial, unproblematic and thus natural. Sedimentation involves the movement from a proposition, a theme, an action or the like constituting something problematic or disputable to it becoming a naturalized and stable context of meaning. This requires a particular *institutionalization analysis.*

On the other hand, there is the problem of being able to identify conditions of action and in particular changes in these, from a position of simultaneously wishing to distance oneself from particular ontological descriptions of spaces of action and maintaining focus on evolving institutional conditions.

This requires a particular *analysis of change*, that is a systematic way of being able to perceive the social organization and the ruptures in social organizing that a given institutionalization process can be said to produce.

Institutionalization Analysis

Within neo-institutional organizational analysis heuristic understandings of the institutionalization process have been developed in terms of a process of field creation, as mentioned above. The most cited conceptualization of the organizational field describes it as consisting of four elements:

> An increase in the extent of information among organizations in the field; the emergence of sharply defined interorganizational structures of domination and patterns of coalition; an increase in the information load with which organizations in the field must contend; and the development of a mutual awareness among participants of a set of organizations that they are involved in a common enterprise (DiMaggio and Powell 1991 [1983]: 65).

Perhaps rather than capturing the creation process per se, the approach seems apt for demonstrating *when* it is possible to talk about an organizational field. Implicitly: when these properties are not present, and an organizational field cannot be said to exist, we must draw on explanations different from the institutional ones. This is a model distinctly oriented toward material conditions – interaction, organizational structure, and information network – while the aspect of meaning primarily becomes a question of the actors in a field gradually coming to recognize each other.

Compared to this approach, Institutional History thematizises more unequivocally the question of meaning. Meaning is a central aspect of the very understanding of institution and institutionalization which is seen as having to do with stabilizing meaning, and making it impact on particular actors and activities.

Within Institutional History meaning is first and foremost associated with language, and the concept of meaning is therefore grounded in language theory, which is why it does not conceptualize individual (subjective) meaning as compared to societal (objective) meaning. Meaning is rather seen as an effect of language use, of articulation.

Most institutional historians draw on Saussure's (1990) concept of signs as constituting meaning through difference and relation in a system of signs (Andersen 1994, Foucault 1982; Andersen 1999). A pattern of meaning is developed when a sign is made equivalent to or different from related signs. The meaning of 'competitiveness' is determined by the system of relation and opposition in which it is placed, such as in relation to concepts as 'reorganization', 'regulation', or 'quality'. At the same time any meaning is arbitrary (the sign could have had a different position) and selective (the position simultaneously excludes other potential positions). The purpose of the linguistic analysis is, through a description of concrete articulations, to discern the particular patterns or regularities both presupposed by and reproduced by concrete language use.

This pattern or regularity is seen as a convention or a language code. A stable and given code determining all meaning in a field does not exist. Rather the code is seen as an emerging pattern the nature of which is to be determined in concrete analysis – as codes may be more or less stabilized, more or less dominant, and more or less subject to controversy and struggle etc. Institutional History has managed this condition by developing an institutional analysis that enables us to map the way in which language codes are created and stabilized, but simultaneously open for transformation. According to this analytical strategy each institutionalized context of meaning can be said to consist simultaneously of three elements the emergence of which can be mapped historically: institution, discourse, ideal (Pedersen 1995; Andersen 1994; Andersen and Kjær 1996; Kjær 1996).[3]

Institution means that a context of meaning has been stabilized to the extent that it is continuously reproduced in a set of concrete institutional arrangements. On the one hand, we may be dealing with formalized institutions, such as freedom of speech or parliamentarianism. On the other hand, we may be dealing with less formalized but still institutionalized contexts of meaning, such as 'the political agenda', 'competitiveness' or 'career', which a group of actors sees as 'things out there', as sine qua non or the like to which everybody must submit. Institutions can thus, as organizational analysis claims, manifest themselves as regulative, normative and cognitive arrangements (and often in configurations of types of institutions). From a constitutional analytical perspective, however, institutional arrangements are understood as 'frozen' speech, that is, as speech which a group of actors continuously reproduces, and which is associated with authority and force via sanctions. It is speech that positions individuals and groups as actors in certain situations and in relation to certain other actors. 'Competitiveness' as an institution places companies, interest organizations, political actors, etc., as actors in relation to something definite and in specific relations in which it is necessary to relate to this 'speech', if you as, for example, an interest organization wish to play a role in wage bargaining.

Discourse designates a particular language code, which puts particular differences and similarities into play. Analyzing discourse entails mapping the linguistic conditions that have made it possible for actors in a particular context to talk seriously about an issue. Discourse is articulation, a verbalization of an issue or a relation, which render it visible and define it. 'Career', for instance, can be seen as a discourse, that is, as a way

3. It should be emphasized that this analytical sequence is often presented in the reverse order – but my point in the following will be that the ambition of institutionalization analysis is not so much to identify the institution but to arrive at an understanding of the ideals that may 'inform' a process of institutionalization. In other words, the ideal is what the analyst arrives at last in his or her analysis.

of talking about work and competencies in a time perspective in which something emerges and is objectified, and the individual is put into a certain relation to working life. The concrete talk about career consists of a series of categories, distinctions, arguments and stories that combined help to focus on something specific. In this context, the language code is ways of categorizing, distinguishing, etc. The language code is the principle(s) for production of propositions that seem to justify the concrete proposition, the concrete distinction, etc. The language code is not stable, and pushing the analysis backward in time often shows how the elements of the code change position. If you push the analysis of the 'career' discourse only a few decades back and look at the debate about personnel policy or the working environment in the 1970s and the 1980s, career changes from being about development and adaptability to being about job security and predictability. Here the individual is not a key figure (and problem); rather, it is the 'employer' or other bodies.

Ideal means that a certain language code is anchored in a certain basic ideal or regulative conception. The ideal is an analytical construct that, in a sense, attempts to capture the basic 'tendency' of a discourse which seems to enable (and constrain) a particular process of discursive elaboration. We can talk about the ideal as the fundamental distinction of a discourse, but it is not necessarily distinctions that can be positively observed at a given point in time, but rather something that is mostly taken as a given or silent point of departure. Contrary to discourse or language code that can be analyzed solely on the basis of concurrent propositions, approaching the ideal demands historical analysis. Only through continuously rolling back variations of discourse does it become possible to locate signs of changes in how discursive articulations are 'anchored'. Only by rolling back contemporary understandings to a point at which central propositions suddenly appear as somewhat incomprehensible in contemporary optics, are we in a position to begin outlining the contours of a certain ideal that constitutes a certain process of articulations. In more tangible terms, the 'problem' is how institutional historians analytically become able to postulate that a certain discourse is anchored in a specific ideal (Pedersen 1995). The assumption is that articulation can be seen as continuous attempts to order the world in the image of an ideal, which tends to lead to the formulation of problems as actual states of affairs are never quite 'efficient', 'competitive', 'flexible' etc. Rolling back the contemporary articulation of, for example, competition policy, we may reach the point where restraints on competition are no longer themselves a problem, but rather the question of how to avoid 'unfair competition'. In other words, we have reached the point where it no longer makes sense to single out problems in contemporary optics. A different ideal seems to be at work, which articulates the issues by distinguishing between good and bad competition and not between good and bad 'regulation' of competition.

Institutional History is first and foremost characterized by analyzing history backwards. The analysis moves from the institutionalized and authorized discourse backward through variations that can be interpreted as a gradual establishment and dissemination of a discourse to the point where it reaches its limit of making sense in view of contemporary authorized talk. The most important purpose of the analysis is thus to 'dig up' the ideal and show how it regulates institutionalized meaning. By demonstrating that meanings are historical and tied to a certain period and a certain set of linguistic distinctions, it becomes possible to recognize authoritative propositions as propositions that basically could have been different, i.e. that what 'competition' means is never a given but the result of a process of discursive elaboration (and struggle).

This backward movement implies great selectivity in the analysis as the point of departure is typically contemporary institutionalized contexts of meaning, which is why institutional analysis in most cases also primarily tracks the discourses that have survived and become institutionalized. This selectivity can be remedied by trying to track, at different points in time, different competing ideals and problems; different discourses and conflicting tendencies in institutionalization. However, this demonstration of alternatives is in some sense not the main purpose of the analysis. Precisely because the winner won, it is pertinent to roll back and perhaps destabilize the victorious history.

Nevertheless, institutional histories have been told in a straight forward chronological manner (for a critique of this tendency, see Bredsdorff 1998: 45 cont.). However, it seems unreasonable to postulate that at a given point in time a certain ideal, for example, about media and politics developed, which was translated into a certain media policy discourse that finally became institutionalized in the shape of a network of institutional arrangements, including 'the agenda'. How could the analyst know that this ideal was exactly the one to look for, or how could one postulate the presence of the ideal prior to it being articulated and simultaneously stress that the ideal has no positive existence? The chronological way of telling institutional histories has implied that they have been seen as genuine historical accounts similar to those produced by professional historians – and not highly selective readings of layers of meaning. At the same time, institutional history has become associated with the very aura of necessity and development that it intended to question. History as an evolutionary process or a grand social learning process seems to sneak in by the back door – or perhaps even by the front door.

The Analysis of Change

The analysis of institutionalization makes it possible to demonstrate the historicity of a given context of meaning. The analysis of change shows how a certain process of institutionalization can be said to imply a change – or in the terminology of institutionalization analysis, how the institutionalization of ideals implies a displacement in social orders. The ambition is here to single out the constitutive effects of a certain ideal. This particular analysis of change can be motivated in two ways.

On the one hand there is the concrete need to clarify how a change in ideals implies a change in the ordering of rationality contexts, in the possibility of being an actor in a society or in a field at a given point in time. If one, for instance, traces the emergence of a 'new' ideal about sustainable development in environmental policies during the 1990s, and this ideal seems to be positioned on top of 'earlier' ideals, it must be relevant to know whether such a change actually implies a rupture, or whether the 'new' ideal with its discourses and institutions simply becomes part of or gradually displaces the existing order. The task is, in other words, both to discover the new, and to relate to the question of continuity and rupture in an institutional historical perspective.

On the other hand, there is another and just as urgent motivation for the analysis of change, which is the fact that institutionalized contexts of meaning in themselves typically imply strong stories not only about change, but also about continuity (Andersen 1997: 9 cont.). It is often postulated that pronounced changes have taken place in, for example, the nature of the organizational or economic environment, and in the demands on the individual person or firm. During the 1980s and the 1990s industrial policy was, like many other policies, constructed as a structural policy, the main purpose of which was to continuously transform companies, industries and public institutions to fit a volatile world characterized by technological change, international competition, etc. Here the purpose of the change analysis is to observe concrete changes – without automatically becoming part of the dominant stories about change or theories of change – in order to reflect on the relationship between change discourses and the actual change of the discourse (Esmark 1999).

The analysis of change can be operationalized in various ways. The most elementary form of change analysis is to use the terms of institutionalization analysis, not only to describe variation over time, but also to compare different ideals, discourses and institutional arrangements in order to demonstrate shifts in rationality contexts – before and after the institutionalization of particular ideals. Here, historical extrapolation is a useful approach to the construction of 'presents' because it enables comparison of pure types or ideal types of meaning of particular periods (Andersen 1994). The purpose is not just an average characterization of a period, but the extrapolation of particular discursive or institutional traits to identify rupture of continuity compared to other extrapolated periods.

Such an analysis may show the interplay of change and continuity. Institutional historical analyses have thus described how contemporary talk about 'market orientation' and 'liberalization' apparently subscribes to an ideal of free market competition simultaneously with being inscribed in institutional arrangements developed around an ideal about socio-economic balance (see for example Kjær and Pedersen 2001).

The change analysis may, however, go beyond merely comparing institutionalized contexts of meaning and pointing out continuity and discontinuity. As indicated above, the ambition is also to be able to ascertain displacements in forms of governance and social ordering, and to identify emergent principles of political organization. The institutional historical strategy of analysis initially evolved within the political science setting with an ambition to analyze shifts in political organization that have challenged the 'Rechtsstaat' or similar classical political ideals. These ideals remain important within political science, law and – to some extent – everyday political understanding (Pedersen 1985, 1989, 2000). The point of departure for the analysis of forms of governance is that a given institutional meaning context not only constitutes a context for (rational) action, but is also part of a certain form of governance. Discourses and institutions do not just constitute a certain selection of roles and possible actions but can even be seen as certain ways for a society to coordinate individual and collective behavior. An institutional meaning context has a specific functionality that becomes manifest in the way in which it designates entities and regulates their interrelationship. The description of changes in forms of governance often requires analyses of concrete discursive processes in a meaning context, which indicates how public and private actors are constituted, and how the relationship between these actors and their environment is described. There are different suggestions for how this part of the analysis should be carried out.

The *first version* operates with a distinction between *structure, process, and mechanism* (e.g. Berrefjord, Nielsen and Pedersen 1989; Pedersen, Andersen, Kjær and Elberg 1992: 1985 cont.). This version describes 1) a certain institutional meaning context consisting of stabilized ideas and institutional arrangements (structure); 2) the processes by which a certain structure is disseminated, reproduced, and changed, and 3) the mechanisms through which concrete processes are implemented. The conceptual apparatus draws some inspiration from discussions within other types of institutional analysis, such as the characterization of different forms of institutional structure or the debate on institutional mechanisms, such as path dependency. This conceptual approach has produced analyses of how a 'negotiated economy' has developed on top of a 'market economy' and a 'mixed economy', such as within labor market policy and industrial policy.

Based on an institutional analysis it has been demonstrated how certain ideals of socio-economic co-ordination have been institutionalized in a network of institutions that make it possible to articulate, for example, the relationship between business performance and socio-economic balance in terms of socio-economic problems and solutions. Furthermore, based on studies of concrete policy fields, three types of negotiated economic processes are identified: language games, negotiation games and concrete negotiations through which the structure of the negotiated economy is developed, maintained and disseminated. Finally, a number of concrete mechanisms operating in negotiated economy processes have been identified tentatively: learning, legitimization, etc., which are concrete ways in which actors can enter into negotiated economic processes. The notion of the negotiated economy as a form of governance, which operates through institutionalized processes of articulation, has been constructed analytically through systematic comparisons with, in particular, the market economy or the Rechtsstaat as ideal typical forms of governance.

The *second version* is inspired by recent sociological systems theory (first and foremost represented by Niklas Luhmann) and concerns in particular the concepts of *boundary, structure, action, and identity* (Andersen 1995; see also Andersen 1996). Common to these concepts is that they are all system components that make it possible to observe a given entity such as an administrative unit as a system of communication. The point is to observe the stabilization and change of systems. This also means that transformations of industries, political organizations or forms of government are observed in the optics of systems theory. Here, the decisive question is how displacements in meaning contexts can be seen as 'semantics' that from a systems theoretical perspective are tied to transformations of system structure be it in society in toto or in individual organizations (Esmark 2002). One example is the analysis of fundamental shifts in the way in which the public administration is constituted – from an externally defined administration functioning as part of a governance hierarchy, to a 'self-created administration', the administrative units of which are designated as organizations that participate in the formulation of their own action conditions and own governance in the image of a reorganizing public sector (Andersen 1995).

Analyses of change have produced diagnoses of contemporary society that single out features of the current social organization which challenge with familiar dogma social organization (law, market, hierarchy, public administration). Among other things, this has focused attention on the way in which contemporary society is held together or controlled via institutionalized opinion-building. That is by the embeddedness of autonomous actors in orchestrated processes of communication that define needs, interests, action possibilities, and responsibility. In Institutional History it has thus been a point to demonstrate that the production of 'imagined communities' ranging from the 'information society' or the 'knowledge society' to the 'dream society' have been an integral part of political governance. The ambition has not been to create new, seductive visions, but to trace the society, which may already have been constructed, quietly and through multiple institutionalization processes in various areas (Andersen, Kjær and Pedersen 1996). In that sense, the Institutional History contributed to furnish early diagnoses of what is currently discussed as under the broad heading of 'governance'.

Part of the social sciences and broader public debates subscribe to the great narrative of decline: the decline of the market, of a sovereign state governed by law, of the civil servant, of professional autonomy, etc. Institutional History may identify ruptures and transformations, but the question of decline (or for that matter 'development') remains one that only can be posed within a certain context of meaning (Pedersen, Kjær, Esmark, Horst and Carlsen 2000; Pedersen, Esmark and Kjær 1999). In other words, the change analyses are neither stories about universal evolution nor the decline into dystopias, but descriptions of the ideals that are in the process of becoming institutionalized and the constitution of society, organization or individual that they entail.

Conclusion

In my introduction to Institutional History I have, in general, played down conceptual questions as well as the many problems pertaining to the concrete interaction with 'data', for example, in relation to textual analysis. This negligence is deliberate in the sense that I wanted to direct focus towards an intermediate layer of analytical strategy: that which thematizes, justifies and classifies series of analytical choices – without anticipating all the more concrete choices to be made. The purpose is to stress that the 'identity' of Institutional History is found at this very level and not in the type of discourse analysis or the type of process analysis or the way in which a concrete text is selected and read.

Institutional History is characterized by relating to debates and fields where there have been long traditions for institutional analysis. Here,

Institutional History supplies a specific analytical strategy which emphasizes, in particular, institutional creation and institutional change. The analytical strategy reformulates key concepts of institutional analysis by borrowing from, among other things, language theory, which makes it, I claim, a more radical constitutional analysis that distances itself from the propensity of old- and neo-institutionalism for either (post-hoc) rationalization or exposure of institutions.

A special characteristic of Institutional History is that the analytical strategy is not primarily justified meta-theoretically, theoretically or methodologically, but by the ambition of wanting to be able to diagnose a certain age: the particularly fluid processes of social organizing that seem to have developed after the 1960s. It is probably here that one also finds its lasting contribution. While other approaches both inside and outside the broad field of institutional analysis may offer more elegant or coherent conceptual apparatuses, Institutional History has been able to produce new readings of contemporary Danish society in terms of 'Negotiated Economies' or 'Negotiated Administration' that have challenged the dominant neo-liberal storyline of modernization and globalization, and have suggested novel ways of perceiving the field of possibility for contemporary policy making and governance.

References

Andersen, N.Å. 1994, 'Institutionel historie – en introduktion til diskurs- og institutionsanalyse', *COS-forskningsrapport*, 10/94, Copenhagen.

Andersen, N.Å. 1995, *Selvskabt forvaltning. Forvaltningspolitikkens og centralforvaltningens udvikling i Danmark 1900-1994*, Nyt fra Samfundsvidenskaberne, Copenhagen.

Andersen, N.Å. 1996, *Udlicitering. Når det private bliver politisk*, Nyt fra Samfundsvidenskaberne, Copenhagen.

Andersen, N.Å. 1997, *Udlicitering – Strategi og historie*, Nyt fra Samfundsvidenskaberne, Copenhagen.

Andersen, N.Å. 1999, *Diskursive analysestrategier, Foucault, Koselleck, Laclau, Luhmann*. Nyt fra Samfundsvidenskaberne, Copenhagen.

Andersen, N.Å. and P. Kjær 1996, 'Institutional Construction and Change: An Analytical Strategy of Institutional History, *COS-forskningsrapport*, 5/1996.

Andersen, N.Å., P. Kjær and O.K. Pedersen 1996, 'Forhandlingsøkonomi – Teori eller samfundsdiagnose?', in *Dansk Sociologi*, Vol. 7:3, pp. 81-91.

Berrefjord, O., K. Nielsen and O.K. Pedersen 1989, 'Forhandlingsøkonomi i Norden – en indledning', in K. Nielsen and O.K. Pedersen (red.), *Forhandlingsøkonomi i Norden*, Jurist- og Økonomforbundets Forlag, Copenhagen.

Bredsdorff, N., 1998, *Om studiet af forvaltningen*, Skriftserie fra Roskilde Universitetsbibliotek, 27, Roskilde.

Brunsson, N. and J.P. Olsen 1993, *The Reforming Organization*, Routledge, London.

Czarniawska, B. and G. Sévon 1996, *Translating organizational change*, De Gruyter studies in organization, 56, de Gruyter, Berlin.

DiMaggio, P.J. 1991, 'Constructing an organizational field as a professional project. US Art Museums 1920-1940', in W.W. Powell and P.J. DiMaggio (eds.) 1991, *The New Institutionalism in Organizational Analysis*, Chicago University Press, Chicago.

DiMaggio, P.J. and W.W. Powell 1991, 'Introduction', in W.W. Powell and P.J. DiMaggio (eds.) 1991, *The New Institutionalism in Organizational Analysis*, Chicago University Press, Chicago.

DiMaggio, P.J. and P.W. Walter 1991 (1983), 'The iron cage revisited – institutional isomorphism and collective rationality in organizational fields', in W.W. Powell and P.J. DiMaggio (eds.) 1991, *The New Institutionalism in Organizational Analysis*, Chicago University Press, Chicago.

Esmark, A. 1999, 'Tvang til tid – forandringsfetischisme eller forandringsanalytik?', in *GRUS*, 59, 1999, pp.78-98

Esmark, A. 2002, *At forvalte Europa – den danske centraladministrations omstilling til det europæiske samarbejde*, Ph.D. Dissertation at the Department for Political Science, Copenhagen.

Esmark, A., P. Kjær and O.K. Pedersen 1999, 'Det politiske kommunikationssystem', *Politica*, Vol. 31:2, pp. 147-160.

Fligstein, N. 1990, *The Transformation of Corporate Control*, Harvard University Press, Cambridge.

Foucault, M. 1982, *The Archaeology of Knowledge. And the Discourse on Language*, Pantheon Books, New York.

Hall, P.A. 1993, 'Policy Paradigms, Social Learning, and the State. The Case of Economic Policymaking in Britain', in *Comparative Politics*, 25 (3), April 1993, pp. 275-296.

Kjær, P. and O.K. Pedersen 2001, 'Translating Liberalization. Neoliberalism in the Danish Negotiated Economy', in J.L. Campbell and O.K. Pedersen (eds.), *The Rise of Neoliberalism and Institutional Analysis*, Princeton University Press, Princeton.

Kjær, P. 1996, *The Constitution of Enterprise – An Institutional History of Inter-firm Relations in Swedish Furniture Manufacturing*, Ph.D. Dissertation, Stockholm University.

Manicas, P.T. 1987, *The History and Philosophy of the Social Sciences*, Basil Blackwell, Oxford.

March, J.G. and J.P. Olsen 1989, *Rediscovering Institutions. The Organizational Basis of Politics*, The Free Press, New York.

Meyer, J.W. and B. Rowan 1991 (1977), 'Institutionalized Organizations: Formal Structure as Myth and Ceremony', in W.W. Powell and P.J. DiMaggio (eds.) 1991, *The New Institutionalism in Organizational Analysis*, Chicago University Press, Chicago.

Meyer, J.W., J. Boli and G.M. Thomas 1987, 'Ontology and rationalization in the Western cultural account', in G.M. Thomas, J.W. Meyer, F.O. Ramirez and J. Boli (eds.), *Institutional Structure. Constituting State, Society and the Individual*, Sage, Newbury Park, CA, pp. 12-37.

North, D.C. 1990, *Institutions, Institutional Change and Economic Performance*, Cambridge University Press, New York.

Pedersen, O.K. 1985, *Institutionel historie*, Forlaget Samfundsøkonomi og Planlægning, Roskilde.

Pedersen, O.K. 1989, 'Fra individ til aktør i struktur. Tilblivelse af en juridisk rolle', in *Statsvetenskaplig Tidskift*, 3.

Pedersen, O.K. 1991, 'Nine Questions to a Neo-institutional Theory in Political Science', in *Scandinavian Political Studies*, 4 (2).

Pedersen, O.K. 1995, 'Problemets anatomi – eller problemet, der er et problem', in *Tendens*, 7 (1).

Pedersen, O.K. 2000, 'Den samfundsøkonomiske forvaltning – om forvaltning og interesseorganisationer', in Peter Bogason (red.), *Stat, Forvaltning og Samfund efter 1950*, Jurist- og Økonomforbundets Forlag, Copenhagen.

Pedersen, O.K., N.Å. Andersen, P. Kjær and J. Elberg 1992, *Privat politik. Projekt forhandlingsøkonomi*, Samfundslitteratur, Copenhagen.

Pedersen, O.K., P. Kjær, A. Esmark, M. Horst and E.M. Carlsen 2000, *Politisk* journalistik, Forlaget Ajour, Århus.

Perrow, C. 1986, *Complex organizations. A critical essay*, 3rd Edition, McGraw-Hill, New York.

Peters, B.G. 1999, *Institutional theory in political science. The »new institutionalism*, Repr. Continuum International 2001, London.

Powell, W.W. and P.J. DiMaggio (eds.) 1991, *The New Institutionalism in Organizational Analysis*, Chicago University Press, Chicago.

Saussure, F. d. 1990, *Course in General* Linguistics, Duckworth, London.

Scott, W.R. 1992, *Organizations. Rational, natural, and open systems*, 3rd Edition, Prentice Hall, Englewood Cliffs.

Scott, W.R. 1994, 'Organizations and Institutions. Towards a Theoretical Synthesis', in W.R. Scott and J. W. Meyer, *Institutional Environments and Organization*, Sage, Thousand Oaks, CA.

Scott, W.R. 1995, *Institutions and Organizations*, Sage, Thousand Oaks, CA.

Scott, W.R. and S. Christensen 1995, *The institutional construction of organizations. International and longitudinal studies*, Sage, Thousand Oaks, CA.

Selznick, P. 1992, *The Moral Commonwealth. Social Theory and the Promise of Community*, University of California Press, Berkeley.

Thompson, J.D. 1967, *Organizations in Action*, McGraw-Hill, New York.

Wagner, P., B. Wittrock and R. Whitley 1991, *Discourses on Society. The Shaping of the Social Science Disciplines*, Sociology of the Sciences, 15, Kluwer Academic Publishers, Dordrecht.

Williamson, O.E. 1975, *Markets and Hierarchies*, Free Press, New York.

Williamson, O.E. 1985, *The Economic Institutions of Capitalism*, Free Press, New York.

CHAPTER 6

The Institutionalization of Regional Trade Agreements: Surprise and Stickiness in NAFTA and Mercosur

Francesco Duina

Associate professor, Bates College, USA and Copenhagen Business School, Denmark

Introduction

Most scholars accept the idea that the European Union (EU) has become 'institutionalized'. What exactly this might mean, of course, varies greatly across the literature. By and large, however, it refers to the growth and spread of processes, rules, and organizational entities that have acquired lives of their own – that are functioning and evolving according to principles and patterns that are no longer under the direct control of the member states. The sheer volume of research on the topic is stunning. After all, the most important consequence of the institutionalization of the EU is a loss of control by the member states, with important implications for questions of national sovereignty.

The EU is no longer the only prominent instance of regional integration. Starting in the 1990s as the Cold War came to an end, countries rushed to form regional trade agreements (RTAs) – spaces where a combination of goods, services, capital, and labor can move free from various tariff and non-tariff barriers. The growth of RTAs has surely been impressive. Between 1990 and 1994, officials from the World Trade Organization were notified of 33 new RTAs, more than doubling the total to 68. Then, between 1995 and 2001 another 100 RTAs formed. Today, almost every country on earth belongs to an RTA.

Scholars have devoted considerable attention to the new RTAs. Much of the research has however focused on three questions which, though surely important, do not address the issue of institutionalization: the causes of the widespread embrace of integration, the impact of integration on vulnerable groups such as labor and women, and whether regional integration should be seen as a step towards or an obstacle to the rise of a global economy (Duina 2006). The intergovernmental nature of most, if not all, of those RTAs probably explains why scholars have so far shown little interest in investigating the possibility of institutionalization: with no major formal policymaking, administrative, or judicial bodies comprised of officials who are supposed to work on behalf of any given RTA and not their countries of origin (something that by contrast happens in the EU's Parliament, Commission, and Court of Justice), the new RTAs certainly seem unlikely to develop processes, rules, and organizational entities that evolve independently from the oversight and will of the member states.

In this chapter, I suggest that we should in fact take seriously the possibility of institutionalization in the new RTAs. A fundamental insight of sociology – thoroughly central and often a starting assumption in much of Ove Pedersen's work[1] – is that most organizations, especially complex ones such as RTAs, become institutionalized over time. The very intergovernmental character of RTAs, along with countless expressed declarations by national officials, points to a clear desire on the part of the member states to pursue integration with very tight oversight and command of what is happening. Evidence of institutionalization would suggest that integration is following a course that is both unplanned and unwanted by those member states. Once underway, institutional dynamics generally

1. See, for instance, the extensive study by Pedersen and his colleagues on the Europeanization of national administrations, where the starting premise is not whether but *how* those administrations develop in ways that are both complex and reflective of factors that extend beyond any single member state or entity (Jacobsson, Lægreid and Pedersen 2004).

intensify. An institutional investigation of RTAs seems, therefore, very much in order.

In the following pages, I argue that the new RTAs are showing early signs of institutionalization. Much of the literature on the institutionalization of EU draws from historical institutionalism and its beliefs in the independent and often irrational (from an economic or efficiency perspective) evolution of organizations. I borrow from those insights to propose that the new RTAs, regardless of their intergovernmental character, have developed institutional arrangements that are both 'sticky' (i.e., difficult to get rid of even when the member states no longer want them) and surprising (i.e., generating unforeseen and generally unwanted outcomes). Such stickiness and surprise have created considerable frustration among the member sates, since they have affected important dimensions of political, legal, and economic life.

To provide support for my argument, I turn to NAFTA and Mercosur – the two most important RTAs besides the EU – and consider developments in areas as diverse as dairy products, investor rights, tariffs, and macroeconomic policy coordination. The chapter is organized as follows. I begin with a discussion of historical institutionalist research on the EU. I then use that discussion to develop my claims about institutionalization in the new RTAs. In the following section, I present evidence in support of my claims. In the conclusion, I explore the challenges of institutionalization and the possibility of alternative architectures for RTAs.

Institutionalization and Regional Integration

Without a question, much research on the EU points to a process of institutionalization. Institutionalists come in many guises, of course, and generalizations about their work are quite risky to make. In the case of the EU, however, we can safely say that a major strand of research is historical institutional in nature. What sorts of arguments have these scholars made about the evolution of the EU? Let us recall the general point that historical institutionalists are by and large interested in high-level principles of how institutions *evolve* over time. With this in mind, we can identify three primary points in the literature.

Perhaps the most important and widespread is the notion of path dependency. The idea is that processes, rules, and organizational arrangements made at one point in time constrain and shape what follows later, as if the initial stages of an institution define its 'trajectory' over time (Pierson 1996). From this perspective, actors can play a role in influencing outcomes, but only within a narrowly predetermined range of possibilities. This perspective has been deployed to account for numerous aspects of European integration. Some of the most recent and interesting studies focus on the development of the EU budget system (Ackrill and Kay 2006), the content of the Nice and Amsterdam Treaties (Sverdrup 2002), the evolution of the Common Agricultural Policy (Bulmer 1998: 373), and the gradual move towards a federal and democratic EU (Holzinger and Knill 2002).

A second central point of historical institutionalist analyses of the EU concerns the notion of autonomy. Here the question is the extent to which, once launched, organizational entities within the EU accrue power and become less controlled by the member states. The mechanisms through which this happens vary by scholar. Among the most discussed are the election-focused and thus short-term horizons of officials initially involved in the design of institutions (Pierson 1996; Heisenberg and Richmond 2002: 204). The result, as Alter argued in her seminal research on the European Court of Justice, is that those institutions capitalize, often as quietly as possible, so as not to 'arouse political passions', on openings and opportunities to expand their competencies and depths of influence over particular issue areas (1998: 131). A second mechanism is the unplanned but ever increasing volume and specificity of issue areas that fall within the competency of EU institutions.

A third point has to do with reinforcing loops between institutions, and between institutions and their environments, with the ultimate result that institutions, once launched, tend to grow. The contributors to Sandholtz and Stone Sweet's (1998) important volume on supranational governance in the EU described in a variety of ways, for instance, the mutually reinforcing relationship between trade volume, the legal output of the EU, the decisions of the ECJ, and other activities of the EU. Bulmer made a similar point about the European Commission and the European Court of Justice: 'historical institutionalism helps to forge a link between jurisprudence of the European Court and the legislative process', showing that one helps the other grow (1998: 373).

It is certainly too early for anyone to determine whether any of the above dynamics are taking place in the new RTAs. Evidence of path dependency, for instance, generally concerns developments over decades rather than a few years. Yet, the three arguments above build on certain basic insights about the workings of institutions which might, in fact, apply and be observable in the new RTAs. Two of these insights concern the stickiness and unpredictability of institutions.

Let us first turn to stickiness. Path dependency and the idea of reinforcing loops point to the persistence of institutional arrangements over time. They underscore the fact that institutions, once created, are quite difficult to get rid of or even change in any significant manner. Theories about the autonomy of EU institutions also make that point, though perhaps less directly: their descriptions of how institutions become stronger over time are, after all, about how those institutions become more and more entrenched in their settings. These arguments about stickiness are made with the member states in mind: institutional persistence is seen as happening in ways that frustrate those countries – if national officials were to have the opportunity, they would redesign those institutional arrangements. In light of these considerations, my first claim is that *the new RTAs are already exhibiting sticky institutional arrangements of considerable consequence for the member states.* We should take those arrangements seriously, for they are likely to be the early phases of significant institutionalization in RTAs.

Much the same can be said about the element of surprise in the new RTAs. Arguments about autonomy and reinforcing loops are at least in part about the unexpected and unplanned. They underscore the fact that institutions function and evolve over time in ways that depart from their original scripts. Institutions typically do not become autonomous overnight; reinforcing loops, in turn, happen slowly over many years. Yet, the element of surprise that is inherent to both types of dynamics can in principle be observed in much shorter time periods. Again, we are of course interested in situations that prove problematic for the member states – that somehow indicate a departure from the stated preferences and desires of the member states. My second claim is the following: *the new*

RTAs have developed institutional characteristics that have unexpectedly challenged the desires and preferences of the member states in important issue areas.

Let us now consider evidence in support of these claims. Our attention turns to NAFTA and Mercosur – the two most important RTAs after the EU.

Stickiness and Surprise in NAFTA and Mercosur

NAFTA is the largest free trade area in the world. Comprising Canada, Mexico, and the United States, it was put into effect in 1994 with the aim of liberalizing the trade of most goods, capital movement, and selected services by 2003. NAFTA is purely intergovernmental. Only NAFTA's arbitration panels, whose ad-hoc participants are expected to act with NAFTA's interest in mind, exhibit a supranational dimension. Started in 1991 with the signing of the Treaty of Asunción, Mercosur brings together Argentina, Brazil, Paraguay, Uruguay and, as of 2006, Venezuela, into the world's second largest common market after the EU. Eager to keep the member states in control of integration, the founders explicitly designed Mercosur as intergovernmental. National officials thus make up the Common Market Group, the Common Market Council, and the Joint Parliamentary Commission. The intergovernmental architecture of both NAFTA and Mercosur has not prevented them from developing sticky and surprising institutional arrangements. To show this, we turn first to NAFTA.

NAFTA's Sticky Dairy Policies

The United States is clearly the most powerful member of NAFTA. Yet, on several occasions, it has attempted to change processes, rules, and organizational entities. Those institutions proved sticky: once established, they could not be easily undone. The recent row over dairy offers a very good example. The story begins with the early phases of the integration process, when the governments of both Canada and the United States found it convenient to exempt a variety of dairy products from trade liberalization between the two countries. The position of both countries reflected decades of domestic protectionism of dairy producers, which included a variety of quantitative restrictions on imports, price setting, measures to subsidy exports in times of overproduction, and more (Financial Post 1996).

Findings themselves aligned in terms of their preferences, the two countries eagerly adopted Article 702 of NAFTA, which directly incorporates into the agreement a number of articles found in the 1989 free trade agreement between the two countries (CUSTFA). One of those articles states that the 'the Parties retain their rights and obligations with respect to agricultural, food, beverage and certain related goods under the General Agreement on Tariffs and Trade (GATT) and agreements negotiated under the GATT, including their rights and obligations under GATT Article XI (CUSFTA Article 710)'. Article XI of GATT, in turn, states that countries have the right to use an array of restrictions on dairy products. During the negotiations, there was indeed little discussion of alternative approaches. As Ira Shapiro, Ambassador from the United States Trade Representative Office, would unambiguously state in a testimony before the House Committee on Agriculture's Subcommittee on Dairy, Livestock, and Poultry, 'there were no agricultural market access negotiations between the United States and Canada during the NAFTA negotiations' (Federal News Service 1996).

A protectionist policy around dairy was thus set. The United States' position started to change, however, during the mid-1990s. Attracted by the opportunities that come with having a bigger market, the larger dairy producers began pushing for open borders. The federal government responded by reviewing its various policies. Yielding, it took unilateral steps to open the domestic market to Canadian products. Unfortunately, the Canadian government proved totally disinterred in this change of direction. Its response was to impose tariffs on dairy products that reached 350 percent. In 1996, tariff-rate quotas reached 343 percent for butter, 275 percent for cheese, and 270 percent for milk and cream. The Canadian government indicated that those quotas would be lowered, but only to 299 percent, 246 percent, and 241 percent respectively, by the year

2001 (US Department of Agriculture 1997: 19-20).[2] The message was clear: Canada would take full advantage of NAFTA's Article 702.

The situation became quickly intolerable for the United States. In a move that a few years before would have been unthinkable, United States officials filed a complaint against Canadian tariffs on imported dairy products, arguing that they went against certain provisions found in NAFTA. The Canadians reacted with dismay. Claude Rivard, President of Dairy Farmers of Canada, angrily stated that 'the United States is trying to secure through the NAFTA dispute settlement process something that was never agreed to through eight years of bilateral, trilateral and multilateral trade negotiations.' These were agreements made, he added, 'openly and in good faith' (Canada NewsWire 1996). An upset Richard Doyle, executive director of the same organization, would in turn note: 'The story is always the same with the Americans. They sign an agreement, and then when they find it doesn't suit them exactly, they turn around and try to get out' (The Gazette 1996).

The complaint landed before a dispute resolution panel. The five judges (two of whom where from the United States) unanimously concluded that the tariffs were perfectly in line with the NAFTA texts. The United States was left with no options but to accept a provision it no longer wanted. If the Canadians were happy, farmers and politicians in the United States felt quite differently.

The Unforeseen Implications of NAFTA's Chapter 11

NAFTA's Chapter 11 appears to be fairly straight-forward. Designed to promote investments across borders, it says that the member states shall treat foreign investments as if they were domestic ones. To that end, it asks those countries not to adopt laws, regulations, or procedures that discriminate or otherwise target in an exclusive fashion those investments (Article 1102).

Given its seemingly uncontroversial content, Chapter 11 was hardly debated by the legislatures and administrations of the member states. Consider the case of the United States, for instance. When the Senate Fi-

2. These reductions were necessary to keep in line with agreements made at the Uruguay Round of negotiations regarding GATT's Article XI.

nance Committee (along with several other committees of jurisdiction) reported the NAFTA Implementation Act (S. 1627), Chapter 11 was mentioned only once. During the debate in both the House of Representatives and the Senate, Chapter 11 was discussed only in passing (Congressional Record 1993: 159-161 and 163-164). In April 2004, the junior senator from Massachusetts, John Kerry, summarized how little attention was given to Chapter 11: 'when we debated NAFTA, not a single word was uttered in discussing Chapter 11'. When asked why, he admitted that it was 'because we didn't know how this provision would play out. No one really knew just how high the stakes would get' (Liptak 2004).

Chapter 11 has in fact generated highly contested, expensive (in the United States alone, claims amount to billions of dollars), and publicized outcomes. This is for two reasons. First, foreign investors can at times *happen* to be the only entities affected in any significant way by a particular law, court decision, or regulation that is in no way directed at them. When this occurs, Chapter 11 gives those investors an opening to claim discrimination or otherwise unjust treatment. This was of course not planned by the officials approving the chapter. The second reason follows from the first: Chapter 11 empowers foreign private individual and corporate investors to sue a foreign government (and its local entities), administrations, and courts over rules, laws, decisions, and other outputs produced in line with domestic requirements. This is not only a major and unprecedented departure in international law (where countries can sue each other but private entities cannot sue countries) but in the case of court decisions in particular it gives those foreign actors *rights which domestic actors do not have*. None of this was understood by those approving Chapter 11 as law. The result is that well over 40 cases have been filed in Canada, Mexico and the United States under Chapter 11, causing furor among legislators, law experts, and sections of civil society. We explore here three important examples.

Perhaps the most surprising effects of Chapter 11 concern judicial decisions. Two cases in particular illustrate this. In 1996, the Canadian funeral company Loewen Group was hit with a US$500 million verdict in a Mississippi civil suit. The group appealed to a NAFTA arbitration panel under Chapter 11, claiming that biased jurors and an unfair court drove the outcome. In 1990 in turn, Mondev, a Canadian real estate company, won a claim against the City of Boston for breach of contract. In 1998, the Supreme Judicial Court of Massachusetts reversed the judgment. Mondev brought its case to the United States Supreme Court, which, by refusing to hear it, let the reversal stand. Mondev then submitted its claim to arbitration under Chapter 11. In both instances, the NAFTA tribunals backed the United States. What gave great significance to the cases, however, was the fact that, *for the first time ever*, foreign actors were able to challenge, on the basis of international law, judicial decisions made within the United States. In the Mondev case, this meant that a foreign actor could challenge those decisions *further* than would have been possible for domestic actors (who, after failing to have the country's highest court hear the case, would have had to desist). Astonishingly, the panel for the Loewen case went so far as to assert that judicial decisions are covered under Chapter 11, though the text says no such thing explicitly. Is this what Chapter 11 was intended to allow?

We consider here the reactions of legal academics and judges. Leading scholar John Echeverria of Georgetown outright stated that 'this is the biggest threat to United States judicial independence that no one has heard of and even fewer people understand' (Liptak 2004). Chief Justice Ronald M. George of the California Supreme Court noted that 'it's rather shocking that the highest courts of the state and federal governments could have their judgments circumvented by these tribunals' (Liptak 2004). Chief Justice Margaret Marshall of the Massachusetts Supreme Court said, with reference to the Mondev case, that 'to say I was surprised to hear that a judgment of this court was being subjected to further review would be an understatement' (Liptak 2004). Most revealing were the words of Abner Mikva, former Chief Judge on the United States Court of Appeals for the District of Columbia and a former congressman, who was actually one of the three NAFTA judges on the Loewen panel: 'If Congress had known that there was anything like this in NAFTA', he said, 'they would never have voted for it' (Liptak 2004).

Most Chapter 11 cases have impacted legislative autonomy. The 1997 Canadian Parliament banning of import and inter-province transport of MMT, a gasoline engine performance enhancer, on grounds of its high neurotoxin content, shows how great that impact can be. Ethyl Corporation of Richmond, Virginia, was Canada's sole supplier of MMT. A few weeks after the adoption of the ban, Ethyl filed a Chapter 11 investor-state claim seeking US$250 million in compensation for discrimination. After initialing arguing against the claim before an arbitration panel, the Canadian government settled by paying US$13 million in legal damages and fees and *agreeing to reverse* the ban. The outcome shocked just about everyone in the legislature and the public. No one had realized that Chapter 11 could have such intrusive effects on domestic law. MP Bill Blaikie was for instance appalled by the 'harassment and intimidation of the government with respect to the issue of MMT' and said he was witnessing a 'sabotaged Canadian democracy' that had given 'excessive power to unelected and unaccountable international trade organizations ... [thereby] erod[ing] the ability of Canada's elected representatives to act in the public interest' (Hansard 1999: 1094). 'Canadians', Blaikie (1999) added, 'have had enough of this self-inflicted powerlessness'. MP Clifford Lincoln stated that 'I can't believe that a foreign corporation can almost dictate its terms and we as a sovereign nation are completely powerless to do anything about it' (Duffy 1998). Other MPs, such as Charles Caccia and Alexa McDonough, echoed these comments while, in parallel, public watchdogs voiced their anger outside of the legislature (Public Citizen 2005: 22). But there was little that the government could do to revisit Chapter 11 and remedy the situation.

Mercosur's Common External Tariff: Stickiness and Frustration

Mercosur is a common market. As such, its member states agreed to adopt a common external tariff (CET) regime. The CET would harmonize the member states' different trade tariffs with the outside world, thereby making competition within the Mercosur space more even. There was little doubt among Mercosur's architects of the virtues and promise of the CET. Negotiations focused instead on what would be the appropriate level, with Argentina supporting a lower CET than Brazil. President Lacalle of Uruguay compared his country's entrance into the common market to gaining independence, stating that, because of it, Uruguay was 'entering an important stage with enormous possibilities' (Madrid EFE 1994). Argentine Foreign Relations secretary, Jorge Campbell, declared that the new Mercosur would become 'the most powerful tool that Argentina possesses to reach dynamic and sustained growth over time' (Campbell 1995).

The CET imposed on the member states a major requirement: that no country could engage in bilateral negotiations with third parties. Any bilateral agreement would simply break the CET. Decision 32/00 of 2000 spelled out that requirement in no unclear terms: the 'foundation of a common market implies, among other things, the necessity of presenting a common external political front'. It followed that no member states would be permitted 'to sign new preferential accords ... that have not been negotiated by Mercosur'.

Problematically, but for Brazil, the member states' unwavering commitment to the CET began to change with time – but in different ways and at different junctures, so that there has been no possibility of revisiting the framework. Uruguay – a traditionally open economy – has been perhaps the most eager to have access to new markets, especially the United States. The government supported, for instance, the Free Trade Area of the Americas (FTAA) project. The Uruguayan government started to voice its dissatisfaction with the status quo in 2001. At the FTAA meeting that year, President Jorge Batlle told a regional forum on free trade that Uruguay 'need[s] a bilateral agreement with the United States' (MercoPress 2001). His country, he added, was becoming resentful of certain states acting as 'obstacles' to Uruguayan trade liberalization. Batlle then sought the help of Chilean and Mexican experts to aid in the negotiation process. Batlle backtracked soon thereafter, calling for some more flexibility but ruling out a unilateral United States-Uruguay trade deal. In parallel, however, Batlle's economy minister continued to voice the government's dissatisfaction. April 2002 brought more complaints from Batlle: 'since I see no collective negotiations, I need to re-establish bilateral negotiations [with the US] and I have to do so quickly' (BBC Monitoring 2002). In May 2003, the Uruguayans backtracked again, agreeing to continue the 'four plus one' negotiations with the US. The same year, however, Batlle insisted that it would be sometime before 'we will have to subject our trade and general political decisions to a higher order' (Grassi 2003). Thus, in February 2007 Uruguay signed a Trade and Investment Framework Agreement – what is essentially a prelude to a real free trade agreement. But Uruguay cannot afford to upset its major trading partners, especially Brazil, and thus has little choice but to accept the status quo.

Argentina voiced its own problems with the CET in 2001, following its major currency crisis and the search for new markets to help the economy recover. In May of that year, Minister of Economy Domingo Cavallo thus declared in Washington, DC, that Mercosur 'should follow Chile's lead and negotiate bilateral trade treaties with the US'. 'If Mercosur can't do it together,' Cavallo added, 'Argentina can't discard the possibility of going it alone' (Wisnefski and Loughran 2001). To show his determination, Cavallo then unilaterally exempted capital goods, including computer and telecom equipment, from Argentina's items subject to the Mercosur CET. The Brazilians called this a clear violation of Mercosur law, but the move proved quite popular back home. Argentina relented after its economy began to recover.

Paraguay also has recently expressed its desire to leave the CET. Its economy has fared quite poorly since joining Mercosur. Its clothing, beef, and organic sugar industries need new markets. Vice President Lius Alberto Castiglioni accordingly expressed his country's desire for a 'waiver' and the right to 'negotiate trade agreements with the United States and other countries' (Economist 2005). The government has sometimes joined Uruguay in its efforts to revise the CET framework. The requests have raised serious concerns with Brazil, whose Foreign Minister made it clear that 'Paraguay must understand that the choice is between Mercosur and other possible partners' (Economist 2005). The warning has so far proved effective, frustrating Paraguay's continued interest in revisiting the CET.

Economic Integration without Macroeconomic Coordination? Surprise in Mercosur

Mercosur promotes economic integration without requiring the member states to coordinate their macroeconomic policies in any serious fashion. Article I of the Treaty of Asunción does ask the member states to pursue the 'co-ordination of macroeconomic and sectoral policies' in areas such as 'fiscal and monetary matters, foreign exchange and capital'. But little has in fact been done to pursue that goal, especially when it comes to inflation rates and exchange rates. What might explain this approach? On the one hand, most RTAs are primarily about trade. Mercosur merely follows that trend. More importantly, though, was the optimism on the part of Mercosur's architects that economic integration by itself would foster significant stability in the zone and lead naturally to convergence in macroeconomic policies. The comments of Argentine Economy Minister Domingo Cavallo in 1991 reflected precisely this line of thinking: 'co-ordination will come almost automatically if we continue to pursue the present policies and, fundamentally, maintain ... fiscal discipline' (Latin America Regional Reports 1991).

The early years of integration seemed to prove those assumptions correct. Between 1990 and 1995, intra-Mercosur trade increased by 350 percent. The Brazilian and Argentine economies were growing and were quite dependent on one another; the correlation of their GDP growth rates was 0.9 between 1996 and 1998 (Devlin et al. 2001). In 1996, President Carlos Menem of Argentina would thus buoyantly proclaim that 'we are not only growing, we are growing together with other countries in the region' (Boustany 1996). On the macroeconomic side, governments pursued fixed exchange rate regimes and observers agreed that there had been 'de facto convergence on macroeconomic, particularly exchange rate policies' (Bouzas 2003: 71).

Things began to change after Mexico's 1995 peso crisis, which sent signals worldwide about the risks of an overvalued currency. The Brazilian government announced that the real would be devalued by 7.5 percent against the dollar each year. But the currency remained overvalued. This, coupled with poor fiscal discipline and large budget deficits, set Brazil up for a major crisis after Russia defaulted on its debt in 1998 and devalued its ruble. Investors began to withdraw capital from emerging markets. Between August and October, US$50 billion was taken out of Brazil. In response, the Brazilian government spent over US$36 billion defending the real, increased taxes, cut spending dramatically, and took US$41.5 billion in International Monetary Fund money. To prevent inflation, the Central Bank in turn raised interest rates to strikingly high levels.

The approach could not be sustained. The interest rates greatly hurt various industrial sectors and anyone needing to borrow. Brazil was in crisis: 'for the first time in Mercosur's history, the major macro-economic indicators of gross domestic product growth, productivity, external trade balances, and related measures of stability were all declining' (Guira 2003:

171). The response was unilateral action *without consultation* with the Mercosur partners (O'Keefe 2003). President Cardoso responded by devaluing the real 8.5% against the dollar in January 1999. Limiting the devaluation to 8.5 % proved impossible, however. By March, the real had lost 45% of its value. Now, heavy trade dependence among the member states was matched by 'absolutely incompatible' macroeconomic policies (de Andrade et al. 2005: 87). The situation proved disastrous for everyone in Mercosur.

Argentina's trade balance with Brazil decreased by over 75 % in one year (O'Keefe 2003). Uruguayan President Jorge Batlle noted a loss of 50 % of the country's exports overnight. Cheap imports from Brazil were in turn flooding into the other member states. Protests against Brazil mounted. 'With the death of the Plan Real,' declared then-Uruguayan foreign minister Alvaro Ramos (referring to Brazil's previous currency stabilization strategy), 'Brazil changed the rules of the Mercosur game ... by threatening the fate of its partners' (Montero 1999). Fernando de la Rua warned, a week before becoming Argentina's president, that his country's industries would be devastated (Dyer and Warn 1999). 'Argentine import-competing sectors,' reported observers, 'reacted vocally fearing that a flood of 'cheap' imports from Brazil ... would wipe out domestic firms from their own market. Export-oriented business, in turn [were] hurt by a devaluation that priced them out of the Brazilian (usually their largest) market' (Albin and Bouzas 2004: 170).

Greatly constrained by Mercosur's regulatory framework, Argentina, Paraguay, and Uruguay responded to the new 'game' without the full box of tools historically at their disposal. They thus resorted to sloppy, inconsistent, and largely illegal barriers to trade. In July 1999, Argentina for instance introduced quotas limiting textile imports from Brazil. Disputes between Argentina and Brazil engulfed auto, steel, sugar, electronics, and footwear. Brazil reacted to the Argentine measures by imposing restrictions on 400 Argentine products. The weak, ad hoc dispute mechanisms of Mercosur were unable to successfully intervene. Ultimately, Argentina, Paraguay, and Uruguay had little choice but to wait for Brazil's currency to stabilize. By 2001, ironically, Argentina itself would face devaluation, with major consequences for the other member states.

Reflections on the Design of RTAs

As intergovernmental projects, NAFTA and Mercosur have no supranational institutions. The previous analysis has suggested, however, that an intergovernmental architecture has not prevented these RTAs from developing early signs of institutionalization – from beginning to have processes, rules, and organizational entities that gradually take on lives of their own and, in the process, prove frustrating to the member states. Leveraging the insights of historical institutionalism, our attention turned to important examples of institutional stickiness and surprise in areas as diverse as dairy, investors' rights, tariffs, and macroeconomic policymaking.

Moravcsik (1998) was correct, then, when he famously urged us to stop thinking of the EU as a case *sui generis*. He was less convincing, however, in justifying his call by emphasizing the intergovernmental character of the EU. I suggest that RTAs resemble each other by virtue of their tendency toward institutionalization and, as a result, by engendering dynamics that are potentially detrimental to member state interests. Integration, in other words, is a messy affair, and we would do well to think more carefully about the gap between intentions and formal structures *and* actual outcomes. In this last section, I would like to reflect on two possible implications of this gap.

The first is that the gap points to instability. If integration generates unwanted institutional arrangements, the member states are likely to waiver in their commitment. History supports this interpretation: failed RTAs far exceed successful ones, whether in the Americas, Africa, Asia, and even Europe. Let us recall that Mercosur's smaller member states have already threatened to leave the block on several occasions. In the EU, Great Britain has historically shown much ambivalence, while the French and Dutch citizens have recently expressed their ambivalence towards the EU by rejecting the proposed constitutional treaty. Failed RTAs are expensive – politically, diplomatically, and financially. Understanding the nature of that instability is a must.

The second point is about possible alternatives. Is the current blueprint for regional integration, with what seems be a common propensity towards institutionalization, the only possible one? We should recognize that most RTAs rely on enduring, wide reaching agreements reached by elected politicians in a short period of time without sufficient planning for adjustment costs. Matters could be different. Specific decisions – such as those on certain economic sectors, for instance – could include clause for periodic reviews, with the possibility of revisions and even abrogation. In addition, decisions could routinely be made independent of each other – so that member states could participate in some dimensions of integration but not others. Fundamental decisions related to integration could, in turn, require the approval of at least two political leaderships in every member state (this, we should note, did happen in the case of NAFTA's three member states). Finally, mechanisms for collecting and redistributing significant funds could be introduced. Table 1 identifies the advantages and drawbacks of the traditional form of integration and a looser alternative model.

The message from Table 1 is clear. The alternative model would allow the member states to establish an evolving and mutable relationship with a given RTA. Certainly there would be drawbacks to this approach: fewer sectors of the economy might be involved, member states can easily opt out of certain dimensions of integration, governments may be less willing to compromise, and so on. On the whole, however, we might see more stable and enduring RTAs, as member states increase their overall control of the process of integration.

Table 1
Models of Regional Integration

	Current Integration Model (e.g. EU, NAFTA, Mercosur)	Alternative Integration Model
Permanence of Decisions	Decisions are generally taken as permanent; cumbersome and difficult steps required for revisions Advantages: predictability (for market and other actors); cohesion of measures in a given policy area Disadvantages: as economic and political reality change, decisions can prove harmful	Possibility of easily revisiting, revising, and/or abrogating decisions Advantages: decisions closely reflect economic and political realities on the ground; higher compliance rates Disadvantages: incoherence in a given policy area; different regulatory frameworks may act as non-tariff barriers to trade
Extent of Issue Linkage	All-or-nothing approach makes it very difficult to win exemptions from given issues once part of broader integration project Advantages: deeper integration; easier to overcome obstacles from individual member states on specific issues Disadvantages: likelihood of domestic pressures against parts of the agreement	*A-la-carte* integration: member states can choose which dimensions of integration (specific sectors, policies, etc.) they participate in Advantages: less domestic resistance to integration Disadvantages: selective integration, inefficiencies due to inter-dependence between dimensions of integration
Initial Approval / Approval of Major Revisions	Can be done by one political leadership (typically with support from legislature) Advantages: expediency (both domestically and internationally) Disadvantages: agreements more likely to come under attack later and be poorly implemented over time	Requires at least two consecutive political leaderships (with support of legislatures) Advantages: stronger commitment by the member states Disadvantages: lower likelihood that agreements are reached or, when possibly needed, revised
Redistributive Mechanisms	Very limited pooled funds and mechanisms to deal with impact of integration on selected industries Advantages: upfront costs of integration are limited Disadvantages: impact of integration can lead to unrest and pressures for dissolution of agreement	Collection and redistribution of significant funds Advantages: decreased strains on commitment to integration Disadvantages: richer countries may prove less interested in integration; fewer incentives for member states to prepare for adjustments to integration

Source: Duina and Buxbaum (2008)

References

Ackrill, R. and A. Kay 2006, 'Historical-institutionalist perspectives on the development of the EU budget system', in *Journal of European Public Policy*, 13(1), pp. 113-33.

Albin, E.R., and R. Bouzas 2004, 'Argentina's foreign trade strategy: the curse of asymmetric integration in the world economy,' in V.K. Aggarwal et al. (eds.), *The Strategic Dynamics of Latin American Trade*, Woodrow Wilson Center Press and Stanford University Press, Washington and Stanford, pp. 159-74.

Alter, K.J. 1998, 'Who are the »Masters of the Treaty«? European Governments and the European Court of Justice', *International Organization*, 52 (1), pp. 121-146.

BBC Monitoring (International Reports) 2002, *Uruguay's Battle tells Brazil's Cardoso Uruguay seeks alternatives to Mercosur*, 3 April.

Blaikie, B. 1999, Bulk water exports, Retrieved 11 February 2007 from http://www.billblaikie.ca/node/72.

Boustany, N. 1996, 'Argentina: prospering from lessons learned', in *The Washington Post*, 6 December.

Bouzas, R. 2003, 'Economic integration in the Southern Cone: can Mercosur survive?', in A. Margheritis (ed.), *Latin American Democracies in the New Global Economy*, North-South Center Press, Coral Gable, FL, pp. 63-81.

Bulmer, S.J. 1998, 'New institutionalism and the governance of the Single European Market', in *Journal of European Public Policy*, 5 (3), pp. 365-86.

Campbell, J.S. 1995, 'We obtained a lot in Mercosur', *Clarín*, (Foreign Broadcast Information Service, Latin America, FBIS-LAT-95-020), 19 January.

Canada NewsWire 1996, *A deal is a deal*, 26 February.

Congressional Record. 103rd Congress, 1st session 1993, 139, pp. 159-161 and 164-164.

de Andrade, J.P. et al. 2005, 'Disintegrating effects of monetary policies in the Mercosur', in *Structural Change and Economic Dynamics* 16 (1), pp. 65-89.

Devlin, R. et al. 2001, 'Macroeconomic stability, trade and integration', in *Integration & Trade*, 5 (13), pp. 35-96.

Duffy, A. 1998, 'Liberal MPs rage over gas additive reversal', in *Ottawa Citizen*, 24 July.

Duina, F. 2006, *The Social Construction of Free trade: The European Union, NAFTA, and Mercosur*, Princeton University Press, Princeton NJ.

Duina, F. and J. Buxbaum 2008, 'Regional Trade Agreements and the Pursuit of State Interests: Institutional, Perspectives from NAFTA and Mercosur', forthcoming in *Economy and Society (38)*.

Dyer, G. and K. Warn 1999, 'Mercosur feeling the pinch since Brazil's devaluation', in *Financial Times*, 13 August.

Economist 2005, *Improbable allies: Paraguay and the United States*, 1 October.

Federal News Service 1996, *Prepared testimony of Ambassador Ira Shapiro Office of the United States Trade Representative before the House Committee on Agriculture Subcommittee on Dairy, Livestock, and Poultry*, 25 September.

Financial Post (Toronto) 1996, *Supply management regime gets a reprieve*, 27 July.

Grassi, R. 2003, 'Mercosur: Uruguayan leader critical of Mercosur partners', in *Inter Press Service*, 15 October.

The Gazette (Montreal) 1996, *Agricultural agencies warn of job losses if US wins*, 30 January.

Guira, J. 2003, *Mercosur: Trade and Investment amid Financial Crisis*, Kluwer Law International, The Hague.

Hansard, 36th Parliament, 2nd session, 1999, 136.

Heisenberg, D. and A. Richmond 2002, 'Supranational institution-building in the European Union: a comparison of the European Court of Justice and the European Central Bank', *Journal of European Public Policy* 9 (2), pp. 201-218.

Holzinger, K. and C. Knill 2002, 'Path dependencies in European integration: A constructive response to German Foreign Minsiter Joschka Fischer', *Public Administration*, 80 (1), pp. 125-52.

Jacobsson, B., P. Lægreid and O.K. Pedersen 2004, *Europeanization and Transnational States: Comparing Central Nordic Governments*, Routledge Press, London.

Latin America Regional Reports 1991, in *Brazil (May 2)*, Latin American Newsletters Ltd., London

Liptak, A. 2004, 'Review of US rulings by NAFTA tribunals stirs worries', in *New York Times*, 18 April.

Madrid EFE 1994, 'Uruguay's President discusses launch of Mercosur', *Foreign Broadcast Information Service*, Latin America, FBIS-LAT-94-244, 18 December.

MercoPress 2001, *Mercosur is over*, 18 April, Retrieved August 6, 2007, from http://www.mercopress.com/detalle.asp?NUM=680

Montero, D. 1999, 'Trade: Brazil irks Mercosur partners', in *SUNS – South-North Development Monitor*, 4366, 3 February, retrieved March 6, 2006, from http://www.sunsonline.org/trade/process/followup/1999/02030299.htm

Moravcsik, A. 1998, *The Choice for Europe: Social Purpose and State Power from Messina to Maastricht*, Cornell University Press, Ithaca, New York.

O'Keefe, T.A. 2003, *A Resurgent Mercosur: Confronting Economic Crises and Negotiating Trade Agreements*, The Dante B. Fascell North-South Center, University of Miami, Miami, FL.

Pierson, P. 1996, 'The Path to European integration', in *Comparative Political Studies* 29 (2), pp. 123-64

Sandholtz, W. and A. Stone Sweet (eds.) 1998, *European Integration and Supranational Governance*, Oxford University Press, Oxford.

Sverdrup, U. 2002, 'An institutional perspective on treaty reform: contextualizing the Amsterdam and Nice treaties', in *Journal of European Public Policy*, 9 (1), pp. 120-140.

Public Citizen 2005, 'NAFTA Chapter 11 investor-state cases: Lessons for the Central American Free Trade Agreement', in *Global Trade Watch* (Publication No. E9014), February, retrieved August 6, 2007, from http://www.citizen.org/trade/nafta/

U.S. Department of Agriculture, Economic Research Service 1997, *Agricultural Outlook*, (January-February), retrieved August 6, 2007, from http://www.ers.usda.gov/publications/agoutlook/jan1997/

Wisnefski, S. and T. Loughran 2001, 'Argentina's Cavallo marks territory on free trade front', in *Dow Jones International News*, 9 May.

SECTION 2

Politics and Ideas

CHAPTER 7

What do we know – or not – about Ideas and Politics?

John L. Campbell

Professor, Dartmouth College, USA and Copenhagen Business School, Denmark

Introduction

One of the most important debates in political science and sociology today is the degree to which self-interest, rather than ideas, such as norms, values, cognitive frameworks, identities and the like, motivates political behavior. I first encountered this debate in a sustained form during an early visit to Copenhagen in 1993 when I gave a series of seminars about institutional change and the state. I was frequently challenged at these gatherings by Ove Pedersen and his colleagues for assuming, as rational choice theorists do, that the world was all about the rational pursuit of self-interest. In particular, they took me to task for failing to consider the importance of discourse and ideas in shaping people's perceptions of their interests and strategic actions in the first place.

To be honest, I did not fully appreciate what they meant other than to extend the classic Berger and Luckmann (1966) arguments about the social construction of reality, perhaps through the structure of language, which seemed to me not all that helpful in terms of understanding things like the determinants of tax policy and institutional change, which I was studying at the time. These things seemed to me to be all about people jockeying for position so as to advance their self-interests, or the interests of others, as best they could within a particular institutional (i.e., rule based) context. But it became clear to me from all of this that there were literatures that were relevant for understanding institutions and policy-making, and that spoke to the issue of how ideas as well as interests made the world go around.

Since then I have read a lot of this literature and now realize two things. First, ideas are important, but interests are too. Indeed, interests are just another type of idea, although one that is often rooted in people's perceptions of their material situations. Second, there is plenty of work to be done in order to understand how ideas other than interests affect policymaking and institutional change.

This paper identifies some of these problems. As such, it constitutes a critique of those who have criticized rational choice theory – including some rational choice theorists who have engaged in a certain amount of critical reflection on the shortcomings of their own theoretical paradigm. It focuses on the contributions of those who have argued that ideas matter at least as much as interests – a position advocated increasingly by sociologists schooled in organizational analysis, and some political scientists working in the areas of comparative political economy and international relations. I refer to their work as ideational analysis in contrast to rational choice analysis. Although there are important differences among these critics of rational choice theory, they share an orientation to political analysis that emphasizes the importance of formal and informal institutions, which include taken-for-granted normative and cognitive constructs, as principal determinants of political behavior (e.g., March and Olsen 1984, 1989). Yet the critics of rational choice theory are not without their own problems and these must be reconciled in order to convince the rational choice skeptics, who still believe that politics is all about interests, that other types of ideas also matter.

The chapter proceeds as follows. I begin by briefly reviewing the basic rational choice approach. Next I discuss some of the criticisms that have been made of it by rational choice theorists themselves who have accepted that, in addition to self-interest, other types of ideas are important determinants of political-economic decision making. And I identify three problems with these criticisms. These are (1) a failure to explain the origins of ideas, (2) conceptual confusion about different types of ideas, and

(3), insufficient attention to specifying the mechanisms by which ideas affect decision making. Third, I show that these same three problems are prevalent in the criticisms of rational choice theory that come from non-rational choice scholars – that is, scholars who believe that ideas other than self-interest are often the key determinants of decision making. And I argue that these must be resolved if there is any hope of convincing the more hard-core rational choice skeptics that ideas matter. Fourth, I suggest how these problems might be resolved in ideational analysis. I have developed some of these arguments in other papers, which is to say that my early experience in Copenhagen had a profound effect on my work (e.g., Campbell 1998, 2002a, 2002b, 2002c, 2004 chap. 4). Finally, I raise some questions that still require answers in order for ideational analysis to better account for how ideas affect policymaking.

Rational Choice Theory

Generally speaking, rational choice theory sees politics as being determined by instrumentally motivated individuals acting according to a utilitarian, cost-benefit logic. In this view politics are driven by self-interested actors whose preferences, weighted by their respective resources, determine political outcomes. Politics is a competition where outcomes are often the result of processes, such as voting, log rolling and interest group lobbying, through which individual preferences are aggregated and institutionalized. This does not mean, however, that actors necessarily get what they want. The aggregation process may yield outcomes that are unintended by some actors. In any case, both public policies and political institutions, that is, the rules of the game within which politics occur, are created through this process and subsequently constrain action (e.g., Alt and Shepsle 1990; Booth et al. 1993; Buchanan 1988; Knight 2001, 1992).

Although rational choice theory is derived from neoclassical economics, which argues that outcomes are generally functional and efficient insofar as they represent the pareto-optimal result of the aggregation process, rational choice theories of politics are less optimistic about the efficiencies of political markets. For example, Kenneth Arrow (1951) found it logically impossible to aggregate individual preferences into a general social welfare function and others have discussed a variety of dilemmas associated with voting and other political means of aggregation that tend to yield less than optimal outcomes (e.g., Buchanan 1988; Mueller 1989). Similarly, some rational choice theories of politics borrow heavily from the new institutional economics, which argues that actors often make decisions in order to reduce transaction costs, especially the costs of monitoring and enforcing contracts (Alchian and Demsetz 1972; Chandler 1977; Coase 1937; North 1990). This approach also acknowledges that political decision making does not necessarily result in the most efficient outcomes because previously existing institutions constrain the range of alternatives from which actors choose (e.g., Ostrom 1990).

Rational choice theory has been the target of wide-spread criticism (Green and Shapiro 1994; Hollis and Nell 1975). For our purposes, the most basic is that it neglects the importance of ideas other than material interests (e.g., March and Olsen 1984, 1989). Even some rational choice theorists, notably Douglass North (2005: 5, 1990: 42-44, 1981), lament this problem and have argued, for instance, that the neglect of ideas, such as long-standing norms, is one reason why rational decision making does not always yield the most efficient or optimal outcomes.[3] As a result, North (2005; Knight and North 1997) and others have tried to incorporate an analysis of ideas into their theories without abandoning the basic rational choice framework. But in doing so, they run into three additional problems.

Internal Criticisms of Rational Choice Theory

To begin with, it is often charged that rational choice theory fails to account for the origins of preferences. Rather than endogenizing an analysis of preference formation, rational choice theorists simply ignore the issue

3. Of course, rational choice theorists also try to explain sub-optimal outcomes in other ways that have little to do with norms or other types of ideas (e.g., Knight 1992).

(Thelen and Steinmo 1992: 7-10).[4] The same criticism can be leveled at those rational choice theorists who have recognized that ideas like norms matter and may influence preferences (Kiser 1994; Levi 1988, 1997; North 1990; Ostrom 1990: 33-35). They understand that what actors believe may be just as important as what they want (Vanberg and Buchanan 1989: 51). But they typically neglect the *origins* of these beliefs and ideas (but see Knight and Ensminger 1998). North (1990, 1981), for instance, argued for much of his career that norms have been an important constraint on decision making throughout history, but shed little light on where those norms came from in the first place.

Second, the few rational choice scholars, who accept that ideas other than interests matter, argue that things like an actor's normative and cognitive structures are important sources of bounded rationality problems, and that these affect political decision making (Jones 1999; Knight and North 1997). However, rarely, if ever, do they carefully differentiate among these and other types of ideas. North (2005) has provided the most extensive argument from within a rational choice framework about the important effects that ideas have on decision making. But he uses terms such as beliefs, ideas, mental constructs, norms, and culture almost interchangeably when in fact they are fundamentally different types of ideas that have different types of effects on decision making. Cognitive structures, for instance, may limit what an individual can imagine in the first place whereas normative structures may limit what individuals find to be acceptable within that initial set of cognitively imaginable ideas (March and Olsen 1984, 1989). Hence, there is much *conceptual confusion* about different types of ideas that matter.

Third, although some rational choice theorists recognize that normative and cognitive structures mediate action, they need to better specify in their theories the *mechanisms* by which all of this happens. Indeed, North (2005) has tried to flesh out what some of these mechanisms might be by

4. In response, some rational choice theorists have tried to explain how preferences as well as strategies are determined by the institutional contexts within which actors find themselves (e.g., Bates et al. 1998; Frieden and Rogowski 1996; Garrett and Lange 1996) as well as the relative balance of bargaining resources at the disposal of contesting actors (e.g., Knight 1992, 2001).

delving into cognitive psychology and brain science to see how cognitive structures and beliefs constrain how people learn and respond to uncertainty in their environment. But by doing so he neglects the sociological mechanisms, discussed below, that may be operating as well.

External Criticisms of Rational Choice Theory

There is a vast literature on how ideas affect institutional change and policymaking (Campbell 2002c). Much of it revolves around the sociological argument that actors behave according to a logic of appropriateness; that norms constrain behavioral options; that taken-for-granted cognitive scripts constrain people's perceptions of their problems, interests, and strategies of action; and that these norms and scripts often diffuse through fields of organizations, such as nation-states, in ways that yield a certain convergence across countries in beliefs and practices (e.g., Thomas et al. 1987). However, much of this literature suffers from problems quite similar to those found in the self-criticism of rational choice theory discussed above. Hence, as we shall see, the parallels between these two bodies of work are striking.

A great deal of this literature builds upon March and Olsen's (1984, 1989) classic distinction between the logic of consequentiality and the logic of appropriateness. The logic of consequentiality, typically associated with rational choice theory, is the notion that in order to make political decisions actors calculate present costs against future benefits and select the option that maximizes benefits relative to costs. The logic of appropriateness is the notion that actors make political decisions that they believe are appropriate and legitimate rather than necessarily consistent with a cost-benefit analysis. They do so because they face situations of scarce information, bounded rationality, and uncertainty – situations in which their interests are ambiguous rather than self-evident and transparent. For March and Olsen, what actors deem to be appropriate depends on prevailing norms, taken-for-granted routines, and cognitive schema through which they interpret their situations (see also Meyer and Rowan 1977). While provocative, this literature is lacking in three important respects, which very much parallel the problems of rational choice theory discussed above.

The Problem of Mechanisms

The first problem is that the ideational view typically fails to specify the *mechanisms* by which norms, cognitive schema, and the like work their magic. In particular, while some claim that cognitive constructs diffuse among nation-states in the international political community, it is not clear how this happens. All that is demonstrated empirically is that over time organizations tend to adopt similar structures and practices. Insofar as nation-states are concerned it is because the "world polity" sets normatively legitimate standards to which member nation-states are supposed to subscribe in order to obtain legitimacy (i.e., acceptance) from the international community, as represented, for instance by the United Nations, OECD, or other such organizations.

Missing from all of this are convincing explanations about exactly how the diffusion process works. Most scholars simply assume that this process involves the well-known forces of mimetic and normative isomorphism. Mimetic isomorphism is a process whereby organizations of a type, such as nation-states, imitate each others practices and, as a result, tend to exhibit the same set of practices over time. They choose to imitate each other because they are unable to rationally calculate the best or most efficient practice due to information uncertainties or other ambiguities in their environment. Normative isomorphism leads to the same outcome, but because organizations learn from experts in various ways what the most acceptable practices are (DiMaggio and Powell 1983; Thomas et al. 1987). In other words, organizations often adhere to a logic of appropriateness instead of a logic of consequentiality. But researchers typically assert this without demonstrating empirically that this is actually what is happening in the cases they are studying (e.g., Mizruchi and Fein 1999).[5]

5. In at least one empirical study John Meyer, the foremost proponent of this diffusion perspective, and his colleagues (Meyer et al. 1997: 645) admitted that although their approach may be sufficient for determining the degree to which diffusion and convergent isomorphism occurs among nation-states, it is not well equipped to identify the causal sequences and processes involved. Other

For instance, Frank Dobbin's (1994) *Forging Industrial Policy* is a book that directly criticizes interest-based accounts of policy making and institutional analysis. In that book he argues that the different organizational structures of the French, British, and American railroad industries were the result of different nationally-specific political cultures favoring different models of state-economy relationships (e.g., statist, laissez faire, etc.). This is an important book in part because it attacked rational choice based arguments. But it suffered from a serious problem.

Dobbin believed that cognitive and normative structures – rather than interests – motivated action in his cases. And he believed this because key actors said things in public testimony and pronouncements about how railroads ought to be organized that seemed to reflect the nationally-specific values about state-economy relationships of the nations in which they lived. In other words, such statements, he believed, showed that people were acting according to a logic of appropriateness, not a logic of instrumentality. But he had taken at face value that these people were telling the truth in very public places (e.g., parliamentary or congressional debates). He never raised the possibility that people, perhaps especially politicians, might say one thing publicly but something quite different in private in order to conceal their true motives from public view (e.g., Kuran 1995). So it is hard to be sure whether the mechanism operating in his story was a kind of normative, taken-for-granted, script-based sort of action rather than the raw pursuit of self-interests albeit cloaked in normatively legitimizing rhetoric.

The Problem of Conceptual Confusion

A second problem in the ideational literature is that of *conceptual confusion*. There is terrible confusion about what these normative, cognitive, and other ideational constructs actually are. The literature is a conceptual mess in dire need of clarification. People talk of cognitive mind sets, taken-for-granted scripts, normative principles, logics of appropriateness and instrumentality, paradigms, and more, but often without differentiating clearly among them.

researchers have recently started to tackle these issues (e.g., Djelic and Sahlin-Andersson 2006; Halliday and Carruthers 2007; Bartley 2007).

Dobbin's work, for instance, suffered from failing to distinguish between different types of ideational concepts. On the one hand, he talked about taken-for-granted cognitive and normative constructs, such as the French proclivity for centralized state planning, as being the chief determinant of organizational outcomes. But, on the other hand, the public pronouncements of politicians that he offered as evidence for his argument could just as easily have been strategic frames used as normative cover for the pursuit of material interests. Had he distinguished between cognitive or normative constructs and strategic frames, perhaps his analysis and conclusions would have been much different.[6]

The Problem of Origins

Finally, is the problem of *origins*. While everyone writing about the importance of ideas accepts that new ideas can transform policies and institutions, nobody really has much to say about where these new ideas come from in the first place. Diffusion theorists, for instance, simply assert that new ideas emerge in the world polity and then diffuse around the globe (Meyer et al. 1997a, 1997b; Soysal 1994). This is an all too mysterious process that needs to be specified more carefully.

There are some partial exceptions. Neil Fligstein (1990) suggested that new ideas in the business world tend to emanate from people in business schools, who teach them to their students and publish them in business journals. New ideas work their way into organizational practices from there. Mauro Guillén (1994) made a similar argument about the diffusion of organizational models for corporations across countries. And Peter Hall (1989) and colleagues wrote about the development of Keynesianism and its spread across countries – although they emphasized much more the diffusion of Keynesianism than its development per se. Finally, Sarah Babb (2007) showed how the International Monetary Fund adopted a set of orthodox, anti-inflationary policy prescriptions during the early postwar period when Keynesianism was the norm in most academic and

6. Despite my concerns about Dobbin's book, it is an important one. It was one of the first extended empirical studies that showed how taken-for-granted normative ideas may influence political, economic, and institutional outcomes in a cross-national political-economic context.

policy-making circles. She attributed this to the power of professionals within the organization, the propensity to routinize policy prescriptions under conditions of bounded rationality, and the influence of key donor states, notably the United States of America. But she had much less to say about where these ideas came from in the first place.[7]

In sum, there are three problems with the work on ideas that has been produced by both rational choice and non-rational choice scholars. One is that it fails to specify the mechanisms by which ideas affect outcomes. Another is that it suffers from considerable lack of conceptual clarity. And the third is that it does not account satisfactorily for the origins of new ideas.

Attempts to Resolve These Problems

How might we solve these problems? What follows is a discussion of some possible solutions. Some are more developed than others and I make no claim to have entirely solved any of them. In any case, this discussion sets the stage for the last section of the paper in which I list a series of questions that remain for those of us who are interested in how ideas operate with causal effects in the world.

Clearing up the Confusion about Types of Ideas

The problem of conceptual confusion has to be solved first. That is, one cannot go about seeing either how ideas affect outcomes, or how they originate without specifying what types of ideas we are talking about in the first place. There are four ideal types of ideas that matter for people trying to understand political-economic outcomes (Campbell 1998). These can be distinguished along two dimensions. First, whereas *cognitive* ideas specify causal or means-ends relationships, *normative* ideas specify how things ought to be. Second, whereas in politics some ideas are hotly debated and, therefore, are located in the *foreground* of political debate, other ideas are much more taken-for-granted and are located in the *background*

7. Recent work in the sociology of professions, particularly the economics profession, is beginning to shed light on where new ideas come from that influence policy making. See, for example, Yonay (1998) and Fourcade (2006).

of political debate. These distinctions have often been collapsed in one way or another in the literature.

Working with these distinctions, four types of ideas can be distinguished. (1) Policy *programs*, such as specific proposals for a flat tax or progressively graduated income tax, are cognitive ideas located in the foreground of political debate. (2) *Paradigms*, such as neoclassical or supply-side economics, are cognitive ideas located in the background of political debate insofar as they are taken-for-granted views for most policy makers and their advisors. (3) *Public sentiments*, such as a general aversion to budget deficits, are normative ideas located in the background of policy debate. (4) *Frames*, such as the metaphorical pronouncements of political spin doctors and others about how high taxes are anathema to American values, are normative ideas located in the foreground of political debate. The point in developing these distinctions is simply to suggest that this sort of scheme might be useful in untangling notions that have been conflated in the literature and, therefore, that have blocked empirical work that might have better determined the degree to which ideas, broadly construed, or self-interests drive policymaking and institution building in particular historical episodes.

This is not a perfect conceptual scheme. One might argue that these distinctions are too severe and that there is more slippage between cognitive and normative ideas and between foreground and background ideas than this typology allows for. Moreover, ideas in the background may shift into the foreground over time and vice versa. For example, from the 1940s through the mid-1970s, neoclassical economics and Keynesianism were paradigmatic mainstays of conventional economics and policymaking in most advanced capitalist countries. But during the 1970s and early 1980s Keynesianism emerged from the paradigmatic background and was subject to considerable criticism both among academics and politicians in their respective foregrounds. To a degree, Keynesianism was abandoned and supply-side economics took its place. Hence, these ideas floated between the cognitive foreground and background. Moreover, Keynesianism was the normatively appropriate way to manage the macro economy in both countries until stagflation set in during the 1970s (Campbell 2004: chap. 5). Again, slippage problems are evident. How to handle this sort of slippage problem requires more thought. That said, remember that I am talking about *ideal types*. Furthermore, the two dimensions from which the four types are derived are probably more akin to continua than to rigid dichotomies.

Specifying Causal Mechanisms and Processes: Bringing Agency Back In
But what about the mechanisms by which different types of ideas affect outcomes? Different types of actors are primarily responsible for the creation, maintenance, and dissemination of different types of ideas. These actors and their maneuvering in various political and other arenas are the ones who are responsible for the effects that ideas might have in any particular policymaking episode.

For instance, Mark Blyth (2002) showed in his analysis of the rise of neoliberalism in Sweden and the United States that different types of actors were associated with different types of ideas. Professional economists were associated with different economic paradigms; different politicians were associated with different policy programs; and so on. Especially important was the central role that "think tanks" played in all of this (see also Campbell 1998, 2004: chap. 5; Campbell and Pedersen 2007). But the important point here is that, in contrast to many diffusion theorists, scholars who take actors and agency seriously avoid excessively structuralist arguments about how ideas influence the policy-making process. By focusing on specific actors they bring agency back into the analysis and, therefore, begin to specify some of the mechanisms by which ideas have effects.

Some diffusion theorists have recognized this. For instance, some of them have started to explore how international non-governmental organizations (INGOs), such as Amnesty International, the United Nations, and the World Wildlife Federation, are important actors whose mission is to spread ideas about how nation-states ought to behave with respect to human rights, environmental, and other policy programs (Boli and Thomas 1999). Hence, they argue that INGOs are the bearers of ideas and are responsible for spreading them among nation-states. INGOs are also often responsible for bringing political pressure to bear on nation-states that may be reluctant either to adopt such practices into law, or to enforce them once they have been adopted (Keck and Sikkink 1998).

That said, focusing on actors and agency is not entirely sufficient to solve the mechanism problem. This is because the effects of background ideas are more structural and less susceptible to manipulation than are ideas in the foreground. Hence, for example, taken-for-granted ideas about national identity may underpin policymaking with real effects – such as providing a common sense of purpose during periods of crisis that enable policymakers to overcome their day-to-day partisan differences and come together to solve pressing national problems (Campbell and Hall 2007). The point is that different types of ideas may operate through different mechanisms. All of this needs to be sorted out more carefully than has been the case so far in the literature.

Explaining Where New Ideas Come From

The final problem, better understanding where new ideas come from in the first place, remains to be solved. I have written a bit on institutional change. And I have argued that institutions tend to evolve in ways best described as a process of *bricolage.* That is, institutional entrepreneurs (actors) seeking to change an institution typically do not throw out the old one and replace it with something completely new. Rather they draw upon whatever institutional principles and practices they have at hand, and then blend or recombine them in ways that yield something different, but not totally different, from that with which they started (Campbell 2004: chap. 3).

I think academics do very much the same thing. We read each other's work, and take bits and pieces of it, blend them together, and come up with modifications, new insights, and quasi-original ideas that advance our fields of study. In fact, I think this is how most new ideas are very often created in academia, business, and politics, not to mention the arts and sciences. For instance, scientific breakthroughs at the Pasteur Institute during its heyday were due to cross-fertilization among different types of scientists who were brought together to teach and do research collaboratively (Hage 2006). Rarely are new ideas cut from whole cloth. They tend much more often to be the result of a process of bricolage.

We need to know much more about how this process actually operates. Clearly it is embedded in social relations such that people who tend to be the most creative, I suspect, tend to be those who are well situated among different networks of scholars, scientists, politicians, or artists such that they are exposed to a variety of ideas which they might then use for their own creative purposes as bricoleurs (e.g., Collins 2000). It is also influenced by the jetsam and flotsam left over from alternative ideas and models that have since been tried and either abandoned or marginalized (Schneiberg 2007). Many policy ideas for welfare state building, urban planning, agricultural development, and more were developed in the United States during the early twentieth century through a process of blending European ideas with principles and practices inherited from the past in America. The European ideas diffused to the United States through interpersonal networks of scholars, politicians, philanthropists, and business leaders (Rodgers 1998). But we need to know much more about how network location and social relationships affect all of this.

Beyond that, however, as Robert Wuthnow (1989; see also Babb 2007) has argued, a theory of idea formation needs to pay attention, first, to the organizational and individual *actors* who generate and advocate different kinds of ideas. Second, we must recognize that for new ideas to emerge they must be attached to *resources*. The dissemination of new ideas requires political and economic support. Third, new ideas often tend to result from the recombination of bits and pieces of already existing ideas—a process by which the development of new ideas is typically a *path-dependent process* where new ideas differ from but still resemble the old ones. Finally, for new ideas to become influential the bearers of these ideas must have access to places, such as the media, government, corporate board rooms, or anywhere else people use ideas to make decisions. As a result, the *institutions* that configure these venues are critical insofar as they act as filters allowing some, but not all, new ideas to penetrate.

Remaining Questions

While I am fairly comfortable with my approach to thinking about different types of ideas, I am less comfortable when it comes to our understanding of the mechanisms by which different types of ideas affect policymaking and institutional development. And I am much less confident in our understanding of how new ideas are generated in the first place. In particular, much work is needed to answer the following questions, which are derived from the preceding discussion.

1. How do we know empirically when paradigms are at work? What are the mechanisms by which they influence policymaking and institutional development? That is, how do we know when actors have succumbed to a particular taken-for-granted policy paradigm or not? And how do we know when they have experienced some sort of paradigm shift?
2. Similarly, how do we know when public sentiments (or national identities) are at work? What are the mechanisms by which these taken-for-granted norms and values influence policymaking and institutional development? There is, of course, a great danger in generalizing about public sentiment, public opinion, national values, and the like, so this is tricky business. These may not be monolithic wholes shared by nearly everyone in a society. And they may sometimes be subject to disagreement and debate, hence creeping into the foreground of policy debates.
3. What are the conditions under which ideas of various sorts become taken-for-granted thereby exerting structural effects? Conversely, what are the conditions under which taken-for-granted ideas become less taken for granted and become subject to conscious reflection and articulation?
4. How can we empirically determine the degree to which actors are acting based on ideational considerations of one sort or another rather than in the pursuit of their own self-interests? Put differently, how can we determine empirically the manner in which ideas and the pursuit of interests *interact* to produce policy and institutional outcomes? Do we need different methodologies for determining how this happens for different types of ideas? In particular, do we need one methodology for determining whether background ideas affect policymaking and institution building and another methodology for determining whether foreground ideas have such effects? Similarly, do we need different methodologies to determine whether cognitive ideas, on the one hand, and normative ideas, on the other hand, have effects?
5. How do new ideas get created? What are the social circumstances most likely to generate new ideas? That is, how do social networks, resource flows, political influence, institutional arrangements, and other things affect how new ideas are formed?

Note that there are important methodological implications for many of these questions. A full-blown discussion of the methodologies that would be required to arrive at answers to these questions is well beyond the scope of this chapter. Others have started to discuss these issues at length (e.g., Berman 1998, 2001; Blyth 1997; Campbell 2004: chap. 4). For instance, traditional historical description based on interviews may be sufficient to determine how ideational frames are used as tools to mobilize political support for a particular policy program. But content analyses of government documents or newspaper editorials may be necessary to determine the degree to which a particular cognitive paradigm or normative sentiment permeates and, thus, influences either the public debate or more insulated policy-making discourse surrounding a particular policy-making episode. These and other methodological issues are far from resolved.

Conclusion

I have argued that there are at least three important analytic problems that must be resolved before rational choice skeptics will be convinced that ideas matter in political decision making. And I have offered some suggestions how some of these problems may be resolved. Yet many questions remain. In the end, all of this amounts to a kind of manifesto for ideational analysis. If critics of rational choice theory want to convince the rational choice skeptics that ideas matter, then these questions require resolution. The good news is that at least among some rational choice theorists there is sympathy for the ideational project and, therefore, a window of opportunity for engaging rational choice theorists in a constructive fashion around these issues.

But to avoid misunderstanding let me be clear about what I am *not* arguing. On the one hand, none of what I have said is intended as a critique of rational choice theory per se. Instead, the fundamental point of this chapter is to reflect on some of the shortcomings in arguments that have been raised *against* conventional rational choice theory. It is a critique of those who have argued in favor of the influence of ideas – including myself. On the other hand, although I am sympathetic to the notion that ideas matter, I do not reject the argument that sometimes actors are rational or that they operate on the basis of their interests. To the contrary, I believe that we need to develop a better understanding of the relationship between interests and other types of ideas as determinants of political decision making. So I disagree with those who argue that the effects of ideas and interests are mutually exclusive.

Finally, I accept North's (2005: 5) assertion that rational choice theorists really know very little about how ideas other than interests affect decision making. But I am not convinced that ideational analysts have fully understood how ideas affect decision making either. There is more work to be done on these issues by all of us.

References

Alt, J.E. and K.A. Shepsle (eds.) 1990, *Perspectives on Positive Political Economy*, Cambridge University Press, New York.

Alchian, A. and H. Demsetz 1972, 'Production, Information Costs, and Economic Organization', in *American Economic Review*, 62, pp. 777-95.

Arrow, K.J. 1951, *Social Choice and Individual Values*, Yale University Press, New Haven.

Babb, S. 2007, 'Embeddedness, Inflation, and International Regimes: The IMF in the Early Postwar Period', in *American Journal of Sociology*, 113, pp. 128-64.

Bartley, T. 2007, 'Institutional Emergence in an Era of Globalization: The Rise of Transnational Private Regulation of Labor and Environmental Conditions', in *American Journal of Sociology*, 113 pp. 297-351.

Bates, R.H., A. Greif, M. Levi, J.-L. Rosenthal and B. R. Weingast 1998, *Analytic Narratives*, Princeton University Press, Princeton NJ.

Berger, P. and T. Luckmann 1966, *The Social Construction of Reality*, Anchor, Garden City, NY.

Berman, S. 2001, 'Ideas, Norms, and Culture in Political Analysis', in *Comparative Politics*, 33 (2), pp. 231-250.

Berman, S. 1998, *The Social Democratic Movement: Ideas and Politics in the Making of Interwar Europe*, Harvard University Press, Cambridge.

Blyth, M. 2002, *Great Transformations: Economic Ideas and Institutional Change in the Twentieth Century*, Cambridge University Press, New York.

Blyth, M. 1997, 'Any More Bright Ideas? The Ideational Turn of Comparative Political Economy', in *Comparative Politics*, 29 (2), pp. 229-250.

Boli, J. and G.M. Thomas (eds.) 1999, *Constructing World Culture: International Nongovernmental Organizations Since 1875*, Stanford University Press, Stanford.

Booth, W.J., P. James and H. Meadwell (eds.) 1993, *Politics and Rationality*, Cambridge University Press, New York.

Buchanan, J. 1988, 'The Economic Theory of Politics Reborn', in *Challenge*, 31 (2), pp. 4-10.

Campbell, J.L. 2004, *Institutional Change and Globalization*, Princeton University Press, Princeton.

Campbell, J.L. 2002a, 'Convincing the Skeptics: Ideas and the Critique of Rational Choice Theory', in *Sociologie et Sociétés*, 34 (1), pp. 35-50.

Campbell, J.L. 2002b, 'A Clarification and Response to the Critics', in *Sociologie et Sociétés*, 34 (1), pp. 169-173.

Campbell, J.L. 2002c, 'Ideas, Politics and Public Policy', in *Annual Review of Sociology*, 28, pp. 21-38.

Campbell, J.L. 1998, 'Institutional Analysis and the Role of Ideas in Political Economy', in *Theory and Society*, 27, pp. 377-409.

Campbell, J.L. and J.A. Hall, 2007, *The Political Economy of Scale and Nation, With Special Reference to Denmark*, unpublished manuscript, Department of Sociology, Dartmouth College.

Campbell, J.L. and O.K. Pedersen, 2007, *Knowledge Regimes and Comparative Political Economy*, unpublished manuscript, Department of Sociology, Dartmouth College.

Chandler, A.D. 1977, *The Visible Hand: The Managerial Revolution in American Business*, Harvard University Press, Cambridge.

Coase, R.H. 1937, 'The Nature of the Firm', in *Economica*, 4, pp. 386-405.

Collins, R. 2000, *The Sociology of Philosophies: A Global Theory of Intellectual Change*, Harvard University Press, Cambridge.

DiMaggio, P.J. and W.W. Powell 1983, 'The Iron Cage Revisited: Institutional Isomorphism and Collective Rationality in Organizational Fields', in *American Sociological Review*, 48, pp. 147-160.

Djelic, M.-L. and K. Sahlin-Andersson, 2006, *Transnational Governance: Institutional Dynamics of Regulation*, Cambridge University Press, New York.

Dobbin, F. 1994, *Forging Industrial Policy: The United States, Britain, and France in the Railway Age*, Cambridge University Press, New York.

Fligstein, N. 1990, *The Transformation of Corporate Control*, Harvard University Press, Cambridge.

Fourcade, M. 2006, 'The Construction of a Global Profession: The Transnationalization of Economics', in *American Journal of Sociology*, 112, pp. 145-94.

Frieden, J.A. and R. Rogowski, 1996, 'The Impact of the International Economy on National Policies: An Analytical Overview', in R.O. Keohane and H.V. Milner (eds.), *Internationalization and Domestic Politics*, Cambridge University Press, New York, pp. 25-47.

Garrett, G. and P. Lange 1996, *Internationalization, Institutions and Political Change*, in R.O. Keohane and H.V. Milner (eds.), Cambridge University Press, New York, pp. 48-75.

Green, D.P. and I. Shapiro 1994, *Pathologies of Rational Choice Theory: A Critique of Applications in Political Science*, Yale University Press, New Haven.

Guillén, M. 1994, *Models of Management: Work, Authority and Organization in Comparative Perspective*, University of Chicago Press, Chicago.

Hage, J. 2006, 'Radical Innovation and Institutional Change: French Bio-Medicine, 1888-1919', *Paper presented at the annual meeting of the American Academy of Arts and Sciences*, St. Louis, February.

Hall, P.A. (ed.) 1989, *The Political Power of Economic Ideas: Keynesianism Across Nations*, Princeton University Press, Princeton.

Halliday, T. and B. Carruthers 2007, 'The Recursivity of Law: Global Norm Making and National Lawmaking in the Globalization of Corporate Insolvency Regimes', in *American Journal of Sociology*, 112, pp. 1135-1202.

Hollis, M. and E. Nell 1975, *Rational Economic Man*, Cambridge University Press, New York.

Jones, B.D. 1999, 'Bounded Rationality', in *Annual Review of Political Science*, 2, pp. 297-321.

Keck, M. and K. Sikkink 1998, *Activists Beyond Borders: Advocacy Networks in International Politics*, Cornell University Press, Ithaca.

Kiser, E. 1994, 'Markets and Hierarchies in Early Modern Tax Systems: A Principal-Agent Analysis', in *Politics and Society*, 22 (3), pp. 284-315.

Knight, J. 2001, 'Explaining the Rise of Neoliberalism: The Mechanisms of Institutional Change', in J.L. Campbell and O.K. Pedersen (eds.), in *The Rise of Neoliberalism and Institutional Analysis*, Princeton University Press, Princeton NJ.

Knight, J. 1992, *Institutions and Social Conflict*, Cambridge University Press, New York.

Knight, J. and J. Ensminger 1998, 'Conflict over Changing Social Norms: Bargaining, Ideology, and Enforcement', in M.C. Brinton and V. Nee (eds.), in *The New Institutionalism in Sociology*, Russell Sage Foundation, New York, pp. 105-26.

Knight, J. 1992, *Institutions and Social Conflict*, Cambridge University Press, New York.

Knight, J. and D. North 1997, 'Explaining Economic Change: The Interplay Between Cognition and Institutions', in *Legal Theory*, 3, pp. 211-226.

Kuran, T. 1995, *Private Truths, Public Lies*, Harvard University Press, Cambridge.

Levi, M. 1997, *Consent, Dissent and Patriotism*, Cambridge University Press, Cambridge.

Levi, M. 1988, *Of Rule and Revenue*, University of California Press, Berkeley.

March, J.G. and J.P. Olsen 1989, *Rediscovering Institutions*, The Free Press, New York.

March, J.G. and J.P. Olsen 1984, 'The New Institutionalism: Organizational Factors in Political Life', in *American Political Science Review*, 78, pp. 734-49.

Meyer, J.W., J. Boli, G.M. Thomas and F.O. Ramirez 1997a, 'World Society and the Nation State, in *American Journal of Sociology*, 103 (1), pp. 144-181.

Meyer, J.W., D. Frank, A. Hironaka, E. Schofer and N. B. Tuma 1997b, 'The Structuring of a World Environmental Regime 1870-1990', in *International Organization*, 51, pp. 623-651.

Meyer, J. and B. Rowan 1977, 'Institutionalized Organizations: Formal Structure as Myth and Ceremony', in *American Journal of Sociology*, 83, pp. 340-63.

Mizruchi, M.S. and L.C. Fein 1999, 'The Social Construction of Organizational Knowledge: A Study of the Uses of Coercive, Mimetic, and Normative Isomorphism', in *Administrative Science Quarterly*, 44, pp. 653-683.

Mueller, D. 1989, *Public Choice II*, Cambridge University Press, New York.

North, D.C. 2005, *Understanding The Process of Economic Change*, Princeton University Press, Princeton.

North, D.C. 1990, *Institutions, Institutional Change and Economic Performance*, Cambridge University Press, New York.

North, D.C. 1981, *Structure and Change in Economic History*, W.W. Norton, New York.

Ostrom, E. 1990, *Governing the Commons*, Cambridge University Press, New York.

Rodgers, D. 1998, *Atlantic Crossings*, Belknap Press, Cambridge.

Schneiberg, M. 2007, 'What's on the Path? Path Dependence, Organizational Diversity and the Problem of Institutional Change in the U.S. Economy 1900-1950', in *Socio-Economic Review*, 5 (1), pp. 47-80.

Soysal, Y. 1994, *Limits of Citizenship*, University of Chicago Press, Chicago.

Thelen, K. and S. Steinmo 1992, 'Historical Institutionalism in Comparative Politics', in S. Steinmo, K. Thelen and F. Longstreth (eds.), in *Structuring Politics: Historical Institutionalism in Comparative Analysis*, Cambridge University Press, New York, pp. 1-32.

Thomas, G.M., J.W. Meyer, F.O. Ramirez and J. Boli (eds.) 1987, *Institutional Structure: Constituting State, Society, and the Individual*, Sage, Newbury Park.

Vanberg, V. and J. Buchanan 1989, 'Interests and Theories in Constitutional Choice', in *Journal of Theoretical Politics*, 1, pp. 49-62.

Wuthnow, R. 1989, *Communities of Discourse*, Harvard University Press, Cambridge.

Yonay, Y. 1998, *The Struggle Over the Soul of Economics: Institutionalist and Neoclassical Economists in America Between the Wars*, Princeton University Press, Princeton.

CHAPTER 8

Norms of War: An Institutionalist Account

Edgar Kiser and Eric Gleave

Professor and Graduate Student, University of Washington, USA

Introduction

On 25 October 1415, the English army in France found their retreat blocked by French troops and faced a much larger French army on the field outside Agincourt. With a numerical advantage of at least 3:1, the French proceeded to decisively lose the battle as their knights repeatedly charged the line of English knights while being cut down first by longbow volleys, then by desperate peasant archers, out of arrows, fighting hand-to-hand using only daggers and mallets against fully armored knights. The French knights continued to focus their attack on the English knights, never directly confronting the English peasant archers who were inflicting such heavy casualties. What could explain the decision to avoid combat with the English archers in favor of assaults on the knights?

In the late 14th century, the Aztec empire was spreading in central Mexico. Engaged in over a decade of warfare with tribal federations, the form of conflict was not mass warfare but was a highly stylized confrontation between a few of the best fighters on each side. These battles resulted in few deaths and took no advantage of Aztec skills with projectile weapons and the ability to field large armies. What could explain this normative practice of prolonged military engagements without escalation on either side where battle was rarely mortal and, even when it was, nobility were deliberately spared? Why, for example, would the loser of the smaller ritualized conflict simply accept defeat instead of escalating to large-scale war?

At the level of the individual, the army, and the state, there are very few actions that involve higher stakes than warfare. Individuals can die, armies can be annihilated, states can go bankrupt (which, as Skocpol [1979] notes, often leads to revolutions) or be conquered and lose sovereignty. Yet in spite of these high stakes, soldiers, armies, and states often do not try to win wars by any means necessary. As both of the examples above illustrate, they often abide by norms that limit their actions and thus decrease their odds of victory. From the perspective of rational choice theory, the actions described above (and many other discussed later in this chapter) appear to be anomalous. Can this sort of normative action be explained with a more nuanced rational choice model, or are these irrational actions that can be accounted for only by cultural theory?

We use rational choice institutionalism to explain (1) the existence and content of norms governing action in warfare and (2) variations in compliance with norms of war. The main goal of this paper is theoretical, to outline and assess various answers to these two questions. In addition to this, we will use a few empirical cases, the Battle of Agincourt 1415 and Aztec Flower Wars in the 14th and 15th centuries, to illustrate the causal mechanisms producing norms of war and determining compliance with them.

Defining Norms of War

Norms of war refer to general agreements shared by more than one state that govern the nature of acceptable conduct (both prescriptive and proscriptive) during war. The types of norms that especially interest us are those that limit actions in ways that appear to decrease the odds of victory. As with all norms, there are sanctions for violating them, but the type of sanction and who enforces it will vary. The sanctions include reputation costs for a state to the use of force, and the sanctions can be enforced by the other state participating in the war, states not involved in the war, non-political organizations (religious organizations, NGOs), or broader political organizations such as the United Nations. In some cases, the norms can be codified as formal international laws enforceable by international judicial institutions.

Several aspects of warfare are regulated by norms of war: who should fight, based on class (Samurai) and age (Geneva Conventions against military recruitment of children), weapons (papal injunctions against the use of crossbows in medieval Europe, conventions against chemical weapons, landmines, indiscriminant fire), treatment of non-combatants (medieval norms of ransom, Geneva Conventions on prisoners of war, non-combatants, and mercenaries), combat duration (campaigning seasons, holidays, and regularized truces such as Greek Olympics), who can kill whom (prohibitions against killing unarmed combatants in flight or nobility slaying peasantry), the number of soldiers deployed (such as classical monomachy, single combat between champions), how soldiers should dress (British red coats) and where fighting can take place (Greek hoplites fought only on level ground).

Explaining the Existence of Norms of War

There are two main types of arguments about the existence and particular content of norms of war: one stresses instrumental rationality and efficiency and the other emphasizes values and culture. It is of course possible that each of these arguments could account for some norms of war. Our focus will be primarily on rational choice accounts, but we begin with a brief discussion of cultural arguments.

Cultural arguments tend to focus more on the effects of norms (and the internalized values or identities with which they are sometimes associated) on behavior rather than on the causes of norms. However, it is possible to outline a cultural account of the origins of norms of war. For example, norms of war could be a subset of more general cultural norms and values, reflecting the general characteristics of the latter. These more general cultural norms could be derived from »national cultures,« or could reflect religious or philosophical systems that are shared by several states. Meyer's (Meyer, Boli, Thomas, and Ramirez 1997) form of cultural institutionalism suggests that cultural values in the high status countries could spread to much of the rest of the world (for example, western or

American values may dominate the contemporary world polity), but they might be loosely coupled with actual behavior in times of war. Discursive institutionalism (Kjær and Pedersen 2001) would argue that norms of war are the product of the dominant symbolic and meaning systems in any historical era. Historians often use cultural explanations of norms of war, mostly by relating particular norms to broader cultural features of particular societies and/or historical periods in a purely descriptive manner. See the case studies below for examples and criticisms of this form of cultural explanation.

Rational choice arguments about the norms of war begin with the premise that wars (armed conflicts between states) are always fought for reasons; they are instrumental actions oriented toward certain goals (primarily wealth and power). There are two types of rational choice arguments about the genesis of norms of war at two different levels of analysis, each pointing to different causal mechanisms. However, the two types of arguments are interrelated as nested games (Tsebelis 1990). The broader game is between states (the rulers of states, more specifically) who make decisions about whether to fight wars and how to fight them (abiding by the norms of war or not). The rulers themselves do not fight wars, however; they are conducted by soldiers commanded by generals, a classic agency relation with the attendant problems. So the second game embedded in the first is a game played between generals and soldiers. Of course, what happens in each game has important effects on the other game.

The first looks at states as the units of analysis and analyzes war as a game between states. Warfare is a negative sum game for both players combined, and thus arises only when other means of resolving disputes between states are unavailable or unsuccessful. The first explanation of the norms of war suggests that they are agreements oriented toward reducing the costs of warfare for both states involved, essentially minimizing the negative externalities associated with resolving disputes in this manner. However, since the structure of this game is essentially a prisoner's dilemma, the obvious question is why both sides do not consistently defect on norms of war.

The second game relaxes the simplifying assumption of states as unitary actors and looks at war from the point of view of individual soldiers and the generals who attempt to control them. Wars are fought by individual soldiers who are agents of commanders on the battleground, and these commanders are themselves agents of political leaders. The norms of war might therefore arise to help mitigate the agency problems that are present at this level in warfare. We will outline these two arguments below.

The Game between States: How Norms Can Reduce the Costs of War

If warfare were always a Hobbesian, anarchic, »no holds barred« affair, the costs to both states entering into it would be extremely high. Norms of war could reduce these costs by prohibiting some of the most costly actions or by revealing information that allows the dispute to be resolved more quickly (thus lowering the costs to both parties). For example, norms could prohibit the use of the most destructive types of weapons, limit the size of armies, limit the duration of fighting, and limit attacks on non-combatants or the destruction of valuable resources. Both parties in the war could benefit if norms like these existed and were enforced.

Since war is such a costly negative sum game, one could reasonably wonder why it occurs at all. In any situation, both parties could assess the situation, including the odds of each winning the war and how much it would cost each to participate, and knowing these things could negotiate an outcome without paying the costs of actually fighting. In other words, in a world of perfect information and rational actors, war should not occur. In the real world of bounded rationality, however, wars will occur as a result of poor information and/or miscalculation. The actors involved will often come to different conclusions about their odds of winning or the costs of fighting. If both actors believe they will win, think the war will cost them less than it will, over-estimate the benefits of winning, or underestimate the costs of fighting, war will be more likely to occur.

If this is true, anything that increases the information both actors share about the costs of war and its likely outcome will decrease the odds of fighting or the duration of the war after it begins, allowing disputes to be resolved at lower cost. Perhaps norms of war do exactly this by serving as signaling devices. For example, if both armies march out into the middle of a large field in neat rows wearing bright uniforms, it is easy for both parties to compare the relative size of armies and thus assess the likely outcome. The norms are oriented to producing the clearest possible signals, since the clearer the signal, the greater the odds of avoiding an unnecessary war (one that would not be fought if both parties had better information).[1] Fights among animals are often preceded by substantial ritual posturing and display. One case of this is the »parallel walk« done by red deer, allowing a comparison of their relative size and often avoiding fighting when one is clearly larger (Gould 1998: 192). Another example along the same lines is that tigers mark their territory by reaching as high as they can and scratching trees. An invading tiger can thus know her size relative to her rival without even seeing the other tiger (Maynard-Smith and Harper 2003).

However, the size of armies alone does not always determine the outcome because the soldiers in one army might be better fighters than the soldiers in another. As a result, it is often necessary to begin fighting in order to gain the necessary information on the relative power of the two sides. Any norms of war that control or limit this early stage of fighting can reveal the necessary information without high costs. The use of ritualized fighting by just a few hand-picked soldiers, illustrated in the case of the Aztec flower wars discussed below, is a classic example.

The obvious question about these arguments is why would any state comply with them? The structure of the interaction seems to be a standard prisoner's dilemma, since it is in the mutual interest of both parties to comply with the norms to minimize total costs, but each party could gain an advantage (potentially enough to win the war) by violating the norm. In this situation, especially when the gains to violating the norm are so great, the standard rational choice argument is that both states will 'defect' and the norms will be useless. Yet the historical record shows that in many (although certainly not all) cases, states do comply with the norms of war. How can we explain this variation? The following section provides one reason that states might abide by the norms of war, by focusing on the ways in which some of these norms might mitigate agency problems in the embedded general-soldier game.

1. Of course, as in any signaling situation, actors can try to strategically manipulate signals. For example, they can try to make their army look larger than it is in order to deter a potential opponent, or make their army look smaller than it is in order to encourage a battle they know they can win.

The Game between Generals and Soldiers: How Norms Can Increase the Odds of Winning Wars

A different type of rational choice argument avoids the problem of why states don't defect on the norms of war by specifying a causal mechanism that applies directly to the interests of particular states (as opposed to the shared interests of the two warring states). Instead of reducing the overall costs of warfare for both parties, some norms may in fact increase the odds of victory. The interesting cases here are norms that seem to make armies less efficient – for example, how can an army that dresses its soldiers in bright uniforms and marches them out in the open be more effective than one that has soldiers wearing camouflage and hiding behind trees?[2]

One of the biggest problems faced by states in warfare is how to motivate their soldiers to fight. This applies not only to getting them to join the army in the first place (which is why conscription is often necessary) but also to getting them to put themselves in a position in which they might be killed in order to increase the odds that their state will win the war. This is a classic agency problem – how can states (principals) induce soldiers (their agents) to risk their lives for state objectives? There are several possible answers to this question. First, non-rational motivations including emotions and values can get soldiers to fight, and states often spend a lot of resources trying to instill patriotic values and feelings in their soldiers (and in the voters or subjects who have to pay the economic costs of wars). Second, states can make soldiers partial residual claimants by giving them shares in the proceeds of the war, and this was often done in pre-bureaucratic armies. But in many cases, neither of these causal mechanisms will be strong enough to get soldiers to pay the ultimate cost of risking their lives in battle. In these cases, some norms of war may help states get their soldiers to fight.

Agency problems exist because of information asymmetries – the agent knows their actions better than the principal and it is costly for the principal

2. There are other reasons that fighting in fixed, close formations might be more efficient, in addition to the factors addressed below. For example, it allows for the volley firing of weapons which maximized potential enemy casualties in pre-rifle eras.

to monitor the actions of the agent. One way to mitigate the problem is by making the actions of the agent easier to observe. Some norms of war do exactly this. Dressing soldiers in bright uniforms and marching them out into the middle of large open fields in fixed formations may make it easier for the enemy to kill them, but it also makes it much easier for their own general to watch them. On the other hand, soldiers wearing camouflage and hiding behind trees may be difficult to kill, but they are nearly impossible for their superiors to monitor, and thus may well simply continue hiding behind a tree until the battle is over.

In many cases, the benefits of better monitoring may outweigh the costs of tactics like these, and these norms of war would increase the efficiency of an army and thus the odds of winning a war. Whether or not this is the case depends on how self-motivated the soldiers are, getting back to the first two ways of mitigating agency problems discussed above. When agents are highly motivated, due to values, emotions, or the promise of material gains as partial residual claimants, they will be expected to fight even when monitoring is poor. In cases like that, norms of war increasing the visibility of soldiers will be inefficient, since the costs of making them more visible to the enemy will not be outweighed by the benefits of making them more visible to their own commanders. One the other hand, when soldiers are not highly motivated to fight, norms of war increasing visibility will be efficient. Thus, we expect violations of the norms of war oriented toward solving agency problems to be greatest when armies have highly motivated soldiers.

Explaining Compliance with the Norms of War

Compliance with norms of war can be explained in terms of either culture or instrumental rationality. As above, our focus will be on the latter, but we begin with a brief discussion of the former. How would cultural arguments explain variations in the extent of compliance with norms of war? One of the main determinants would be how the identities of the fighters related to the identities of those they were fighting. For example, if the culture of a state taught that all human beings were equal and thus should be treated the same way, then the state would comply with norms regardless of whom they were fighting against. However, if the culture stressed ethical dualism and the people they were fighting were identified as »others«, then the norms would not be seen as applying to them and the state would feel under no obligation to comply. One proposition that would follow from this is that compliance with the norms of war should be high when combatants share the same cultural identities and low when they do not.[3]

From a rational choice perspective, compliance with norms of war is more problematic. The first possibility is that warfare is best modeled not as a one-shot prisoner's dilemma but as an iterated prisoner's dilemma game. If this is true, the sanctions for violating the norms will come from the other participant in the war. If both parties are playing a tit-for-tat strategy or some close variant, when one state violates the norms they can expect the other to do likewise and the situation will quickly change from a low-cost equilibrium to a high-cost equilibrium, making them both worse off. Both states will recognize this, and if their discount rates are sufficiently low, they will refrain from violating the norms.[4]

When discount rates are high, however, states are not expected to comply with norms of war in repeated game situations. A state that is about to be conquered is facing an obvious last period problem, and thus will be expected to do whatever is necessary to avoid that fate, including violat-

3. Identities are never entirely fixed, and it is common practice in the course of a war, or even in the period leading up to it, to dehumanize the opponent, in order to facilitate the brutal action against them necessary to win the war, perhaps including the violation of norms of war.
4. Since this argument takes states as corporate actors, it assumes that states can prevent individual soldiers from violating norms of war, even when it might be in their interests to do so (for example, to increase their personal safety). In other words, it assumes that states can adequately control their agents. This simplifying assumption will often be problematic. For example, soldiers in some cases could increase their safety by violating the norms of war by killing civilians they think might harm them or prisoners who are a burden on their resources. On the other hand, soldiers ordered by states to violate norms of war may be reluctant to do so because they would pay the costs of retribution by the other army.

ing the norms of war.[5] More generally, states that are losing wars are more likely to violate norms of war.[6]

It is also possible that norms of war can be enforced by third parties. These third parties can be other states (in some cases, involved in treaty alliances), other non-state organizations (religious organizations or human rights groups), or trans-state political entities (such as international courts or the United Nations). The ability of these third parties to enforce norms of war will depend on the types of sanctions at their disposal. For example, sanctions are less likely to be used or to be effective against strong states, so strong (especially hegemonic) states are expected to be less likely to comply with norms of war. The recent actions of the United States in Iraq in violation of several well-accepted norms of war concerning both non-combatants and prisoners of war seem to support this proposition.

Agency theory provides another account of how the norms of war are enforced. Norms governing tactics in warfare not only make monitoring less costly, as discussed above, they also facilitate sanctioning. Fixed formations make it impossible for soldiers in the front lines not to advance, since they are constantly being forced to move ahead by the soldiers behind them (note the advice of Sun Tzu to not allow soldiers an exit option when flight is likely). In fact, in some armies the soldiers marching behind have orders to kill the soldiers in front of them if they fail to advance.

Historical Illustrations and the Norms of War: Emergence and Compliance

The most useful ways to test arguments about the norms of war would be to either to take a large, systematic sample of cases and look for variations in causal factors and outcomes or to do a detailed case study of one or a

5. In a slightly different example, the allies used nuclear weapons at the end of World War II in order to minimize total casualties on both sides by forcing an earlier surrender.
6. An interesting counter-example, raised by Steve Pfaff, comes to mind: why didn't Hitler use nerve gas and chemical weapons against the United States or the Soviets at the end of World War II?

few episodes in which detailed historical narratives could reveal the causal mechanisms at work. This chapter does not attempt either strategy. As an exploratory theoretical paper, we will simply use two historical illustrations (the Aztec Flower Wars and the medieval battle between England and France at Agincourt) to show that our arguments can help illuminate the causes of the emergence of norms of war and variations in rates of compliance with them.

Aztec Flower Wars

Historical accounts from the Aztecs, rival tribal federations, and invading Conquistadors all refer to the seemingly strange practice of 'flower wars'. These conflicts involved fixed numbers of warriors, equal on each side, fighting closely observed battles with blunt objects on sanctified battlefields – a classic example of both sides agreeing on a norm limiting the number of soldiers they would deploy. When escalated, these battles produced captives for sacrifice. The consecration of the battlefield also made any fallen warrior a sacrifice to the gods, helping to quench their thirst for human blood (Hassig 1988).

Cultural perspectives explain flower wars in pre-Columbian Mesoamerica as largely a function of religious beliefs. When quizzed by Cortez as to why the Aztecs would wage a flower war rather than conquer a neighboring federation, Montezuma II explained that it permitted the training of young soldiers and provided a steady supply of human sacrifices (Hassig 1996). The Aztecs believed that the gods required sacrifices of human blood to survive and that the world would end without them. This need was supplied through wars of conquest and flower wars in much the way that the imperial Roman economy was supported by imports of battle-captured slaves. The cultural interpretation that religious belief prevented the Aztecs from effective conquest has persisted in part because the Spanish conquered the Aztecs using an alliance with a tribal federation which had been engaged in a lengthy flower war them.

This practice served several rational aims, however. Conditions in central Mexico made it difficult to maintain a strong army at a distance from the capital. Having no draft animals, no roads, and no wheels, Aztec forces could travel at best two-by-two down regional trade paths using porters to carry necessary supplies of corn. This meant the army could not travel far from supply sources or campaign for long. Politically, the Aztecs ruled through tribute without puppet governments. While this left the conquered people less likely to overthrow local power structures, it also meant local leaders were more likely to take opportunities to shirk tribute or rebel.

These attributes combined to mean that conquest was a costly and risky business. Subjugating a strong tribal federation could take decades of warfare and even then result in ongoing rebellions. Flower wars were a solution to this. Aztecs conquered weaker neighbors, surrounding stronger regions with hostile territory. They then forced all neighbors to likewise wage war on the target, and eventually through isolation and multiple engagements forced capitulation from a weakened federation that lacked other options. The group being attacked had little incentive to escalate the conflict and risk the full wrath of Aztec forces, even if a full invasion would eventually fail. Flower Wars thus allowed the minimization of costs to both invaders and the invaded while the Aztecs worked to cut off the federation from external support.

The ritualized combat also served as a protracted signaling game akin to the parallel walk by red deer discussed above. Weapons were limited to the least lethal weapons requiring the most skill. While a barrage of atlatl darts could clear a field of combatants efficiently, these did not require skill and thus were forbidden in Flower Wars. Using only evenly matched groups of skilled warriors, the Flower War allowed each side to assess the skill and training of the other.

Flower wars could also function as a negotiation tool, akin to how animals determine territorial boundaries through low cost contests (Maynard-Smith and Harper 2003). As invaders, Aztec forces faced an uphill battle since defenders have an advantage, even net of resource capacity (Wazlavek and Figler 1989). Of course, the larger force is more likely to win, so this home-court advantage usually had no effect and the Aztecs conquered rather than engaged in ritualized battle. Determining a victor when combatants are evenly matched can lead to longer, more violent conflicts (Stamps and Krishnan 1994), and negotiation through talk alone is unlikely to create lasting deals due to the human capacity for deception (Farrell and Rabin 1996). Higher cost signaling of force and intent can be achieved through lengthy but low cost conflict (Engquist et al. 1990).

Thus, Flower Wars allowed the Aztecs and strong tribal federations to size one another up and negotiate borders and tribute without incurring the high costs of total war.

Agincourt

The events at the Battle of Agincourt are frequently used to illustrate aspects of medieval chivalry, whether to lament its demise or highlight the extent of internalization of those norms. The decision of the French knights to pursue only combat with other knights is easily explained by invoking chivalry. Killing poorly armed peasants would not bring honor to a knight, and may even incur infamy. This normative impetus combined with the honor and tangible profit possible from ransoming an English knight gave the French knights only one clear choice.

Agincourt also highlights the agency problem in warfare. Once the battle had turned and it was clear the English might not lose, news came to Henry that the baggage boys had been killed. Interpreting this to mean the French were attacking from his rear and had disregarded the rules of combat, Henry ordered the execution of all captives (Keegan 1976). The English knights refused to give up the potential ransom they could get for the captured French knights, so the order was not carried out until Henry formed a detail of a few hundred archers to dispatch the captives. The refusal of the English knights to execute the prisoners and the refusal of the French knights to attack their executioners both reflect the weight of individual decisions over the collective good.[7]

Other sights from the field of Agincourt illustrate medieval signaling. The use of horses, for example, demonstrated the capacity to train, both horse and rider, and carry sufficient provisions. The wealth in armor, weapons, and horses should have caused the English to capitulate at Agincourt; but chivalry ensured the survival of the nobility, and would likewise have left the large portion of peasant archers executed in France.

7. This illustrates that fact that norms of chivalry had complex effects on war outcomes from the perspective of states, sometimes motivating nobles to fight and thus mitigating agency problems, but at other times leading to actions that decreased the odds of victory. Contemporary norms of patriotism, when they exist and are enforced, have more uniformly positive effects from the perspective of states.

The costly signals of horses and armor turned to liabilities, however, as archers killed or panicked charging horses and the heavy armor cost many French knights their lives, drowned in the deep mud. Once the archers began attacking in hand-to-hand combat, the armor designed to deflect heavy blows and arrows were ineffective at blocking jabs from daggers into the small remaining holes.

The outcome and decisions of the battle are easily described as a series of choices for the individuals on either side. Stripped to the key players, this means the French knights and the English archers. The French knights could either attack the archers or assault the line of English knights. The first option leads to no honor, no ransom, likely loss of their horses, and real possibility of death; the potential costs are high and the potential benefits absent. The second option risks capture for the possibility of ending the battle and capturing English knights for ransom; the potential costs are low and the reputation and material benefits are high. Whether to charge straight into the line of English knights or turn towards the archers, then, is an easy decision.

The archers had a similar structure to consider. Knowing they could not be ransomed, the cost of losing was death for the archers. Winning meant a share in the spoils and a return home. With incentive structures like this, it isn't much of a surprise that the archers, upon seeing the English line falter, charged into the fray with only small arms and turned the tide of the battle.

Discussion

While both medieval chivalry and Mesoamerican Flower Wars are easily explained with cultural explanations specific to the particular historical eras, these do little to generate more general explanations that can be transported to other times and places and produce predictive models for norms. Rational choice explanations, on the other hand, can account for the origins, continuation, and end of normative patterns. While the stories above have illustrated mostly static norms, similar cases show the end of norms or their violation for rational reasons. For example, the chivalrous practice of ransoming was blocked, on pain of death, by Edward III at the

Battle of Crécy in order to ensure all efforts were towards defeating the French. Given the high likelihood of losing this battle based on numbers, this violation is to be expected. Likewise the Aztecs gradually escalated flower wars from no casualties to slaughter of non-nobles to full combat as they perceived their opponent getting weaker. Norms are more likely to be violated, then, by a losing party seeing no other way out and, counter-intuitively, by a victor who no longer faces threat of sanction.[8]

Conclusion

The norms of war can be best understood as arising and being enforced in the context of a two-stage game. In the first stage of the game states (or in some cases tribes or terrorist organizations) are trying to win wars, but at as low a cost as possible. In this stage of the game, norms emerge to minimize the total costs to both parties of resolving conflicts via warfare. They will be enforced when the game is repeated, and the costs of violating the norm are greater than the costs of abiding by it. This game alone is not sufficient to explain all norms of war, however, because in many cases its assumption that states are corporate actors ignores another important game – that between generals and soldiers in the field. This is a classic agency problem, since soldiers do not have the same incentives as states or generals to win wars, but would prefer instead to minimize their risk of death. Many norms of war exist to mitigate this agency problem by making it easier for generals to monitor and sanction the actions of soldiers in the field.

Our two historical examples are not offered as tests of our model, but simply as illustrations of some of the causal mechanisms we posited. This exploratory study of the norms of war is intended only to demonstrate the importance of the issue and the potential plausibility of our theoretical account. Further historical work will be necessary to fully assess our claims.

8. Whether this applies to contemporary conflicts, where super-national organizations exist with the capacity to sanction, is an empirical question.

The norms of war are not only relevant in historical cases, but in the contemporary conflicts as well. Moreover, the issues they raise are not only theoretical but ethical as well, as this concluding example illustrates. In late June of 2005, a small band of US Navy SEALS found themselves in a difficult situation (O'Shaughnessy 2007). Deep into hostile territory in Afghanistan, they were discovered by a small group of goatherds, including a boy. If they let these civilian non-combatants go and their position was revealed, they faced combat at overwhelming odds from nearby Taliban forces. If they killed them, they faced trial for murder by US and possibly international courts for violating the rules of engagement. After debating the issue, they decided to let the civilians go. Within hours they were attacked on three sides by Taliban armed with rocket propelled grenades and automatic weapons (Tyson 2006). Three of the four seals died on that mountain and sixteen more soldiers died in the rescue effort.

References

Enquist, M., O. Leimar, T. Ljunberg, Y. Mallner and N. Segerdahl 1990, 'A test of the sequential assessment game: fighting in the cichlid fish Nannacara anomala', in *Animal Behavior*, 40, pp. 1-14.

Farrell, J. and M. Rabin 1996, 'Cheap Talk', in *The Journal of Economic Perspectives*, 10 (3), pp. 103-118.

Gould, S.J. 1998, *Leonardo's Mountain of Clams and the Diet of Worms*, Random House, New York.

Hassig, R. 1988, *Aztec Warfare: Imperial Expansion and Political Control*, University of Oklahoma Press, Norman and London.

Hassig, R. 1996, 'Aztec Flower Wars', in *MHW: The Quarterly Journal of Military History*, 9 (1), pp. 8-21.

Keegan, J. 1976, *The Face of Battle*, Viking Press, New York.

Kjær, P. and O.K. Pedersen 2001, 'Translating Liberalization: Neoliberalism in the Danish Negotiated Economy', in J.L. Campbell and O.K. Pedersen (eds.), in *The Rise of Neoliberalism and Institutional Analysis*, Princeton University Press, Princeton, pp. 219-248.

Maynard-Smith, J. and D. Harper 2003, in *Animal Signals*, Oxford University Press, New York.

Meyer, J.W., J. Boli, G.M. Thomas, and F.O. Ramirez 1997, World society and the nation-state, in *American Journal of Sociology*, 103, pp. 144-181.

O'Shaughnessy, P. 2007, 'An American Hero: Navy SEAL was an officer and a gentleman right to the end', *New York Daily News*, 16 April 2007.

Skocpol, T. 1979, *States and Social Revolutions*, Cambridge University Press, Cambridge.

Stamps, J.A. and V.V. Krishnan 1994, 'Territory Acquisition in lizards: I. First encounters', in *Animal Behaviors*, 47, pp. 1375-1385

Tsebelis, G. 1990, *Nested Games: Rational Choice in Comparative Politics*, University of California Press, Berkeley.

Tyson, A.S. 2006, 'Two SEALS Receive Navy Cross: Pair died fighting Taliban in Afghanistan', in *Washington Post*, 14 September 2006, p. A12.

Wazlavek, B.E. and M.H. Figler 1989, 'Territorial Prior Residence, Size asymmetry and escalation of aggression in convict cichlids (Cichlasoma nigrofasciatum Gunther)', in *Aggressive Behavior*, 15, pp. 235-244.

CHAPTER 9

What *Should* the State Do? A Political Economy of Ideas and Institutions

Sven Steinmo

Professor, European University Institute (EUI) Florence, Italy

Introduction

Over the past several years there has been a substantial shift in ideas amongst policy elites about the proper role of government in the society and the economy. Though it is extremely difficult, if not impossible to find a corresponding dramatic change in public attitudes, policy elites now appear to believe that government both cannot, and should not, do many of the things that it once did.[1] Ronald Reagan and Margaret Thatcher are no longer in office, but the ideas that were proposed by the Right, appear to now dominate the Center of the political spectrum. Indeed, there appears to be a growing consensus among elite policy makers – on all sides of the political spectrum – that the state should not do many of the things that it used to do. In other words, the argument is not simply that we *cannot do* what was once done, but now we *ought not* do what was once done.

1. See, for example, National Election Studies, historical data (now available on the WEB, www.umich.edu/~nes/).

The following paper examines the evolution of this new thinking in a particularly significant arena domestic policy making – tax policy. The focus here is not on whether 'the state is dead' (Korten 1995). Nor does this paper address the question of the revenue implications of internationalization (Swank and Steinmo 2002). Instead, this paper examines the evolution of policy maker's *ideas* about taxation policy during the twentieth century. My central argument is that there is an iterative and contingent relationship between policy ideas and institutional change. Further, I believe we must see this relationship in evolutionary terms. Ideas do not come out of thin air – they are generated within a policy context. At the same time, any given policy context is the product of a previous set of ideas. Finally, neither ideas nor context can be held constant. In order to understand what the state does (or more specifically why so many states have taken a neo-liberal turn) we need to examine the evolution of both policy ideas and their subsequent institutional manifestations. This argument leans heavily on the previous works of John Campbell and Ove Pedersen – particularly their seminal book, *The Rise of Neo-Liberalism and Institutional Analysis*, which details many of the basic points I will make here. I take a somewhat longer view than *The Rise of Neo-Liberalism*, in part because I want to show the deeper history to the current intellectual ideas. But the reader will undoubtedly find a significant overlap between the arguments presented here and those offered earlier by Campbell and Pedersen (Campbell and Pedersen 2001).

In recent years, »ideas« have become the focus of a great number of works in both comparative politics and international relations.[2] Unfortunately, as Campbell points out, the term 'ideas' has come to stand for a number of *different* variables (eg. norms, values, beliefs, preferences, culture, attitudes) but few of these authors have defined precisely what they specifically mean by »Ideas« (Campbell, 2001). In this analysis 'ideas' are defined as probablistic arguments. Ideas are thus understood in much the same way that we use the term 'ideas' in everyday English. When one says: »I have an idea«, what we are really saying is »I have a solution to

2. See for example, (Campbell 1998) or (Berman 2001).

our collective problem.« [3] When one says »That is a good idea!« what we are really saying is »I believe that is a good solution to the problem.« Ideas are always probabalistic solutions because in a world of enormous complexity, nested games, and some rather basic uncertainties, we cannot hope to truly predict the future. The best we can do is offer convincing arguments that this particular solution (idea) is better than some alternatives. Whether others will agree and/or can be mobilized to support a particular idea will depend on a number of other clearly related variables including their beliefs (about how the world really works), their values (about how it 'ought' to work), and, of course, their individual strategic calculations of their 'interests. '

Ideas, thus, are intimately related to both interests (even raw economic 'self-interest') and values – but are not the same as either. Too often the literature on ideas has juxtaposed ideas and interests as if they were *alternative* explanations. This distinction is false. It *may* make sense to pose 'values' and 'interests' as separate and distinct variables in a static analysis of a specific choice matrix. For example, we might try to analyze whether an actor chose A or B because of her value commitments or as a product of her calculations of her economic self-interest. (But even in a static analysis we can easily see how these two variables intersect and overlap and shape one another.)[4] Ideas as used here may be the mechanism through which actors interests and values confront one another.

Ideas can change for several reasons: a) There can be new information that forces us to update our positions. b) For a variety of reasons we can be forced to confront the inconsistencies in our beliefs. c) We can be *persuaded.*

This paper argues that experiences with one era's tax regime shaped both economists and policy makers ideas about tax reforms for the next era. This analysis has two fundamental objectives: First, it explores how and why virtually all advanced countries embarked on a series of major

3. We use 'idea' in this sense as probabalistic solutions to collective action problems of all sorts – from 'Where shall we go to dinner?' to 'What kind of electoral system would best?'
4. See Mark Blyth (Blyth 2003) chapter 2 for a critique of the distinction between idea's and interests.

tax reforms in the late 20th and early 21st century. This paper explains these current reforms in terms of an evolutionary outgrowth of the previous tax regimes dominant in the capitalist world. Secondly, the paper seeks to contribute to the growing body of literature which explored the ideational roots of policy change. I do not argue that ideas determine policy outcomes. Instead, I argue that purely rationalist interest based explanation of policy change fails to capture substance of that change. I show instead that ideas may be both the agents and the transmission belt of that change.

In a recent essay, Joel Slemrod has shown quite substantial attitudinal shifts of tax policy professionals over the past decades (Slemrod 1995). He shows, for example, that whereas in the 1930s tax professionals were largely opposed to sales and consumption taxes and in favor of progressive income and wealth taxes, today a large percent of tax professionals are skeptical of high marginal income tax rates and quite supportive of regressive consumption taxes.

This essay demonstrates that in each major epoch of 20th century, there were specific policy ideas which 'fit' the political and economic context of the time. These ideas evolved out of policy maker's and tax professional's experiences with their then extant revenue systems. The central contention here is that history is a dynamic process and thus the very policy solutions initiated in one era created new opportunities and problems that formed the foundation for new policy ideas in the next era. Policy ideas are not abstract value or ideological judgements which are simply floating around and waiting to be used by entrepreneurial policy activists. Instead, substantive historical experience with revenue policies in time 1 substantially shape policy elite's beliefs/ideas about policy options in time 2. In this sense the current epoch of tax reform is no different from the tax reform epochs of previous decades. This is an evolutionary process: The political/economic context in which policies are made also affect the political/economic context (read 'ecology') of the next era. In short, there is a dynamic and iterative relationship between tax policy ideas, tax policy outcomes, and the very structure and shape of the modern capitalist welfare state.

This paper first gives a brief overview of this history of modern taxation. The emphasis here is to show how the ideas about what made for 'good' tax policy emerged in the context of both the changing structure of advancing capitalism *and* the political demands placed on policy makers. In short, new ideas became possible as the economy changed and revealed new sources of revenue which simply could not exist in a pre-modern economy. These new revenue sources, in turn, made possible new levels of government involvement in the economy which, in turn, shaped what policy makers and interest group activists understood to be possible and desirable.

Next the paper examines the politics of tax reform in the United States up the historic Tax Reform Act of 1986 (TRA '86). The point here is both to see how the idea for this historic act grew out of the concrete and specific abuses of the tax system that had evolved up to this point (in no small part due to Reagan's own policies in his first administration) and to show that once passed, the TRA acted as an ideational rallying point (if not template) for similar tax reforms around the world. Here we see that the belief about what is possible critically shapes what is desirable. The final section offers an overview of the evolution of tax policy internationally. The paper shows both that while the specifics of tax policy changes vary to some extent, there is remarkable degree of ideational coherence in tax reforms witnessed in countries as different as Sweden and New Zealand and Argentina and Germany, and that while the details of course vary, the patterns are astonishingly similar. I also argue that though 'globalization' has been a useful symbolic tool in the struggle for tax reforms, it cannot in itself explain the outcomes witnessed so far and wide.

The Ability to pay and the Idea of "Fair Taxes"

Over the last 100 years, the ways in which states have raised revenues has been transformed. At the close of the last century revenue systems were not really *systems* at all. They were instead a collection of disparate excises, charges, duties and taxes on an amazing array of items and services – everything from men's hair powder, to windows, to salted cod. These various »taxes« were highly inefficient, easy to avoid, extremely inequitably applied and did not generate very much revenue. No state collected more than ten percent of GDP from all of the literally hundreds of revenue sources combined.

As the new century dawned, new political forces came to the fore demanding voting rights for the working classes *and* fairer distribution of tax burdens. Indeed, taxation quickly became a major battleground of both economic interests and ideology at the beginnings of the twentieth century. Precisely as predicted by the great fiscal economist Knut Wicksell, the expansion of the franchise ushered in an era of new policy demands with respect to taxes. Whereas tax policy had previously been the domain of Chancellors and Finance Ministers far removed from their mass publics, the advance of democratic politics brought with it the idea that taxes should do more than simply raise revenues. Unsurprisingly, the poor bore much heavier tax burdens than the rich. But, as unions, working and middle class parties mobilized, their political representatives increasingly demanded that taxes be used as instruments to change what they believed was the maldistribution of income and wealth brought about by capitalism. Indeed, the very origins of what we now call »modern« tax policies (that is efficient, universal and equitable taxes) were an attempt to address the growing problem of inequality in modern society

When introduced at the turn of the century these progressive income and profits taxes were in fact quite minor in revenue terms but were to be paid only by the very richest individuals. They were therefore accurately described as »class taxes«.[5] Indeed, in his 1927 Presidential Address to the American Economic Association. T.S. Adams observed the following:

5. See (Brownlee 1996). In the U.S., for example, the Supreme Court ruled the first permanent progressive income tax unconstitutional in 1896. Justice Field justified this ruling in the following way: "The present assault upon capital is the beginning. It will be but the stepping stone to others, larger and more sweeping, till our political contests will become a war between the poor and the rich". Similarly, in Britain the House of Lords refused to pass Lloyd George's "Super Tax" and thus evoked a constitutional crisis. The crisis was eventually resolved when the Commons permanently stripped the House of Lords of its authority over budgetary matters (Sabine 1966). Still, tax rates were quite low by today's standards (e.g. top marginal rates were no higher than 6 percent in Sweden; 7 percent in the U.S.; 10 percent in the U.K.).

> [M]odern taxation or tax-making in its most characteristic aspect is a group contest in which powerful interests vigorously endeavor to rid themselves of present or proposed tax burdens. It is, first of all, a hard game in which he who trusts wholly to economics, reason and justice, will in the end, retire beaten and disillusioned. *Class politics is the essence of taxation* (Adams 1928: 1 my emphasis).

This truth, he went on, applies not only to the political game of tax-making. It affects vitally the economist's thinking about taxation. Economists offered theoretical justifications for progressive taxes as well. Modern capitalism resulted in enormous economic wealth *and* inequalities, they argued. The implication of this thinking, they argued, was that taxes should be levied according to the taxpayer's »ability to pay« (Elvander 1972; Stein 1969). Market forces, it was argued, produced a variety of economic 'externalities' and it was not only appropriate but advisable that public policy be used to mitigate against these. Taxes, they increasingly believed, were an appropriate instrument in this regard (Blough and Shoup 1937).

As World War I broke out, the principle of »let the rich pay« was taken to some remarkable extremes. It is also clear that these value judgements were in many ways reinforced by the extreme fiscal needs of the nation at war. »Total War«, as it was sometimes called, was extremely expensive. Thus, new »Excess Profits Taxes«, »War Preparedness Taxes«, and »National Defense Levies« were implemented as 'temporary' taxes.[6] For most belligerents, income taxes on the very wealthy were increased to historic levels. By 1918 the top marginal income tax in the U.S., for example, reached 77 percent, in Britain the top rate reached a some-what more moderate 60 percent by 1920. In both cases, it was widely argued that it was unfair to have working class men fight this »rich man's war« while the rich stayed home and got even richer.[7] In many countries, these taxes quickly became the major sources of national government finance even

6. There were several different types of "excess profits" taxes used in these years in these countries. They are far too complicated to explain here, but in each case an attempt was made to tax all, or nearly all, the profits made as a result of the hostilities.
7. In the U.S. the income tax was called "rich man's conscription" (Waltman 1985: 45).

though they were paid only by corporations and by fewer than five percent of citizens.[8] But certainly the most important result was the remarkable growth in national state revenues.[9]

During the 1920s, capital's political clout reasserted and progressive taxes were rolled back in most countries. But in no cases did fiscal policy makers attempt to abandon the principle of »Ability to Pay«. By now the idea that taxation policy had a legitimate function as an instrument of redistribution in modern society was no longer seriously questioned. Clearly there was much disagreement over how progressive taxes should be, but not even the American financier Andrew Mellon, who became Secretary of the Treasury under Hoover, argued that taxes should not be progressive – he simply argued that they should not be *as* progressive as they had become during the war years.

The Great Depression quickly reinvigorated the tax policy debate. The voice of those who wished to use tax policy as a punitive instrument with which to »soak the rich« grew louder and louder. Unsurprisingly, given the huge political dissatisfaction with capitalism and capitalists at the time, taxes on the rich were increased. Tax rates – even on the very rich – would not, however, be pushed back up to the levels they had seen during the Great War. In many countries, tax authorities began to seriously evaluate the various revenue options available to them for funding expanded social and economic programs. In the U.S. Roosevelt was personally devoted to both a balanced budget *and* redistributional taxation: he favored 'soak the rich' taxation – shifting the tax burden to the wealthiest individuals and corporations according to 'ability to pay' (Brownlee 1996: 74). Tax policy, in other words, increasingly became pro-active.

8. In 1918, income and profits taxes contributed 44.8 percent of total state and local government revenue in Sweden. In the same year, the income and profits taxes contributed 63.1 percent the federal government's ordinary receipts in the U.S. In Britain these taxes contributed 64.9 percent of total tax revenue in 1920.
9. To take but one example, US Federal government receipts grew from $761 million in 1916 to $5,130 million by 1920. Federal outlays grew from $713 million to $8,493 million in the same period. (Source: Budget of the United States, 2000, Historical Tables, Table 1.1.)

Economists too were apparently persuaded by the idea that taxes should be used as instruments of redistributive policy. According to the data provided by Slemrod in his essay comparing tax professional's opinion in 1934 and 1994, the earlier generation of tax economists were more likely to favor progressive taxes and oppose regressive taxes than economists today. For example, only 12-13 percent felt that there should be a retail sales tax but fully 66 percent believed that capital income should be taxed at a higher rate than ordinary (earned) income (Slemrod, 1995).

A Time of Sacrifice

World War II changed the tax policy climate dramatically. The costs of fighting this war were enormous, and it was clear to virtually all concerned that no one would be able to escape massive increases in their tax burden. The fiscal problem was that traditional revenue sources were clearly incapable of financing the new kind of 'mass war.' Fortunately (?) the new income tax systems which were by now in place could be adapted. The brilliant idea, which occurred to policy makers across the globe, was that if the average worker could be brought into the income tax net, huge revenues would come to the state each month. Once again, the income tax was originally intended as a tax on the rich, but the new idea was to bring everyone into this tax net. The political problem, however, was how could policy makers persuade average citizens that this was 'fair'? The answer? To massively increase the tax rates on companies and the very rich.

Very high taxes on capital and capital income were re-introduced everywhere. There was a firm political commitment in all democratic nations to the principle that capitalists should not get rich by supplying the instruments of war. In many cases the various profits taxes introduced in these years, reached close to 100 percent of net earnings. Wealthy individuals were also subjected to very steep increases in their tax burdens. In Britain, for example, the top marginal tax bracket was pushed up to 97.5 percent in 1941. In the U.S. the top bracket peaked at 94 percent in 1944.

Though clearly intended originally as taxes on the rich, Ministers of Finance or Treasury officials also saw the enormous revenue potential of income taxes. The 'idea' soon developed that income could be withheld by employers and paid directly to the government even before the worker collected it in his weekly check. Two factors are critical to understanding how these 'ideas' came to the fore: First, as capitalism advanced, a larger and larger share of the workforce moved from agriculture to wage employment. Wages are far easier to assess and tax than agricultural income – especially small farmer income. Thus, quite simply modern capitalism made a 'modern' mass income tax possible. Secondly, the revenue needs required to finance modern warfare were tremendous. Income taxes, financial policy officials quickly realized, could be collected with each worker's paycheck via the PAYE (Pay As You Earn) system. Such a system had enormous financial advantages to the state. With this system employers could effectively act as revenue collectors for the state and the state would not have to wait for the monies until the end of the fiscal year. Finally, massive increases in government revenues could be politically and morally justified. It was 'fair' to tax income, as long as everyone paid. Moreover, given the now common egalitarian beliefs among elites, it was even more 'fair' if the rich paid a higher percentage of their income than the poor. The eventual result, though not without considerable controversy in some cases, was the lowering of tax thresholds such that even modest income earners would now have taxes deducted from their weekly check. In short, during WWII the income tax ceased being a »class tax« and became a »mass tax«. Whereas until the end of the 1930s income taxes were still paid by only the very richest in society, by the end of the war at least 60 percent of income earners were now paying this tax. These changes massively increased the revenue raising capacity of central governments in Europe and America. Tax revenues as a share of GDP nearly doubled in most countries between 1930 and 1945 (Mitchell 1998).

The implementation of these new policy ideas fundamentally transformed the future of the modern state. No one could have predicted the long term consequences of this new revenue system, but at this point, it is virtually impossible to under-estimate its long-term impact. Taken together the revenue reforms of the 1930-1945 era transformed the politics of taxation in all industrial democracies. By steeply increasing tax rates on companies and the very wealthy at the same time that they extended the income tax net downward, central/national governments became responsible for both redistributing wealth and income across classes and generations and, as we shall see, managing both the macro and micro economic outcomes. As we shall see below, the structural fact of high tax revenues and high tax rates now provided a new foundation upon which new policy ideas could evolve.

After the War – now what?

At the close of the war, voters and interest groups alike expected governments to roll back taxes to somewhere near pre-war levels. This, of course, did not happen. Instead, all western democratic governments, held on to the high levels of taxation that the war had made politically possible (Peacock and Weisman 1961). Even where conservative parties gained majorities in Parliament, tax rates were not pulled down substantially.[10] Why were taxes not rolled back when the war was over? The key is that by the end of the 1940s there was a widespread consensus (belief) among policy elites that the state now had a meaningful and appropriate role in managing the capitalist economy. Moreover, now, given the high levels of taxation brought in during the war, these elites had a new mechanism to aid in this management.

The experience of wartime planning and economic management opened the door to a new set of ideas about the proper role of the state in society. The well known economist John Maynard Keynes, then, offere a new set of ideas which could help states translate their experience into a positive program of state intervention. Whereas the dominant idea before the war was that the state should not manipulate the economy, Keynes' ideas was that if the state actively managed demand it could produce higher long term growth and lower unemployment in the short run. How could any politician resist such and idea?

»Keynsian« economic management quickly became widely accepted in most advanced capitalist nations. The basic tenet of this economic idea was that governments had both the right and the ability to influence the

10. In most cases the wartime "Excess Profits" duties and taxes were scaled back and/or folded into more permanent corporate profit tax systems.

macro economy (Hall 1986; Hall 1989). It did not take major intellectual leaps, then, to conclude that the government might also be able to influence more micro economic outcomes. Tax policy was seen as a major instrument with which to accomplish this end. Modern governments discovered that, given the high marginal rates of taxation, the tax structure could be manipulated to provide incentives for a wide range of economic activities. In effect, governments now were in a position to impose a deal on capital: if you invest in places, times, or activities that we determine, you will pay lower taxes. If you chose to ignore our incentives, you pay higher taxes.

Tax policy thus quickly became a major instrument of social and economic management. Tax incentives could be (and were) used to affect decisions about where to invest, when to invest, and what to invest in (Howard 1997). There were far too many complicated incentive mechanisms developed in various nations to discuss here: They ranged from general investment tax credits, to inventory, to reserve funds, to special depreciation allowances, to tax deductions for investments in particular regions, products, and companies. But it is important to note that all countries engaged in these micro-manipulations of the economy via the tax code irrespective of party, ideology, and level of economic wealth. Economists did not doubt that taxes could be used as instruments of what they called »Social Control«, the real questions were which instruments were best and which were less so.

Certainly there were those who continued to argue that high taxes damaged economic performance. But, as a number of empirical studies have indicated, there was very little empirical evidence that could be used to support this proposition (Barro 1991; Ferleger and Mandle 1993; Lindert 2004). For most of the post-war period there has simply been no correlation between tax burdens and economic performance.

Taxation and Inflation: Revenue as a free Lunch

As early as the 1930s economists and tax advisors became concerned about the complex relationships between taxes and inflation. On the one hand, taxation contributed to inflation by raising the price of goods. This was particularly clear for taxes on goods and services. But even income taxes might encourage employees to demand higher wages to, in effect, compensate for the taxes that they would inevitably pay. At the same time, inflation increased the costs of government programs and the government needed sources of revenue that would grow along with the costs of providing services. Progressive income taxes helped governments with this revenue problem (Brownlee 1996: 98). The very idea of a progressive income tax is that those who earn larger incomes should pay a higher percentage of that income in taxes. But what happens when it is inflation that drives people's incomes up? The answer is that income earners not only pay more in taxes, but also they pay a larger share of their income in taxes.... even if their real incomes have not gone up. This was known as »bracket creep«. From a revenue point of view, this is excellent news. From a public relations point of view, this is potentially explosive.

The way policy makers solved (or at least assuaged) this dilemma in the 1950s, 60s and 70s was to cut taxes periodically. As before, no one thought of this possibility when these taxes were introduced, but experience led them to new understandings, new possibilities and new ideas. In this way politicians could have their cake and eat it too. In other words, inflation and economic growth would drive up revenues and politicians could then take credit for lowering taxes. In this way public revenues would be held largely constant (as in the US, or could be allowed to grow (as in most European countries) all the while, politicians could take credit for helping their supporters by passing tax cuts. These cuts tended, naturally, to go to the politically powerful more often than to those who most 'deserved' them in a economic/inflationary sense.

By the late 1970s, however, the problems with this revenue strategy came to a head.

Low economic growth combined with high inflation created a political one-two punch. Inflation pushed individuals into higher and higher tax brackets – and thus increased taxes as a share of their real income – while low economic growth made it more difficult to increase real gross income. Unsurprisingly, resentment for taxes increased. Beginning with the »Proposition 13« tax revolt in California, taxpayers around the US, and eventually across the globe, began to rise up against the »unfairness« of the tax systems that their governments were creating with their inflation finance tax cuts for the special interest. Whereas tax systems were justified 'fair' because of their adherence to the principle of 'ability to pay', it became increasingly obvious that this principle was being pushed aside by the revenue needs of the state on the one hand, and the desire of political leaders to buy off their most important constituents on the other. Thus once again, the basic structure into which modern tax systems had evolved provided the foundation for new ideas about what a good tax system should and could do.

Rethinking Tax Policy – the Origins of Tax Reform

By the 1960s and 70s, taxes were increasingly seen by political leaders as low cost (politically) solutions to virtually every problem. In country after country – under both left and right governments – policy makers invented a dizzying array of tax policy instruments. It would take volumes to simply catalogue the astonishing number of tax instruments enacted in the 1960s through to the early 1980s that were designed to promote or support different types of economic activity within the OECD (Reese 1980; Witte 1983). The truth was that tax expenditures became far more than social and economic instruments in the pursuit of commonly held public goals – it was increasingly obvious that they were more and more likely to be political plums whose intent was to satisfy particular constituencies.

Ironically, the very tax incentives introduced to promote economic growth in this era tended to exacerbate the political dilemma facing virtually all OECD nations. Whether tax incentives had the general economic effects their sponsors claim or not, they clearly had the specific effects of complicating tax codes, making it easier for sophisticated taxpayers to avoid paying taxes and, finally, radically reducing taxes for *some* taxpayers. Consequently, reports of huge corporations and multimillionaires (and even American Presidents) who payed little or no taxes became virtually commonplace throughout the OECD. In short, tax policies justified with reference to the goal of promoting economic growth had the direct effect of undermining another widely accepted goal for tax policy – equity. Taxes were increasingly felt to be »unfair«.

The second reason the Left came to question tax expenditures was that they grew increasingly skeptical about how well they actually worked. As the numbers of tax expenditures grew, the argument that they in fact effectively directed investment, for example, became increasingly doubtful.

Tax policy makers grew increasingly concerned with the revenue consequences of expanding tax expenditures. The American case was perhaps the most dramatic by the 1980s the total revenue loss from tax expenditures to the Treasury *exceeded* the total revenues brought in by the Federal Income Tax (Witte 1983). In other words, other taxes had to be raised in order to pay for tax expenditures. The most obvious consequence of this fact was directly political. To stabilize revenues in the face of increasing spending demands *and* increasing tax leakage (especially at the top end of the income scale) effective tax rates borne by the middle classes were allowed to creep up.

Ultimately economists began to question the very propriety of the use of the tax code to accomplish government's goals. If the government wished to subsidize this activity, or that industry, it ought to do it publically – through the normal spending process – not through 'off budget' (ie. out of sight) mechanisms like tax expenditures (Howard 1997).

In sum, both tax policy experts in government and many on the political Left became increasingly skeptical of tax expenditures (loopholes) because they were seen as giveaways to the rich, they were ineffective as policy tools, they cost ever larger sums to the Treasury, and they were outside normal public scrutiny.

The Political Right Takes the Agenda

A sea change in the political climate swept the western world in the 1980s. It is clearly outside the scope of this short paper to analyze all the sources and consequences of this ideological shift – but I believe its manifestation in tax policy provides us with important insights into the broader phenomenon. In many ways, it can be argued that tax policy was the leading edge in these new political tides. In short, old policies created new problems. New ideas were introduced to help solve these new problems.

It would be wrong to suggest that Ronald Reagan came to power in 1981 with a clear mandate from the people. Many factors contributed to his electoral victory including the Iranian hostage crisis, disaffection with the previous administration, and the continuing economic crisis facing the United States. It is clear, however, that Ronald Reagan came to power with an agenda – he wanted to cut taxes and balance the Federal budget (Birnbaum and Murray 1987). What it meant to 'cut taxes' was still somewhat unspecified: Whose taxes should be cut, and by how much, were still issues to be decided. How he would reduce the deficit, it turned out, was even less clearly worked out.

During his electoral campaign, Reagan campaigned vociferously on behalf of the 'overtaxed middle class'. On June 25, 1980, he specifically promised that if he was elected, he would introduce an across the board 30 percent cut in personal income tax rates. Few knew what this would mean in reality, but it sounded good. Even fewer thought that Congress would ever agree to a tax cut of this magnitude – even if Reagan were to follow through with his promise and introduce it once he was elected. What happened next surprised virtually everyone. As if taking a page from Andrew Mellon's 1924 book, Reagan advanced the counterintuitive argument that cutting taxes would actually stimulate growth and therefore increase revenues taken in by the state. Following this logic, Reagan thus introduced the most sweeping tax cut in modern American history. The process by which the »Economic Recovery Tax Act« (ERTA) was passed tells us a great deal about the nature of the tax policy that had developed up to this point (at least in America). Promising to cut taxes is like singing to the choir. How could any politician be expected to resist such a brilliant idea?

The logic was simple. In order to pass a huge tax rate cut, the administration offered to add literally hundreds of tax expenditures to the tax bill to »sweeten« the package (Stockman, 1986: 44). What started out as a side deal here and a side deal there, however, ended up becoming an avalanche. By the time they were through, Congress passed and Reagan signed a 25 percent across the board tax rate cut and hundreds upon hundreds of special tax expenditures (appropriately called 'loopholes' in this context) to particular clients. The total value of this »Economic Recovery Tax Act« was to reduce government revenues by over $750 billion dollars over the next five years.

Along with this massive tax giveaway (and maybe because of it) Congress was also persuaded by the Treasury officials and the Republican advisors to introduce what turned out to be one of the most significant tax innovations passed in a generation: They indexed the personal income tax rate schedules. When first proposed, this idea was dismissed as politically unthinkable. (What good politician would give away his cake?) But in the massive frenzy of passing ERTA this little noticed provision was passed with remarkably little discussion or debate. The Reagan administration wanted to reduce government spending through any means possible. So why not stop government from collecting new revenue simply through bracket creep?

As it turned out, the Reagan administration proved remarkably unable to actually cut government spending directly... but with this measure they were able to strangle government over the longer run. »The enactment of indexation provides a striking example of how radical change sometimes hangs on precarious events,« Paul Pierson tells us. »Indexation enjoyed only a brief window of political opportunity; by 1982 the mounting budget deficits would have made the change impossible. Once enacted, however, it had truly revolutionary effects« (Pierson 1994: 153).

The immediate consequence of the 1981 tax reform was the massive increase in the public deficit. Though Reagan clearly wanted to cut many government programs, Congress was far less accommodating in this regard. Cutting people's taxes was a far easier thing to do than take away programs that they had become used to. The Federal government's annual deficit grew from $40 billion in 1979 to $207 billion by 1983.

Increasing the public debt to this extent, fundamentally, framed and constrained all policy making in the United States for at least the next decade and a half. From this point forward, the central questions facing proponents of welfare state programs in American became: 1) How can we cut spending to help balance the budget and 2) If we want to introduce new spending, how will we pay for it? Some »revenue enhancing« measures were introduced in 1983 and 1984, by Senate Finance chairman Bob Dole, in an explicit attempt to take back some of the grossest cases of fiscal giveaway that occurred in 1981. But, certainly as long as Ronald

Reagan was President, it was very clear that any future initiatives could not contribute to the growth of the welfare state.

The new political economy of welfare state spending can be understood as a direct consequence of the massive tax giveaway introduced by Ronald Reagan in the first forty days of his first term in office.

The ideas of indexing income taxes and cutting tax rates fundamentally altered the fiscal future of the modern state. Never again would political leaders be able to cut taxes year after year and have revenues grow none-the-less. From here on out, maintaining a welfare state would be a far more difficult political proposition (Campbell and Pedersen 2001).

The detailed twists and turns that tax reform politics took over the next year have been the grist of many excellent books on American politics and policy making (cf. Birnbaum and Murray 1987; Conlan, Wrightson et al. 1990). I shall not recount these stories here. The bottom line, for our purposes, was that the Reagan administration took on what had been a Democratic policy agenda and manipulated it for their own purposes. There were, however, two critical differences between the Bradley-Gephardt tax reform proposals and the proposals eventually put forward by the administration: First, while the Democratic proposal was intended to *restore progressivity* to the tax system by eliminating loopholes and reducing rates on the middle and lower income earners, the administration's proposal eliminated many loopholes and proposed across the board rate reductions. (It was widely reported that Reagan's central personal goal was to cut the top marginal rate to 35 percent, which would mean he had cut the rate by 50 percent since he come to office.) Secondly, the Bradley-Gephardt tax reform was intended to raise revenue and restore fiscal balance to the Federal budget. Reagan specifically prohibited the administration from considering any tax reform proposals that would raise revenues... Apparently the increasing deficit (which now stood at $212 billion in 1986) was serving its purpose. A balanced budget (despite Reagan's earlier claims) was no longer a priority issue.

Democratic reformers and policy experts alike were now in a remarkably awkward position. They had been arguing for decades that the Federal Tax system needed to be reformed and simplified and that loopholes undermined its legitimacy and its fairness. Now the Republicans were proposing a tax reform that promised to make the tax code more simple and, by some measures at least, more fair. Though many pundits predicted at the time that tax reform of this magnitude would surely fail, the particular combination of forces came together in a way not unlike the »Nixon visits China« phenomenon (Minarik 1990: 169). After many, many twists and turns, the TRA eventually made it through Congress and was signed by the President. Truly, what eventually passed was remarkable. Tax rates were lowered for most individuals and corporations and this was financed largely by the elimination of hundreds of tax expenditures/loopholes. Though marginally regressive, the distribution of these cuts was mostly proportional to income. It could scarcely be argued that the new American tax system was »fair« it almost certainly was more fair than the one it replaced.

It is important to remember, however, that the American tax system was improved *in comparison to the tax system since 1981*. When we remember that the tax code had become radically more inefficient, complex and unfair than it had been only five years earlier, the marvel of the 1986 tax reform loses some of its sheen.

The Spread of new Ideas

Once the Americans had reformed their tax system, other countries were remarkably quick to follow suit. One of the most respected economists in the international tax policy community, Vito Tanzi, describes the process as follows:

> There is no question that the tax reform movement in the United States that started in 1981 and culminated in the U.S. Tax Reform Act of 1986 has sent shock waves to other countries. Because that movement represented in part the political expression of a powerful Government, and, perhaps equally important, because it appeared to be built on a foundation of discontent with various aspects of existing tax systems, it provided the officials of other countries with both a challenge and an opportunity to introduce changes in their own tax systems. One does not exaggerate in stating that very rarely has the world seen so much interest in tax reform as in the past couple of years, and very rarely has there been such a convergence of views on at least some aspects of the tax systems that need to be modified (Tanzi 1987: 5).

For the most part, the studies that examine each of these reforms are single case studies which explain tax their country's tax reform in domestic terms. But the more interesting story is found in the fact that after having pursued remarkably similar policy goals in taxation policy for over fifty years, virtually every country in the world effectively changes strategy and begins to emphasize different set of policy objectives from those that had dominated the agenda previously.

It would not be accurate to say that totally new goals suddenly rose to the forefront of the tax policy agenda. Rather the emphasis given to various competing goals shifted quite dramatically. Whereas (after raising revenue) tax policy had been principally driven by the goals of social 'equity' and the desire to use taxes as instruments of economic policy, by the 1990s economic 'efficiency' was now the dominant concern. To be sure, equity is still *part* of the agenda, but now 'horizontal equity' dominates the minds of tax policy makers as opposed to their previous concern with 'vertical equity'.[11]

Cedric Sandford summarized the tax reforms passed across the globe in what he calls a »movement ...without precedent in fiscal history«. He suggests in his book, *Successful Tax Reform*, that »even more remarkable than the widespread nature of tax reform, has been the similarity which justify its description as a movement« (Sandford 1993: 9, 10). He lists the main features of this tax movement as follows:

- Rates of personal income tax have been scaled back (particularly at the top end).
- The number of steps in the income tax scale has been reduced.
- The income tax base as been broadened. (Loopholes and exemptions are reduced.)
- Reductions in income tax revenues have been finance by increases in other taxes (VAT, Social Security, etc.)
- Corporate tax rates have been lowered and tax incentives for corporations have been correspondingly cut back. (Sandford 1993: 10-20)

11. Vertical equity implies progressivity (that "fair" taxes should tax those with greater ability to pay *more* than those with lesser abilities to pay). Horizontal equity, in contrast, refers to treating those with equal incomes equally – often irrespective of their ability to pay.

The convergence of views was indeed remarkable. It is, of course, not surprising that Right-leaning governments, such as those in power in the U.S. and the UK at the time, should favor tax reductions for the rich. But, these views were increasingly shared by key policy makers throughout the democratic world (and beyond) of virtually all political persuasions. In the last five years, this author interviewed Ministry of Finance officials in seven OECD countries from Australia and Japan to Sweden and Denmark. *In every single case,* I have heard a remarkably similar argument. This view is best summarized in the following statement made by former Swedish Minister of Finance, Kjell Olof Feldt: »The very high level of progressive taxation just doesn't work.«[12]

One of the consequences of this tax reform process: Tax rates on upper income individuals and corporations have been drastically slashed. It is possible, however, that the cuts in tax rates are being distributed progressively in some countries. I have found no evidence, however, to suggest that this has happened. It appears instead, as Williams has noted in a survey of tax reforms in the EC conducted for the accounting firm Price Waterhouse:

> At the same time as some disillusion was spreading about the efficacy of our main taxes, other pressures were building up ... Our objective now is to be neutrality [sic], with taxes that do not penalize one person rather than another. They give [priority to] equality of opportunity rather than equality of result ... A 'fair' tax is one which presents us with a 'level playing field' and does not concern itself with the quality of the teams (Williams 1991: 24).

Unfortunately, the enormous complexity of both tax systems and the stunning number of specific tax reforms introduced over the past decade, make it impossible to provide a full accounting of all tax changes introduced. Still, while there are some who may focus on a particular major piece of legislation (say, U.S. 1986, Sweden 1991, Germany 2000) and argue that this specific reform was »neutral« between income classes, virtually all analysts agree that the *cumulative* effects of the many tax policy changes introduced in OECD nations over the past decade and a half have made these tax systems less progressive (Boskin 1990). As Sandford

12. Interview with author, May 1988.

admits, the first »main blot« on the tax reform movement has been »its tendency to increase inequalities in income and in wealth« (Sandford 1993: 222).

The result was that tax policy makers across the world began to think more carefully both about the changing nature of capital's interests in the new global economy and to better understand the effects of capital taxes on both those with mobile and immobile capital assets. We saw above that corporate taxes had become major instruments of domestic economic policy in all industrial states. What this effectively meant was that there were some types of firms and some types of investments that were tax advantaged. Obviously, there was considerable variation across countries and even over time as to who actually benefitted the most. But the general pattern was to yield tax incentives for domestic investment (particularly during economic slowdowns) in plants, equipment, and machinery. Due to these various tax programs, domestic manufacturing, construction, and retailing (not coincidentally – those industries which tended to have large well organized union presence) were generally tax advantaged. In short, domestic investment was advantaged over foreign investment.

By the 1980s, however, the very structure of capital's interest had begun to change. Not only are modern corporations bigger in the global economy, they are also more interconnected and more interdependent. This also effects their tax policy interests. Firms that formerly would have been quite content with tax incentive policies that released them from paying taxes as long as they invested in domestic plants and equipment no longer find these kinds of incentives appealing. In a largely insulated economy, manufacturing firms would be quite happy with accelerated depreciation for capital investment, for example. But a global manufacturing firm, in contrast, prefers a lower tax rate with fewer incentives which »lock in investment«. The point here is that the more internationalized firms become, the less they are likely to prefer taxes that advantage domestic suppliers and/or consumers over those beyond national frontiers.

As we saw above, the tax policies of the 1970s and 1980s discredited the increased use of specific tax incentives. They appeared not to work *and* they substantially added to these political problems facing modern governments. Policy makers throughout the OECD thus were under dual, and in many ways contradictory, pressures with respect to tax policy. On the one hand, there was growing disenchantment with specific tax incentives from the Left. On the other hand, it was becoming equally obvious that both technological and policy changes were making it possible for capital and capitalists to place their money and investment in areas where they received the highest possible *after tax* return. As a result, policy makers began to see the multiple advantages of abandoning or severely restricting their use of taxation policy as an instrument of economic management. Tax incentives were cut in a move to »let the market (and not the government) decide« where, when, and what economic actors should do. In other words, the carrot and stick of tax policy has been increasingly being abandoned by modern governments.

It has long been argued that tax incentives do not create new activity, but simply give some economic actors rewards for doing what they might have done anyway. In previous decades, fiscal economists and policymakers alike responded to these criticisms by arguing that the entire point of tax incentives was to produce distortions and to give tax advantages to those who are doing what society determined should be encouraged or compensated for. But in the past several years this view has been scarcely heard. How could it be that the consensus has shifted so dramatically such a short time? The answer is clearly that governments believe they can no longer effectively manage or control private economic decision makers through the tax system. A »good tax system« has moved from being one that explicitly introduced distortions into the capitalist market place to one that minimizes these distortions. In short, a »good tax system«, it is widely believed by the left and the right, keeps the government out of private economic decision making.[13]

13. Vito Tanzi surveys the recent literature and suggests that changes in the international economy are so profound that there are serious doubts about whether capital taxation can continue to exist at all. For example, Roger H. Gordon has asked, "Can capital income taxes survive in open economies?" In the same spirit, Jack M. Mintz asked, "Is there a future for capital income taxation?" For Guttorm Schjelderup, "the fear is that capital mobility may lead to capital flight from high to low tax countries in such large amounts that it deprives a nation of its tax base and, as a consequence, its welfare system" (Tanzi 1995). Tanzi goes on to argue that it is especially small open countries that are the most vulnerable: Similar fears have been expressed by other authors, inclu-

Where did the »old« Ideas go?

The reader will remember that the original justification for 'reforming' the tax system (in America as elsewhere) was that it had become so littered with tax expenditures/incentives/ loopholes that it was widely perceived as unfair by tax policy makers and tax payers alike. Also remember that by fairness citizens at least meant that the rich were not paying their fair share and the poor and middle classes had been increasingly been forced to pay too much in taxes (Hadenius 1986; Roper 1988; Lewis, 1978). What, it seems reasonable to ask, has become of this goal? The answer, bluntly put, has been that it is often downplayed or forgotten. Vertical equity has virtually been taken off the agenda.[14] »Common intellectual themes [of the tax reform movement]« report Boskin and McLure in their book, *World Tax Reform*, »included concern about the adverse incentive effects of high marginal tax rates and about distortions caused by differential tax treatment of economically similar activities, *and a downplaying of vertical equity as a central objective of tax policy*« (Boskin 1990: 3, my emphasis). As the OECD argued in 1989:

> The pursuit of greater neutrality has been based on the growing acceptance of the fact that a proportional tax system is more likely to be optimal from an efficiency point of view than one which is graduated and selective. ... Also, the idea of minimizing the impact of the tax structure on economic behavior has been a distinctly unfamiliar idea to many OECD governments until recently. Governments have often used the tax system deliberately to alter consumption or investment patterns (OECD 1989).

ding Frenkel, Razin, and Sadka. These fears are related to the taxation of capital in all countries but acquire special urgency in small countries. Small countries may find it particularly difficult for to maintain high tax rates on capital income, and some of them may be tempted to become "tax havens" for foreign capital, thus making it more difficult other countries to maintain their tax rates. As Razin and Sadka have put it, "No capital income tax, whatsoever, can be efficiently imposed by a small open economy if capital flight to the rest of the world cannot be stopped." Of course, for capital to move out of a given country the net-of-tax rate of return in the rest of the world must be lower than that in the country. The idea that especially small countries will be exposed to the effects of deep integration on capital taxation is a recurrent theme in the literature on international taxation (Tanzi 1995).

14. Vertical equity usually implies that those with greater incomes should pay a larger share of their income in taxes.

It was certainly true that there were so many 'loopholes' in modern tax systems (especially the American and British) that tax reforms *could have* cut out the inefficiencies *and* increased the progressivity of the tax systems, but in no case that I am aware of did this actually occur. Indeed, most often exactly the opposite came about. To be sure, rate cuts were partially financed with reductions in tax expenditures, but in most cases they were also replaced with increases in consumption taxes or social insurance fees. Taken together these moves has meant a downward redistribution of tax burdens for most countries.

In a recent conference Richard Musgrave, the author of the most widely used fiscal economics text in the world, comment on the current tax reform movement in the following way: »The major factor [behind the reforms] has been a change in political climate towards a less egalitarian view of distributive justice« (Musgrave 1990: 317).

What *should* the State do?

We are currently witnessing the evolution of a new logic upon which democratic states raise revenue. No matter who holds the reigns of power, all modern governments appear to have concluded that a »good« tax system must both cut taxes for the wealthy and for internationally mobile capital and retreat from using tax policy as an active instrument of economic management. They have apparently decided that the market should be ever more responsible for economic outcomes. Governments, even Social Democratic governments, are moving to get out of the way. In short, tax reform means changing the character of the relationship between the state and the private economy: public authority is being yielded to private interests.

It is clearly the case that pro-market and anti-state-interventionist ideas are now dominant, but it is not true that these ideas are new. Capital and the ideological Right have made these same arguments since the turn of the century. But up until recently, those who called for more socially and economically »neutral« tax systems have been overwhelmed by those who saw it as the legitimate responsibility of the state to try to shape both the distribution of income/wealth in society and to encourage certain kinds of economic activity over others. Reading the current economic literature on tax policy, one might conclude that these new/old principles driving tax policy in the 1980's and 1990's have won because they are superior ideas: the idea that taxes should be based on the principles of »ability to pay« and state management of the economy are simply intellectually bankrupt. Sandford puts it thus: »*Above all, however, tax reform reflected a change in economic philosophy*. In most countries, certainly amongst the leaders, tax reform was part of a programme of pushing back the boundaries of the state... Disillusionment with the results of state intervention had led to a decline in belief in the efficacy of state intervention and a revival of belief in the efficacy of markets« (Sandford 1993: 20, emphasis in original).

It is not true that the tax policy changes that have occurred around the world over the past twenty years or so are purely the product of a new attack on the part of capital and/or the rich against the middle and lower classes. Instead, as this paper has attempted to demonstrate, it was also the increased disaffection with extant tax systems (and what they had become) that opened the door to new thinking about taxation and tax policy. It was the horrible mess that many countries had made of their tax systems in the 1970s and early 1980s that created the disillusionment with taxes than some new systematic attack by forces on the Right. Both the Left and the Right, after all, contributed to building the increasingly complex, inefficient and inequitable systems that these countries had developed.

Public dissatisfaction with taxes in the early 1980s was rooted in the belief that the poor and the middle classes were paying too much and the rich and corporations were paying too little – i.e. vertical equity. But *elite* dissatisfaction with taxes was more rooted in distrust of the efficacy of the tax expenditures that now littered the tax codes and the economic inefficiencies they created. In a fundamental sense, fiscal economists and Treasury/Finance officials grew increasingly skeptical of their political masters. It is not clear that tax policy experts believed tax incentives were by definition bad. But they clearly believed that they were wrongly used and misused by the political leadership. It would be better, they came to believe, to have no (or very few) tax expenditures than to have a tax system littered with tax loopholes designed for the politically powerful.

It would be equally wrong to suggest that economic realities did not play a role in the specific character of the reforms that were eventually passed. As I have tried to show, the realities of economic internationalization substantially contributed to the change in what tax policy makers thought was desirable. As Vito Tanzi puts it, »[t]ax competition from other countries may force some countries into choosing tax structures (and, perhaps, tax levels) that their policy-makers might consider less desirable than the ones they would have chosen if their economies had remained closed« (Tanzi 1995: 134).

Rarely, however, do policy makers think in terms of »if we only could have «. Instead their thinking is fundamentally framed within the economic/intellectual climate in which they work. Just as in the 1930s when it is seemed self-evident to economists that taxes should contribute to social justice, today it is self-evident to them that the state should 'level the playing field.' The President of the American Economic Association T.S. Adams, put this point quite well in his address to his association in 1928: »The dominating factor of economic interest in taxation determines to a large extent the role or place of idealism in taxation. Ideals are effective when they further the economic interest of powerful groups« (Adams 1928: 4).

Ideas about policy are formed in a political and institutional context. As we have seen, experiences with poorly designed and implemented tax policies helped shape politicians', economists' and tax officials' attitudes and beliefs about what reforms were necessary and desirable. This is because beliefs about what is desirable are constructed within the context of historical experience. What we want is fundamentally framed by what we can imagine achieving – and what we can imagine achieving is informed by what we have done before. At the same time, policies are also framed in an economic context. In the present era, the context in which tax reform is constructed is one of increased international economic mobility. The result has been the growing conviction among policy makers that markets will outrun political boundaries no matter how well policies are designed.

In short, both the apparent failure of the political structure to make efficient and fair use of tax policy and the realities of globalization have ultimately shaped what policy elites now believe can be done *and what ought to be done.*[15] Whereas in the first seven decades of this century, there was a widespread consensus that taxes *should* be used as a social policy instrument that had an essential function in redistributing income and wealth in capitalist democracies, today there appears to be a growing consensus (among elites, at least) that taxes *should* not be used for these purposes.

One Path or many?

One should not misinterpret the argument in these pages to suggest either that modern states have no option but to follow the logic of neo-liberal tax policy, nor that all modern states have followed exactly the same path. To draw either of these conclusions would be a significant misinterpretation of the arguments presented here. First, in this essay I have tried to explore *why* certain tax policy ideas have grown and prospered across the advanced capitalist world. While it is quite clear that these ideas have been broadly similar in places as different as the USA and Sweden, it is equally clear that the *interpretation* and *implementation* of these ideas has often been significantly different in different countries. For example, in an essay I published in 2003 titled »Bucking The Trend: Swedish Social Democracy in the Global Economy«. I argued that Sweden was *not* following the neo-liberal logic of rolling back the welfare state in the face of globalization (Steinmo 2003). But clearly neo-liberal ideas have had significant influence in Swedish political economy. Indeed, my evidence supports Kjær and Pedersen when they say, »noe-liberalism should not be conceived as a universally meaningful totality of ideas that diffused across nations and through time, but as a more loosely connected set of concepts, distinctions, and ideas that gained meaning as they were selected, articulated, and then stabilized in unique ways« (Kjær and Pedersen 2001: 221).

15. It is interesting to note that there has been a recent flurry of academic writing among political scientists that appears to argue that tax policy makers do not have to respond to internationalizing incentives by calling taxes and/or redistributing the tax burden. Apparently, however, elite policy makers have not read these analyses.

Secondly, I have argued here that ideas, institutions and policy choices must be understood in an evolutionary manner. A keystone of the evolutionary perspective is *contingency* (Lewis and Steinmo 2007). By this I mean to suggest not only that specific outcomes are not predictable, but also that the local ecology can be equally important to explaining an evolutionary event as the broader global ecology in which it develops. While we know that 'global warming,' for example, will raise average temperatures around the world, we cannot know for certain whether global warming will raise average temperatures in any particular place on the globe. The same can be said for 'globalization'. Clearly the increasing mobility of capital and labor will continue to have enormous consequences for the entire world, but this does not mean that we can specifically predict the particular outcomes of 'globalization' in a specific place in the world.

My aim here has not been to predict what will occur. My goals have been far more humble: I have argued that the political/economic context in which tax policies are made affect the environment (ecology) in which future tax policy choices are made. Political leaders problem-solve and bring forward policy ideas as potential solutions to new problems. These ideas may be new policy solutions that have become available due to previous policy choices, or they may be older ideas that have been more or less dormant for a period. In either case, policy ideas should be seen as »problem solutions« – a kind of rational probabilistic calculation linking problems with potential solutions. New ideas come to the fore because a) older ideas are discredited by experience, b) a new political/economic context opens up new opportunities for innovation or c) the political balance of power shifts, thus those that are advantaged by certain policy ideas are able to push their agenda over others.

Finally, we also must remember that ideas and the policies they imply are not neutral: They advantage some interests over others. One cannot disaggregate ideas from interests as if they were separate and *independent* variables (as one might in a simple regression model) because ideas and interests are both interactive and interdependent. It is tempting to argue, for example, that the recent trends towards lower marginal tax rates for capital and high income earners witnessed around the world is a direct result of 'globalization'. But to do so would be to ignore the way that the negative experience policy makers have had with high marginal tax rates in the 1970-1990s in terms of growing belief that high tax rates led to new inequalities and to the growing belief that policy makers could not be 'trusted' to implement tax policies either fairly or efficiently. These beliefs intersected with one another at a time when the world was in fact become more 'global', thus policy makers and advisors did not believe that it would be possible to close every loophole. Thus the fact of globalization in many ways became a justification for policies which tax professionals and tax policy advisors had long wanted to make. In this view then, the 'ideas' are not derivative of the interests, instead interests may be constructed in a particular way to justify specific ideas.

References

Adams, T.S. 1928, 'Ideals and Idealism in Taxation', in *The American Economic Review*, 18 (1), pp. 1-8.

Barro, R. 1991, 'Economic Growth in a Cross Section of Countries', in *The Quarterly Journal of Economics*, 106 (2), pp. 407-444.

Berman, S. 2001, 'Ideas, Norms and Culture in Political Analysis', in *Comparative Politics*.

Birnbaum, J. and A. Murray 1987, *Showdown at Gucci Gulch: law makers, lobbyists and the unlikely triumph of tax reform*, Random House, New York.

Blough, R. and C. Shoup 1937, 'A Report on the Federal Revenue System: Consultants' report to Undersecretary of the Treasury', Box 63, in *Tax Reform Programs and Studies, Records of the Office of Tax Analysis/Division of Tax Research, General Records of the Department of the Treasury*, Record Group 56, National Archives, College Park, MD.

Blyth, M. 2003, 'Structures do not come with an instruction sheet: Interests, ideas and progress in political science', in *Perspectives on Politics*, 1 (4), pp. 695-706.

Boskin, M.J. 1990, 'New directions in tax policy', in *World tax reform*, edited by M. J.

Boskin M.J. and C.E. McLure Jr., ICS Press, San Francisco.

Brownlee, W.E. 1996, *Funding the modern American state, 1941-1995: the rise and fall of the era of easy finance, Woodrow Wilson Center* series, Woodrow Wilson Center Press; Cambridge University Press, Cambridge and New York.

Campbell, J.L. 1998, 'Institutional Analysis and the Role of Ideas in Political Economy', in *Theory and Society*, 27 (7/8), pp. 15-56.

Campbell, J.L. and O. Pedersen 2001, 'The Rise of Neo-Liberalism and Institutional Analysis', in J.L. Campbell and O.K. Pedersen (eds.), *The Rise of Neo-Liberalism and Institutional Analysis*, Princeton University Press, Princeton.

Elvander, N. 1972, *Svensk skattepolitik 1945-1970 [Swedish tax politics 1945-1970]*, Raben and Sjögren, Stockholm.

Ferleger, L.A. and J. R. Mandle 1993, 'No Pain, No Gain: Taxes, Productivity, and Economic Growth', in *Challenge*, 36 (3), pp. 11-19.

Hall, P. 1986, *Governing the Economy*, Oxford University Press, New York.

Hall, P. 1989, *The Political Power of Economic Ideas*, Princeton University Press, Princeton.

Howard, C. 1997, *The hidden welfare state*, Princeton University Press, Princeton, NJ.

Kjær, P. and O. Pedersen 2001, 'Translating Liberation: NeoLiberalism in the Danish negotiated economy', in J.L. Campbell and O. Pedersen (eds.), *The Rise of Neo-Liberalism and Institutional Analysis*, Princeton University Press, Princeton.

Korten, D. 1995, *When corporations rule the world*, Kamarian Press, West Hartford.

Lewis, O. and S. Steinmo 2007, *Taking evolution seriously*, Florence, Italy.

Lindert, P.H. 2004, *Growing public: Social spending and economic growth since the eighteenth century*, Cambridge, UK and New York.

Mitchell, B.R. 1998, *International historical statistics: Europe, 1750-1993*, 4. edition, Macmillan, Basingstoke.

Musgrave, R. 1990, 'Comments', in J. Slemrod (ed.), *Do Taxes Matter?*, MIT Press, Cambridge: MA.

OECD 1989, *Economies in transition: Structural adjustments in OECD countries*, Organization for Economic Cooperation and Development, Paris.

Peacock, A. and J. Weisman 1961, *The growth of public expenditure in the United Kingdom*, National Bureau of Economic Research, Princeton.

Pierson, P. 1994, *Dismantling the Welfare State? Reagan, Thatcher and the Politics of Retrenchment*, Cambridge University Press, Cambridge.

Reese, T. 1980, *The politics of taxation*, Quorum Books, Westport, Connecticut.

Slemrod, J. 1995, 'Professional Opinions About Tax Policy: 1994 and 1934', in *National Tax Journal*, 48 (1), pp. 121-147.

Stein, H. 1969, *The fiscal revolution in America*, University of Chicago Press, Chicago.

Steinmo, S. 2003, 'Bucking the trend: Swedish social democracy in a global economy', in *New Political* Economy, 8 (1), pp. 31-48.

Swank, D. and S. Steinmo 2002, 'The new political economy of taxation in advanced capitalist democracies', in *American Journal of Political Science*, 46 (3), pp. 642-655.

Tanzi, V. 1995, *Taxation in an integrating world*, Brookings Institution, Washington DC.

Williams, D. 1991, *Trends in International Taxation*, International Fiscal Association, British Branch, London.

Witte, J. 1983, 'The distribution of federal tax expenditures', in *Policy Studies Journal*, 12, pp. 131-46.

CHAPTER 10

How Should the Economy Work? Policy Imagination and Dynamics of Institutional Change

Leonard Seabrooke

Professor, Copenhagen Business School, Denmark

Introduction

This essay discusses what happens if we test our assumptions about how politics and institutions change over time. The notion here is that testing such assumptions is important for scholars of institutional change because it may alert us to change that occurs 'off the path' of assumed cultural traits and trajectories. Such information may tell us that while cycles of rise and fall, national economic characteristics, and cultural path dependence are often used as ideal types to guide our cognitive frameworks for analysis, an ideal type is not a 'cookie cutter' of assumptions about how economies work in practice. Rather, ideal types are intended to be interpretive frameworks with which to understand rather than determine change (see, recently, Crouch 2005: 57; Seabrooke 2006: 49-53, 193-98). Revealing how ideal types fail and how they should be reconfigured, to only fail again when they do not help us understand what is actually going on, can provide us with new information about institutional change. Such information can help us stretch our policy imagination in dealing with contemporary problems since the key policy problem is not modelling change according to abstractions, but implementing policies within a living, breathing, and thinking society.

This essay also argues that different nations of political economy scholarship can positively learn more from each other than is sometimes depicted. Within British and European scholarship, for example, many 'heterodox' scholars have called for a greater appreciation of history in political economy scholarship (Amoore, et al. 2000; Murphy and Tooze 1991), while 'orthodox' North Americans have argued that political economy scholarship lacks policy relevance and is too concerned with demonstrating intellectual acrobatics (Katzenstein, Keohane, and Krasner 1998, 684). If 'heterodox' scholars are arguing for more sensitive understandings of historical change, and some 'orthodox' scholars are arguing for more policy relevant material, then we may have a loose consensus on how political economy may be improved by learning from different social experiments over time, in order to expand policy imagination to deal with contemporary problems.

In putting forward this case I identify three trends in the broader political economy literature that can narrow policy imagination if transformed into 'plug and play' theories, where the scholar applies an established theory or body of thought to whatever the case is in question. The three trends are: 1. viewing the present as natural or within a cycle, 2. seeing history as overtly path dependent; and 3. viewing history as driven by 'Great Men' or 'Great Women'. I must stress here that my representation of these trends are gross exaggerations of tendencies in political economy scholarship (as are the figures I use to depict them). Once these trends have been examined, I present a proposal for how we can widen policy imagination in political economy. Behind this proposal is the idea that a key question for understanding how institutions, politics, and economies change over time is to imagine that we can ask the question 'how should the economy work?' to the subjects of analysis. While not always possible (we do not have time machines, but can ask this question in our own time), the idea is that we are not looking for systems of interest politics based on our own conception of what interests are. Rather, we are looking for information about how norms, values, and discourses are changing that can tell us about issues of legitimacy and identity, social attitudes, and about informal impulses that come from the everyday population to those in power and those in formal institutions (Seabrooke, 2007c). This proposal to reveal the social sources of institutional change requires two conceptual manoeuvres. The first is to find an actor's *intentional rationality* rather than make an assumption of a 'natural' actor with a 'bounded' rationality (Beckert 1996: 819-22). This, I argue, requires us to start from a position of *idiographic* methodological individualism, to stress how the individual's intentions, norms, and acts of legitimation must be historically specified. The second manoeuvre is to learn from the work on 'social mechanisms', to produce transferable lessons from specific historical contexts about types of behaviour that are relevant to understanding the contemporary world economy. Together these manoeuvres may widen policy imagination in political economy by enhancing the capacity for counterintuitive insight. The article is organised according to the three trends and two manoeuvres.

Trend One: Viewing the Present as Natural or Cyclical

In making a case for the importance of understanding historical change, Reinhard Bendix argued against viewing the past through the lens of the present:

> By looking at past events from a contemporaneous viewpoint we create a dynamic picture, or by looking backward at the result we create a static picture. Looking backwards always presents an overdetermined depiction of fate; by this perspective we leave out of focus the possibilities of action which existed at the time. I am only determinist in this methodological sense (Bendix 1984: 56).

For Bendix, imagining placing oneself into the past to create a dynamic picture is primarily a concern with being open to the idea that there are a range of policy options within the period that are not part of our current policy choice set. For Bendix the spread of fascism in the twentieth century was in part created by an inability to see beyond what appeared to be a natural policy choice set (Bendix, 1984).

While we can easily identify historically sensitive work in political economy that seeks to tackle current policy issues by learning from the past (e.g., Germain 1997), much political economy considers current policy options as the dominant policy options. Akin to Bendix, John Hobson argues (Hobson 2002: 5-15) that much political economy scholarship falls into traps that he identifies as *chronofetishism* and *tempocentrism*. They are, respectively, that the present can only be analyzed by examining the present, and that past is viewed through the lens of the present. *Chronofetishism* leads to arguments that naturalise the present order and its institutions, exaggerating the specific characteristics of the present and neglecting alternatives to what is considered a natural order. *Tempocentrism* leads to a failure to appreciate historical difference by smoothing out discontinuities between historical epochs.

Figure 1: History as Cyclical

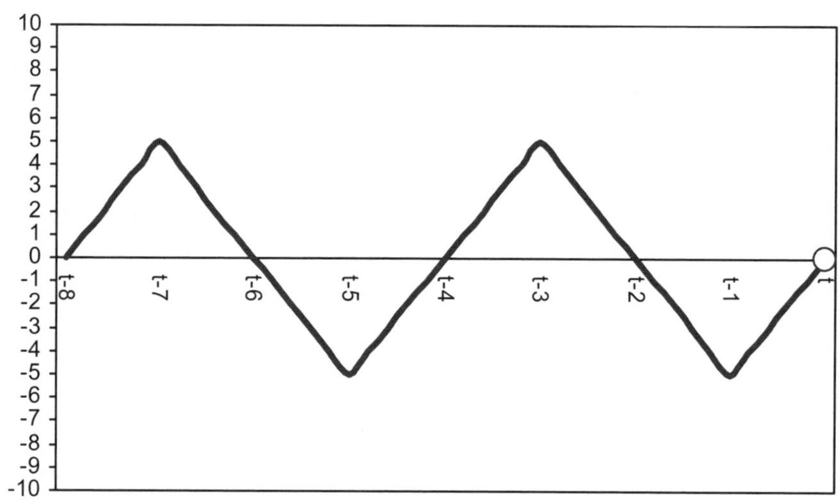

Figure 1 depicts a chronofetishist and tempocentric scenario where history is viewed as a cycle, or within a climateric. On the y-axis we have a policy choice set (which may be infinite in their recombination and design, but restricted to ±10 here). On the x-axis we have eight time periods, representing the past and running up to the present at *t*. The actor at the white circle at *t* looks back into the past finding history to be a cycle that operates within a fixed policy choice set (±5). While this is obviously an exaggeration, the point here is that the actor excludes some policy choices from his or her menu (those above or below ±5). The actor has created a 'bounded rationality' to confirm a view that the only information relevant for policy imagination can be found in the present since the past follows a natural cycle. The cycle itself provides the policy options.

Within political economy the 'orthodox' work on hegemony has been identified for some time now as a perpetrator of the tendencies illustrated in Figure 1 (Hobson, 1997, 200). Comparisons of U.S. hegemony in the 1960s and 1970s with British hegemony in the mid-nineteenth century were commonly based on the notion that both had gone through a 'Golden Age' and were naturally entering a period of decline (Gilpin 1975; cf. Seabrooke 2001: 7-9). Despite a wide array of differences between the two hegemonies, the implication was that the U.S. was going to decline, because Britain did within what appeared to be a natural climacteric (Gilpin 1981). Because of this natural cycle the British case did not so much provide lessons to the U.S. as provide a rationale for the limited policy options available to potentially fight U.S. hegemonic decline in the present. As such, theorists of U.S. hegemonic decline made predictions based on a contemporary model they had mapped onto the past to provide their predictions with empirical rigour. Hegemonic decline would lead to the rise of a new hegemon (Japan), a hegemonic partnership (with Japan), a descent into anarchy, or the sustenance of international cooperation (Gilpin 1981; Gilpin 1987; Keohane 1984). Most of these predictions were wide of the mark. Had the hegemony theorists investigated the prior cases with more sensitivity to historical and social change they may have recognised the importance of France to mid-nineteenth century trading systems (Hobson 1997, Chapter 7), the capacity of the British state to generate credit from the population as a means of financial power despite debts (Seabrooke 2006, Chapters 3 and 5), and fundamental differences in the formal and informal coordination of an international monetary system.

While much of the literature associated with the hegemony debates is commonly associated with 'orthodox' schools of thought, the trend of naturalising the present and viewing the past through the lens of the present also applies to more 'heterodox' Marxist-inspired literature. In particular, work on 'long cycles' and 'world systems' often posited the view that history was engaged in an unfolding evolution or trapped within a cycle where capitalist exploitation was the key driver (Wallerstein 1979; Modelski and Thompson 1996; Van der Pijl, 1998). Once again Figure 1 is relevant for how these scholars view historical change since the systems of power created by capitalist exploitation drive history through cycles (with, notably, disagreement on whether capitalism would implode or not). And as capitalist exploitation provided the key logic, solutions on how to break the system could be found in the present because the system was naturally playing out. The policy choice set was bound within an imagination that favours economic relations within a dominant mode of production. While this is undoubtedly a harsh criticism, the worst aspect here, often implicit rather than explicit, is the notion that the capitalist system 'duped' the masses into their choices. This is a view that, despite protests to the contrary, occurs in much Gramscian work that relies on the concept of 'hegemony' as a form of social control 'forced or imposed on subaltern classes' (Germain and Kenny 1998: 18-19). If hegemony is treated as options individuals make from a choice set (even if they are bad choices), then we may have more insight into how capitalist exploitation works beyond a naturalised historical logic.

Trend two: History as Path Dependent

Political economists often treat history as though past information informs contemporary policy choices within a path dependent sequence. Reinhard Bendix provides sage advice once again in steering us clear of historical traps. Bendix (1977) argued that one of the key flaws of modernization theories of the postwar period was their treatment of history as a progression. For Bendix this view produced serious problems since, at the same time, modernization theory called for 'traditional' states to produce the 'functional equivalents' of Western institutions that were thought to be the drivers of economic growth (Bendix 1977: 416). Bendix's key point here is to argue that the 'right' institutions cannot simply be grafted onto a society if they have legitimacy.

Within most 'orthodox' political economy the concept of path dependence is frequently applied as a logic for understanding historical change. Here history provides information on changing institutional forms, where the assumption is that the institutions provided all the information the actors within them needed to select appropriate policies. And while we can readily acknowledge that point A does indeed come before point B, we should not catch ourselves in the trap that what happened at point A will determine what happens at point B, C, and so on, on the grounds of increasing returns (cf. Pierson 2004; Thelen 2004). Nor should we assume that the institutions undergoing change have the capacity to provide themselves with the policy information required for reflexive transformation. The tendency in many political economy analyses is to rely on externally given moments of uncertainty and crisis, on 'critical junctures' or 'triggers', that come along and break up the current institutional equilibrium and establish a new path for institutional change (Cortell and Peterson 2002). By tracing these 'triggers' we can unravel the evolution of an institution in which a policy choice made at point *t-8* informs the choice made at *t-7*, and so on.

Figure 2: History as punctuated equilibrium/evolution

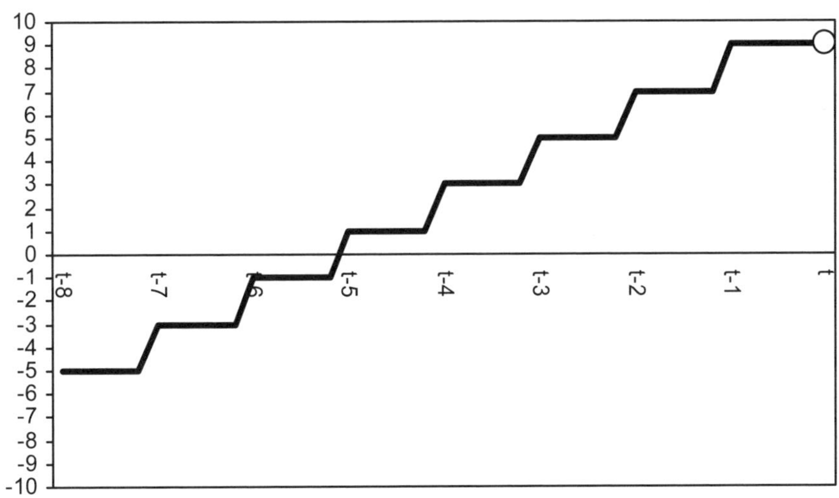

A situation of extreme path dependence within an evolutionary trajectory is illustrated in Figure 2. Once more on the y-axis we have a policy choice set (again restricted to ±10), with change over eight periods of time represented on the x-axis. The actor at the white circle at *t* looks back into the past to see that policy options have been determined by an historical trajectory, and that breaks in policy continuity have been provided only at key moments. In this case the linear evolution of the institution in question provides all the information the actor needs in selecting policy options. And once again the actor's rationality is 'bounded' by this information.

Within political economy, the rationalist institutionalist and historical institutionalist camps often display a tendency to overplay the importance of path dependence. For the rationalists, such as Douglass North (1990), institutions change according to transaction costs, with institutions changing during periods of exogenously generated uncertainty as they seek to improve their information. Culture is viewed as important to how institutions transform over time, but primarily to explain why they did not conform to a more rational model. Avner Greif's work (1994; 2006), for example, traces how the cultural characteristics of groups of Genoese and Maghribi traders led to the development of different trading institutions. Culture here is viewed as a form of 'cognitive dissonance' when it does not conform to evolving rational expectations (Greif 1994: 916-17). As I have argued elsewhere, culture and norms are left to explain the noise distorting decision – making within a rational capitalist mindset; that 'norms are error terms' (Seabrooke 2006: 24). This view of history therefore posits the individual in the present as holding superior information about rational decision-making than those examined in the past 'regardless of the specific case or the outcome being problematized' (Somers 1998: 752). To put it bluntly, the actor in the present can see evolution because he or she is the most evolved.

Historical institutionalists rely on the concepts of path dependence, 'sequencing', and punctuated equilibrium or evolution to study how institutions transform over time (Steinmo, Thelen, Longstreth 1992; Cortell and Peterson 2002; Mahoney and Rueschemeyer 2003). Here both exogenous and endogenous sources of change are considered, with shocks to an institutional equilibrium provided by external crises or internal manoeuvrings from actors inside the institution that have policy ideas that 'fit' with the pre-existing institution (Hall 1989). The institutions therefore provide the information to the actors making the choices, including a 'logic of appropriateness' concerning how they should behave (March and Olsen 1989, see also Campbell 2004). As above, the institution itself provides all the information, so tracing the policy choices that established 'critical junctures' in institutional form provides a view of history as progress (or degeneration).

The work on 'state capacity' in political economy, which I have associated with strongly in the past, provides another example, as does the work on 'varieties of capitalism'. The 'state capacity' literature, inspired by historical sociologists like Michael Mann (1986) and Theda Skocpol (1979), sought to provide a logic to how states can respond to external pressures of economic interdependence and globalisation (see Seabrooke 2001; Gill 2002). Here, the role of 'pilot economic agencies' to development was highlighted, as were relations between the capitalist class and the state in producing economic outcomes (Evans 1985; Weiss 1998). Akin to the 'functional equivalents' mentioned by Bendix above, pilot economic agencies were seen as necessary for success but difficult to create if the culture in question was not predisposed to them. Similarly, the blossoming literature on 'varieties of capitalism' posits national economic frameworks within which firms seek to find institutional complementarities (Hall and Soskice 2001). The two predominant frameworks within the world economy are thought to be 'liberal market economies' (LMEs) and 'coordinated market economies' (CMEs), typified, respectively, by the United States and Germany (cf. Blyth 2003). Despite this literature's emphasis on individual firms selecting institutional complementarities, policy information is derived from the national economic framework. One could argue here that historical change is viewed as following a progression of institutional forms where change to the form is itself established by the institution. Given such circularity, 'off the path' developments are rarely considered, including important differences in how subnational systems have evolved that may be contrary to expectations (see Whitford 2005; Seabrooke 2007b).

To sum up the extremes of this second trend, by smoothing out history, like smoothing a 'line of best fit' in regression analysis, important information is lost and policy imagination is narrowed. This applies not only to the 'outliers' that stick out as abnormal within the data set, but also variations around the 'line of best fit' that provide important contextual information on why some policies and practices worked and others did not.

Trend three: History as driven by great Men and Women

Recently, there has been much talk in political economy about how ideas and norms inform institutional change over time. Certainly a body of work is now identified or self-identifies as 'economic constructivist' or 'constructivist political economy'. This work typically assesses how ideas and norms have influenced how institutions have changed over time, focusing predominantly on how elite actors have acted as ideational entrepreneurs in enacting change.

In studying how norms influence political, social, and economic change through history, Norbert Elias warned that that they must be treated as 'double-edged'. Rather than embodying a 'good', they 'bind people to each other and at the same time turn people so bound against others' (Elias 1996: 160; also Katzenstein 1996: 3, 18-19). As such, how they split and fragment social groups is just as important in understanding historical and social change as learning how norms can provide a source of cooperation. The bulk of work in economic constructivism has not sufficiently treated ideas and norms as 'double-edged', but prefers to concentrate on how ideational elites can influence institutional change through the propagation of an idea or norm. As such, history is often viewed as driven by the propagators.

Figure 3: History as Driven by Great Men and Women

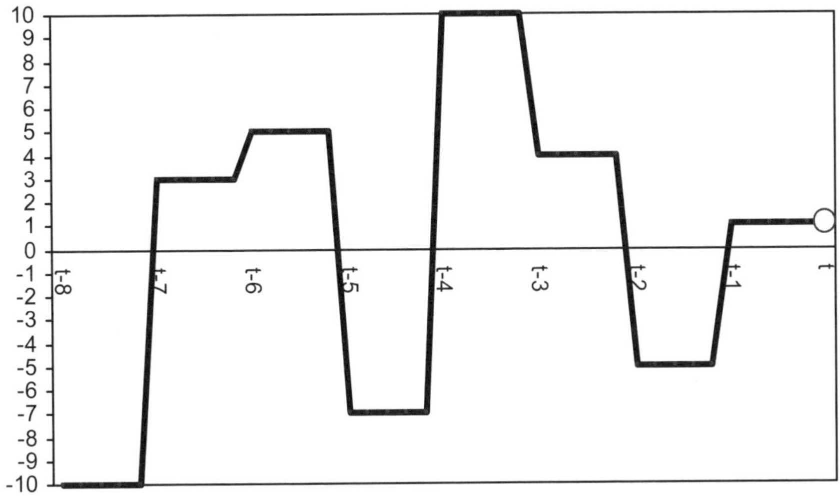

Figure 3 presents an extreme and exaggerated view of history as constructed by ideational entrepreneurs' idea and norm propagation at key moments in time. As in earlier diagrams, on the y-axis we have a policy choice set (within the bounds of ±10), while change over time is divided into eight periods along the x-axis. The actor at the white circle at *t* looks back and sees little continuity in how institutions have changed over time. Rather, movement within the policy choice set is wide open (ranging across the policy choice set in this example), because the actor's rationality is not 'bound'. There is a thin continuity exhibited between the constructed 'shocks' that create institutional change, but this is not a 'sticky' form of path dependence because the institutions follows the ideas, held by the entrepreneur, rather than necessarily responding to political, economic, and social dynamics. Indeed, there is not sufficient information on whether institutional change established by ideational entrepreneurs in the 'foreground' must be 'backgrounded' by social change (Campbell and Pedersen 1996).

Given the emphasis on ideational entrepreneurs as the drivers of change through time, one could criticise some economic constructivist work for falling into the old 'Great Man of History' trap. From this point of view historical change is explained through the identification of certain individuals to the exclusion of broader society that may have: a) informed the ideational entrepreneur's ideas; and b) have the capacity to create policy failure, so that ideas and policy options for institutional change remain 'in the air' rather than 'on the ground' (Seabrooke 2007c). Furthermore, this approach to history places less emphasis on what Susan Strange referred to as 'non-decisions', the 'failures to take a decision, which, no less than active policy – making have affected – and still affect – the outcomes of the international political economy' (Strange 1988: 22). Tracing changes to the formal operation of institutions, even when they incorporate a great deal of flexibility or ambiguity, may not provide an accurate picture of how actors within the world economy operated in practice (cf. Best 2005).

The concept of uncertainty is critical to the economic constructivist account of historical change, but also produces a bias in how history is treated. Uncertainty is typically treated not as a problem to be overcome by acquiring better information, but as an *unprecedented* situation in which ideational entrepreneurs must re-examine their worldviews and use 'ideas as weapons' to battle it out with others in finding a solution and a new path for institutional change (Blyth 2002). Ideational entrepreneurs are then able to emerge from their uncertainty with a 'master frame' with which to direct future institutional changes (Parsons 2003). The work on European integration, which is a common topic within the economic constructivist literature, is indicative. The focus is typically on tracing how powerful elite actors, such as French President Valéry Giscard d'Estaing or European Commission President Jacques Delors, influenced the path towards integration, with special emphasis on critical junctures (McNamara 1998; Parsons 2003). A materialist punctuated equilibrium is therefore replaced by an ideational punctuated equilibrium model of change (Seabrooke 2007c). And in replicating a punctuated equilibrium model policy imagination is diminished in a school of thought in which one would assume that imagination is viewed as a key social skill.

Within this literature ideas are understood as weapons and are assumed to shape 'shared expectations'. However, the active *sharing*, a two-way relationship, is only being done within a select group. Society at large, the 'masses', are obeying rather than sharing, with the public conceptualised narrowly as influenced by elites rather than also influencing elites (see Finnemore and Sikkink 1998: 903; cf. Seabrooke 2007c). This leads to a view of 'legitimacy by proclamation'; where the pronouncements of policy direction by a victorious ideational entrepreneur are assumed to have an auto-legitimating character (Seabrooke 2006: 38, 40-42). But as Max Weber tells us, in unravelling historical and social change, the important question is not how ideational entrepreneurs push their norms on others, but why people obey (Weber 1994: 354). This question demands that we recognise that those doing the obeying have a choice and brings us to our proposal for bettering our understanding of the social sources of institutional change.

Manoeuvre one: Intentional Rationality

Like Max Weber's question of why men and women obey those who seek to govern them, the question 'how should the economy work?' seeks to get inside processes of rationalisation and reveal how changes in conventions and norms inform institutional change. In principle it seeks to identify the everyday 'thinkability' of institutional change (Hopf 2002: 15). As such, the starting methodological position is ideally individualist but *idiographic* rather than *nomothetic* (Seabrooke 2006: 44-47, 201-3). Rather than assuming, as rationalist institutionalists tend to, that there are natural forms of behaviour, an idiographic position asserts that there is nothing 'natural' about man whatsoever.

Jens Beckert's (1996, 2003, 2005) work on uncertainty and the moral embeddedness of markets provides some conceptual clarification on how we might think about rationalisation and rationality. Beckert proposes we try to understand the *intention* of actions, rather than the actor's access to information (1996: 819-22). This 'intentional rationality' provides a distinction from the typical discussions of 'bounded rationality' within political economy literature (Goldstein and Keohane 1993; Odell 2002), primarily because the 'bounded' implies that taking the blinkers off would provide a superior and 'natural' rationality. Rather, intentional rationality is contextualised within a local system of meaning in which actors want to improve their welfare (Beckert 2003: 770-1, 773-5). Situating the intentions of the actor then requires us to try to understand the everyday environment in which the choices are made since the 'situation itself constitutes pre-reflexive aspirations and tendencies which are present in the actor' (Beckert 2003: 774). An actor's routines and conventions are not inviolable, however, and the individual may shape them when dissatisfied with the result of the 'normal' way of doing things. Intentional rationality calls us to understand the moral components of economic beliefs and actions.

The concept of intentional rationality marries well with what I have inelegantly called 'axiorational' behaviour: belief-driven actions that are informed (not determined) by conventions and norms (Seabrooke 2006: 44-47; Boudon 2001: 93-110). Like intentional rationality, the notion of axiorational behaviour intends to provide us with the idea that instrumental and value forms of rationality are entwined, and that they cannot be understood as fixed conditions, or universalised or naturalised. From this point of view, norms are not simply constraints and obligations, but instead common forms of behaviour within a larger aggregation. Norms are larger schemes of 'how to do things', rather than proclamations of what ought to be done from ideational entrepreneurs that provide information actors may *choose* to act upon through conventions (Seabrooke and Sending 2007). Once more, the selection of conventions is the actor's choice and reflects changes in axiorational behaviour (Seabrooke 2006: 47-51). Actors are therefore not trapped within a 'logic of appropriateness' from which they cannot escape (Sending 2002).

Following this emphasis on agency, attempting to unravel the intentional rationality of actors in time and space is also important if we seek to provide a substantive conception of legitimacy. While legitimacy is a concept commonly associated with a set of beliefs or rhetorical claims, legitimation require *belief-driven actions* rather than talk alone (cf. Jackson 2006). Claims to legitimation made by those who govern (see Barker 2001) must be conferred or rejected by those who are governed over (Beetham 1991). Mapping out the intentions behind belief-driven actions therefore provides not only a story of how rulers maintain power, but how they are constrained (Bendix 1978). It is this notion of legitimacy as the contestation of power that is critical to understanding institutional and social change, particularly because it encourages us to see mechanisms of governance at work rather than conditions of rule. Given this the question 'how *should* the economy work?' may also be recast as 'what are the intentions behind your actions as you seek to transform your economy to realise your life chances?' As we cannot help but transform our economies, overwhelmingly in small incremental ways, understanding one another's intentions is important (Hobson and Seabrooke 2007, Chapter 1). And understanding how intentions are translated into particular types of action requires us to specify social mechanisms of change.

Manoeuvre two: Social Mechanisms in Contextual Constellations

Political economy may learn from Weberian methodological tools, as well as the work on social mechanisms found in economic and political sociology. First, to what political economy can learn from Weberian methodological tools. While the notion of 'ideal types' is commonly understood within political economy, their operationalisation is less clear. Ideal types are intended to be the *scholar's* construction, abstractions derived from empirical observation, which are then used to highlight variations in empirical phenomena by means of imputation from comparison (Weber 1973: 191; Weber 1978). As abstractions, ideal types rely on thick narratives to tell the scholars where the types fail to represent reality (Crouch 2005: 57). Ideal types are made to be broken. The notion of the 'Weberian state', for example, is such an abstraction that must be contextualised within the constellation of the period being considered (Hobson and Seabrooke 2001: 259-263). Similarly, we may identify an 'ideal typical' form of financial investment that draws capital from ordinary citizens and sends it through varied financial institutions and out to the world economy (Seabrooke 2007a). But such an ideal type would rarely be seen in reality. Instead it is used as a benchmark against which to compare different political and economic systems in different periods of time, in order to highlight how they differ in their contextual constellations.

Second, to social mechanisms and contextual constellations. As discussed by Randall Collins, the role of unique constellations of events underpins Weber's analysis of the rise of modern capitalism (exemplified in Weber 1961; cf. Weber 1998):

> Weber saw the rise of large-scale capitalism ... as the result of a series of combinations of conditions which had to occur together. This makes world history look like the result of configurations of events so rare as to appear accidental. Weber's position might well be characterized as historicist, in the sense of seeing history as a concatenation of unique events and unrepeatable complexities (Collins 1992: 97-8).

So while Weber discusses capitalism as a type of economic system, he stresses how it changes and recombines within different contextual constellations. Change in history is viewed as recombinant, as a ramble rather than a march, in which the scholar can use ideal types and social mechanisms to highlight what is unique about the policy choices made and what alternative paths may have been followed.

Figure 4: History as Contextual Constellations

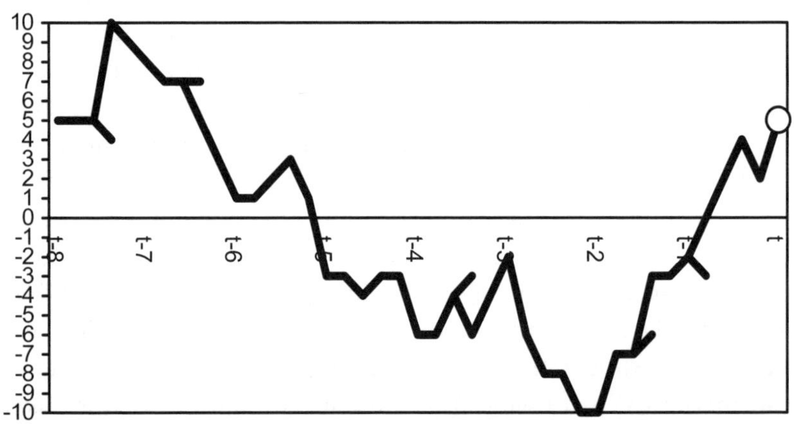

Such a view of history is illustrated in Figure 4, which provides a highly exaggerated depiction of historical change as a ramble. As with the figures above, on the y-axis we have a policy choice set, while on the x-axis we have eight time periods, which takes us from the past to the present at *t*. The actor at the white circle at *t* looks back into the past and sees that the policy in question has roamed across the choice set, recombining itself at points that do not necessary coincide with the time periods we have predefined. The actor also notes that some policy options from the choice set ran consecutively, with some leading to dead – ends while others informed future policies. As such, the kinds of 'non-decisions' that Susan Strange referred to as essential to understanding change in the world economy become important (1988: 22). Given that policy options range across the choice set, that they do not match up with preconceived ideas of 'critical junctures', that often two policies are experimented with at the same time, and that the pace of change in policy options is irregular, our actor at t is required to do two things. The first is to consider the role of counterfactuals in why one path was taken and not the other. Posing counterfactuals provides the means to test alternative explanations that can enhance historical understanding of contests between different groups (Fearon 1991). They are particularly powerful because they ask us to locate the intentions of the actors involved.

Second, the actor at t may find more use in exploring social mechanisms, that is, 'small and medium-sized descriptions of ways in which things happen' within a specified context (Elster 1989: 3). The key notion behind the use of social mechanisms is that they help to avoid functionalist traps, where institutional outcomes are explained by their consequences. Instead, social mechanisms seek to understand types of behaviour among individuals and groups of individuals within a contextual constellation (McAdam, Tarrow, and Tilly 2001; Hedström and Swedberg 1998).

For example, in a recent work I identify three social mechanisms involved in the politics of taxation, credit, and property regimes that typify struggles between groups of individuals on below median income (but not poor), the state, and 'rentier' interests who seek to concentrate financial wealth away from broader society (Seabrooke 2006; Seabrooke 2007a). The three social mechanisms of *contestation*, *redistribution*, and *propagation* are evident within England and Germany prior to the Great War and in the U.S. and Japan in the last quarter century. *Contestation* is evident in times when people on below median income call upon ideational resources to reject state policies and rentier behaviour, *redistribution* involves the state's shifting of assets and access to resources from one social group to another, and *propagation* is where the state makes claims to the legitimacy of its actions, providing ideational resources to people on below median income to confer or to reject the claim and, in doing so, feedback information for further contestation (Seabrooke 2006: 49-53). In each case how the mechanism operates differs according to the social and historical context, and the question of how these actors believe the economy should work informs their actions since each step is not only a fight over material resources but also the presentation of normative claims. The point here is also that by identifying smaller behavioural processes within what would commonly be considered a clunky independent variable (i.e., 'state intervention') we can identify counterintuitive information. For example, I argue that that U.S. financial power in part relies on regulation that enhances creditworthiness assessment for people on below-median incomes – especially for the 'lower-middle classes' – that demonstrates positive forms of state intervention (Seabrooke 2006, Chapter 5). Such a finding does not sit well with the idea of the U.S. as the ideal typical 'LME' or the world's most 'neoliberal' economy (Hall and Soskice 2001). And once we learn of counterintuitive developments within one economy then we also have a different take on what informs the character of the world economy. Without including information about non-elites' belief-driven actions, we are always left trying to identify the strongest player in the game, rather than how the game is being played.

Conclusion: Expanding Policy Imagination

This chapter hopes to enhance policy imagination by widening the scope of political economy scholarship. By treating history as contextual constellations, in which our aim is to identify the intentional rationality of actors and the social mechanisms through which they affect change, we can hope to reveal new information that can expand policy imagination to deal with contemporary problems. It has been argued here that asserting the independent causal effect of 'ideas' or 'norms' or 'material' factors to counter prior arguments creates unnecessary abstractions and narrows the range of a policy choice set. The 'what matters' debate in political economy may produce tighter explanations of what occurred, but increasingly unconvincing understandings of how institutions and societies change over time. This chapter makes a case for why studies of historical change in political economy should not favour a view of policy choice sets as confirming to a climacteric, a national trajectory, or under the control of ideational entrepreneurs. Rather, as Colin Crouch (2005) has recently clarified, selection within a policy choice set is highly recombinant over time and can often break with perceived fixed path dependencies.

Finally, because institutions change through politics, the relationship between those who claim the right to govern and those who can choose to provide or withdraw their consent is crucial to understand. Policy imagination can be enriched by viewing legitimacy as contestation rather than established by elite command or proclamation (Seabrooke 2006, Chapter 2). Understanding how society at large provides impulses to elites and to formal institutions for policy change over time can widen policy imagination our contemporary world in a progressive manner. In doing so we seek to enhance political economy as an enterprise concerned with the betterment of the human condition rather than the replication of scholarly abstractions.

Notes

This chapter draws excerpts from Leonard Seabrooke 2007, 'Why Political Economy Needs Historical Sociology', *International Politics*, 44 (4), pp. 390-413. The piece has greatly benefited from conversations with Mark Blyth, Anna M. Carnerup, Benjamin de Carvalho, John M. Hobson, Carmen Huckel, Peter Katzenstein, Peer Hull Kristensen, George Lawson, Halvard Leira, Arthur Mühlen-Schulte, Ole Jacob Sending, and Shogo Suzuki. Special thanks go to André Broome for his extensive comments on earlier drafts.

References

Amoore, L., R. Dodgson, R. Germain, B.K. Gills, P. Langley and I. Watson 2000, 'Paths to a Historicized International Political Economy', in *Review of International Political Economy*, 7 (1), pp. 53-71.

Barker, R. 2001, *Legitimating Identities*, Cambridge University Press, Cambridge.

Beckert, J. 1996, 'What is Sociological about Economic Sociology? Uncertainty and the Embeddedness of Economic Action', in *Theory and Society*, 25 (6), pp. 803-40.

Beckert, J. 2003, 'Economic Sociology and Embeddedness. How Shall We Conceptualize Economic Action?', in *Journal of Economic Issues*, 37 (3), pp. 769–787.

Beckert, J. 2005, 'Trust and the Performative Construction of Markets', in *MPIfG Discussion Paper*, 05/8, Max Planck Institute for the Study of Societies, Cologne.

Beetham, D. 1991, *The Legitimation of Power*, Macmillan, London.

Bendix, R. 1977, *Nation-Building and Citizenship*, University of California Press, Berkeley.

Bendix, R. 1978, *Kings and Peoples*, University of California Press, London.

Bendix, R. 1984, *Force, Fate and Freedom*, University of California Press, London.

Best, J. 2005, *The Limits of Transparency*, Cornell University Press, Ithaca.

Blyth, M. 2002, *Great Transformations*, Cambridge University Press, Cambridge.

Blyth, M. 2003, 'Same as it Never was? Typology and Temporality in the Varieties of Capitalism', in *Comparative European Politics*, 1 (2), pp. 215-225.

Boudon, R. 2001, *The Origin of Values*, Transaction Publishers, New Brunswick.

Campbell, J.L. 2004, *Institutional Change and Globalization*, Princeton University Press, Princeton.

Campbell, J.L. and O.K. Pedersen 1996, 'The Evolutionary Nature of Revolutionary Change in Postcommunist Europe', in J.L. Campbell and O.K. Pedersen (eds.), *Legacies of Change*, Aldine de Gruyter, New York.

Collins, R. 1992, 'Weber's Last Theory of Capitalism' in M. Granovetter and R. Swedberg (eds.), *The Sociology of Economic Life*, Westview Press, Boulder.

Cortell A. P. and S. Peterson (eds.) 2002, *Altered States*, Lexington Books, Lanham.

Crouch, C. 2005, *Capitalist Diversity and Change*, Oxford University Press, Oxford.

Elias, N. 1996, *The Germans*, Columbia University Press, New York.

Elster, J. 1989, *Nuts and Bolts for the Social Sciences*, Cambridge University Press, Cambridge.

Evans, P.B. 1995, *Embedded Autonomy*, Princeton University Press, Princeton.

Fearon, J.D. 1991, 'Counterfactuals and Hypothesis Testing in Political Science', in *World Politics*, 43 (2), pp. 169-95.

Finnemore, M. and K. Sikkink 1998, 'International Norms Dynamics and Political Change', in *International Organization*, 52 (4), pp. 887-917.

Germain, R.D. 1997, *The International Organization of Credit*, Cambridge University Press, Cambridge.

Germain, R.D. and M. Kenny 1998, 'Engaging Gramsci: International Relations Theory and the New Gramscians', in *Review of International Studies*, 24 (1), pp. 3-21.

Gill, G. 2002, *The Nature and Development of the Modern* State, Palgrave Macmillan, Basingstoke.
Gilpin, R. 1975, *U.S. Power and the Multinational Corporation*, Macmillan, London.
Gilpin, R. 1981, *War and Change in World Politics*, Cambridge University Press, New York.
Gilpin, R. 1987, *The Political Economy of International Relations*, Princeton University Press, Princeton.
Goldstein, J. and R.O. Keohane 1993, 'Ideas and Foreign Policy: An Analytical Framework', in J. Goldstein and R.O. Keohane (eds.), *Ideas and Foreign Policy*, Caornell University Press, Ithaca.
Greif, A. 1994, 'Cultural Beliefs and the Organization of Society: A Historical and Theoretical Reflection on Collectivist and Individualist Societies', in *Journal of Political Economy*, 102 (5), pp. 912-50.
Greif, A. 2006, *Institutions and the Path to the Modern* Economy, Cambridge University Press, Cambridge.
Hall, P.A. (ed.) 1989, *The Political Power of Economic Ideas*, Princeton University Press, Princeton.
Hall, P. and D. Soskice (eds.) 2001, *The Varieties of Capitalism*, Oxford University Press, Oxford.
Hedström, P. and R. Swedberg 1998, 'Social Mechanisms: An Introductory Essay', in P.
Hedström and R. Swedberg (eds.), *Social Mechanisms*, Cambridge University Press, Cambridge.
Hobson, J.M. 1997, *The Wealth of States*, Cambridge University Press, Cambridge.
Hobson, J.M. and L. Seabrooke 2001, 'Reimagining Weber: Constructing International Society and the Social Balance of Power', in *European Journal of International Relations*, 7 (2), pp. 239-274.
Hobson, J.M. and L. Seabrooke (eds.) 2007, *Everyday Politics of the World Economy*, Cambridge University Press, Cambridge.
Hopf, T. 2002, *Social Construction of International Politics*, Cornell University Press, Ithaca.
Jackson, P.T. 2006, *Civilizing the Enemy*, A. Arbor, University of Michigan Press.
Katzenstein, P.J. 1996, *Cultural Norms and National Security*, Ithaca: Cornell University Press.
Katzenstein, P.J., R.O. Keohane and S.D. Krasner 1998, 'International Organization and the Study of World Politics', in *International Organization*, 52 (4), pp. 645-685.
Mahoney, J. and D. Rueschemeyer (eds.) 2003, *Comparative Historical Analysis in the Social* Sciences, Cambridge University Press, Cambridge.
Mann, M. 1986, *The Sources of Social Power*, vol. 1, Cambridge University Press, Cambridge.
Mann, M. 1993, *The Sources of Social Power*, vol. 2, Cambridge University Press, Cambridge.
March, J.G. and J.P. Olsen 1989, *Rediscovering Institutions*, Free Press, New York.
McAdam, D., S. Tarrow and C. Tilly 2001, *Dynamics of Contention*, Cambridge University Press, Cambridge.

McNamara, K.R. 1998, *The Currency of Ideas*, Cornell University Press, Ithaca.

Modelski, G. and W.R. Thompson 1996, *Leading Sectors and World Power*, University of South Carolina Press, Columbia.

Murphy, R. and C.N. Murphy (eds.) 1991, *The New International Political Economy*, Lynne Reinner, Boulder.

North, D.C. 1990, *Institutions, Institutional Change and Economic* Performance, Cambridge University Press, Cambridge.

Odell, J.S. 2002, 'Bounded Rationality and the World Political Economy: The Nature of Decision Making', in D.M. Andrews, C.R. Henning and L.W. Pauly (eds.), *Governing the World's Money*, Cornell University Press, Ithaca.

Parsons, C. 2003, *A Certain Idea of Europe*, Cornell University Press, Ithaca.

Pierson, P. 2004, *Politics in Time*, Princeton University Press, Princeton.

Pijl, K. Van der 1998, *Transnational Classes and International Relations*, Routledge/RIPE Series in Global Political Economy, London.

Seabrooke, L. 2001, *US Power in International Finance*, Palgrave Macmillan, Basingstoke.

Seabrooke, L. 2004, 'The Economic Taproot of US Imperialism: The Bush Rentier Shift', in *International Politics*, 41 (3), pp. 293-318.

Seabrooke, L. 2006, *The Social Sources of Financial Power*, Cornell University Press, Ithaca.

Seabrooke, L. 2007a, 'Everyday Legitimacy and International Financial Orders: The Social Sources of Imperialism and Hegemony in Global Finance', in *New Political Economy*, 12 (1), pp. 1-18.

Seabrooke, L. 2007b, 'Institutional Change and the Social Sources of American Economic Empire: Beyond Stylised Facts', in *Political Studies Review*, 5 (1), pp. 11-24.

Seabrooke, L. 2007c, 'The Everyday Social Sources of Economic Crises: From »Great Frustrations« to »Great Revelations« in Interwar Britain', in *International Studies Quarterly*, 51 (4), pp. 795-810.

Seabrooke, L. and O.J. Sending 2007, *Norms are Doing Things vs. Norms as Things to Do: Cultural Toolkits and Strategic Action in World Politics*, unpublished manuscript, Norwegian Institute of International Affairs, Oslo, March.

Sending, O.J. 2002, 'Constitution, Choice and Change: Problems with the »Logic of Appropriateness« and Its Use in Constructivist Theory', in *European Journal of International Relations*, 8 (4), pp. 443-470.

Skocpol, T. 1979, *States and Social* Revolutions, Cambridge University Press, Cambridge.

Somers, M.R. 1998, 'We're No Angels: Realism, Rational Choice, and Relationality in Social Science', in *American Journal of Sociology*, 104 (3), pp. 722-784.

Steinmo, S., K. Thelen and F. Longstreth (eds.) 1992, *Structuring Politics*, Cambridge University Press, Cambridge.

Strange, S. 1988, *States and Markets*, Pinter Publishers, London.

Thelen, K. 2004, *How Institutions Evolve*, Cambridge University Press, Cambridge.

Wallerstein, I. 1979, *The Capitalist World* Economy, Cambridge University Press, Cambridge.

Weber, M. 1961, *General Economic History*, Collier Books, New York.

Weber, M. 1973, *Gesammelte Aufsätze zur Wissenschaftslehre*, J.C.B. Mohr, Tübingen.
Weber, M. 1976, *The Protestant Ethic and the Spirit of Capitalism*, George Allen and Unwin Ltd., London.
Weber, M. 1978, *Economy and Society*, vols. I and II, University of California Press, Berkeley.
Weber, M. 1994, *Political Writings*, Cambridge University Press, Cambridge.
Weber, M. 1998, *The Agrarian Sociology of Ancient Civilizations*, Verso, London.
Weiss, L. 1998, *The Myth of the Powerless State*, Cornell University Press, Ithaca.
Whitford, J. 2005, *The New Old Economy*, Oxford University Press, Oxford.

CHAPTER 11

Liberal Machiavellianism

John A. Hall

Professor, McGill University, Canada

Introduction

Ove K. Pedersen has spent much of his career thinking about the roles played by varied sorts of states within the historical record. Apparently this intellectual preference derives not just from an early exposure to Hegel, but also from nothing less than *yearly* re-reading *The Phenomenology of Spirit*. If this is an extraordinary feat in Anglo-Saxon eyes, it is certainly a meritorious one. For Hegel's views on the state are determinedly realistic, particularly when contrasted to Marx's fantasies about `the withering away' of the forces of coercion. Nonetheless, the contribution to state theory that I wish to make in this essay derives from Machiavelli rather than Hegel. The Florentine is more concerned with the business of rule than Hegel, perhaps because the latter is so sure that the Prussian state represents the end point in the history of state formation. Accordingly, a Machiavellian perspective allows us to think about modern states – that is, states whose character has certainly advanced beyond the absolutism of early nineteenth century Prussia.

Perhaps everything in life has an opportunity/cost attached to it. If one is deeply grateful for the sophistication of the Cambridge school of intellectual historians on account of their ability to discover context and intention, one sometimes misses simpler and old fashioned views of political theorists. In this case, I will bracket (at least for now) discoveries about Machiavelli's republicanism – that is, about the Machiavelli of *The Discourses*, the prophet of active citizenship and liberty – so as to concentrate on the adviser to princes. *The Prince* itself is concerned most of all with how to hold new territory, from which derive various principles of rule that led to Machiavelli gaining the reputation as a bad man. I have always had a divided view about this. On the one hand, there is a very great deal to be said for the view that politics is not moral, that its language is violence, and that it is a mistake to enter this world with a view to saving one's soul. In this matter Machiavelli's great descendants are of course Max Weber (1946) and Raymond Aron (1983: 22-3), both of whom wrote on the nature of the political with enormous force. On the other hand, and perhaps because of this very understanding, it seems to me that there *is* much to approve morally in some of the points made by a purportedly bad man. Machiavelli is right when insisting that it is dangerous to seek to please too easily, to dispense goodies of one sort or another to the extent of bankrupting the state – thereby leading to arbitrary policies likely to create resentment and opposition. The more general point that Machiavelli makes in connection with this is – to use modern words – that politics do not matter most of the time for most citizens. Hence any injury, any act of visceral coercion, should be inflicted at the start of a period of rule, so that it can then be forgotten during extended periods of benign regularity.

This is the insight that leads to Liberal Machiavellianism, a principle whose central insight is best stated bluntly at the start before then assembling material designed to justify endorsing it. One element to modernity is surely the entry of the people onto the political stage, both as classes and nations. Liberal Machiavellianism claims that political integration is the best route to order, that softer political rule de-radicalizes. Liberalism is desirable, to emphasize the point, for Hobbesian reasons.

A moment's reflection even at this point can make something clear. If there is a striking interest here in the nature of rule, this does not rule out proper social science. Very much to the contrary: rule can only be effective if it is based on genuine social understanding. To that end I begin with the challenges posed to old regimes in Europe by socialism and nationalism – that is, by the people in their two (and often interrelated) forms – so as to establish sociological truths. This then leads to more pointed comments about the nature of state policies. I conclude with reflections on social theory, seeking to bring to our attention theories too often forgotten in a world in which assumptions about the political derive from Greek sources – that is, from a world in which political participation was seen as the ultimate good.

The Sociology of Working Classes to 1914

The most obvious, appropriate and helpful place to begin is with the greatest theorist of socialism, Karl Marx. The expectation of Marx and most Marxists in the years before the First World War was clear: workers had no countries, and so would inevitably be forced to unite as a solidary class because of the inherent contradictions of the capitalist mode of production. In retrospect, we can see that the decision of workers to fight for their countries in 1914 was the first piece of writing on the wall indicating limits to the secular religion that is Marxism. But what matters here is something entirely different, namely the variation in working class behavior in the years before the onset of war.

Let us construct an imaginary scale of radicalism or political consciousness – as we must if we wish to be true to historical experience – and then turn to an explanation of its character.[1] At one end of such a scale is the United States, bereft of any mass socialist movement then and now. More radicalism is apparent in British politics which had generated a Labour Party in the early years of the twentieth century. But the radicalism of British workers was not deep, as can be seen by looking at two cases at the other end of the scale. Marx's greatest hopes were reserved for German workers, not surprisingly as they possessed genuine political consciousness, expressed in 1912 in the electoral surge of the SPD. Samuel Gompers and Arthur Henderson knew of Marxist ideas, but resisted them as foreign and dangerous; in contrast, Marx's ideas were well known to many manual workers in Germany. Still, the farthest point on the scale belongs to Russian rather than to German workers. The point can be made bluntly: in 1917 the workers of St Petersburg and Moscow

1. This scale is based on the work of Mann (1993, chapters 15, 17, and 18).

put up barricades in the streets, creating the situation of dual power famously described by Trotsky in his *History of the Russian Revolution*. Such workers were genuinely revolutionary, prepared to act without intellectual guidance, and clearly less respectable and orderly than their German colleagues. These staccato points lead to a single conclusion, namely that Marx was wrong, even for his own time. There was no single working class, rather working classes of particular countries. Let us see what was involved by country so that the variation can then be properly explained.

Workers in the United States were militant at the industrial level, but lacked any alternative political consciousness because the state was, so to speak, their own: for virtually all white males in the United States gained the vote in the 1830s, the age of Andrew Jackson. Doubtless there were other factors: class solidarity was undermined by immigrant labor, whilst one should not discount Werner Sombart's insistence that socialism in America drowned amidst reefs of apple pie (1976). Still, the other cases suggest that the nature of the political regime is the key variable. Thus in Britain the moderation encouraged by the granting of trade union rights, but not votes for all manual workers, was interrupted by the 1902 Taff Vale court decision which seemed to threaten trade union rights. The Labour Party resulted from this moment of putative repression. But any further move towards greater radicalism was prevented by the softer regime of the Liberals in the decade before the war, not least in its restoration of union rights. Equally, regime behavior best explains the radical cases. Anti-socialist laws in Germany from 1878-1890 meant that workers were forced to take on the state precisely because their industrial rights were curtailed. But Imperial Germany was a *Rechtstaat*, and this encouraged legalistic, respectable politics. Imperial Russia was of course very different, autocratic and arbitrary rather than merely authoritarian. The fact that one might be shot for distributing leaflets encouraging a strike meant that the regime as a whole had to be destroyed, not merely its particular flavor of the moment. A necessary caution must be entered here, not least as it so massively supports the general argument. Adapting a phrase of Sartre helps capture the point. Russian workers had existences rather than any single essence. When the regime seemed open to the granting of rights, as it was in the early part of the century, radicalism declined markedly (McDaniel, 1988). Lenin in effect wrote about those moments in *What is to be Done?*, his classic 1903 analysis of workers lacking political consciousness, so stuck in economism that a vanguard party was necessary if revolution was to be achieved. It was the abrupt ending of such political openings that drove workers to revolution.

What is going on is fairly clear. Workers jumped at the chance of reform rather than revolution, preferring to gain industrial benefits through union activity rather than risk being shot at on the barricades. It is equally clear that the character of working class movements derived more from the nature of the political regime with which they interacted than from capitalist social relations. From this derives the point that matters in the context of this essay. Political inclusion contained, even tamed working class demands. It may be worth amplifying the point. It takes a very great deal to make working classes radical, let alone revolutionary – indeed, I can only really think of Russian workers before 1914, Protestant workers in Northern Ireland setting up barricades against power-sharing agreements in the 1970s and the Polish workers of Solidarity as true political agents. Capitalism when left to itself does not occasion violent conflict from below. Clearly, liberalism is justified for Machiavellian reasons.

Two qualifications need to be made to the highly simplified picture that has been presented. The first is historical. Elite treatment of working classes changed notably after the First World War, with fascist regimes sometimes seeking to mobilize rather that to contain popular pressure. The second qualification concerns liberalism itself. It is important to remember that there were in fact two sides to liberal behavior. If one side allowed entry into politics, another side was capable of extreme viciousness towards small groups of extremists. The British state sent Chartist leaders to Australia, whilst worker deaths in the United States in the nineteenth century were second only to those in Tsarist Russia (Mann, 1993, chapters 15 and 18). This complete strategy of liberalism in practice – at once offering an opening to the many whilst seeking to crush the few – is of course entirely in accord with the spirit of *The Prince*.

The Sociology of Nations

An oddity of modern social science is the relative lack of neglect shown to the national question given that its impact on the historical record has been so much greater than that of socialism. The neglect can be explained. For one thing, nationalism came to be associated with imperialism, and with Nazism in particular; curiously social science seems not to wish to study social actions that it deems – correctly – to be morally repulsive. For another, the national question has been very largely solved in the advanced West – which is where most organized social inquiry takes place. Denmark is no exception to this rule, having solved its own national questions as the result of its marvelous capacity to lose wars and thereby to downsize its territory to a homogeneous core.

But the neglect need not cause us much worry, for the analytic sociology emphasized here goes a very long way to explaining the incidence of nationalism – understood initially as secession, that is, as the search by nations for survival and security of their own ways of life, whether historic or newly created. One can begin with the classic case of the Czechs in the nineteenth century.[2] There was nothing inevitable about the creation of a Czech nation-state. Very much to the contrary, virtually every Czech national leader in the nineteenth century merely sought for cultural autonomy under the protection of the Hapsburgs. The logic to this position was very clearly articulated by Frantisek Palacky in 1848 when arguing for a Slav Congress in Prague – in opposition of course to the liberal meeting held in Frankfurt at that time. The Czechs feared being absorbed by Germany, and were quite as afraid of Russia. If Austria did not exist, Palacky argued, it would have been necessary to invent her.

Nonetheless, the Czechs did eventually gain their state, and it is important to explain this development. National movements reflect the character of the states with which they interact quite as much as do the movements of working classes. The Czech national movement was not particularly radical, that is, it did not seek independence, so long as there was sufficient hope that the Hapsburgs would allow for cultural auton-

2. My view of Czech nationalism is much influenced by Peter Bugge's important *Czech Nation-Building, National Self-Perception and Politics, 1780-1914* (1994).

omy within their empire. For long periods there was every reason to believe that such hopes were realistic: linguistic and educational rights were granted, as was a measure of self-government. In the last analysis, however, the Hapsburgs baulked at the granting of real autonomy: in the early years of the First World War it became clear that the constitutional monarchy for which the Czechs longed was being rule out of court. It was these circumstances that finally convinced Tomas Masaryk that national independence had to be sought. The situation as a whole can accordingly be captured in theoretical terms derived from Albert Hirschman (1970). Loyalty is created by voice, the desire for exit by it absence. This of course is but another way of expressing the central argument of this paper. Liberal policies are the best way of containing nationalist excess. Liberal Machiavellianism once again gains intellectual support.

Even cursory reference to other cases can make it clear that there is nothing peculiar about the Czechs. The Finns were granted very great autonomy by the Tsars for most of the nineteenth century, and accordingly were exceptionally loyal subjects. But a drive for independence was created at the turn of the new century in response to imperial policies designed to homogenize and integrate all imperial territories. The sudden privileging of Russian as the official language of the empire threatened to diminish the status of Finns who of course reacted in consequence. The Ukraine had never been accorded cultural rights, but was faced by something much worse by the end of the century. Russians were a minority in their own empire – unless Ukrainians could be seen as `little Russians', thereby making the construction of a nation-state that much easier (Lieven 2000). Absolute repression created a drive for exit. I have been witness to exactly the same considerations in Quebec. The core liberalism of the Canadian state makes it very hand indeed to mobilize sufficient support for genuine independence, especially now that the French language is securely protected in Quebec. This is not to say that secession is impossible. What is needed – and what independentist leaders continually seek – is some insult, some moment of repression that will make those who wobble believe that voice is denied to such an extent that exit has become absolutely necessary.

Reprise

The general view being put forward is sufficiently novel as to deserve both re-statement and amplification. The best way to approach the former task is to recall and to celebrate the sociological insights of Ralf Dahrendorf's *Class and Class Conflict in Industrial Societies*. Amplification is best addressed by considering new work in the sociology of revolutions.

Dahrendorf's opposition to the Parsonian view of societies as held together by normative consensus led him to produce a series of abstract propositions about the nature of social conflict. The particular claim of interest here concerns the intensification of conflict. A single conflict is, so to speak, trivial and manageable. Real intensity results when different types of conflict are layered on top of each other (Dahrendorf, 1959, chapter 6). An example given by Dahrendorf himself remains useful. French society has seen intense political conflict because religious and political divisions were layered on top of each other. To be on the left meant that one would inevitably be anticlerical, for the right received the backing of the Catholic Church. The underlying point remains that conflict diffuses through society unless state actions concentrate matters. Differently put, the liberalism of a political regime can defuse tensions throughout society, thereby creating fundamental political stability.

Dahrendorf's principle can easily be illustrated with reference to the field with which he was purportedly concerned, namely that of modern class conflict. Consider Solidarity. The fact that Polish workers were not allowed to have their own unions meant that they had to `take on' the state, because politics and economics were combined in actually existing socialism. The extraordinary consequence of this was that a group of workers in a nearly defunct industry did a very great deal to destroy the socialist state of Poland – thereby putting one of the nails in the Soviet Model, and perhaps in socialism more generally. The point being made – that conflict diffuses through society unless it is artificially concentrated – can be reinforced by considering class conflict in modern Britain. I remember claiming in the early Thatcher years that any massive increase in unemployment caused by her policies would be sure to lead to protest on a very large scale. Unemployment surged, but without much popular reaction. The answer to this conundrum lay most immediately in the fact that the unemployed lost union support, and tended moreover to be older – together with the state's intelligent provision of various social programs for the young. But something much larger was at issue. Social contracts between labor, capital and the state have as a side effect the politicizing of industrial relations – they make the state responsible for levels of employment, and give workers the right of access to political power. Thatcher abolished this connection, the world of `beer and sandwiches' in Downing Street: levels of employment resulted from the impersonal forces of global capitalism, held to be beyond the power of any state to control (Bradley and Gelb 1980).

That the principle of Liberal Machiavellian has reach beyond the sociology of classes and nations can be shown by a cursory look at important recent work on the sociology of revolutions. The flavor of such work is neatly captured in the title of a leading treatise in the field, Jeff Goodwin's *No Other Way Out* (2001). Being shot at, tortured and imprisoned is something to avoid at all costs, if at all possible. But when it is not possible to escape from such treatment, and when life can be dangerous in any case, people do become revolutionaries. The absence of the ability to participate in politics turns people into revolutionaries: normal politics is accordingly a safety valve, diminishing the intensity of conflict. A member of the traditional elite of his society, Vaclav Havel, only moved into outright opposition because there was no other way to be heard. More generally, Goodwin himself is particularly effective in demonstrating the importance of regime rather than of mere social relations in explaining the incidence of revolution. Capitalist social relations and/or levels of poverty in Central America can not explain the incidence of revolution, for the simple reason that these conditions are essentially similar throughout the region – with revolution occurring in some rather than other countries, in Nicaragua rather than in Costa Rica. One factor that explains this should now be obvious to us: Costa Rica has a long history of liberal politics, in contrast to the Nicaragua of Somoza – which excluded and so radicalized another member of another elite family, Daniel Ortega. If here too Liberal Machiavellianism gains support, it is important to note that Goodwin's complete account pays attention to one further factor. Liberalism most certainly did not characterize Salvador, but that country avoided revolution. What distinguished Salvador from Nicaragua was the presence of genuinely meritocratic, and truly vicious, forces of coercion, in contrast to the nepotistic, `Sultanist' arrangements within Nicaragua. Pure force can sustain a regime, leading in the Salvadorean case to a period of brutal civil war. Nonetheless, the Weberian point – that force is less stable in the long run than legitimate power – remains true, with contemporary Salvador gaining real stability only in the last years when liberal openings have been created.

Past and Present

It takes but a moment to realize how terribly Europe managed the entry of the people onto the political stage. Workers were radicalized in both Imperial Germany and Imperial Russia, causing political difficulties in the former, and a revolution in the latter that led to horrors still not properly told. If nationalist movements did not cause the onset of war, they certainly added to the range and intensity of conflict within Europe during its darkest days, between 1914 and 1945. The principle of one culture per state was fulfilled only by means of population transfer, ethnic cleansing and mass murder, all habitually carried out in the midst of the fog of war. There is accordingly something altogether odd about Europe seeing itself as a fount of wisdom, prepared to offer advice to the developing world. Nonetheless, Europe has now firmly established liberal democratic rule, and it is important to locate some elements of that achievement, before turning to one surprising and substantial achievement of some parts of the developing world.

One fundamental element that helped to create stability for European liberal democracy has been the role played by the United States. European history has been witness to endless wars, of an increasingly destructive character in the industrial age. The United States solved Europe's security problem – and solves it still. Beyond this, however, are factors internal to Europe. Two World Wars provided the incentive, particularly on the part of the Franco-German condominium, to create that greater level of international co-operation within Europe that is the European Union. Crucially, liberal politics emerged from the discrediting of extreme left and extreme right, that is, of those forces which sought to make virtue the business of the state. The defeat of fascism was so total as to rule it out of court completely, with Christian Democracy perhaps doing more than any other force to cement liberalism in postwar Europe. The extreme left was not defeated in battle in the same manner, with the undermining of communist parties in Europe in the immediate postwar years having a good deal to do with American interventionist policies, but it was very largely discredited by the events of 1956, wholly so by the suppression of the Prague Spring. In these circumstances class compromise was possible, blessed above all by the golden years of economic growth characteristic of the *Belle Epoque* of postwar Europe.

Europeans have a right to be proud of real achievements in the postwar period. But pride most certainly should not be excessive, as we can see if we turn from class to nation. There are achievements in this area as well. Geopolitical order has allowed states to be less unitary, with real autonomy being granted to regions of Britain and Spain. But the fundamental reason for the lack of continuing conflict over the national question is altogether brutal. The national question no longer exists in most of Europe: it was 'solved' by the horrors of twentieth century politics. Before 1914 perhaps twenty-five million Europeans lived in states ruled by people not co-cultural with themselves. This was considerably reduced by the creation of new states in 1918 and 1919. Still, many of those states had significant minorities within them, and it took the Second World War to create real national homogeneity in Central and Eastern Europe. We have of course witnessed the completion of this dreadful history in the third set of Balkan wars that followed the dissolution of Yugoslavia (Mann, 1999).

It is at this point that one can point to a marvelous development present in some parts of the developing world. The almost total inability of Europeans to create political regimes within which different nations can live and prosper stands in marked contrast to the situation elsewhere. The classic and most important example is that of India, whose situation is best understood with reference to David Laitin's superlative work on linguistic repertoires (Laitin, 1993). In a nutshell, Laitin argues that active Indian citizenship requires a linguistic repertoire of three plus or minus one languages. Two languages that are clearly necessary are those of Hindi and English, both of which have all-India official status. But most people live within states which have their own language – Tamil for

Tamil Nadu, etc., etc. One needs capacity in only two languages when one's state is Hindi-speaking, but four languages if one happens to be a minority in a non-Hindi-speaking state. Language is of course but one factor which can serve as an integrating symbol for a national movement. Still, it is a vital symbol, making India's success very remarkable indeed.[3] Thanks to the fact that this great part of the developing world has *not* followed the pattern of Europe's past, hundreds of millions of people have avoided violent deaths. The pacifying effects of liberalism are confirmed once again.

Some details and qualifications need to be added to this picture. Support is given to the picture painted of India by the rather different behavior of that state in Kashmir: the lack of liberalism there is the direct cause of secessionist feelings. Then a crucial misunderstanding should be avoided. Though there are a significant number of countries in the developing world that operate with linguistic regimes not dissimilar to those of India, there is no denying the fact that many other states have sought to copy the European route of nations homogenization, often with disastrous consequences. Finally, the bleak comments concerning nationalism in Europe need to be modified. The European Union more or less possesses a linguistic regime that is similar to that of India, a two plus or minus one linguistic repertoire – the language of one's state plus English comprising the standard two, minus that if one is English, with a third language necessary if one is a minority within all national states except for Great Britain (Laitin, 1997). There is accordingly a sense in which a liberal Europe has now become an Austro-Hungary which works – in part though because it has few geopolitical ambitions that would require unitary statehood. But it takes a moment to realize that problems remain within Europe, and detailing one of these can usefully close this section. Laitin is entirely right to suggest that languages can be learnt, allowing for several nations to live within the same political roof. But his model tends to miss class factors that can play a role

3. No claim is being made that the liberalism of language policy is the only factor responsible for political stability in India. The presence of an army that remains the backbone of the state, as well as a measure of unity bred by participation in a mass nationalist movement, clearly have enormous significance as well.

within nationalism. Specifically, it is less easy to be truly fluent in another language, with capacities in writing as well as speaking, than he imagines. Class advantage, the ability to take holidays in other countries and to spend one's children to summer schools in such countries, helps create linguistic repertoires. One form of nationalism that seems to gain prominence in the early years of the new millennium is that of the excluded, that is, those whose class background makes them wish to preserve the benefits of traditional nation-states. Tensions are developing between the internationalism of liberalism and its ability, whether through negative or positive means, to secure social cohesion domestically. Liberalism faces considerable new challenges, and these will require rethinking of some of its core components.

Conclusion: Theories, Restatement Apologia in Anxiety

It may be as well to place the argument in relation to other theorists since this will immediately lead to a summary restatement – which in turn will occasion something of an apologia. Three thinkers can usefully be considered, Smith, Tocqueville and Weber.

One of the oddities of much of social science is the relative neglect of the sociology of Adam Smith. No thinker has done more in my view to understand and to help us to understand the stability of capitalist society. We can reach the core of this thought by insisting that there is no 'Adam Smith problem', that is, there is a perfect fit rather than a clash between the emphasis on sympathy in *The Theory of Moral Sentiments* and the praise given to self-interest in *The Wealth of Nations*. What matters for human beings, in Smith's eyes, is the approval of one's fellows, and this is most often gained through the possession of riches. Social life resembles, to use a modern metaphor, an escalator: distinction is gained by possessing something that those below lack. Smith's world is one of jealousy, rather than one of envy – that is, in which it is normal to try to catch up with the person above one on the slippery slope rather than to create policies designed to level the field, or to change the rules of the game. The clarity with which Smith viewed this system is astonishing. Wealth was but a nonsense in his view:

> [Riches] are immense fabrics, which it requires the labour of a life to raise, which threaten every moment to overwhelm the person that dwells in them, and which wile they stand, though they may save him from some smaller inconveniencies, can protect him from none of the severer inclemencies of the season. They keep off the summer shower not the winter storm, but leave him as much, and sometimes more exposed than before, to anxiety, to fear, and to sorrow; to diseases, to danger and to death (1976: 183).

Nonetheless, the illusion – and illusion it was, utterly dominant in the vulgar for all that the wise could see through it – was beneficial: it created not just industriousness but political stability. Here we have the most brilliant exposition of the view that civil society when left alone will not much concern itself with politics, together with a near Machiavellian view of the advantages of deception. This would be complete Liberal Machiavellianism if more attention were given to political inclusion as the key mechanism leading to political passivity. As it is, Smith's argument is strongest on the way in which society works once a capitalist regime has been established.

A second thinker whose thought has resonates with some of the points made here is Tocqueville. The great French liberal stressed in multiple ways that social forces gain their character from the nature of the states within which they are embedded. One rather neglected example of this concerns civil associations. Such associations were dangerous in France, conspiratorial and convinced of their right to rule, whereas in the United States they served as the training ground for responsible citizenship. The difference was easily explained. Groups which were forced underground became radicalized, prone to believe that they represented the popular will; such delusions were removed by openness, which transmitted a sense of reality (2000: 184-6). More generally, Tocqueville's masterpiece *The Old Regime and the Revolution* insisted that the inability of groups to co-operate with each other resulted from the way in which they had been treated by the state in the past (1998: 170-1). The divide and rule tactics of the Kings of France had taught social groups to distrust, even to hate each other. It was this political culture which made it impossible to consolidate liberal democracy in 1789 – and in 1848. But if Tocqueville resembles Dahrendorf in stressing the importance of regime behavior, he is in fact not a Liberal Machiavellian in the last instance – as we shall see in a moment.

The thinker who stands closest to the general argument is Max Weber. He was well aware that German workers had been turned in a radical direction by the regime's anti-socialist laws, and his views on a reconstructed Germany made it quite clear that a measure of inclusion would make them loyal to the regime Weber (1978). This might seem to make him an exemplar of the Liberal Machiavellianism. But this is not quite so. For Weber despised political passivity. If workers had been unnecessarily radicalized, his fundamental belief was that loyalty to Germany would be active rather than passive – through endorsement of the national principle that he himself held so dear. More generally, his view of democracy emphasized the importance of charismatic leadership, the highlighting of which would allow movement rather than stagnation in a society.

These thinkers illustrate perfectly elements within Liberal Machiavellianism, namely the realization that civil society 'normally' operates according to its own logic, the insistence that political consciousness is created by the demands of an interfering state, and the discovery that liberal inclusion can defang or contain radicalism. It is of course the combination of these insights that makes Liberal Machiavellianism a complete and original position.

It is not a nice position, being so to speak left-handed or paradoxical in endorsing liberal practices almost in opposition to the spirit in which they were created and for which they were intended. Perhaps this does not matter. Surely it is better to be intellectually powerful than politically correct, especially in an intellectual environment in which hope so often triumphs over historical experience. But it is as well to note the fundamental presupposition that lies behind Liberal Machiavellianism, namely that civil society can and will operate on its own, if the state allows that to happen. This is accurate sociology in normal times. But times are not always normal. The classic instance of this not being so is of course that of Weimar Germany. Political order could not be achieved passively, by allowing economic growth to paper over political cracks. In these circumstances, the lack of positive enthusiasm for liberal democracy came to matter. So in the end we are returned to the Machiavelli of the *Discourses*, and to Tocqueville's great warning about self-interest properly understood (2000: 514-7) – that is, to an appreciation that negative rule is not always enough, powerful and unrecognized though it is for most daily circumstances of modernity.

References

Aron, R. 1983, *Memoires*, Julliard, Paris.

Bradley, K. and A. Gelb 1980, 'The Radical Potential of Cash Nexus Breaks', in *British Journal of Sociology*, vol. 31.

Bugge, P. 1994, *Czech Nation-Building, National Self-Perception and Politics, 1780-1914*, Ph.D. Dissertation, University of Aarhus.

Dahrendord, R. 1959, *Class and Class Conflict in Industrial Societies*, Stanford University, Standford.

Goodwin, J. 2001, *No Other Way Out: States and Revolutionary Movements, 1945-91*, Cambridge University Press, Cambridge.

Hirschman, A. 1970, *Exit, Voice and Loyalty: Respones to Decline in Firms, Organizations and States*, Harvard University Press, Cambridge (MA).

Laitin, D.D. 1993, *Language Repertoires and State Construction in Africa*, Cambridge University Press, Cambridge.

Laitin, D.D. 1997, 'The Cultural Identities of a European State', in *Politics and Society*, vol. 25.

Lieven, D. 2000, *Empire: the Russian Empire and Its Rivals*, John Murray, London.

Mann, M. 1993, 'The Sources of Social Power', in *Volume Two: The Rise of Classes and Nation-States, 1760-1914*, Cambridge University Press, Cambridge.

Mann, M. 1999, 'The Dark Side of Democracy: the Modern Tradition of Ethnic and Political Cleansing', in *New Left Review*, no. 235.

McDaniel, T. 1988, *Autocracy, Capitalism and Revolution in Russia*, University of California Press, Berkeley.

Smith, A. 1976, *The Theory of Moral Sentiments*, Oxford University Press, Oxford.

Sombart, W. 1976, *Why Is There No Socialism in the United States?*, Macmillan, London.

Tocqueville, A. 1998, *The Old Regime and the Revolution*, Chicago University Press, Chicago.

Tocqueville, A. 2000, *Democracy in America*, Chicago University Press, Chicago.

Weber, M. 1948, `Politics as a Vocation', in H.H. Gerth and C.W. Mills (eds.), from Max Weber, Oxford University Press, New York.

Weber, M. 1978, 'Parliament and Government in a Reconstructed Germany', in G. Roth and C. Wittich (eds.), *Economy and Society*, University of California Press, Berkeley.

CHAPTER 12

Transnational Regulation: Europeanization of Nordic Central Governments

Per Lægreid, Runolfur Smari Steinthorsson & Baldur Thorhallsson
Professor, University of Bergen, Norway, Professor, University of Iceland, Iceland and Professor, University of Iceland, Iceland

Introduction

This chapter addresses how the tasks and functions of control and regulation in ministries and central agencies in Denmark, Finland, Iceland, Norway and Sweden have changed as a result of increased integration into the European Union (EU). The Nordic countries represent a regional cluster that is highly integrated politically but less so regarding polity (Dyson and Goetz 2003). There are significant differences between the Nordic countries in how their polities adapt to increased European integration due to variations both in form of affiliation, length of membership, and depth of membership involvement (Jacobsson, Lægreid and Pedersen 2001, 2003). Thus the scope and depth of EU-related regulatory activity might differ between the countries, but also between ministries and agencies and between policy areas.

The focus in this chapter is on a narrow definition of regulation as a) goal formulation, rule making, and standard setting; b) monitoring, information-gathering, scrutiny, inspection, audit, and evaluation; and c) enforcement, behaviour-modification, and the application of rewards and sanctions (Hood, Rothstein and Baldwin 2001: 23). We set out to do two things: 1) to describe the degree of EU regulation in the Nordic countries by focusing on the scope of EU rules and regulations in the domestic administration, the monitoring and control, and the compliance and enforcement; 2) to analyse the variation in regulation, emphasising the importance of structural, cultural, and environmental features in the central government administration. Thus we primarily address the reception, or downloading, of EU regulation domestically by focusing on procedures, practices and activities developed to absorb the EU regulations into the daily work of central administrative bodies (Börzel 2002a). Our focus is on polity features and on how formal and informal regulatory structures, procedures and practices are affected by increased integration into a European regulatory system (Börzel and Risse 2003).

In considering *rule making,* we first examine the degree of change in existing domestic rules and regulations or the introduction of new rules as a consequence of the EU over the past five years. Secondly, we ask if the EU/EEA work has implied changes in the arrangements for control and regulation within the unit's area of responsibility. Thirdly, we examine the degree to which the making and changing of laws, rules, regulations, directives and standards comprises a primary task in the divisions.

The *implementation and monitoring* variables denote whether control, supervision, performance reporting, accounting, auditing and application of rewards and sanctions forms a main emphasis of the section's EU/EEA related work. Secondly, has the extent of control and regulation increased or decreased? Thirdly, we ask how much of their workload has been related to implementation and enforcement of EU/EEA decisions and regulations.

Regarding external *enforcement of and compliance* to rules and regulations, we first ask if the European Commission or national authorities have investigated special EU-related cases in their area of work. Secondly, we question how the court system has been involved in regulation and control concerning EU/EEA related cases. To what degree have national courts and the European Court of Justice been involved?

The data basis is a comparative survey undertaken in Denmark, Sweden, Finland, Norway and Iceland. Having one old member of the EU (Denmark), two new members (Sweden and Finland) and two nonmember states (Iceland and Norway are members of the internal market by the European Economic Area (EEA)) presents us with a unique opportunity for a quasi-experimental design. By studying the five Nordic countries, we include small European countries that share a cultural and geographic region as well as many features of parliamentary government. They differ, however, in their formal relationship to the EU, their length of membership, the size of their administrations, and the national context represented by the administrative tradition and strategy on EU integration.

The survey comprises all ministerial divisions as well as divisions in central agencies and directorates. The survey was first conducted in 1998 and replicated in 2003. We describe the response patterns by asking each individual division about its own experiences with EU/EEA cases. The respondents were asked to answer on behalf of the unit and not on behalf of themselves. A total of 1408 divisions in the five countries replied to the questionnaire in 1998. In 2003 1321 units responded. In 1998 the response rate varied from 86 per cent in Norway to 72 per cent in Iceland. Five years later the response rate varied from 81 per cent in Sweden to 61 per cent in Finland.

The outline of the paper is as follows: firstly, we discuss the development towards transnational regulation by focusing on regulatory development in the EU and its implications for the Nordic countries. Secondly, we present the theoretical perspectives used and the hypotheses that we put forward. Thirdly, we present the empirical results, and finally, we discuss the findings and draw conclusions.

Transnational Regulation

It is necessary to go beyond the rather state-centric approach of the regulatory state approach and to allow for a more transnational regulatory state or regime (Eberline and Grande 2005, Christensen and Lægreid 2006). This approach does not only focus on the European level or on the national level, but argues that there is a horizontal and vertical differentiation of regulatory authority integrating into the European multi-level system of policy-making. The EU is blurring the boundaries of competence and adding new dimensions to regulatory policy. Regulation nowadays includes not only regulation by the state, but also by organizations outside the state (Scott 2003). National administrations are highly integrated into the European regulatory system when it comes to rule making, implementation and enforcement.

Regulation is the most important type of policy-making in the EU, and in the last decade the EU itself has been the subject of a variety of reforms affecting both its own regulatory regime and those of the member states (Armstrong 2000). The creation of the single European market required the liberalization of the utilities sectors, the abolition of national monopolies, and the establishment of independent regulatory agencies in the member states to promote competition. National agencies serve domestic governments, but they also take part in the formulation and implementation of EU policies (Egeberg 2006). Thus the EU has affected the domestic regulatory system.

It is difficult to discern a convergence towards a single and identical regulatory approach in the various countries (Lodge 2001). Different domestic institutional constellations, such as the degree of fragmentation, hierarchy, and policy overlap, tend to create their own logic and dynamic in the process of regulatory reform (Jordana and Sancho 2004). Domestic institutions and traditions represent »filters« producing different outcomes in different countries. Both the domestic arrangements and the national facilitating factors affect the translational regulatory regimes (Börzel and Risse 2000, Knill and Lehmkuhl 1999, Eberline and Grande 2005, Humphrey and Pagdett 2006).

The EU depends on domestic institutions to implement its rules and regulations and there is an increased attention in the EU towards the proper application of existing rules (Sverdrup 2004). There is also a growing literature on the implementation of EU regulations in domestic administrations, focusing on the transposition of EU rules into national legislation and adhering to, complying with, and enforcing them in the different member countries (Bursens 2002; Börzel 2002b; Falkner et al. 2004; Sverdrup 2005; Tallberg 2002). In this paper we will primarily address the question of EU-related rule making, implementation performance and how and to what extent the Nordic governments are being affected by increased European regulation.

Despite the evidence that the Nordic countries are among the best performing countries when it comes to transposing EU directives (Sverdrup 2004) and implementation of EU rules and regulations (Börzel 2002b, Sverdrup 2002), there are variations in their regulatory policies and practices. This is because they have not followed the same adoption pattern to the EU and their form of affiliation differs.

As a consequence of the EEA agreement, Icelandic and Norwegian legislation has to be aligned with that of the EU in a number of areas in order to ensure a congruent legal framework. These two countries have to incorporate all EU legislation of relevance to the market project (Egeberg 2005). Thus, there are similarities between the member and non-member countries when it comes to the domestic transposition of the EU rules. One difference, however, is that the member countries cover a broader scope of policy areas than the non-members.

In order to understand the degree of EU regulation in the Nordic countries, it is obvious that we have to move beyond a simple enforcement perspective to account for the variation in the adoption and practice of regulation. It is necessary to look at the functions of control and regulation from a broader viewpoint.

Understanding EU-Regulation in the Nordic Countries

To provide an understanding of the variation in EU regulation in the Nordic countries, we will distinguish between three perspectives: structural-instrumental, cultural-institutional, and environmental, which stresses the importance of external pressure (Christensen and Lægreid 2001, Jacobsson, Lægreid and Pedersen 2003).

A structural-instrumental perspective

The concept of bounded rationality (March and Simon 1958) implies that decision-makers have limited time and attention and cannot address all goals, all alternatives, and all consequences. They face problems of capacity and understanding and have to make some choices. The formal organizational structure represents one important selection mechanism. Formal structures and procedures organize some actors, cleavages, problems, and solutions into decision-making processes in the public sector, while others are excluded. According to this perspective, formal structure matters. It is not enough to focus on the narrow internal organizational structure of the civil service; their external organization may also play an important role in their behaviour.

Based on this general perspective we will adopt three structural variables: form of affiliation to the EU, administrative level, and administrative size. *Form of affiliation* represents the external organization, and we will distinguish between member countries (Denmark, Sweden and Finland) and EEA members (Iceland and Norway). The first group of countries participates fully in the regulatory decision-making process, while EEA countries only have a consulting role in the preparation phase. The EEA countries have to adopt the EU regulations concerning the internal market but are more loosely coupled to other policy areas. In addition, the EU has more capabilities, longer traditions, and stronger enforcement capacities than the EFTA (Sverdrup 2004). Thus our first hypothesis is that member countries will have a stronger workload of transposition of EU rules and regulation than EEA countries.

Administrative level refers to the internal organization of the civil service. A major distinction in the Nordic central administration is between ministries and central agencies. The main idea is that ministries should prioritise policy advice and planning, but also rule making, while the primary tasks of agencies are policy implementation and monitoring. The different regulatory functions are split between different administrative levels, but there is also a general trend to delegate more regulatory activities to agencies. Thus the hypothesis is that EU-related regulatory activities are more common in agencies than in ministries, especially when it comes to monitoring.

Furthermore, according to the importance of administrative capacity we develop the third structural variable: *size of administration*. In the case of the Nordic states there is a considerable difference in the size of the central administrations in Sweden, Finland, Denmark and Norway on the one hand, and in the central administration in Iceland on the other. Thus, we assume that the small size of the Icelandic administration affects its capacity and how it adapts in regulatory issues and distinguishes it from the other Nordic administrations (Lægreid, Steinthorsson and Thorhallsson 2004). Accordingly, our hypothesis states that Iceland has greater difficulties in adapting to EU/EEA regulatory issues than the other Nordic states because of its limited capacity.

A cultural-institutional perspective

A second set of factors concerns the historical and cultural traditions of political-administrative systems (Selznick 1957). In institutional approaches informal norms, identities and the logic of appropriateness are important (March and Olsen 1989). Norms and values within agencies and central government and internal dynamics are important. Path dependencies constrain what is appropriate and possible to move to agency status and how the agencies will operate. The reform road taken reflects the main features of national institutional processes, where institutional »roots« determine the path followed (Krasner 1988). What happens in one country's administration is not a blueprint for developments in others. Regulatory activities reinforce underlying distinctive national trajectories and historical legacies, and the effects of formal structure are mediated and constrained by contextual factors (Thatcher and Stone Sweet 2002).

We will distinguish between an *East Nordic and a West Nordic administrative culture* tracing back over several hundred years (Jacobsson, Lægreid and Pedersen 2003). The eastern Nordic dualistic model finds its clearest expression in the Swedish national administration. A clear distinction is made between the government and its offices on the one hand and the central agencies on the other. The agencies are formally autonomous of the individual ministers but are subordinated to the government as a whole. Traditionally Finland has been placed in the East Nordic model, but recent changes have weakened this link. The West Nordic model finds its expression in Denmark, Norway and Iceland. In this monistic model ministries are formally responsible for their subordinate agencies based on the principle for ministerial responsibility. One possible consequence of this difference between the east and West Nordic administrative tradition is that the adaptation to EU regulations will be easier in the more integrated West Nordic model than in the east, with stronger and more independent central agencies. The West Nordic Model is in many ways more compatible with the European polity style based on the principle of ministerial responsibility. Thus the hypothesis is that Denmark, Norway, and Iceland will score higher on EU/EEA-related regulatory activity than Sweden and Finland.

Moreover, administrative norms and values in terms of willingness to adapt to new traditions and to implement the bulk of regulations may have profound influences on the success or failure of particular regulations. The Nordic states have been more reluctant to participate in the European integration process than those on the Continent (Jacobsson, Lægreid and Pedersen 2001). As a result, Finland is the only Nordic state to take a full and active part in all aspects of the European integration process. Our concern is the extent to which Euro-scepticism in the Nordic states has influenced the central administrations´ willingness to adopt EU/EEA regulatory issues. In other words, *political and administrative engagement* in European integration may affect the responses of central administrationsto EU/EEA regulatory issues. Thus, our hypothesis is that the central administrations of the partial engagement countries, Iceland, Norway, Denmark and Sweden, are more reluctant to adopt EU/EEA regulatory issues than the pro-European Finland.

External pressure from the EU

A third set of factors describes the autonomy and control of agencies primarily as a response to external pressure from the EU. Seen form this perspective, development within the EU plays a decisive role in what happens in the national administration. The development of the EU, its aspirations and its dynamics, together with its ideas and regulations, explain the actions of the national administration. We will distinguish between three variables: *policy area, time, and length of membership*. First, the pressure from the EU as a regulatory body varies between policy areas. It started and is strongest in the EU's core, related to the four freedoms: free movement of people, capital, goods, and services; the internal market, and the utilities sectors. Competition policy was the first 'supranational' policy in the EU (McGowan and Wilkes 1995). The regulatory pressure will be stronger in the area of economic regulation than in other areas. Thus the hypothesis is that the regulatory activities are more extended within the economic market-oriented industry, business areas and environmental issues than in the soft welfare state sectors such as health or education, and in security and defence issues where decisions are still dominated by domestic decision-makers.

Secondly, we expect *time to* make a difference. The EU is a dynamic organization and the integration process has acquired a new pace in the last five years, representing a stronger regulatory pressure in 2003 than in 1998.

Over time the EU bodies have developed improved methods for controlling compliance and improving their skills and capacities. Based on such an enforcement model, time matters. There will be increasing enforcement power over time due to enhanced integration. Thus our hypothesis is that the regulatory activities were more extensive in 2003 than in 1998.

We might also argue that length of membership matters (Jacobsson, Lægreid and Pedersen 2001, 2003). Denmark, with more than 20 years longer in the EU than Sweden and Finland and also the EEA countries, has much more experience with handling EU-related matters. Denmark is a transposition leader in the EU (Bursens 2002). In the period 1997-2004 Denmark had the lowest transposition deficit of the EU member states (Sverdrup 2005). European matters have to a greater extent become an integrated part of the daily work in ministries and central agencies in Denmark. Thus the hypothesis is that Danish units will generally report less EU-related regulatory activity due to their experience, and that the EEA partners and the other countries, due to their newness as members, will report a stronger EU-related regulatory activity. In particular, we expect Denmark to score low on rule enforcement.

Summing up, the regulatory activities are the result of a blend of external pressure, path dependencies, and structural constraints (Olsen 1992). We will argue that we have to combine these features to understand the scope, level, and variation of regulatory activities.

EU-Regulations in Domestic Administration

The first question that we would like to cover in our review of the empirical material is the extent to which the units are applying EU-regulations among the different dimensions of rule making, rule implementation and monitoring, and rule enforcement.

Rule making

Nearly half of the divisions that have been affected by the EU/EEA agreement state that they have rule-making as a primary task. Divisions dealing with regulations on the internal market are more likely to emphasize rule-making than those concerned with other policy areas (Table 1). One out of four divisions has introduced new procedures for control and auditing because of EU/EEA work. Units dealing with regulations concerning the internal market have to a greater extent adopted new procedures than those involved with other sectors. This is also the case in Finland compared with the other states. Moreover, agencies are more likely to have introduced new procedures for control and auditing than ministries.

Nearly half of the divisions state that there have been major changes in existing rules and regulations or that many new rules have been introduced in their field of work over the past five years in consequence to the EU/EEA. More than half of the units dealing with regulations related to the internal market have introduced new rules or made significant changes to their original procedures, while only one third of those concerned with other policy sectors have introduced new rules or made considerable changes to existing ones. Moreover, Table 1 (below) indicates that there is a stronger regulation pressure in 2003 than in 1998. The central administrations in Finland and Iceland have introduced more new rules or changed their original rules to a greater extent than the other three administrations.

Table 1: Is rule-making a primary EU related task, has the EU/EEA work implied new procedures for control and auditing or has there to a large extent been changes in existing rules and regulations or introduction of new rules as a consequence of the EU/EEA? Percentage.

	Rule making as a primary task	New procedures for control and audit	Major changes in rules and regulations
Country:			
Denmark	42	17	48
Sweden	44	25	42
Finland	49	41	57
Norway	46	20	43
Iceland	55	21	57
Total	**46**	**24**	**44**
Administrative level:			
Ministry	51	20	42
Agency	44	26	47
Year:			
1998	46	24	42
2003	46	24	47
Policy area:			
Internal market	53	29	53
Other	37	18	33

Our data supports the concept that rule making and regulation are important in Europeanization (Laffan 2001), especially in relation to the internal market. The increased intensity of the rule making activity is evident but moderate in divisions dealing with regulatory activities. On the other hand, the pressure on departments regarding control and auditing is has not increased over time. According to Sverdrup (2004), who reports a diverging development between the European countries in the ways they handle conflicts, the Nordic countries seek to resolve conflicts by consensus.

Monitoring

The data indicates that monitoring is a less extensive task than rule-making. Only 13 percent of the divisions report that monitoring, overseeing and control have been primary tasks in the last five years, according to Table 2. On the other hand, the extent of control and auditing has increased in one out of every four divisions.

Table 2: Monitoring as primary task of the division's EU'EEA related work and increased control and audit of EU/EEA related work. Percentage.

	Monitoring, overseeing and control as primary task during the last year	The extent by which control and audit has increased during the last five years
Country:		
Denmark	12	14
Sweden	15	21
Finland	15	47
Norway	10	20
Iceland	12	37
Total	**13**	**25**
Administrative level:		
Ministry	9	21
Agency	15	27
Year:		
1998	12	25
2003	15	26
Policy area:		
Internal market	17	31
Other	9	18

Policy areas belonging to the internal market are significantly more affected than other sectors. Nearly half of the divisions in Finland have experienced further control, while Denmark, being an early EU member state, has increased control and audit considerably less than the others. Iceland is also an interesting case in this respect, scoring high on increase in the extent of control and auditing. In general, agencies tend to have monitoring as their primary task to a greater extent than ministries do. They have also experienced greater control and audit than ministries in the last few years.

Our data indicates that nearly 2 out of every 10 divisions that have been affected by the EU/EEA report that a large part of their workload has been related to implementation and enforcement of European issues in the past year. Formally it seems that the development in the Nordic countries may be seen more as a step towards a hierarchical regulation and control system accompanied by agencification. The focus is towards implementation of regulation, which resonates with Sverdrup (2004), in that all states have reduced their implementation deficit. The importance of monitoring seems to be increasing, and the respondents reveal little freedom of interpretation in the implementation. Nevertheless, the information that monitoring in the Nordic countries is a less extensive task than rule making indicates that resolution of implementation and enforcement issues is more informal and pragmatic than formal and ideological (Sverdrup 2004).

Enforcement/compliance

The study shows that nearly 20 percent of the divisions have been subject to control from EU/EEA authorities in the last year reported (Table 3). Denmark stands out as only 8 percent of its divisions have been controlled, compared to around 30 percent of divisions in Iceland, Norway, and Finland. Interestingly, ESA has exercised control over Iceland and Norway more often than EU regulatory agencies have over Sweden and Denmark.

Table 3: Has EU-related control within the division's area of work been executed in the past year from EU authorities or from national authorities? Percentage.

	By the EU Commission, EU regulatory agencies or ESA	By national regulatory agencies
Country:		
Denmark	8	2
Sweden	22	14
Finland	30	23
Norway	29	6
Iceland	32	4
Total	**19**	**8**
Administrative level:		
Ministry	21	9
Agency	19	8
Policy area:		
Internal market	26	11
Other	11	6

EU-related control to a greater extent comes form EU/EEA bodies than form national regulatory agencies. EU/EEA authorities and national regulatory agencies both tend to be more concerned with regulations on the internal market than regulations and decisions belonging to other policy areas. Nearly one out of every four divisions in Finland has been controlled by national regulatory agencies, while only 2 percent of Danish divisions have had the same experience. Finland and Sweden, belonging to the East Nordic Model, are more likely to have had control exercised by domestic regulatory agencies than states in the West Nordic Model.

The fact that Norway and Iceland have more often been controlled by ESA than have Sweden and Denmark by EU regulatory agencies, seems to offer some support for the statement that ESA is »more catholic than the Pope« (Sverdrup and Graver 2002). Also, of some interest in this regard, are the findings reported by Sverdrup (2002) that the majority of the cases taken up by ESA are by their own initiative. The situation reported by the agencies when it comes to EU/EEA related cases presented to national courts and EU-courts is that more than 50 percent have arisen as a result of external complaints and initiatives. There seems to be a sceptical but obedient adoption of EU rules and laws by the Nordic authorities.

Structure, Culture, or Pressure from the EU?

The main question in this section concerns the relative importance of the various independent variables for the different regulatory features.[1] There are some significant relationships related to variables derived from all three perspectives.

Structure. The EU member states are experiencing more pressures than Norway and Iceland in only two of our cases, especially in terms of control from the Commission and in a higher workload related to implementing rules. Although form of affiliation therefore makes a difference, it is not nearly as decisive as one might expect (Jacobsson, Lægreid and Pedersen 2003). For instance, form of affiliation does not seem to effect changes in existing rules and regulations or in the introduction of new rules; new procedures for control and audit; rule-making or monitoring as primary task; freedom experienced concerning implementation.

Administration level makes a difference for most of our regulatory indicators. The most noticeable is that ministries experience more workload related to the implementation process than agencies do. Also, ministries have more often experienced having cases within their area of work brought to EU and national courts than agencies have, which may not come as a surprise because of their greater jurisdictions. In addition, ministries have somewhat more freedom of manoeuvre than agencies and rule-making is more a primary task compared to agencies. Ministries are also slightly more likely to have experienced changes in existing rules and regulations or in the introduction of new rules than agencies. Ministries and agencies seem to be under similar pressure from the Commission and national authorities in the implementation process. Thus our hypothesis on administrative levels is only partly supported. Ministries are more involved in rule-making than agencies, but the monitoring and implementation give a more mixed picture than we would expect.

Contrary to our hypothesis on size, the small size of the Icelandic administration does not make much difference except in that the extent of control and audit has increased within the Icelandic administration, and

1. This is done by multivariate analysis. The regression analyses are documented in Lægreid, Steinthorsson and Thorhallsson (2005).

in that there have been changes in the existing rules and regulations or introduction of new rules. The Icelandic central administration seems to be experiencing similar pressure from the EU/EEA engagement and to be adapting to it in a similar fashion, despite being considerably smaller than the other Nordic administrations. This supports previous findings that the Icelandic administration is now fully capable of taking part in the EEA (Thorhallsson 2004).

Summing up, structural features make some difference but do not reveal any distinctive variations between the Nordic countries. The distinction between ministries and agencies seems to be more important than the country's form of affiliation to the European Union. As a result, our hypotheses are only partly supported: Regulatory activities are slightly more common in agencies than ministries; the form of affiliation has little effect; and the small size of the Icelandic administration is not a limiting factor in coping with the adaptation process to EEA regulations.

Culture. Our analysis shows that central administrations in Finland and Sweden have experienced greater pressure from EU membership than have administrations in the West Nordic Model. This is especially the case concerning the enforcement factors, i.e. control from the Commission and national authorities and cases brought to national courts. Also, the east Model countries experience greater workload on implementing rules and new procedures for control and to some extent monitoring as a primary task. Our hypothesis that the adaptation to EU regulations would be easier in the West Nordic model than in the East Nordic model seems only to be partly supported. The high enforcement pressure indicate that the West Nordic model face some problems in adopting the EU-regulations.

This analysis is, however, complicated by the fact that the administrative model in Finland is in between Sweden and the West Nordic countries. Adding to this, Finland, being the only Nordic state to be fully integrated into the EU framework, would presumably be most willing to adapt to EU regulatory pressure. Thus, the hypothesis stating that Finland will experience more changes in its regulatory activities than the others seems to be supported by the empirical analyses. The reports reveal that control and audit has increased considerably more in Finland than in the other states. Also, quite a number of new procedures for control have been established and Finland reports stronger EU-related control from national authorities. Furthermore, fewer Finnish divisions have experienced several cases under their jurisdiction being brought before the EU Court than the other EU member states. The willingness of Finland to become a good European as soon as possible is demonstrated in the country's increased control in monitoring EU regulations, i.e. setting up new procedures for the purpose, and in not allowing cases to reach the EU Court, i.e. settling disputes at the early stages.

Summing up, administrative and political culture make a difference both when it comes to rule-making, monitoring and enforcement. There is a significant variation between Finland and the other countries on several dimensions, and also between countries representing the East Nordic and the West Nordic administrative model.

EU pressure

Our analysis shows that policy area is a distinctive factor in determining the level of EU pressure. Divisions dealing with policy areas in the internal market experience considerably more pressure than those concerned with other issues. In particular, they have introduced a greater number of new rules or changed the original rules and regulations and experienced stronger control pressure from the Commission than the others.

Time is not such an important factor as one might expect because of new phases of European integration. Generally, the Nordic states did not experience greater pressure from the EU in 2003 than in 1998. To understand the weak affect of time, we also have to take into consideration that in 1998 all the countries except Denmark were in a phase of introduction, trying to adjust to all the new laws and regulations which followed membership and EEA agreement. This pressure might have been weakened in 2003 but could have been succeeded by stronger integration in the years after 1998.

Our hypothesis that Denmark is experiencing considerably less EU pressure because of its long engagement with European integration generally gets little support. Denmark is, though, experiencing less control from the Commission than the other states and reports a lighter workload concerning the implementation and enforcement of EU decisions and regulations.

Summing up, policy area seems to be a decisive factor in understanding the variation in EU-related activity in the Nordic countries. This supports our hypothesis that the pressure from the EU is greater on the internal market than on welfare and other areas.

Conclusion

When it comes to domestic regulation, Europeanization concerns mainly the transposition of European directives in national legislations, and to a lesser degree implementation and monitoring. The workload on external enforcement and oversight is even lighter, probably due to the fact that oversight by the EU and court cases mostly concern transpositions rather than the actual implementation at the shop floor levels.

National structure and culture are revealed to carry little importance and are somewhat overshadowed by an emerging transnational regulatory system. Whether the state is a member of the EU or not, whether it is small or large, regardless of political culture, agency or ministry, the EU/EEA is transforming their rule-making, monitoring and enforcement procedures. The big story is that national structure and culture are minor influences as they are swamped by Europeanization.

This being said, regulatory pressure from the EU is definitely stronger in the policy area of the internal market and free movement of people, capital, goods, and services, than in other policy areas. This reflects the fact that EU regulatory activities remain concentrated within the core of the common and internal market, including environmental issues (Christensen 2005). Policy area has a particularly strong influence on rule-making as a primary activity, changes in EU-related rules over the past five years, activities and EU-commission control.

Our findings indicate the need to blend different perspectives to analyse the Nordic states' involvement in EU/EEA regulatory activity, and to obtain a clearer picture of their activity regarding rule making, implementation, and enforcement of EU/EEA regulations (Christensen 2005). The study reveals that the impact of EU regulation is high and that all countries report increased activities of transposition over time. The increased role of agencies is supported, but more workload on ministries is also revealed. The workload is somewhat higher in the East Nordic countries than in the West Nordic sphere.

Interestingly, the data indicate that a similar amount of EU pressure is exerted on both the EU outsiders and on the member states, despite the reality that Norway and Iceland implement considerably fewer EU regulations than their counterparts. EU affiliation does not really 'make a difference' and EEA-membership is just as strong a factor of Europeanization as EU-membership when it comes to regulation. Form of affiliation only makes a difference in the cases of the EU member states experiencing greater pressure from EU/EEA regulatory agencies than is the case in Iceland and Norway. They also experience a higher workload in implementing rules than the non-EU countries do. EU membership results in a greater number of EU regulations being implemented but not in a considerable difference in adaptation of the central administration. In other words, all the central administrations of the EU/EEA member states feel the pressure of membership. Denmark, having had more than 30 years to adapt to EU membership, experienced similar EU pressure to the other states in the last five years.

Furthermore, divisions in Norway and Iceland report similar levels of activity concerning rule-making, implementation and monitoring as the other countries, despite the fact that they are not members. Finland and Sweden report higher levels of enforcement activity than the other countries. The reported pressure from external enforcement bodies is low in Denmark, and it is worth noticing that there is considerably more pressure from external enforcement (EU/ESA) in Norway and Iceland than from national regulatory agencies.

The Nordic countries are indeed integrated into the European regulatory system to a considerable degree, despite the history of reluctance. This is especially true when it comes to aspects related to rule-making and transposition of rules, but less so on implementation and enforcement of those rules. The research supports the viewpoint that the national administrations in all the Nordic countries have to some extent become a part of an »EU-administration« which is supposed to deliver efficient implementation of EU rules and regulations (Egeberg 2005, Jacobsson, Lægreid and Pedersen 2004). We reveal a system in which increased integration of domestic administration into the EU has produced a set of administrative routines and practices in ministries and agencies to facilitate transposition, implementation and enforcement of EU rules and regulations (Christensen 2005).

One of the characteristics of this study is that it goes beyond a state-centric approach to regulation and provides an opportunity to analyse regulatory activities from a transnational and multi-level perspective. What the study reveals, not surprisingly is that the increasing importance of EU-regulation challenges the concept of the Regulatory State by blurring the boundaries of competence and by adding new dimensions to regulatory policy. The increased autonomization and Europeanization of the regulatory agencies might enhance multiple identities and result in them assuming a double-hatted character through enforcing EU laws in direct interaction with the European Commission, while at the same time performing traditional regulatory tasks as agents for domestic governments (Egeberg 2006). The parallel development of autonomous regulatory agencies in the EU and in the member states might create a direct link between regulatory agencies at different levels, thus bypassing the domestic ministerial structure. This development, in which regulation seems to be on the increase but not necessarily as a direct result of state action, indicates that we are heading towards a transnational regulatory state in which the border between national and EU regulation tends to fade away. This might improve regulatory implementation efficiency, but it might also increase the problems surrounding political accountability, control and legitimacy.

References

Armstrong, K.A. 2000, *Regulation, Deregulation, Re-regulation*, Kogan Page, London.

Baldwin, R., C. Scott and C. Hood, (eds.) 1998, *A Reader on Regulation*. Oxford University Press, Oxford.

Bursens, T.A. 2002, 'Why Denmark and Belgium have different implementation records: On transposition laggards and leaders in the EU', in *Scandinavian Political Studies*, 25 (2), pp. 173-95.

Börzel, T.A. 2002a, *Why Do States not Obey the Law?*, Paper presented at ARENA seminar, ARENA, Oslo.

Börzel, T.A. 2002b, 'Pace-Setting, Foot-Dragging and Fence-Sitting. Member State Responses to Europeanization', in *Journal of Common Market Studies*, 40 (2), pp. 193-204.

Börzel, T.A. and T. Risse 2000, 'When Europe hits home: Europeanization and Domestic Change', *European Integration Online Papers* (EIoP), 4, pp. 1-20.

Börzel, T.A. 2003, 'Conceptualizing the Domestic Impact of Europe', in K. Featherstone and C. M. Radaelli (eds.), *The Politics of Europeanization*. Oxford University Press, Oxford.

Christensen, J.G. 2005, 'Elusive Europe: The Impact of EU-regulation on Danish Public Policy', Paper presented at the conference of progress and Problems in Building a European Legal Order, The University of Luxembourg, June 24-25 2005.

Christensen, T. and P. Lægreid (eds.) 2001, *New Public Management. The Transformation of Ideas and Practice*, Ashgate, Aldershot.

Christensen, T. and P. Lægreid 2006, 'Agencification and Regulatory Reform, in T. Christensen and P. Lægreid (eds.), *Autonomy and Regulation. Coping with agencies in the modern state*, Edward Elgar, Cheltenham.

Dyson, K. and K.H. Goetz 2003, 'Europeanization Compared: the Shrinking Core and the Decline of 'Soft' Power', in K. Dyson and K.H. Goetz (eds.), *Germany, Europe and the Politics of Constraints*, Oxford University Press, Oxford.

Eberline, B. and E. Grande 2005, 'Beyond delegation: transnational regulatory regimes and the EU regulatory state', in *Journal of European Public Policy*, 12 (1), pp. 89-112.

Egeberg, M. 2005, 'The Nordic Countries and the EU: How European Integration Integrates and Disintegrates States Domestically', in S. Bulmer and C. Lequesne (eds.), *The Member States of the European Union*. Oxford University Press, Oxford.

Egeberg, M., (ed.) 2006, *Multilevel Union Administration. The Transformation of Executive Politics in Europe*, Palgrave, London.

Falkner, G. et al. 2004, 'Non-Compliance with EU Directives in the Member States: Opposition through the Backdoor?', *West European Politics*, 27 (3), pp. 452-473.

Hood, C., H. Rothstein and R. Baldwin 2001, *The Government of Risk. Understanding Risk Regulation Regimes*, Oxford University Press, Oxford.

Humphreys, P. and S. Padgett 2006, 'Globalization , the European Union, and Domestic Governance in Telecoms and Electricity', Governance, 19 (3), pp. 383-406.

Jacobsson, B., P. Lægreid and O.K. Pedersen (eds.) 2001, *Europaveje. EU I de nordiske centralforvaltninger*, Jurist- og Økonomforbundets forlag, Copenhagen.

Jacobsson, B., P. Lægreid and O.K. Pedersen 2003, *Europanization and Transnational States: Comparing Nordic Central Governments*, Routledge, London.

Jacobsson, B., P. Lægreid and O.K. Pedersen 2004, 'Robust and Flexible States: The Transnationlaization of Nordic Central Administration', in *Zeitschrift für Staats- und Auropawissenschaften*, 2 (1), pp. 32-55.

Jordana, J. and D. Sancho 2004, 'Regulatory design, institutional constellations and the study of the regulatory state', in J. Jordana and D. Levi-Faur (eds.), *The Politics of Regulation*, Edward Elgar, Cheltenham.

Knill, C. And D. Lehmkuhl 1999, 'How Europe matters. Different Mechanisms of Europeanization', in *European Integration online Papers* (Eiop), 3, pp. 1-17.

Krasner, S. 1988, 'Sovereignty: An Institutional Perspective', in *Comparative Political Studies*, 21, pp. 66-94.

Laffan, B. 2001, 'The European Union polity: a union of regulative, normative and cognitive pillars', in *Journal of European Public Policy*, 8 (5), pp. 709-727.

Lodge, M. 2001, 'From Varieties of the Welfare State to Convergence of the Regulatory State? The »Europeanization« of regulatory Transperency', in *Queen's papers on Europeanization*, 10/2001, London.

Lægreid, P., R.S. Steinthorsson and B. Thorhallsson 2004, 'Europeanization of Central Government Administration in the Nordic States', in *Journal of Common Market Studies*, 42 (2), pp. 347-369.

Lægreid, P., R. S. Steinthorsson and B. Thorhallsson 2005, 'Europeanization of Nordic Central Governments: Towards a Transnational regulatory state?', in *Working Paper*, 10/2005, Rokkan Centre, Bergen.

March, J.G. and J.P. Olsen 1989, *Rediscovering Institutions*, Free Press, New York.

March, J. and H. Simon 1958, *Organizations*, Wiley, New York.

McGowan, F. and H. Wallace 1996, 'Towards a European Regulatory State', in *Journal of European Public Policy*, 3 (4), pp. 560-576.

Olsen, J.P. 1992, 'Analyzing Institutional Dynamics', in *Staatswissenschaften und Staatspraxis*, 3 (2), pp. 247-271.

Scott, C. 2003, 'Organizational Variety in Regulatory Governance: An Agenda for a Comparative Investigation of OECD Countries', in *Public Organization Review. A Global Journal*, 3, pp. 301-316.

Selznick, P. 1957, *Leadership in Administration*, Harper and Row, New York.

Sverdrup, U. 2002, *Compliance and conflict resolution in the European Union*, Paper presented at the Arena seminar 17 September 2002.

Sverdrup, U. 2004, 'Compliance and Conflict Management in the European Union: Nordic Exceptionalism', in *Scandinavian Political Studies*, 27 (1), pp. 104-121.

Sverdrup, U., 2005, *Implementation and Europeanization. A review essay*', Working Paper 25/2005, ARENA, Oslo.

Sverdrup, U. and H.P. Graver 2002, 'ESA – mer katolsk enn paven?', in *Nordisk Administrativt Tidsskrift*, 83 (2), pp. 154-170.

Tallberg, J. 2002, 'Paths to compliance: Enforcement, management and the European Union', in *International Organizations*, 56 (3), pp. 609-643.

Thatcher, M. and A. Stone Sweet 2002, 'Theory and Practice of Delegation to Non-Majoritarian Institutions', in *West European Politics*, 25 (1), pp. 1-22.

Thorhallsson, B. 2004, 'Shackled by smallness: a weak administration as a determinant of policy choice', in B. Thorhallsson (ed.), *Iceland and European Integration: On the Edge*, Routledge, London.

SECTION 3

Politics and Business

CHAPTER 13

The Political Economy of European Integration and Business: How to Explain Policy Developments

Peter Nedergaard

Professor, Copenhagen Business School, Denmark

Introduction: The European Union as a Societal Experiment

The economic-political regulation of the EU now makes up more than 80 percent of the regulations in the Member States of the European Union (EU) regarding production, distribution, and trade with goods, services and capital (Hix 2005: 3). Legislation on the use of chemicals, product standards, rules on the formation of limited companies, information on bank interest rates etc. are determined at EU level. Moreover, the harmonisation of legislation regarding production, distribution, and trade with goods, services and capital has proceeded at a faster pace and with a far higher degree of centralism in the EU than in the United States of America.

For political science, the EU has become the equivalent of the fruit fly in biology. The fruit fly is used by students of biology to demonstrate a variety of genetic propensities that are known as Mendel's Laws. The usability of fruit flies is due to the pace of their procreation, which implies that researchers will have several generations of fruit flies at the disposal of their research within a limited time period. Developments in the EU are similarly progressing at a rapid pace. In the course of a few years, an entity with clear federalist traits has emerged in the economic-political area. The speed of evolution in the economic-political integration in Europe thus also offers the potential for uncovering general social science regularities.

In general, political developments are often characterised by inertia and deadlock in most polities. When certain institutional or political equilibriums are reached, institutions and policies are fixated. A distinctive feature of the EU is that internal and external pressures mean that changes in equilibriums and hence new political developments are more frequently seen. In this regard, internal pressures are inter alia the strong EU institutions that contribute to accelerating the economic-political integration, while the external pressures especially stem from the continuous expansion of the Union with an increasing number of Member States.

In this sense, the EU is a large-scale societal experiment, where different forms of economic-political regulation and cooperation are tested. Business is both subjected to the EU's cross-cutting, business-related economic-political regulation and its sector-specific regulation. The EMU and the legislation on the Internal Market are the best examples of the economic-political regulation, which in the course of a few years has established a radically different regulation of the external environment for businesses in the EU compared to previous regimes. The EU's Common Agricultural Policy (CAP) is a similar good example of a sector-specific policy that has evolved over the 50-year lifespan of the EU, entered a state of perennial crisis and been subjected to a number of reforms. Meanwhile, the CAP is also an important object of inquiry for students of the EU, since it has formed the rules of the game and the institutions of the EU (Nedergaard 1995; Nedergaard 2005).

All of the three EU policies previously alluded to are policies that to a great extent influence companies in a range of means through legal regulation, macroeconomic regulation and regulation of expenditure. Moreover, the three mentioned EU policies also exemplify the variation in the corporate options for influencing the political decisions of the EU and hence the direction of the EU's market integration. Business generally has two options for influencing the political system of the EU in relation to its output of regulations. On the one hand through the democratic process that is expressed in the Council of Ministers and the European Parliament, and on the other through interest groups that are either nationally-oriented or so-called Euro-organisations. In particular, the influence of Euro-organisations has been on the increase in the last 10 to 15 years. Research has shown that business Euro-organisations are particularly adept at aggregating positions and interests that are in demand by the Commission and the European Parliament. However, both institutions also require contributions from individual companies when they are seeking expert advice (Bouwens 2004).

The EU as a political system

When analysing the corporate options for influencing the EU polity in its production of regulations, students need to consider that the EU in exactly this area is a political system and not a state. American political scientist David Easton (Easton 1957) has pointed out that a political system consists of all the actions that affect the authoritative allocation of values for a society. The political system receives inputs in the shape of demands and support that it converts in its institutions to outputs that include actions and decisions (Rasmussen 1971: 86).

The political system hence consists of four elements. Firstly, it requires a stable and clearly defined number of decision-making institutions, which the EU has. The EU is likely to be the most formalised and complex decision-making system in the world. Secondly, citizens and interest groups must direct their desires and interests at and through any political system worthy of its name. For the EU it holds true that this is exactly what an increasing number of social groupings are doing.

Thirdly, collective decision-making in the institutions of the political system must have a significant direct and/or indirect impact on the distribution of political goods. The EU also meets this requirement since, as previously alluded to, it is the source of most business-related legislation in the constituent states, which equals an EU output of 100 distinct pieces of business-related legislation each year. Moreover, budget transfers made by the EU equal up to 5 percent of the GDP for some Member States.

Fourthly, a political system must have a process of continuous feedback between its political output understood as regulation and distribution of funds on the one hand and emerging demands and support on the part of citizens and societal groupings on the other. It is in this area that the EU is most deficient compared to national political systems: it is only the EU associations of business and labour which exhibit continuous and close contacts with EU institutions, and these contacts have tended to increase in recent years. However, other societal groups are also following suit, although developments in this area are hardly progressing swiftly (Bouwen 2004; Eising 2004).

Overall, the EU can be regarded as a political system with respect to business. Meanwhile, the EU is not a state. It does not maintain a 'monopoly on the exercise of legitimate violence', which is the prerequisite for statehood according to Max Weber (1972). The EU is conversely something new and unexplored in international politics, where the entity is on the one hand much more than an international organisation, and yet on the other is clearly not a state. Against this backdrop former Commission President Jacques Delors once characterised the EU as a UFO, an 'Unidentified Flying Object'.[1]

The EU as a supranational organisation

The EU's special character as an independent political system with regard to business-related policies is intimately related to its status as a supranational institution: it is not an intergovernmental organisation like all other international organisations are (Nedergaard 2007a).

The supranational character of the EU is expressed by the positions of power of the EU institutions. The Commission is the executive power and retains the monopoly on making political initiatives. Moreover, in most business-related areas, Member States use Qualified Majority Voting (QMV) in the Council of Ministers, and the European Parliament is usually also integrated in the process in these areas. Finally, the Court has fully independent competencies to ensure compliance with agreed economic-political regulation (Nedergaard 2007a).

1. See Timothy Garton Ash: 'Keep the UFO flying' in The Guardian, 8 June 2004.

Not least, the independence and autonomy of the Commission and the Court have been the subjects of a large body of research. Later in this paper I will discuss the implications not just for Member States, but also companies and citizens, in the fact that established EU institutions that are tasked with correcting, pressuring and exercising jurisdiction over Member States, companies and citizens.

Overall, the EU institutions have been established to produce political results in the form of the adoption of political decisions that are inter alia designed to accelerate economic-political integration. In addition to the formal institutions of the EU, there are also institutional structures in the shape of more or less organised interests that operate in a more opaque manner, but have at least the same impact as the formal institutions. Since the establishment of the EU, business has endeavoured to organise at European level because the impact of common European economic-political regulation has been appreciated.

EU institutions are generally stable. In this regard, I define institutions as channels of a political process. Basic norms and values are, for instance, not included in my definition of institutions as opposed to parts of institutional theory (Campbell 2004: 4).

As mentioned above, one of the most prominent features of the EU is that policies change so rapidly. Such changes, or the implementation of new EU policy initiatives are, however, not necessarily dependent on changes in the EU institutions. Changing preferences on the part of decision-makers and the public are also a factor to a large extent when analysing the rapid development in EU policies. By the term 'preferences', I mean the more or less changeable values, norms and considerations, which individuals, often organised in groups, find that the EU must basically meet through its initiatives. For example, the implementation of the Internal Market cannot be understood unless we take into account that preferences changed over the course of the 1980s in the direction of a more broadly shared desire to use market mechanisms to increase societal wealth, despite the transition costs that would arise.

The logic so far can be summarised in the following equation of politics (Hix 2005: 13; Hinich and Munger 1997: 17):

Preferences + Institutions = Outcome

Hence, political outcomes can change if political preferences are changed and the political institutions remain unchanged. Political outcomes can also change due to changes in the political institutions. Or political outcomes can change due to changes in both political preferences and the political institutions.

In practical research, either the preferences or the institutions are treated as constants for analytical and theoretical reasons. In the case of the EU, research on the role of the political institutions has often dominated vis-à-vis research on preferences and changes in preferences. However, this picture has changed somewhat with the introduction of a new form of cooperation, the Open Method of Coordination (OMC).

The Open Method of Coordination in the EU

The raison d'étre of the Open Method of Coordination is mutual learning between actors engaged in the process, mostly civil servants. The aim is to allow Member States to learn from each other's good and bad experiences via benchmarking, indicators and best practices in a range of policy areas that has gradually evolved from macroeconomic policies, to employment policy and on to social, education and research policies (Nedergaard 2007b).

The traditional means of cooperation in the EU rests on regulation in the shape of formally agreed regulations, directives and decisions in the Council of Ministers that must subsequently be implemented in national legislation. In contrast with this mode of cooperation, the Open Method of Coordination results solely in non-mandatory recommendations – although supported by arguments and documentation – that national actors can choose to observe or ignore.

The Open Method of Coordination means that the preference component of the classical equation of politics has become much more of a factor in EU research compared with previously. This is due to the fact that the stated aim of the Open Method of Coordination is to change the preferences of actors as much as possible in a particular direction.

The backdrop of the establishment of the Open Method of Coordination was in particular British and Northern European dissatisfaction with the increasing number – in their opinion unwarranted – of regulations coined in Brussels. Critics claimed that the danger inherent in this development was an EU characterised by inflexibility and political deadlock, as was often observed in national political systems. This was unfortunate if the EU desired to be a competitive region in the globalizing world (Nedergaard 2006c). The Open Method of Coordination was, in other words, intended as a means to preserve the EU as a societal experiment.

I have from the beginning regarded the concept of learning as essential to grasp if one wants to carry out research on the results achieved within the Open Method of Coordination. The study of the concept of learning led me to Ludwig Wittgenstein (2003, original 1952), the originator of modern constructivist learning theory who, particularly in his posthumously published book 'Philosophische Untersuchungen', explored the basic essence of learning if one accepts the premise that learning occurs in a collectively shared linguistic space and not as the individual's recognition of external conditions or as an intra-mind development, as prescribed by traditional theories of learning.

The starting point, in other words, is that learning is a socially constructed phenomenon where concepts give rise to learning when used and lead to results in practice. This contrasts with much of current research in the Open Method of Coordination, where learning is approached methodologically through interviews (Nedergaard 2006d).

However, if learning occurs as in constructivist perspective, it cannot be uncovered through interviews, since the respondent does not necessarily realise if she or he has expanded or refined her or his conceptual apparatus, or if she or he has acquired new concepts with a view to solving national issues when interviewed. Instead, in a Wittgensteinian perspective, the methodology for analysing learning in the Open Method of Coordination consists of interpreting the dissemination and implementation of concepts in written text as well as possibly an indirect test of from which source, respondents as a whole recognise to have learned from.

If this methodology is applied, it transpires that the learning processes in the Open Method of Coordination are considerably more significant than previously recognised. One finds that there are many traces of mutual learning between the EU's Member States, and the direction and thrust of learning are also clearly discernible. The Member States that obtain the best results in individual policy areas are those that other Member States learn from (Nedergaard 2006d).

The Open Method of Coordination is hence to a considerable extent contributing to moving European countries forward to a more advanced social-liberalist state with more competitive companies, employees and states through changes in the preferences of decision-makers.

The EU institutions and theories of European integration

The other component in the classical equation of politics regards political institutions. This area has received a great deal of research attention for a number of years. Because EU law has been a strong field in EU research there has also been a more than proportional attention on the formal institutions of the EU.

In political analysis, the analysis of the EU institutions over many years occurred on the basis of a number of classical theories of European integration. Ernst B. Haas (1958) analysed and predicted European development as early as the late 1950s in a book with the visionary title: 'The Uniting of Europe'.

Ernst B. Haas conceived the process of European integration in a determinist manner, like a snowball that rolled down a snow-filled mountainside. Haas called the 'snowball' spill-over. The triggers of spill-over mechanisms were not least non-state actors in the shape of interestorganisations, companies and political parties. They gradually shifted interests and loyalties and to a large extent sought influence in the new European centre of power in Brussels, where the Commission was the most important centre of attention.

Meanwhile, the Commission was, according to this theory, an autonomous actor with respect to sustaining the ongoing spill-over mechanisms. The effects of the Internal Market programme of the 1980s have been analysed from this theoretical perspective (Nedergaard 1990; Tranholm-Mikkelsen 1991).

Neo-functionalism, which is the formal name for this approach, forms part of the liberal school in international politics that predicts that processes of Europeanization, internationalization and globalization will gradually lead to the nation state becoming obsolete (Hay 2002: 22).

With respect to the explanatory value of this theory, it on the one hand explains the development of the EU through spill-over mechanisms in the following areas:

Customs union →
Common trade policy →
Common market policy →
Common Agricultural Policy →
Common monetary policy →
Common external economic policy →
Common external policy

On the other hand, this theory has difficulties explaining why stagnation occurs in the process of European integration. Why, for the most part, did no 'snowballs' roll down the EU mountainside from the middle of the 1960s to the middle of the 1980s? The answer to the explanatory problems of neo-functionalism is provided by the other dominant school in international politics: realism, which is called intergovernmentalism in the context of EU research. This approach rejected the logic of automatic integration suggested by neo-functionalism (Hoffmann 1966).

According to intergovernmentalism, states are still important and even the most important actors when explaining the process of European integration, and they have particular self-interests that they seek to fulfil within this process. Hence, according to intergovernmentalism, European integration only occurs when Member States have an autonomous interest in integration.

However, over time, it has become more difficult to assert that Member States act as monolithic blocks in the EU. Research has illustrated that states in the area of EU policy include multiple internal actors that seek to pull EU cooperation in divergent directions. Actual events in the world of politics hence also put pressure on intergovernmentalism.

From these countervailing theoretical pressures, the compromise between the liberal and the realist schools arose at the beginning of the 1990s in the shape of Andrew Moravcsik's liberal intergovernmentalism (Moravcsik 1993). According to this theory, European integration occurs in two steps.

The first consists of the emergence of a 'demand' for EU policies from different internal economic and social actors. The second comprises a 'supply' of EU policies through intergovernmental agreements at the level of government heads. However, liberal intergovernmentalism asserts – as follows from its status as a compromise between the two main schools of international politics – that the EU should still first and foremost be regarded as a phenomenon of international politics.

On the other hand, theoretical developments in later years have instead taken as a starting point that the EU actually has an autonomous political system which I – following Easton – have pointed out previously. The theoretical implications are that the EU should be analysed using concepts, theories and approaches from the field of comparative politics rather than international politics. This conversely does *not* mean that a lot of insight can be gained from analyses of the EU based on the classical theories of European integration. It simply means the theories have lost their status as all-encompassing and all-explanatory with regard to the political results of the EU.

The EU and rational choice theory

An agenda-setting analytical model imported from the field of comparative politics with a view to analysing the political system of the EU and particularly the EU's institutional side could be rational choice institutionalism (Nedergaard 1988; Nedergaard 1990; Nedergaard 1995; Nedergaard 2006a), also just referred to as rational choice, public choice, new political economy or institutional political economy. The starting point for the theory is the application of neoclassical economic theory on the political process. This firstly implies an acceptance that the neoclassical methodological assumptions – methodological individualism and rational utility maximizing – are also applicable in the analysis of the political system. Secondly, it implies that political transactions in the political system are not conceived as fundamentally different from economic transactions in the market. In both systems goods with an individually ascribed value are being supplied and demanded, regardless if the item in question is washing powder, housing, agricultural support or pensions.

However, there is one basic difference between the economic and political systems, since products (e.g. washing powder) in the economic system are supplied by persons who individually finance the sale and acquisition of goods. In other words, the market system is symmetric.

However, in the political system goods (e.g. agricultural subsidies) are supplied and demanded by persons who do not individually finance them. The political system is hence an open battleground for well-organised interests that can here obtain advantages that clearly exceed the cost of organisation. The losers are conversely poorly organised interests, most often tax payers and consumers. The political system is hence also asymmetric. In rational choice theory, the independent variable is often this political asymmetry that is used to explain particular political outcomes.

In EU research, much emphasis has been made on explaining the agricultural policy of the EU both theoretically and with regard to concrete reform initiatives on the basis of rational choice theory. Also the EU's trade policy and the Internal Market policy have been analysed using the theory (Nedergaard 1990; Nedergaard 2006a). These analyses have, however, also demonstrated the limitations of rational choice theory; or the so-called 'scope conditions' of the theory.

Rational choice theory is well suited to explain particular elements of the political process over the course of a few years, but faces more difficulties in interpreting political processes that extend over longer period of time. In the short term, rational choice theory is often both a simple and parsimonious theory. It is meanwhile consistent with dominant economic theory, which makes it well-suited to economic-political analyses. Rational choice theory is also well-suited to institutional analyses in an EU context where it is possible to conceive the EU's political institutions in accordance with game theory where actors are assumed to maximise their utility on an individual and rational basis.

One of the major unanswered questions in EU research with regard to the EU's institutions is why Member States establish EU institutions that in some cases correct and even undermine the very same Member States. We will for now disregard the explanation that asserts that the Member States are completely unaware of the consequences of their actions. This means that we presume a minimum of rationality with regard to the Member States (Nedergaard 1995).

Using as a starting point an example by EU researcher Simon Hix (2005: 112), one can on this basis design a game akin to the 'prisoners' dilemma' that explains the independent and autonomous options for the European Court of Justice and the Commission to set the political agenda and push Member States in the opposite direction of their immediate preferences.

Table 1: An autonomous Commission and an independent Court of Justice: explained by the 'prisoners' dilemma' game

	Member State B		
Member State A		Does not implement legislation for the Common Market (cheating)	Does implement legislation for the Common Market (cooperates)
	Does not implement legislation for the Common Market (cheating)	A: 0 B: 0	A: + 7 B: – 3
	Does implement legislation for the Common Market (cooperates)	A: – 3 B: + 7	A: + 4 B: + 4 Only an independent Court of Justice and an autonomous Commission with a right of initiative can ensure this outcome.

Source: Simon Hix (2005, 112) and own additions.

The prisoners' dilemma explains why Member States have a rational advantage in establishing an independent European Court of Justice or an independent Commission, which can compel Member States to implement the rules of the EU's Internal Market.

The table above illustrates that the situation of an independent European Court of Justice and an autonomous Commission making independent initiatives is the optimal and at the same time the most stable situation for Member States. If the European Court of Justice and the

Commission have inadequate autonomy and independence, the EU risks a situation where no state would implement the legislation on the Internal Market. The same game could be applied to other areas of economic policy in the EU where the Member States need a third party and arbiter to ensure cooperation that is collectively beneficial for the Member States – but which the Member States cannot obtain on their own.

Scope conditions for rational choice theory

Rational choice theory pertains to a theoretical school that is currently in a strong position in political analysis. From an international perspective, theoretical developments in the field of political analysis can to a large extent be reduced to the question of how to modify rational choice theory. One of the most important critiques of the theory is that it does not take ideas, norms and ideologies into consideration: that man is conceived of as a non-historical and selfish entity, that the individual and only the individual forms the fundamental basis of the theory due to its methodological individualism, and that man in this theory is seen as overwhelmingly rational (Blyth 2003).

I find that this critique is warranted in one *very* particular way. I have previously argued that political preferences should be regarded as socially constructed in a concrete historical context; that preferences are moreover articulated in a language that is the result of a collective process, and that ideas can determine the formation of preferences.

I meanwhile retain the position that rational choice theory is the most adept theory for explaining political outcomes in the short term, i.e. over the course of a few years. Rational choice theory is hence a theory where the scope conditions for its explanatory power are more or less constant. When synthesising the two relevant theories with a view to the analysis and explanation of the political outcomes in the EU, the equation of politics previously alluded to will be as follows:

Preferences <u>(social constructivism)</u> + institutions <u>(rational choice)</u> = outcomes

Hence, preference structures are the scope conditions within which institutions can act. Preference structures change in the course of time and therefore the 'range of action' of the institutions also changes when institutions are seen as channels through which political processes flow.

The overall idea of such a social constructivist rational choice theory aiming at the explanation of political outcomes is that even though preferences are socially constituted, they are relatively 'frozen' or fixated after their constitution. They can hence be used as a basis for calculation and optimisation. This frozenness or fixation is relevant in the political process for some years, whereafter a thaw can occur that then forms the basis for new frozen preference structures.

The point of the social constructivist model is furthermore that although learning has occurred collectively through the linguistic processes of concept formation, it is individuals who then act in a sphere of other individuals on the basis of these constituted or internalised preferences.

I will seek to illustrate and elaborate the theory in the following section by using the EU's Common Agricultural Policy (CAP) as an example. If the EU is overall a societal experiment where policy evolves rapidly, the CAP is a societal 'super-experiment' where price subsidies, modernisation of the rural economic fabric, international agreements, regulations for the protection of the environment, animal welfare schemes etc have been implemented only a few years apart over the course of the last 30 years.

In the following, the social constructivist rational choice theory will be applied to the development of the CAP. I will, in the context of the CAP, focus on the largest and most significant reforms of the CAP in the last three decades, e.g. the imposition of the milk quota regime in 1984, the 1992 MacSharry[2] Reform and the 2003 Fischler[3] Reform.

The imposition of the milk quota regime in 1984

Gradually, from the beginning of the 1970s onwards, milk production ran out of control. Year after year, production was larger than consumption,

2. Named after the Irish commissioner for agriculture, Ray MacSharry.
3. Named after the Austrian commissioner for agriculture, Franz Fischler.

and the production increased much more than consumption. As a result, 'Butter Mountains' and large stocks of milk powder became the order of the day in the EU (Grant 1997).

The Commission put forward various proposals to introduce duties on dairies or producers in cases of increasing deliveries of milk. However, the proposals were all rejected because they were impossible to implement – either from an administrative or political point of view. In consequence, at the beginning of 1983 the Commission concluded that only two solutions were open in order to solve the problem over supply of milk in the EU: either lowering the price of milk or implementing quotas (Nedergaard 1985).

Lowering the price of milk was problematic for decision-makers because it would demand a rather large price cut if it were to have any impact on milk production. Basically, the reason for this is that agriculture is characterised by higher fixed costs compared to other businesses. The farmers have to pay these costs no matter what. Hence, she or he will continue his business longer in spite of lower prices than most other sectors of the economy.

Most reports estimated that a price cut of 10 to 20 percent was necessary on the milk that farmers delivered to dairies to attain the required significant reduction in production (Nedergaard 1988). A price cut of that size would certainly damage incomes and the standard of living of many small farmers. In consequence, according to the Commission, a number of special arrangements were to be introduced in favour of small farmers if the price cut was not to result in flourishing national subsidies. This left only one realistic option open: the quota arrangement. The Commission therefore supported this (Nedergaard 1988).

The first Commission proposal for a milk quota arrangement was negotiated in the Council of Ministers in the autumn of 1983 without results. There were deep disagreements between the Member States about the introduction of the measure. The United Kingdom wanted a lower total milk quota. Belgium wanted special considerations vis-à-vis small far-mers. The Netherlands wanted another year of reference as the basis of the quota arrangement. The Irish Republic wanted exemptions and threatened to veto any proposal. France wanted to limit the imports of fodder as it saw these as the main reason for the oversupply of milk. Luxembourg wanted specific considerations vis-à-vis disadvantaged areas. This was also the case for Italy which, along with Greece, also wanted another year of reference that would put it in a better position (Nedergaard 1988).

After these preliminary negotiations the Commission changed strategy and put forward a proposal implying a 12 percent price cut in the case of no quota arrangement being adopted. Such a price cut would lead to significantly lower incomes for most milk producers, and it would especially hurt small milk producers. Hence, the Commission put direct pressure on Member States in order to make them accept the quota arrangement. Compared to other international secretariats of international organisations, only the Commission as an independent policy entrepreneur could make such a decisive, agenda-setting move.

The Commission succeeded with its strategy. After several meetings, the ministers of agriculture agreed to the introduction of a milk quota arrangement in March 1984. This arrangement implied a larger degree of flexibility than originally envisaged by the Commission. Hence, Member States could choose between quotas on individual farms as well as on the level of diaries. The final proposal also meant an increase in the total milk quotas as well as an extra milk quota for Ireland (Nedergaard 1988).

As far as the milk quota arrangement is concerned, as can be seen, the preference structures relied solely on considerations vis-à-vis small farmers and farmers in disadvantaged rural areas. On the top of these considerations, only various technicalities were discussed: the year of reference, the administrative level of quotas, and special treatment of certain Member States etc.

At the same time, the final reform was in line with the expectations of Olsonian rational choice theory (Olson 1965): when a policy comes under pressure to be reformed, the final reform will safeguard the well organised interests at the cost of the less well organised interests due to the asymmetry of the 'political market'. In the milk quota arrangement this meant that consumers did not get the cut in milk prices that the over supply on the milk market made possible.

The 1992 MacSharry Reform

The problems of the CAP did, however, not wither away in the aftermath of the implementation of the milk quota regime in 1984. On the contrary, the CAP came under increasing pressure during the so-called Uruguay Round of trade negotiations at the beginning of the 1990s, when the United States successfully placed trade in agricultural products on the agenda. Within the EU, the UK and the Netherlands were pressing for a reform whereas France was most against it. The EU Member States that were from the beginning against the reform were the UK, Denmark, Belgium, the Netherlands and – to a degree – France. These Member States had either benefited from the traditional CAP (Denmark and the Netherlands), benefited very little from the CAP in general (the UK) and/or were producers of northern products (Belgium and partly France). At the same time, several Member States that were originally against the 1992 reform were also strongly in favour of a GATT agreement. This is the case for the UK, the Netherlands and Denmark. Therefore, these Member States came increasingly under stress as it became clear that a condition for a GATT solution was reform of the CAP (Nedergaard 1995: 137).

In general, the United States had a big influence on the ideas and preferences about how to run an agricultural policy from the 1990s onwards. The reason was that the American way of supporting farmers – through direct payments and not via prices – was broadly recognized by economists and in the GATT and WTO as the least distorting and least welfare decreasing method (Coleman et al. 2004). The low price model of US agricultural policy – combining low prices with direct income support measures – was perceived as much more welfare optimal than the EU's high price model where farmers were supported through high prices. This fact would have great importance for both the MacSharry Reform of 1992 and the Fischler Reform of 2003.

Already the year before the reform of the CAP in 1992, the Commission had put forward guidelines for which new structures of preferences should be embedded in the upcoming CAP reform. The new preferences concerned preserving the rural social structure and the cultural landscape. Farmers should also play an important role, as both producers and protectors of the environment, through the introduction of less damaging production methods.

In general, it should be an independent goal of the CAP to promote less intensive agricultural production. In addition, agricultural support should be better distributed across farmers and regions of the EU. Finally, according to the Commission, the CAP should have a more direct impact on the incomes of farmers (Nedergaard 1995).

First and foremost, the MacSharry Reform – that resulted from both internal and external pressure on the CAP – resulted in a considerable decrease in the prices of grain which was, however, compensated for by direct payments which were made whether farmers had produced something or not. In addition, 15-20 percent of the arable land had to be set aside, but this objective was a requirement only for the large grain producers. Besides, milk and beef producers also had to face price cuts taking into consideration the specific conditions of these less efficient farmers.

As can be seen, environmental concerns were much more embedded into the MacSharry Reform of 1992 than into the milk quota arrangement of eight years earlier. Nonetheless, environmental concerns *could* have been part of the milk quota arrangement. For example, one could have made it a condition for obtaining milk quotas or at least for getting additional milk quotas, that certain environmental criteria were met. However, environmental concerns did not feature as prominently in 1984 as in 1992, when they were integrated into the reform as part of the new policy instruments. In other words, new preferences were formed or constructed in the meantime as part of a gradual development of so-called postmodern preferences (Hay 2002: 216-250).

The most important new instrument in the MacSharry Reform is the area premiums that compensate farmers for price cuts no matter whether they utilise the land or not. Of course, this is meant to be an incentive for less intensive exploitation of the farming land.

In conclusion, after the implementation of the MacSharry Reform, the level of agricultural support was kept at the former level according to the wishes of the well organised farm lobby; however, the payment for the support of farmers was partly transferred from one weakly organised group (i.e. the consumers) to another weakly organised group (i.e. the tax payers). At the same time, the CAP underwent a transformation from a high price policy to a low price one, combined with direct payment *ad modum* the US agricultural policy model; this was due to changes in the structure of preferences as far as the EU decision-makers and their constituencies are concerned.

The 2003 Fischler Reform

In the so-called Fischler Reform of 2003, environmental concerns were highlighted even more than in 1992, in combination with other concerns relating to animal welfare and food security. Just like in 1992, the decisive factor concerning the Fischler Reform came both from outside the EU as a result of the trade negotiations within the WTO, and from inside the EU due to the so-called Mad Cow crisis[4]: the latter played an important role as a de-legitimising factor as far as industrialised agriculture is concerned. The crisis pushed in the direction of more post-modern preferences among decision-makers and their constituencies.

In 2002 the Commission presented a plan for a reform of the CAP. First, it proposed a full de-coupling of the support for farmers, i.e. that they would have no obligation to produce agricultural goods (like grain) covered by the arrangement of direct support. Secondly, it meant that 20 percent of all agricultural support was supposed to be redirected towards general development of agricultural districts. Thirdly, the Commission proposed price cuts for milk and grain. Fourthly, it introduced the concept of 'cross-compliance' which means that the support for farmers should only be given on condition that certain criteria concerning environmental protection, animal welfare and food security are met.

From the very outset, Franz Fischler had support for CAP reform from the United Kingdom, Germany, the Netherlands, Denmark and Sweden; however, the majority of Member States opposed his plans. Nevertheless, in May 2003, Ireland, Belgium, Austria, Greece and Italy changed their stance, and accepted CAP reform, leaving France, Spain and Portugal without a blocking minority in the Council of Ministers (Nedergaard 2006b).

4. The official name was Bovine Spongiform Encephalopathies (BSE).

As always, the final reform was less radical than in the Commission's original proposal. Among other things, agricultural support was not fully decoupled and prices on grain were not cut. In addition, Member States were given more administrative flexibility in order to implement the reform. Nevertheless, the consequences of the reform were clear: agricultural support was now to be paid by tax payers to an even greater extent than in the reform of 1992 (Nedergaard 2006a).

A Comparative Perspective on the Reforms of the EU's Common Agricultural Policy

In comparison, clearly, the CAP reforms of 1984 onwards reflect a dramatic shift as to how central decision-makers and their constituencies think about agricultural support. The structure of preferences in the agricultural policy field of the 2000s are quite different from the 1980s. Within these 20 years preferences structures have shifted radically towards more post-modern values.

At the same time, the institutional conditions in the form of organised interests, European institutions and their interests as well as those of the Member States remain relatively unchanged. Agricultural interests have become somewhat weaker during this period, but they are still more powerful than those groups which are potential opponents of the financial support for farmers, namely consumers and tax payers. Basically, the institutions that constitute the political asymmetry of the 'political market' of the CAP have been left relatively intact.

All three CAP reforms analysed in this paper signify a gradual shift in the structure of preferences in the area. Decision-makers' preferences have to a large extent changed over the 20 years examined as a result of, among other things, the shifting discourses with regard to the problems of the CAP. In other words, changing circumstances have led to changing constructions with regard to which set of agricultural problems should be solved by which policy instruments, whereas the institutions remain relatively stable. Table 2 below contains the changes with regard to the preferences and institutions in the three reforms of the CAP.

When discourses on problems in a policy area are finalised and the preferences have been fixed or frozen for a period of time, the content of the reforms can only be explained on the basis of the potential asymmetry that prevails in the political market place between well organised business interests on the one hand, and weakly organised consumers and tax payers interests on the other. At the same time, the independent Commission and its specific position as policy entrepreneur within the EU political system is also an important impetus for all three CAP reforms. Incidentally, this specific position can also best be explained within the rational choice theoretical framework.

Table 2: Three reforms of the CAP: Changes in Preferences and Institutions.

Reform	Preferences	Institutions
The Milk Quota Arrangement of 1984	1) Specific considerations to small producers. 2) Specific considerations to disadvantaged areas. 3) Preserve high price system.	1) Very well organized agricultural interests. 2) Strong and independent Commission safeguarding the long term interests of the EU. 3) A Council of Ministers structure making it possible for member states to promote short term interests.
The MacSharry Reform of 1992	1) Specific considerations to small producers. 2) Specific considerations to the environment. 3) Gradual transformation of the CAP towards a low price system.	1) Well organized agricultural interests. 2) Organized environmental interests. 3) Strong and independent Commission safeguarding the long term interests of the EU. 4) A Council of Ministers structure making it possible for Member States to promote short term interests.
The Fischler Reform of 2003	1) Specific considerations to small, non-industrialized producers. 2) Specific considerations to the environment. 3) Specific considerations to the food quality. 3) Significant transformation of the CAP towards a low price system.	1) Well organized agricultural interests. 2) Organized environmental interests. 3) Strong and independent Commission safeguarding the long term interests of the EU. 4) A Council of Ministers structure making it possible for member states to promote short term interests.

Source: Own presentation

Conclusions

The economic-political regulations and other institutions of the EU are today the most important frameworks for EU business; moreover, these are also to a large extent subject to greater changes than national regulation. Cooperation in the EU has hence become a sort of a societal experiment that should also be of interest with regard to the testing and development of general hypotheses in social science.

In the economic-political area, the EU can be characterised as a political system, but not as a state. The background for this is not least the EU's character as a supranational organisation, which is illustrated by the powerful positions of its institutions and decision-making procedures where individual countries can be outvoted.

If the basic equation of politics where preferences + institutions = outcome is taken as a point of departure, most EU research has been concerned with institutions conceived as channels that political processes flow through. However, the preference part of the equation, understood as the considerations and values societal groups find political institutions must seek to satisfy, has become increasingly salient. This is due to the introduction of the Open Method of Coordination (OMC), the most significant purpose of which is to further mutual learning between countries: it is hence a deliberate attempt to alter the preferences of decision-makers in Member States.

Meanwhile, research in EU institutions remains highly relevant according to the classical equation of politics. Traditionally, this has happened with starting points in the classical theories of European integration, neo-functionalism, intergovernmentalism and liberal intergovernmentalism. These theories do all suffer from their emergence as theories in the field of international politics that presupposes that the EU should be seen as a phenomenon of international politics and not as a political system, which would be an incentive for the application of theories from the field of comparative politics.

Rational choice theory has been an important contribution in this connection, a contribution which I have argued should also play a role in the analysis of the institutions of the EU. The explanatory strength of rational choice theory is due both to its key concepts such as, for instance, the political asymmetry that contributes to explaining the political outcomes of the EU's political system – and because the formal EU institutions' monopoly on initiatives and their duty to make independent initiatives can be interpreted in a rational manner as it contributes to a more optimal equilibrium.

Meanwhile, I accept the critique of rational choice theory for overlooking the role of socially constituted preference structures. These preference structures hence serve as the scope conditions within which institutions must operate. The preference structures also change and with them the 'range of action' of the institutions.

In other words, the idea with the proposed social constructivist rational choice theory aimed at explaining political outcomes in the EU is that, although preferences are socially constituted, they are also relatively 'frozen', so actors can use thus them for strategising and optimising outcomes. Rational choice theory is in this view adept at explaining political outcomes over the perspective of a few years.

I elaborated the social constructivist rational choice model through an analysis of the three most ground-breaking reforms of the EU's Common Agricultural Policy (CAP): the imposition of the milk quota regime in 1984, the 1992 MacSharry Reform and the 2003 Fischler Reform. The analysis shows that the three reforms to a significant extent reflect the changed preference structures towards post-modern values in area, as environmental concerns, the desire for a regime of low prices combined with direct subsidies, food quality concerns and concern with non-industrialised agriculture have become ever more salient in the political outcomes of the reforms. Conversely, the institutional framework in the shape of organised policy area interests, EU institutions and the Member States' national interests has largely remained unchanged in this period, although with the caveat that agricultural interests have been weakened to some extent and pro-environment actors have become better organised. Political outcomes can hence be explained by changes in preference structures in conjunction with the continued state of political asymmetry.

References

Blyth, M. 2003, 'Structures Do Not Come with an Instruction Sheet: Interests, Ideas and Progress in Political Science', in *Perspectives on Politics*, 1 (4), pp. 695-706.

Bouwen, P. 2004, 'Exchanging access goods for access: A comparative study of business lobbying in the European Union institutions', in *European Journal of Political Research*, 43 (3), pp. 337-369.

Campbell, J.L. 2004, *Institutional Change and Globalization*, Princeton University Press, Princeton and Oxford.

Easton, D. 1957, *'An approach to the Analysis of Political Systems'*, in World Politics, 9, pp. 383-400.

Eising, R. 2004, 'Multilevel Governance and Business Interests in the European Union', in *Governance*, 17 (2), pp. 211-245.

Grant, W. 1997, *The Common Agricultural* policy, Macmillin, Basingstoke.

Haas, E.B. 1958, *The Uniting of Europe: Political, Social and Economic Forces 1950-1957*, Stevens and Sons, London.

Hinich, H.J. and M.C. Munger 1997, *Analytical Politics*, Cambridge University Press, Cambridge.

Hix, S. 2005, *The Political System of the European Union*, 2nd. ed., Palgrave Macmillan, Houndsmills.

Hoffmann, S. 1966, *Obstinate or Obselete? The Fate of the Nationa State and the Case of Western Europe,* Daedalus, 95 (4), pp. 862-915.

Moravcsik, A. 1993, 'Preferences and Power in the European Community: A Liberal Intergovernmentalist Approach', in *Journal of Common Market Studies*, 31 (4), pp. 603-634.

Nedergaard, P. 2007a, 'European Union Administration: Legitimacy and Efficiency', in *Nijhoff Law Special series*, 69, Martinus Nijhoff Publ., Leiden and Boston.

Nedergaard, P. 2007b, 'Maximizing Policy Learning in International Committees: An Analysis of the European OMC Committees', forthcoming in *Scandinavian Political Studies*, No. 4.

Nedergaard, P. 2006a, 'The 2003 Reform of the Common Agricultural Policy: Against all Odds or Rational Explanations?', in *Journal of European Integration*, 28(3), pp. 203-223.

Nedergaard, P. 2006b, 'Market Failures and Government Failures: A Theoretical Model of The Common Agricultural Policy', in *Public Choice*, 127(3), pp. 385-405.

Nedergaard, P. 2006c, 'Policy learning in the European Union: The case of the European Employment Strategy', in *Policy Studies*, 27 (4), pp. 311-323.

Nedergaard, P. 2006d, 'Which Countries Learn From Which? A Comparative Analysis of the Direction of Mutual Learning Processes within the Open Method of Co-ordination Committees of the European Union and among the Nordic Countries', in *Cooperation and Conflict*, 41 (4), pp. 427-447.

Nedergaard, P. 2005, 'Mutual Learning Processes of the European Employment Strategy: Theoretical Approaches and Methodologies', in T. Bredgaard and F.

Larsen (eds.), *Employment Policy from Different Angles*, DJOEF Publ., Copenhagen.

Nedergaard, P. 1995, 'The Political Economy of the EC Agricultural Reform', in F. Laursen (ed.), *The Political Economy of European Integration*, Martinus Nijhof Publ., Leiden and Boston.

Nedergaard, P 1990', *EF's markedsintegration. En politisk økonomisk analyse*, DJOEF Publ./ DUPI, Copenhagen

Nedergaard, P. 1988, *EF's landbrugspolitik under omstilling*, DJOEF Publ./ DUPI, Copenhagen.

Nedergaard, P. 1985, *EF og mælken. En analyse af landbrugspolitikkens etablering, udvikling, problemer og tilpasning som baggrund for indførelsen af en mælkekvoteordning I EF*, Specialeopgave ved Institut for Statskundskab, Aarhus University.

Olson, M. 1965, *The Logic of Collective Action: Public Goods and the Theory of Groups*. Harvard University Press, Cambridge, Mass.

Rasmussen, E. 1971, *Komparativ Politik 1.*, Gyldendal Publishers´, Copenhagen.

Tranholm-Mikkelsen, J. 1991, 'Neo-functionalism: Obstinate or Obsolete? A Reappriasal in the Light of the New Dynamism of the EC', in *Journal of International Studies*, 20 (1), pp. 1-22.

Weber, M. 1972, *Wirtschaft und Gesellschaft*, 5, Aufl. Tübingen.

Wittgenstein, L. 2003, *Philosophische Untersuchungen*, Suhrkamp, Frankfurt a.M.

CHAPTER 14

Party Competition and the Origins of Collective Capitalism in Denmark

Cathie Jo Martin

Professor, Boston University, USA

Introduction

Ove K. Pedersen's insights into the mechanisms by which Danes engage in collective action has made a major contribution to the field of comparative political economy. For Pedersen, informal networks are at least as important as the formal organizations, and these roots of Danish collectivism run deep: modern networks and associations build on the intricacies of family ties and community life, repeated and reproduced through the ages in this closed and stable society (Pedersen et al. 1992).

This essay delves deeper into the institutional roots of Danish collectivism, in particular, drawing attention to the role of party competition in fostering the rise of corporate association among employers and, thereby, in nurturing collective engagement. At the dawn of the Twentieth-Century, employers and their government supporters across the western world sought to develop peak business associations to create political supports for developmental capitalism and to aggregate the corporate voice; yet, these experiments in non-market coordination ultimately resulted in quite different organizational forms. Some countries joined Denmark in developing highly-organized, centralized, and hierarchical »social corporatist« groups, while others produced fragmented or »pluralist« associations, with limited capacity for expressing collective concerns. One wonders, then, why nonmarket coordination succeeded in some places but failed in others.

I argue that while the emergence of modern forms of non-market coordination in Denmark and other European countries, in part, reflected the legacies of preindustrial collective arrangements, these forms were also fostered by the structure of party politics. In short, proportional, multi-party systems were more likely to produce social corporatist associations, while non-proportional, two-party systems were more likely to give rise to pluralist associations. Countries with multi-party competition were more likely to develop dedicated business parties that helped to develop the collective voice of business, and that had political incentives to cooperate with other parties and social actors to form ruling governmental coalitions. In contrast, the large umbrella parties found in two-party systems cut across class lines; consequently, employers were dispersed across parties, had greater difficulty finding common ground, had fewer political reasons to negotiate with labor, and ultimately formed fragmented »pluralist« groups.[1]

The importance of party competition in fostering business organization in particular and the evolution of coordinated capitalism more generally becomes apparent in a comparison of employers' struggles to associate in Denmark and the United States at the end of the Nineteenth-Century. In both countries, employers sought to develop national peak associations in the mid 1890s. Danish and American employers had very similar interests in cooperative national industrial policies and, in both cases, party activists initiated employer organization to help with the party's policy ambitions. Yet the subsequent trajectories of associational development depended on the structure of party competition. The Danish conservative party (Højre) advocated a strategy of cooperation with other parties and social actors and, to this end, sought the development of a centralized, highly-coordinated association (*Arbejdsgiver Foreningen Efter 25 Aar*). The US National Association of Manufacturers was similarly envisioned to be a vehicle for fostering cooperation and unifying manu-

1. This essay builds on the arguments presented in Martin (2006) and Martin and Swank (2007).

facturers politically fractured by diverse party representation, but NAM was also supported by the McKinley campaign to poach business voters in Democratic regions. Thus NAM's policy goals became tarnished by its politicized reputation and its coordinating policy ambitions were consistently rejected by Democratic legislators in the South and West.

These musings on the links between the play of party politics and employer organization have relevance for the origins of managed capitalism and for the emergence of cross-national differences in the models of market economies. Associational development established path dependencies that were vitally critical to the emergence of comparative political economies in the Twentieth-Century, thus their origins are of great importance to comparative political economists. Yet while scholars have sought to understand the organization of national business associations in light of the challenges of industrialization, variations in labor organization, or deep cultural roots; they have largely neglected the influence of electoral competition (but see Martin and Swank 2007; Cusack, Iversen, and Soskice 2004).

This analysis also has important real-world implications for social solidarity and equality. We have shown elsewhere that social corporatist forms of employer organization have a significant impact on welfare state spending and on programs to enhance the labor market participation of the socially excluded (Swank and Martin 2001; Martin and Swank 2004). Therefore it is important not only for social science theory, but for the history and contemporary evolution of the welfare state, to understand the initial development of these organizational forms.

Partisan Competition and Business Organization

National umbrella business associations developed across the western world in the latter part of the nineteenth century, as the political locus of control moved from »community« to »society« in response to a growing consensus that national rather than regional solutions were necessary to cope with the forces of industrialization (Hayes). Economic developmental policies were sought to promote international trade in increasingly global markets and to make workers' skills commensurate with the remarkable technological advances of the era. Regionally-dominated and diverse economies were consolidating into national economies during this period and employers had a greater need to represent their collective interests in national political forums. Thus, business groups developed to promote industrial interests in policy debates and to help companies work collectively on tasks that could not be done individually.

Yet these early experiments in national business organizations resulted in quite different types of peak associations. While some advanced industrialized nations – led by Denmark – ultimately produced a single peak employers' association to represent collective business interests, other countries engendered multiple umbrella groups and a system of representation marked by fragmentation and redundancy. Business groups in many countries were consolidated into hierarchical organizational structures, dominated by centralized peak associations, yet elsewhere employer representation remained fragmented and even multiple umbrella employer organizations claimed to represent business. Over time the countries with centralized peak associations became known as corporatist countries while those with fragmented associational structures became known as pluralist countries.

The scholarly literature tends to line the varying degrees of employers associations to two broad factors: types of industrial development and the nature of labor organization. The first theoretical tradition links cross-national variation in employer organization to economic structural differences including the level of industrialization, the openness of the economy and the level of regional economic diversity. With the onset of industrialization, sector trade associations and, subsequently, multi-sector umbrella organizations appeared as a way to manage the cutthroat competition associated with unregulated capitalism and to facilitate rapid industrial growth. Initially, sectoral trade associations appeared to enable price collusion, to control output, to limit the entry of new firms, to assist with standardization, to promote products, to foster innovation, to manage labor relations, to compile data, to organize research and development, and to offer education and insurance benefits (Bradley 1965; Tedlow 1988; Lynn and McKeown 1988: 2-3). Industrial sectors producing for export markets (such as the British electrical engineering sector) were more likely to form trade associations than those producing for domestic consumption, because business associations provided firms with a forum to unify to battle the common enemy of foreign firms: they facilitated collective action in gathering information about the structure of foreign markets, sharing research and development costs, and coordinating cooperative innovation projects (Davenport-Hines 1988; Gourevitch 1986; Katzenstein 1985). Building on these sectorally and regionally specific groups, many countries then spawned national peak associations.

The second body of scholarship roots variation in types of association to differences in industrial relations systems: for example, some assume that because business organized to fight unions, countries with more highly-organized workers were also more likely to have highly-coordinated employers' associations (Crouch 1993; Ferguson 1983; Stephen 1979). Employers organized differently in response to threats from craft and industrial unions, with corporatist employers' organizations more likely to develop in countries with industrial unions. American labor organized into weak and fragmented craft unions, and employers' associations could afford to be weak as well. Alternatively, Swedish workers formed industrial unions before widespread industrialization and corporatist employers' associations developed accordingly (See Tolliday and Zeitland 1991). In addition, where working class consciousness was fragmented by racial, religious, and ethnic divisions, both labor and business had lower rates of collective organization (e.g., Stephens 1979).

Employer organization has also been linked to the level of skills in the workplace, in that employers dependent on highly-skilled workers had a greater need for coordinating institutions. The skills content of the production process matters to business organization, because firms relying on highly-skilled workers seek collective mechanisms for training, tolerate (or even push for) union organization and collective bargaining structures to secure workforce stability, and, thus, recognize the advantages of nonmarket coordination more readily than firms who use low-skilled workers (Thelen 2004; Iversen and Soskice no date). Pre-industrial patterns of economic organization shaped the development of both business and labor associations, and in particular, the guild system had a profound impact on skills development by facilitating vocational training systems that allowed firms to develop specific assets (Thelen 2004, Iversen and Soskice).

While there is much to admire in these explanations, they are somewhat overly deterministic. For example, while the organization of labor clearly had an impact on the development of employers' organizations, the relationship between types of unions and employer associations is more varied than initially appears (Tolliday and Zeitland 1991). While industrial unions led to corporatist associations in Sweden, craft unions produced highly corporatist peak employer associations in Denmark (Galenson 1952). In addition, while employers clearly sought collective organizations to develop skills, cross-national differences in skills were less starkly different in the nineteenth than in the twentieth century. Coordinated market economies could be found at the regional level throughout Europe and North America in the Nineteenth-Century before the first »industrial divide«; however, only some countries adopted coordinated national production regimes. For instance, American manufacturing processes in many sectors resembled those in continental Europe and a diversity of models or economic dualism may best characterize American manufacturing during this period (Berk 1994; Piore and Sabel 1984). Many American communities also had extensive apprenticeship and training systems during the nineteenth century (Bureau of Labor 1911; Piore and Sabel 1984; Hansen 1997; Martin 2006). Thus the process of employer organization also influenced by the vagaries of politics.

This essay suggests that political factors, such as the structure of party competition, also have a profound impact on the formation and subsequent developmental trajectories of employers' associations. In particular, proportional, multi-party systems are more likely to produce social corporatist associations while non-proportional two-party systems are more likely to produce pluralist associations. The structure of party representation matters to the origins and evolutions of business organization, because the presence or absence of proportionality and multipartism shape the incentives of both employers and party activists. Proportional, multi-party systems cover corporate interests more completely than do two-party systems; thus, actors in these systems encounter different strategic games.

Multi-party systems often include dedicated business parties; these partisan organizations can make credible commitments to their members and coverage of interests is fairly high (Cusack et al.) These dedicated business parties help to aggregate and to unify broad corporate interests; therefore, they may assist in developing the collective voice of business. Dedicated business parties have incentives to form alliances with parties representing workers, farmers and other interests in order to join the ruling coalitions; and one might expect these parties to transfer this spirit of cooperation to employers' associations. Highly organized employers associations may emerge to coordinate labor and industrial relations systems and to help with state development strategies. At the same time, although employer organizations in multi-party systems enhance cooperative arrangements with labor and implement party goals, these organizations should be less directly involved in electoral politics. Therefore, their activities may be viewed as more legitimate.

In two-party systems, the large umbrella parties tend to cut across class lines and employers (and other groups) are often dispersed across parties. Systems of two-party competition generally create representation gaps in electoral politics, and these »representation gaps« in the coverage of interests are exacerbated by party leaders' tendency to formulate positions that appeal to the medium voter (Downs 1957). Interest groups such as business associations may develop to fill voids created by representation gaps, but this path to interest group development may produce more fragmented, less unified, less cooperative and more politicized groups. When employers are dispersed across parties, a common corporate voice may be more difficult to establish. No business party exists to urge the associations to develop accommodating positions with labor. When business organizations develop to substitute for real business parties, employers' associations should be expected to play a bigger role in electoral politics. The excessively politicized nature of business organizations in two-party systems might give rise to greater questions about the employers' associations legitimacy and, in turn, undermine employers' roles in labor and industrial relations and economic development. Thus parties may have incentives to seek the formation of employer associations in both cases, but the characteristics and functions of these groups may differ under two-party and multi-party systems.

In the following pages, we consider the powerful influence of party competition and political leadership on the formation of the peak employers' organizations in Denmark and the United States. Both countries developed associations in the mid 1890s and each represents a quintessential example of a model country: the Danish employers' association was the frontrunner among European organizations in attaining high levels of corporatist coordination, and the United States is often evoked as an exemplar liberal-market-economy with pluralist labor and business organizations. In both countries employers organized to support public policies designed to nurture industrialization and to stabilize relations with labor; indeed, in both workers were organized into craft rather than industrial unions, and manufacturing employees were still highly-skilled in both countries. Yet the associations were also initiated by political leaders to aid party ambitions such as expanding constituent bases and supporting policy agendas, and major differences in partisan competition sent the Danish Employers' Federation and the National Association of Manufacturers down radically divergent tracks.

The Formation of The Danish Employers' Confederation of 1896

The Danish Employers' Confederation of 1896 (Arbejdsgiverforening af 1896), was formed by employers in the building and metal trades together with a member of parliament from the Højre (rightist) party. In 1898 the Handicrafts sectors joined the movement, making the organization of employers in Denmark complete and establishing the outlines of the Dansk Arbejdsgiverforening (Galenson, 1952: 2-3, 48, 70-72). The Danish business community was divided between the handwork craft sectors and the industrialists, but DA explicitly tried to bring together these diverse sectors. From the first, according to the official history, the organization had a democratic commitment that, in contrast to Sweden, involved the handwork sectors as well as industrialists and »the door way always open to small employers« (*Arbejdsgiver Foreningen Gennem 50 Aar*).

Three factors influenced the organization of this association: the disputes about rising industrialism in the Danish economy, the employers' response to the labor movement, and the dynamics of Danish party competition. First, during this time period, Denmark was developing a more substantial manufacturing sector, and employers wanted changes in public policy that would nurture rising industrialization. Danish industry was changing rapidly in the 1890s: trades were growing in economic importance and industrial sectors were becoming more capital intensive. Yet the public policies most relevant to industry reflected the political and economic power of the agricultural sectors (even before the Venstre party gained power in 1901).

Tariff legislation demonstrates the rather diverse interests of agriculture and industry. Farmers resisted tariffs on industrial products in the Tariff Bill of 1908, because they feared that countries would retaliate by placing tariffs on Danish specialty agricultural exports and that manufactured products would cost more as well. Danish industrial exports were low during this period – under 10 percent – and agricultural interests were able to win most policy battles (Ole Hyldtoft, *Danmarks Økonomiske historie 1840-1910*, Aarhus 1999, Chapters 13-14; Gourevitch). Yet Danish manufacturers were not unified in desiring protection; for example, the trade legislation first proposed in 1893 drew a mixed response from employers. Artisans pushed it to secure trading licenses and to get protection; yet the Højre party was torn between the artisan wing that desired protection and the free-trade industrial wing that rejected it (Dybdahl 1969). In any event, the largely domestic focus of Danish industry, according to Galenson and contrary to conventional wisdom, made firms more willing rather than less to join associations (Galenson 1952: 71-2). Due et al. (1994: 73) argue that the small size of Danish firms contributed to the formation of employers' associations, because the firms did not have any other option.

Second, a need to address industrial relations issues also motivated the creation and development of the employers' association, yet again the employers' attitudes toward labor were more mixed than stereotypes about Scandinavian labor relations might lead us to expect. Employers were centrally organized in 1896-98, before their Swedish and Norwegian counterparts and even before Danish workers, yet to conclude from this that these employers were decidedly pro-labor is a mistake. The guild tradition seemed to leave a mixed legacy for Danish firms; thus Bruun argues that the formation of employers associations were a sign of both continuity and change in Danish business history (Due et al. 1994: 75; Galenson 1952: 72-72; Bruun 1931: 409). On the one hand, the guild tradition was undeniably collectivist, and the associations' endorsement of cooperation is in keeping with this pre-industrial guild system; indeed, a short period transpired between the end of guilds (1892) and the centralization of the employer associations (1896-8). On the other hand, the famous Danish spirit of cooperation was notably absent in the 1885 Metal strike and the push for the organization of DA came largely from technologically-advanced sectors rather than pre-industrial sectors with guilds. In addition, the guilds were largely focused on restricting competition, while the early associations wanted to expand trade.

Employers' positions on social issues seemed more inspired by Germanic ideas about workplace stability than by Social Democratic beliefs in equality; indeed, employers supported social policies precisely because they limited class mobility (Levine 1978). Granted, Denmark had a deeper tradition of collectivism, in both the guilds and perhaps more importantly in the ideological/spiritual writings of N.F.S. Grundtvig (Østergård 1992; Knudsen 1991) Yet Grundtvig's collectivism had more purchase in the agricultural world than among city-dwellers, just as the somewhat comparable Populist tradition was largely confined to rural America. Employers' positive attitudes toward workers seemed to reflect a rational calculation of the firms' self interests. The workmen's compensation insurance offers an excellent example of business pragmatism. When the government proposed insurance for employees injured on the job, the nascent association decided that the burden would undoubtedly fall on employers and determined to take a position. In a meeting on September 18, 1896, the leadership brought together its own members plus representatives from the crafts manufacturing association and other kindred parties and proposed that the insurance be independent. This endeavor offered a lasting lesson for employers, in demonstrating the benefits of cooperation on social legislation both as a boon to the worker and to protect employers' interests (Agerholm and Vigen, *Arbejdsgiver Foreningen Gennem 25 Aar 1896-1921*: 16).

At the historical point of formation of national employers' associations, neither ideological, cultural predispositions nor post-guild legacies moved firms to endorse the peaceful, cooperative demeanor that was to become the signature of Danish business in later years. Rather this great transformation occurred, in part, because employers felt that they had no other way to control labor. Employers in the metal trades moved to curb growing labor power in the 1880s when economic recession threatened, and the first big employers' organization, »Foreningen af Fabrikanter i Jernindustrien i Kjøbenhavn,« was formed in January 1885 after the smiths at Borch & Henriksen started striking. Niels Andersen was to recall that this battle between the trades and employers as the best reason for forming a central agreement (Agerholm and Vigen; *Arbejdsgiver Foreningen Gennem 25 Aar, 1896-1921*: 4)

Employers deviated from their frontal attack on unions only when chastened by the virulent conflict with labor in 1885. The trade unions began to strike at metal-making plants, initially on an individual basis and later by forming alliances with other labor organizations in the locality. This domino effect wore down employers' ability to resist labor organization, and in response firms decided to impose a lock-out. The firms lost their five month lock-out to stop labor organization, and were ultimately forced to recognize labor organizations. The metal manufacturers (and the Association of Manufacturers in København Metal Trades) negotiated a collective agreement with the national trade union not because they favored trade unions but because they felt that they had no other option (Due et al. 1994: 73).

After the 1885 battle, some Danish employers gradually made a strategic decision to secure industrial peace through the creation of institutions for collective action. In part this reflected the afore-mentioned small size of firm and impressive labor militancy. Yet labor was far from organized on a national level; indeed, employers were actually more supportive of a centralized wage-bargaining structure than labor during the 1890s. Thus Due et al. argue that the internal structure of the trade unions was shaped to meet the high levels of centralization among employers. In 1898 during a large lockout by the metal industry, DA sought to contain the conflict at a national, multi-industrial level and lobbied for the formation of a joint committee to oversee collective agreements (Fællesudvalget af 1898) (Due 1994: 78-9). The Danish employers also sought a more centralized labor federation that could ask unions to refuse to work for free-riding firms who stayed out of the business group (Galenson 1952: 2-8, 58, 69-72, 91).
This essay suggests that the structure of Danish party competition also contributed to the employers' association's initial formation and to its subsequent evolution as a centralized and highly-coordinated group. At least a faction of the Danish Højre (Right) party desired a politics of coordination – in which a cooperative employers' association was key – in

order to further the interests of the moderate faction of the party and to enhance Højre's negotiating position with other parties in parliament.

The Danish conservative party, Højre (which later evolved into the Konservative Folkeparti) represented most Danish manufacturers, other upper class fractions, and many public officials; yet in the 1890s also had a share of working-class voters. Although the party had dominated Danish politics for many years, the 1890s brought much talk of parliamentary reform, and the party began to decline. For instance, in the 1880s 29,000 Copenhageners belonged to the party, declining to 14,846 by 1897 (Dybdahl 1969: 11). Over time the lower class component got markedly smaller and the businessmen/official constituents grew significantly (*ibid.*: 12). This was a time of intense political struggle that culminated in a constitutional change – »systemskiftet« – in 1901. Before 1901 the government was controlled by Højre, which was able to rule the government without a plurality in the Danish Parliament (Folketing). After the constitutional reform in 1901, no longer could a government be formed if a larger parliamentary coalition could be formed against it. In order to wrest power away from Højre, Venstre was seeking to make a pact with the growing labor movement (Bindslev 1937-8).

During this period was much debate about how to revive the flagging fortunes of the party. Højre contained both a parliamentary organization (the moderate wing) and a set of local committees or conservative clubs (the conservative wing). The parliamentary organization came first, but with the expansion of suffrage, this parliamentary group decided that it needed constituency support and the local party organizations were developed. Initially, the local organizations were both political and social. Although in the early years the parliamentary group had dominated Højre, the local conservative clubs steadily grew in power (*ibid.*).

These two factions had quite diverse interests and ideological positions. The conservative wing wanted a strong national defense and an independent, powerful right. The moderate wing was open to compromise with other parties, accurately recognizing that the march toward democratization in Denmark would ultimately alter the partisan balance of power. The moderate wing of the party also sought to strengthen its message of cross-class cooperation with a message of labor-management coordination.

A leader of the Højre executive committee in the parliamentary organization, Lars Dinesen, wanted to broaden the party's power and cross-class appeal. He set out to centralize the party, to reduce the power of the local committees, and to enhance the negotiating capacities of the central, parliamentary organization. Dinesen wanted to centralize the party in order to facilitate cooperation with a new party of moderate liberals, Venstreformpartiet that had developed as a splinter group from the Liberal (Venstre) party. To this end, he wanted the executive committee to have the right to intervene in candidate selection (among the local parties) in order to chose, if appropriate, candidates that would be acceptable to the new Liberal Reform party. According to Dybdahl, this »electoral pact essentially demanded central leadership.« Local organizations resented this infringement on their authority, and Dinesen was finally forced to resign in 1896 (Dybdahl 1969: 14-15; Bindslev 1937-8).

According to its official history, Højre's involvement in the creation of the Employers' Federation must be viewed against the backdrop of the party's fight for rule against the Liberal Party (Venstre largely for farmers) and the nascent Social Democratic party (*Arbejdsgiver Foreningen i Danmark Gennum 25 Aar*). When the rising social democratic party started to take away Højre's working class constituents and threatened to form an alliance with Venstre to seize control of the government, Højre sought to consolidate its position among industrialists. It may have been that the employers' organization was viewed as giving the party leaders some leverage against the local committees.

The Danish Employers' Federation of 1896 was the brainchild and cause celebre of two men: Vilhelm Køhler and Niels Andersen. Køhler was the director of Frederiksholms Teglværker (Brick factory), head of the bricklayer guild, and a master builder. A strike broke out in February 1896 and Køhler approached the contractor association's head, Niels Andersen, who was a Højre party member of the Danish parliament. The two men determined to develop an employers' association committed to restraining conflict between business and labor. Køhler and Andersen held a meeting on March 6 1986 in Copenhagen (Studiestræde 7) that was attended by representatives for most of the sectoral associations in building, metal working and other trades. Køhler and Andersen proposed that an association be formed to secure labor peace through collective action.

If the association's governing body recognized an ongoing strike as illegitimate or an ongoing lockout as legitimate, members would pledge not to hire workers or purchase materials from the plant that had that strike or lockout. The trade associations belonging to the peak association would each elect a member to represent them, and each member should pay 30 kroner in dues. According to official biographers of DA, Agerholm and Vigen (1921: 11-4), this idea became the guiding light for Danish social development.

A later official biography of DA emphasizes more directly the political origins of the Employers' Federation of 1896. Niels Andersen (a »Højre man« and a civil servant (etatsråd)) founded DA in order to demonstrate that Højre offered a meaningful middle way to lead the country to technological industrial development and labor peace between employers and workers (*Arbejdsgiver Foreningen Gennem 50 Aar 1946*).

These political motivations for the formation of the employers' federation may partially account for the Social Democrat's deep-seated animosity toward the idea. Thus the paper, Social Demokraten, wrote on May 20, 1896:

> Let the workers have their own associations in peace, when through these groups they can request improvements in worker representation and take matters up with a loyal negotiator. Leave on the shelf the arrogant tone of those who want the opposite for workers so that there will be »peace and stability« [quotations in the original] in the workplace. To workers we say, »Keep a watchful eye on the increasing combination of the purchasers of labor power and close ranks.« (Agerholm and Vigen 1921, translation by C.J. Martin).

The creation of DA did not end labor/management strife once and for all; indeed, a huge battle between business and labor arose a few years after the formation of DA. In 1899 a big conflict on the labor market (the Great Lockout or Storlockouten) finally induced employers and workers to engage in their first »hovedaftale« or general negotiation between DA and LO. A strike in Jutland, followed by an employer lock-out, spread throughout the economy and lasted 3 months. There is some evidence that employers drove the lock-out in order to push toward a national system of collective bargaining (so that employers could restrain their workers' wages) and to guarantee managerial control over the organization of work. Ultimately the Højre States Minister Hørring in an informal meeting with Niels Andersen threatened to intervene if the two sides were unable to find a solution. But before this was necessary, the employers and labor associations ended the stand-off with the famous (in Denmark) September Compromise (September Forlig) and the Danish system of collective bargaining was established (Due et al 1994: 80-1). The insitutionalization of the Danish model, following the lockout of 1899, had benefits for both business and labor, but employers enjoyed the greatest victory. The compromise established employers' control over the organization of work and structured conflict along decentralized trade lines. The state's role in overseeing labor-management relations after this was sharply limited and the pattern of voluntarism and significant devolution of power to the social partners was confirmed (Due and Madsen #26).

Højre was replaced in the Twentieth Century by the Danish Conservative party, which more exclusively represented employers in parliamentary debates. Although the party now had less need to appeal to constituents across the class divide, the need to form coalitions with other parties in this multi-party, proportional system continued to encourage cooperative thinking by party leaders. By the 1960s the Conservatives were to brag that they had played a major role in every »decisive step in this expansion« of the welfare state (Friis 1969). Indeed, the cooperative vision of Niels Andersen and his allies was institutionalized in the September Compromise of 1899 and has structured Danish industrial relations (with some changes) down to the present day.

The Formation of the National Association of Manufacturers

As was the case in Denmark, the Republican Party and a group of industrialists developed the National Association of Manufacturers to nurture industrial capitalism and to transfer regulatory privilege from agriculture to manufacturing (NAM, Edgerton 1926). Thus NAM's explicit goals concerned building infrastructure for manufacturing and foreign trade, and its Committee on Resolutions proposed as a basis for organization the ambition that, »our home market should be retained and supplied by our own producers and our foreign trade relations should be extended in every direction.« (»Delegates Got Down to Business« 1895: 8).

Like the Danish case, industrial relations at NAM's inception played against stereotype: Although American employers are viewed as anti-labor and anti-state, NAM sought cooperation among agents in business, labor and the state to foster economic development and only turned against the labor movement eight years after its inception in 1903 (Werking 1977: 21-2; NAM 1926: 61-2). Again contrary to conventional wisdom, many sectors in pre-Fordist Nineteenth-Century America were quite coordinated and relied on highly-skilled workers (Berk 1994; Hansen, 1997). Some states and communities had developed extensive vocational training programs, and employers in some regions entered into private collective arrangements to meet their skills needs. In addition, employers sought union assistance in forming business combinations: they negotiated trade agreements with unions and asked their labor allies to pressure other firms to join the combinations (Gable 1959: 539; Galenson 1952). President Search reflected on this spirit of business-labor cooperation in his presidential address at the 1901 convention:

> Organized capital is confronted by organized labor and it is exceedingly gratifying to note that instead of more determined antagonism there is a larger disposition to consider the points at issue with calm deliberation and intelligent judgment ... To those who are appreciative of the humanitarian aspects of industrial life it must be exceedingly gratifying that so many representative manufacturers are devoting much attention to the problems affecting the conditions under which their operatives live and labor ... There is an economic value in such ideas in addition to the interest which attaches to them from the humanitarian standpoint, and profit can be derived in many ways ... in those modern establishments where progressive ideas have been applied in full force (Search 1901).

In similar fashion to Danish employers, NAM's organizers were guided by a corporatist vision and were intrigued by Bismarck and the German model of industrial relations (Atlanta Constitution). The group would only accept as members associations rather than individuals and the executive committee hoped »to consolidate into one great powerful representative body the total force and influence of American industry, so that when any question of any large national industry shall present itself, American manufacturers will speak and act with a positive assumption that they will be heard and heeded« (»The National Association of Manufacturers and other Organizations« 7/1/1899).

Despite these manifold similarities, the two countries ultimately took divergent paths and, we argue, this break reflects the structure of party competition; thus, the limits of the two-party system explains both the development of NAM as a tool for coordination among business, labor and the state and its ultimate rejection of this cooperative vision. NAM was initially formed to overcome the electoral institutional incapacities of sectionally-dominated two-party competition and to provide assistance for McKinley's nationalist economic ambitions and presidential campaign. The Republican Party advocated a set of national policies to foster industrialization, but could not successfully mobilize employers in the south and west, who voted Democratic. The Republican efforts to create *national* policies to further the industrial economy were hampered as well by the party system's *local* orientation and by the power of corrupt party bosses, who often demanded control over patronage in exchange for political support. McKinley and Hanna helped to initiate the National Association of Manufacturers in order to transcend this regionalism and to build a national constituency composed of interest groups rather than of local networks dominated by party bosses. The need for a national business organization supporting policies for industrial development was especially great in the Southern one-party states, where Democratic party's dominance made another form of organization necessary to affirm a commonality of interests among employers, to link southern business managers to their compatriots in other sections of the country and to connect these employers (largely Democrats) to McKinley's campaign for political economic change (National Association of Manufacturers, »Advice from the South«1895: 154). NAM expected to be rewarded for this contribution and the *National Industrial Review* (a quasi-official publication of NAM) forecast that the organization »will be in future a great factor in our National elections« (*The National Industrial Review* 1895; Steigerwalt 1964: 33).

The origins of NAM reveal McKinley's political involvement and interests. Although the official story was that employers in Cincinnati and Atlanta spontaneously developed the association, NAM later admitted that McKinley had a major role in the effort (NAM 1926: 61). There was much overlap between the NAM organizers and the McKinley Republican campaign, with key personnel important to both efforts. Among the core group of Ohioan organizers of NAM was Thomas McDougall, who had helped to organize an effort to save McKinley from financial scandal a few years before (Olcott 1916: 290). The first president of NAM, Thomas Dolan of Pennsylvania, was curiously elected to office at the organizing convention without even being present; however, his relation with William McKinley was so close that he became one of a few trustees for the McKinley monument after the president's death (»It's President Dolan« 1895: 1; »For the McKinley Monument« 1901: 3). The three leading Georgian employers were likewise very involved with the McKinley campaign. Thomas Martin served as a member of the organization's constitution and bylaws committees, and was the president of the Atlanta McKinley club. Colonel JF Hanson (owner of the Macon Telegraph) was both the NAM vice-president from Georgia and the major speaker at the meeting of the Southern Republican party convention in advance of the 1896 convention (»Manufacturers in Convention« 1895: 2; Bacote 1959: 218) Colonel AF Buck both recommended to McKinley Republican delegates for the St. Louis Republican National Convention and served as a liaison to African American Republican leaders in the state (McKinley letter to RE Wright 1896; Buck letter to McKinley 1896).

At the NAM organizing convention McKinley was the first to speak after the mayor of Cincinnati (Gable 1959: 536). When McKinley arrived, a host of marching businessmen went to meet him and his keynote address drew a standing ovation from the crowd. NAM's second annual meeting in January 1896 was originally scheduled for the fall of 1895 but was rescheduled for »just about the time when the campaign for the Republican nomination for the Presidency will open« and state conventions began meeting to select the nominee (»A High-Tariff Republican President«, 1895: 1). NAM leaders instructed their members that »a greater significance attaches to the outcome of this convention and its ultimate results, than to that of any other convention, either commercial or political, that has ever been held on this hemisphere« (*The National Industrial Review* July, 1895: 148). According to *The New York Times*, the most significant event was »the applause which greeted a mention of the name of Major McKinley. This applause told as plainly as could a preamble and resolution the real purpose of the delegates« (»Manufacturers Cheer for McKinley«, 1896: 1). In a keynote speech Thomas McDougall blamed »business paralysis to-day« on adverse tariff policy and lack of statesmanship:

> Party politics make a foot-ball of the interests of this country. ... and it is now tying the hands of a country that ought to be to-day on the high road to prosperity. And nothing but the voice of our united manufacturing industries will be able to compel these so-called statesmen to act (McDougall 1896: 3-8).

Yet NAM's cooperative moment did not last and the organization nearly floundered on the circumstances motivating its rise and NAM got caught up in the sectional conflict inherent in the American structure of two-party competition. NAM's dubious reputation as a partisan political agent of the Republican Party seeking to establish a base in Democratic states played a big role in the decline of the organization's fortunes. Thus, NAM's second president, Theodore Search, acknowledged, »Suspicions of political purposes have done great injury to the Association and have naturally retarded its progress.« (Steigerwalt 1964: 39).

NAM's organizational growth was furthermore constrained by the failure of Congress to legislate the association's agenda of economic development. NAM eagerly sought the creation of a new Cabinet-level Department of Commerce (finally established in 1903), to coordinate industrial development policy (*The National Industrial Review*, May 1895). After the election of 1896 the organization was so certain that the commerce department would be created immediately, that NAM's Resolutions Committee member, George Johnson, told the *New York Times* that President-elect McKinley had already a secretary with NAM's unconditional endorsement (»A Ninth Cabinet Member: A Contingent Offer Made«, 1897: 1). Yet the bills to create the Department of Commerce and Industry encountered resistance from legislators reluctant to grant favor to industrial interests. By the 1898 NAM annual convention President Theodore Search was to comment wearily, »There is scarcely another government in the civilized world that does not possess a governmental department whose duty it is to exert a special care and to observe a solicitude in behalf of trade and industry« (Search, 1898: 3-32). NAM's efforts to obtain a national charter were likewise defeated by Congressional Democrats, who viewed NAM as an agent of Republican and sectional interests (Search, »President's Report« Proceedings 1900: 12-3). NAM's legislative failures contributed to the association's profound about-face in 1903, when it determined that it could not attain its cooperative goals and finally converted to an anti-labor platform in 1903.

Conclusion

Conventional wisdom assumes a profound ideological split between coordinated market economies and liberal market economies; for example, many treatments of the history of American industrial organization assume that US employers rejected managed capitalism on ideological grounds at an early point in our nation's history and spurned the institutions for coordination sought by European business. We suggest, however, that employers in the nineteenth century across the western world desired coordination, but that differing political structural conditions constrained the development of managed capitalism in some countries.

Employers everywhere had remarkably similar preferences for business-government cooperative arrangements to foster economic competitiveness and export assistance; thus preferences for coordinating policies and institutions were essentially the default position, even in countries such as the United States that would later become bastions of neo-liberal thought. Manufacturers in both Denmark and the United States had positive views of government and sought public policies more favorable to industrial development. Both groups were envious of and influenced by German employers' coordinated efforts to expand industrial capacities and perceived this cooperation as contributing greatly to the expansion of German economic supremacy. Employers in the two countries also shared many similarities in their needs from and attitudes toward labor. Workers were organized into craft rather than industrial unions, and manufacturing employees were still highly-skilled in both countries.

Yet company parted when it came to the issue of party structure, and profound distinctions partitioned Denmark and the United States in the area of democratic electoral and party politics. In Denmark, Højre's political interests in forming alliances with other parties to join ruling coalitions coincided with a coordinated, highly-organized business community. In America, NAM was ultimately unable to form a corporatist-style association because party competition worked against these aspirations.

Our findings suggest that party politics has a substantial impact on the construction of business as a social class and reveal fundamental interconnections between party structures and patterns of employer association. Nonproportional, two-party systems lacking dedicated business parties create different possibilities for representing the economic development goals of employers compared to prospects in proportional, multiparty systems. The degree of national (versus local) party strength may influence the development of national associations to represent national economic goals.

The story of the origins of business organization is also important for reasons transcending esoteric academic concerns. Business organization is an important determinant of levels of social protection across advanced industrial societies (Martin 1995; 2000; Martin and Swank 2004; Swank and Martin 2001). If organization translates into greater support for social protections and an equitable society, it is important to understand how this pattern of fragmentation and limited institutional incapacity initially emerged.

References

Agerholm, S. and A. Vigen 1895, 'Arbejdsgiver Foreningen Gennem 25 Aar, 1896-1921', *Atlanta Constitution,* assorted articles.

Arbejdsgiver Foreningen Gennem 50 Aar 1896-1946, Langkjærs Bogtrykkeri 1946, Copenhagen.

Bacote, C. 1959, 'Negro Officeholders in Georgia under President McKinley', in *The Journal of Negro History,* 44, 3 July, pp. 217-239.

Bensel, R. 2000, *The political economy of American industrialization,* Cambridge University Press, New York.

Berk, G. 1994, *Alternative Tracks,* Johns Hopkins University Press, Baltimore.

Bindslev, A. 1937-8, *Konservatismens Historie i Danmark,* Bd. 2-3.

Buck, C.A.F., Letter to McKinley 1986, January 8, *McKinley Papers,* series 2 V87-P90.

Bureau of Labor 1911, *Industrial Education,* Government Printing Office, Washington.

Croly, H. 1912, *Marcus Alonzo Hanna,* The Macmillan Co., 184, New York.

Crouch, C. 1993, *Industrial Relations and European State Traditions,* Oxford University Press, New York.

Cusack, T., T. Iversen and D. Soskice 2007, 'Economic Interests and the Origins of Electoral Institutions', in *American Political Science Review,* 101, August.

LaPalombara, J. and Myron Weiner (eds.) 1966, in *Political Parties and Political Development,* Princeton University Press, Princeton, N.J.

Davenport-Hines, R.P.T. 1988, 'The Modernization Crisis of British Industry', in H. Yamazuki and M. Miyamoto (eds.), *Trade Associations in Business History,* University of Tokyo Press, Tokyo, pp. 205-226.

Davenport-Hines, R.P.T. 1988, 'Delegates Got Down to Business', in *Cincinnati Enquirer* 1/24/1895, p. 8.

Downs, A. 1957, *An Economic Theory of Democracy,* Harper, New York.

Due, J. and J.S. Madsen, 'Hvorfor er den danske aftale model anderledes en den Svenske?', FAOS Forskningsnotat, 26.

Due, J., J.S. Madsen, C. S. Jensen, L. K. Petersen 1994, *The Survival of the Danish Model,* DJØF Publishing, Copenhagen.

Dybdahl, V. 1969, *Partier og Erhverv,* Universitets Forlaget i Aarhus, Aarhus.

Friis, H. 1969, 'Issues in Social Security Policies in Denmark', in Shirley Jenkins (ed.), *Social Security in International Perspective,* Columbia University Press, New York.

Gable, R., 'Birth of an Employers' Association', in *Business History Review,* 33 (4), pp. 535-545.

Galenson, W. 1952, *The Danish System of Labor Relations,* Harvard University Press, Cambridge.

Gourevitch, P. 1986, *Politics in Hard Times,* Cornell University Press, Ithaca.

Hall, P. and D. Soskice 2001, *Varieties of Capitalism,* Cambridge University Press, Cambridge.

Hansen, H. 1997, *Caps and Gowns: Historical Reflections on the Institutions That Shaped Learning for and at Work in Germany and the United States*, Unpublished Dissertation, University of Wisconsin.

Hartz, L. 1955, *The Liberal Tradition in America*, Harcourt Brace, New York.

Hawley, E. 1966, *The New Deal and the Problem of Monopoly*, Princeton University Press, Princeton.

Hounshell, D.A. 1978, *From the American System to Mass Production*, Unpublished Dissertation, University of Delaware.

Hyldtoft, O. 1999 (Aarhus), *Danmarks Økonomiske historie 1840-1910*, Chapters 13-14.

»It's President Dolan«, *Cincinnati Commercial Gazette* (January 25, 1895), 1.

Iversen, T. and D. Soskice. No date. »Distribution and Redistribution: In the Shadow of the Nineteenth-Century.« Typescript, Department of Government, Harvard University.

Katzenstein, P. 1985, *Small States in World* Markets, Cornell University Press, Ithaca, New York.

Knudsen, T. 1991, 'State Building in Scandinavia' in Knudsen (eds.), *Welfare Administration in Denmark*, Publikationscentralen, Copenhagen.

Levine, D. 1978, 'Conservatism and Tradition in Danish Social Welfare Legislation 1890-1933', in *Comparative Studies*, 20, 1 January, pp. 54-69.

»Manufacturers Cheer for McKinley«, *New York Times* 1/22/1896, 1.

»Manufacturers in Convention«, *Atlanta Constitution*, 1/24/1895, 2.

Martin, C.J. 2006, 'Seetorial Parties, Divided Business', *Studies in American Political Development 20(2).*

Martin, C.J. and D. Swank 2004, 'Does the Organization of Capital Matter?, in *American Political Science Review*, 98 (4), pp. 593-612.

McDougall, T. 1896, 'The Home Market', in *Proceedings of the First Annual Convention of the National Association of Manufacturers of the United State*, January 21, 22 and 23, pp. 3-8.

McKinley, W. letter to Col. J.F. Hanson February 27, 1896, in *McKinley Papers*, Series 2 V87-P90.

McKinley,W. 1896, letter to R.E. Wright, January 4, *McKinley Papers*, Series 2 V87-P90.

'Metropolitan Cash Used for McKinley', 1908, in *New York Times*, April 4.

Møller, I.H. 1994, 'Velfaerdsstatens udbygning', Samfundslitteratur, Frederiksberg.

'Mr. Blaine's 'Deadly Stab', 1890, in *New York Times*, December 26, 4.

NAM 'Advice from the South', in *National Industrial Review*, II, 6 July 1895, pp. 154.

NAM 1896, *Proceedings of the First Annual Convention of the National Association of Manufacturers of the United States*, Chicago, January 2, 22and 23.

NAM 1902, *Proceedings of the Seventh Annual Convention of the National Association of Manufacturers of the United States*, NAM Bureau of Publicity, April 15, 16, and 17, New York)

NAM 1926, 'Reports of Officers', in *Proceedings of the Thirty-first Annual Convention of the National Association of Manufacturers of the United States of America*, NAM, New York.

'The National Association of Manufacturers and other Organizations', in *American Trade* II, 19, 7/1/1899, p. 148.
The National Industrial Review II 1895, 6 July, 148, (no title).
The National Industrial Review I 1895, 4 May, (no title).
'A High-Tariff Republican President' 1895, in *New York Times*, 25 January, 1.
'A Ninth Cabinet Member: A Contingent Offer Made' 1897, in *New York Times*, 23 February, 1.
Olcott, C. 1916, *William McKinley Vol. 1*, Houghton Mifflin, New York, p. 213.
Pedersen, O.K., N. Andersen, P. Kjær and J. Elberg 1992, *Privat Politik*, Samfundslitteratur, Frederiksberg.
Piore, M. and C. Sabel 1984, *The Second Industrial Divide*, Basic Books, New York.
Search, T. 1901, 'President's Report', in *Proceedings of the Sixth Annual Convention of the National Association of Manufacturers*, NAM Bureau of Publicity, New York, pp. 23-4.
Search, T. 1898, 'To the Executive Committee and Members of the National Association of Manufacturers', in *Proceedings of the Third Annual Convention of the National Association of Manufacturers*, NAM Bureau of Publicity, New York, 25, 26, 27 January, pp. 3-32 and 13-14.
Stephens, J. 1979, *The Transition from Capitalism to Socialism*, Macmillan, London.
Steigerwalt, A. 1964, *The National Association of Manufacturers 1895-1914*, Grand Rapids, University of Michigan, Michigan.
Swank, D. and C.J. Martin 2001, 'Employers and the Welfare State', in *Comparative Political Studies*, 34, October, pp. 889-923.
Tedlow, R. 1988, 'Trade Association and Public Relations', in H. Yamazuki and M. Miyamoto (eds.), *Trade Associations in Business* History, U. of Tokyo Press, Tokyo, pp. 139-172.
'They Welcomed M'Kinley' 1895, M. Telegraph, March 18, 1895, p. 1.
Thelen, K. 2004, *How Institutions Evolve*, Cambridge University Press, Cambridge.
Tolliday, S. and J. Zeitlin 1991, *The Power to Manage*, Routledge, New York.

CHAPTER 15

The State and Corporatism – The Role of the State in the Development and Reproduction of »the Danish Model«

Lars Bo Kaspersen and Ulrich Schmidt-Hansen
Professor, Copenhagen Business School, Denmark
Special Adviser, The Ministry of Finance, Denmark

The State and Corporatism

The role of the state in the development and reproduction of »the Danish model«

In the literature on the establishment and development of the Danish variant of corporatism, emphasis has most often been on the role of the social partners. Scholars rarely stress the crucial role which the state has played in the development of the system. We argue that several actors contributed to the development of the 'Danish model', but that these actors were often orchestrated by the state. At crucial moments the direction of these different actors was even determined by the state. In the first part of the article, it is argued that the state has been under-theorized and to some extent neglected in corporatist theory. In particular, we draw upon a conceptualization of the state developed by Michael Mann and Eric Nordlinger's different forms of state autonomy. We propose a state-centered theoretical focus enabling us to grasp the role of the state in the dynamics of the corporatist system. In the second part of the article, we present an analysis of the establishment and evolution of the Danish corporatist system seen from this distinctively state-centered perspective. In the third part we look into the current system during the last decade of the 20th century. With newly-conducted empirical research, we examine the role of the state in the corporatist system during the 1990s in the labour market and within immigration integration policy. We conclude that due to its autonomous power, the state is still a key player in the corporatist system.

Since the 1990s Denmark has often been described as a successful example of a welfare state with an ability to adapt to new conditions of existence brought about by the new global economy.[1] Key economic figures have proved that Denmark has performed well during the last decade. Often it has been asked how Denmark has managed to change a poor economy in the 1970s and 1980s into a successful enterprise in the last 10-15 years. When trying to explain the socio-economic success in Denmark, observers point to 'the Danish model', where the social partners – especially the labour market parties – have a profound say in policy-making. This has been described as cooperative adaptation (Jørgensen 2002), which implies an ability among actors and institutions to react in a stabilizing manner to ensure that important elements in the welfare system survive.« (Jørgensen 2002: 240). This description follows the vast literature on Denmark and other corporatist countries, where corporatist relations are pointed to as the explanation for socio-economic success (see Katzenstein 1985; Lijphardt and Crepaz 1991; Visser and Hemerijck 1997; Due et al. 1993).

The specific set of institutions and institutional practices which can be characterized as particularly 'Danish' and successful in handling socio-economic challenges has a long history, creating a certain framework for coping with current challenges. We argue that the establishment and development of the Danish variant of effective corporatism has not primarily been driven by the social partners as a number of scholars on Danish cor-

1. The research for this article was conducted in 2003-2005 as a part of the EU-sponsored project 'A Framework for Socio-Economic Development in Europe? The Consensual political Cultures of the Small West European States in Comparative and Historical Perspective (No. HPSE-CT-2002-00134)

poratism seem to suggest (c.f. Due et al. 1993, Jørgensen 2002); neither has its development been entirely due to the small size and openness of the economy as, for example, Katzenstein suggests (Katzenstein 1985). Instead we will bring to the fore the crucial role the Danish state has played in the development and reproduction of the corporative system. We shall argue that several actors contributed both intentionally and unintentionally to the development of the 'Danish model', but that these actors were often orchestrated by the state, and at crucial moments even determined by the state.[2] Such an argument requires a stronger conceptual understanding of the state. Thus, if we want to understand the historical development and the dynamics of the Danish model, we need to incorporate the state-as-an-actor and an active player as an important variable.

In the first part of the article we argue that the state has been undertheorized and to some extent neglected in corporatist theory. The society-centered focus originally suggested by scholars such as Schmitter (1974), Lembruch (1984) and Katzenstein (1985) has biased the analyses leading to an inadequate analytical treatment of the state as an autonomous actor. We shall draw upon various forms of state theories in particular from historical sociology. We propose a state-centered theoretical focus enabling us to grasp the role of the state in the dynamics of the corporatist system. In the second part we present a historical analysis of the complexities of the establishment and evolution of the Danish corporatist system seen from this distinctively state-centered perspective. In the third part we evaluate the development of the Danish model in the last part of the 20th century. We examine the role of the state in the corporatist system on the labour market as an example of an old policy area, and on immigration integration policy as an example of a relatively new policy area.

2. The term model implies that it can be imitated. Since each and every state structure and form of effective corporatism has developed along a unique different historical path and is based upon a specific composition of elements embedded in a specific historical context it is difficult to transfer institutional practices from one state and society to another. Consequently, we do not think this is the case with the so-called Danish Model.

The Theoretical Framework

While much theoretical and empirical effort has been put into discussing and evaluating the outcomes of corporatist policy making, less has been reserved for examining the complex processes of interaction that drive the dynamics. In particular, the role of the state in this process is somewhat undeveloped (Torfing 1995: 9). It is not until the mid-1980s that serious attempts are made to develop a more state-centered perspective on corporatist policy-making (Hemerijck and Vail 2005: 5). Colin Crouch's analysis of how historical contingencies of state traditions has had consequences for the organization and shaping of civil society and interest intermediation stands out as one of the clearest examples of this approach (Crouch 1993). He argues that the state plays important roles not only in constructing the corporatist framework but also in the continuous political exchange within this framework, which the state facilitates by using either side payments or threats of bypassing corporatist institutions. This implies that the state is deeply and continuously involved in regulating corporatist policy-making. Crouch describes the dynamic between the corporatist state and societal partners as a »sharing of political space« (Crouch 1993: 50ff), thereby pointing to a complex reciprocal relationship between the state and organized interests, leaving neither with complete power: the determinants of the dynamics of corporatist governance must therefore be found in the interplay between state and interest groups.

In this perspective the state is implicitly regarded as an actor which is capable of conducting relatively autonomous actions. However, the question of autonomy seems rather undeveloped. Is it fair to argue that the state acts autonomously? How and under what conditions does the state frame and facilitate corporatist exchange? When does it use side payments and when does it use threats of bypassing corporatist institutions? Answers to these questions remain unanswered by Crouch's approach. Other scholars have followed in his footsteps (notably Visser and Hemmerijck 1997; Hemerijck and Vail 2005). Following along the same lines as Crouch, Visser and Hemmerijck's analysis of the Dutch miracle (Visser and Hemmerijck 1997) shows how the state in some cases can be a »shadow of hierarchy«, as was the case in Dutch labour market policy (Visser and Hemmerijck 1997: 81ff). Hemmerijck and Vail argue that the capacity of the state is central when comparing the dynamics of German and Dutch corporatism (Hemerijck and Vail 2005: 42-47). As was the case with Crouch's contribution, one must appreciate the sensitivity to the role played by the state. However, questions surrounding the characteristics of state autonomy still remain unanswered.

Here we have to turn to other sources. The problem of autonomy and the state-society relation has been discussed within various traditions of state theory. A number of scholars have argued that the state is not only relatively autonomous, but in certain situations entirely so. This view is mainly advocated by historical sociologists such as Theda Skocpol, Charles Tilly and Michael Mann. In this context we shall draw upon Mann's work. The state and the autonomy of the state are central in Mann's works (e.g Mann 1977; 1984; 1986; 1988; 1992). Mann's project attempts to break with the reductionism characterizing liberalistic, Marxist, and functionalist theories, in which the state is reduced to pre-existing structures in civil society. The state responds to two kinds of interests/pressures (both internal and external), generating a particular autonomous »space« where the state-elite may manoeuvre and play the classes off against each other. The dual conception of the state is conceived as a step away from reductionism. Mann, however, suggests a further radicalization in order to avoid reductionism. The state is only an arena – a space – and this is the source of the autonomy of the state. Broadly, Mann subscribes to a Weberian point of departure for an understanding of the state (Mann 1988: 4). This includes four parts:

- A differentiated set of institutions and staff, forming
- centrality, defined as political relations, radiating outwards from a center to cover
- a territorially-demarcated area, over which is exercised
- a monopoly of authoritatively binding rule making, backed up by a monopoly of physical means of violence.

To Mann, an essential element is the centralized institutions of the state containing a high level of power possessed by the state elite. The power of the state elite and the centralized institutions have two dimensions. One is called despotic power, which is the direct potential and range of action of the state elite. Actions may be carried out without any kind of routine negotiations with groups in civil society (Mann 1993: 59). The other is infrastructural power, which is the capacity of the state to penetrate civil society and to implement political decisions within a given territory. Infrastructural power has made it increasingly possible for states to subordinate the everyday life of the population with extended levels of control and surveillance. It is this form of power that dominates modern capitalist democracies (Mann 1993: 59).

The possession of despotic and infrastructural power lends autonomy to the state. This power and autonomy have their origins in three conditions: 1) the necessity of the state, 2) the multiplicity of the functions of the state, and 3) the territorial centralization of the state. Concerning the necessity of the state, Mann takes his point of departure from a Hobbesian conception of society. The existence of a society is conditioned by the presence of rules that are capable of protecting life and property. These rules originate from a monopoly. Moreover, it is said that states always exist in a system of states, which also imposes certain rules of behaviour onto each state. The autonomous power of the state proceeds from this necessity – »necessity is the mother of state power« (Mann 1984: 196).

Mann claims that the state has several functions. The state as a »binding rule-making authority« covers several areas, each of which are functional with respect to different sectors within society. These are divided into four main categories:

- The maintenance of internal order.
- Military attack/aggression. The external functions of the state.
- The maintenance of infrastructure (of communication). For example roads, rivers, coinage, weights and measures, and messaging systems.
- Economic redistribution. An authoritative distribution of scarce material resources between various age groups, sexes, regions, classes, etc. Moreover, there is also an international element, since it is the state that regulates the relations of trade and currency exchange along the borders.

These four kinds of tasks are undertaken by the state. Thus the state has several functional relations with various groups. The state's room for manoeuvre exists between all these different groups, and this space can be used to play off the various groups against each other. Mann's conclusion is that this room for manoeuvre is the birthplace of state power. But this insight does not capture the distinctiveness of the state as a social organization. As can be seen in the definition of the state given above, the state's institutional centralized and territorial nature is included as an element. This particular element is the precondition of the unique autonomous power of the state. Only the state has a particular inherent centralized authoritative power over a specific territory. In contrast to economic, ideological and military groups in civil society, the resources of the state elite radiate authoritatively outwards from a center, only coming to a halt at a territorially defined border. »The state is, indeed, a place – both a central place and a unified territorial reach« (*ibid.*: 198). More precisely, this property distinguishes the state from other powerful societal groups such as businesses, capital owners, interest organizations, the Church or the nobility. The autonomous power of the state proceeds precisely from the difference in the organizational structure and socio-spatial conditions. »Territorial centralization provides the state with a potentially independent basis of power mobilization being necessary to social development and uniquely in the possession of the state itself« (*ibid.*: 201). The autonomy of the state therefore consists of its necessity, the plurality of functions and territorial centralization. The power of the state elite cannot be reduced to the power of any group and it is therefore autonomous in relation to civil society. Thus, by bringing Mann's work into our framework we have established the autonomous character of the state.

Moving further towards a more differentiated concept of autonomy, Eric A. Nordlinger presents a rather different analytical perspective to the state compared to Mann. Nordlinger stresses that the state must be conceived not only as an organizational apparatus but also – and maybe more importantly – as a collective of persons with special authority.[3] These persons have the right to make decisions that are binding for all of society (Nordlinger 1981: 11). Nordlinger constructs state autonomy as a variable by introducing three types of stately autonomy which can be exercised by the state under different kinds of conditions of state-society relations.[4] The first type of autonomy describes a situation where the state

3. So far Mann will agree with Nordlinger. Mann's conception of the state is a more encompassing one. Nordlinger has a more narrow focus.
4. We are not entirely convinced that Nordlinger escapes the problem of reductionism and therefore he might not be capable of operating with a concept of

deliberately disregards the interests of other groups – e.g. the labour unions, employer federations etc. (Nordlinger 1981: 118ff). Here the state will only succeed if it possesses what Mann characterized as despotic power. The second type describes a situation where the state tries to sway the preferences of, for example, interest organizations, using political leadership and manipulation in order to arrive at a compromise which will serve the interests of the state. (Nordlinger 1981: 99ff). Finally, the third type describes a situation where the state invites interest groups into the decision-making process in return for a commitment to supporting the implementation of the final decisions (Nordlinger 1981: 74ff). We might describe the last strategy as a kind of give and take system in which interest groups forego some of their political freedom and in return receive a privileged position in the political process. Nordlinger's last strategy does in many ways resemble descriptions of corporatist relations between state and organized interests. We could argue that by approaching a corporatist decision-making system from the perspectives provided by Mann and Nordlinger, we are able to capture the complex reciprocal relationship between the state and interest organizations without losing sight of the autonomous powers of the state as represented by the first two strategies provided by Nordlinger. Thus, by introducing Mann and Nordlinger, we are able partly to establish the argument for the autonomy of the state in state-centered corporatist theory, and partly to provide a specification of various forms of autonomy.

The Development of the Danish Corporatist State and the Effective Corporatist System

It is beyond the scope of this article to give a more comprehensive exposition of the Danish variant of effective corporatism. Several other scholars have contributed to the overview and analysis of Danish development

the state which actually allows the state to be autonomous – and not only 'relative autonomous'. However, the way he differentiates between various forms of autonomy is useful for our purpose and the Nordlinger conceptualization of autonomy is a part of our framework.

(see Jørgensen 2002; Due and Madsen 1993, Campbell, Hall, and Pedersen 2006). Instead, we will concentrate on the role of the state in the Danish corporatist system. This perspective requires a historical sociological analysis of the Danish state formation process. We cannot provide such an analysis here, but some important aspects will form our point of departure.[5]

The Danish state evolved through a particular combination of despotic and infrastructural power, which facilitated a specific variant of corporatism. The Danish state formation process was long, but in 1660 fundamental changes occurred when a stände staat was replaced by a more demarcated, territorial and centralized absolutist state. The 1660 regime change was a crucial 'critical juncture' which transformed the Danish state and facilitated the development of a modern society. This society (market and civil) may be described as being 'fully fledged' with the advent of the liberal-democratic Constitution (June 1849) and the Freedom of Trade Act (1857).

1864 is another critical juncture in the Danish state formation process and arguably more important to the development of corporatism. In 1864 Denmark suffered a defeat to Prussia and this led to a set of changes which included a revision of the constitution, political changes with a strengthening of the conservative forces, and also a loss of fertile land and one third of the population. Moreover, it paved the way for a strong popular nationalism. A huge part of nationalist emotion was distributed among popular social movements – in the beginning primarily in the farmers' associations, but later also in the small-holders and the labour movement. Associationalism was reinforced by popular nationalism partly as popular opposition to the conservative ruling class, and partly as a national response to the new conditions of existence after the defeat.

The strong wave of associationalism had already started in the 1850s and 1860s. These decades are called the 'age of associationalism' in Denmark (Hvidt 1990: 95). The many associations founded in the 1850s and in the following decades were very much in opposition to the ruling elite and class – the landowners and the urban elite. In particular, the farmers

5. Further reading on the Danish state formation process, see Kaspersen 2004; 2006; Kaspersen & Ottesen 2001.

formed a large number of associations aimed at improving their economic situation by creating small local saving banks and insurance companies, for example (Hvidt 1990: 94-96). The state approved because it could see the benefits when the population organized and educated themselves in these associations. The Danish state supported many initiatives financially, and the principle of 'help-to-self-help'. It was a sophisticated way of governing and it is an extension of the infrastructural power capacity of the state. By indirect control of the development of important activities the state could strengthen its own resource base, while the local actors were responsible for the organization and the daily business of the activities, whether local saving banks, a sick-club or adult education.

Further Corporatism

Some other developments facilitated the emergence of the 'organizational society' and the effective democratic corporatist system. The political processes after the defeat to Prussia brought about a peculiar situation in which the state and the political elite – Prime Minister J.B.S. Estrup, the Right and civil servants in particular – appeared to be both strong and weak at the same time. The Conservative government outplayed the opposition. In 1875-94 Prime Minister Estrup managed to keep the opposition – despite its majority in the Folketing (the House of Commons) – out of influence by governing through provisional finance acts. Through Estrup's use of provisional acts, the state appeared to be a strong entity wielding much despotic power. It follows from Nordlinger's differentiation of autonomy that the state during the Estrup-years deliberately disregarded the interests of other groups.

Daily politics was characterized by a policy of obstruction from the Left which was, however, too weak to effect a change in the system. Therefore, daily politics became a matter for interest groups and voluntary associations. The farmers' movement played an important role, as did the associations in towns and cities related to the new labour market emerging as a consequence of industrialization and urbanization. A strong political force from below contributed to shaping Danish society during the second half of the 19th century when the parliamentary system was at a stalemate. The apparently strong but passive state facilitated the growth of voluntary associations, both by providing the legal framework and by acting so passively that a space was left open for other actors. The voluntary association was used in this space as a means of organizing class interest into class conflict. The character of class conflict changed during this period. In the 1860s and 70s the main dispute was between farmers and the landowners, but during the 1880s and 1890s capital-labour emerged as a new conflict dimension.

Several interrelated social and political processes merged in Denmark during the 1860s, 70s, 80s and 90s. The development of voluntary associations and their relationship with the state have already been mentioned. The liberal-democratic constitution gave an impetus to the development of voluntary associations because their formation was stated as a right in the constitution. Moreover, the 1849 Constitution and The Freedom of Trade Act (1857) destroyed the last remnants of the medieval guild structure. The guilds were, however, of major importance for a number of people living in towns and cities. For centuries masters, craftsmen, journeymen and apprentices were organized in guilds: as well as the knowledge transfer and the learning processes which this involved, the guilds also functioned as social welfare providers by providing some security in terms of sick pay, poverty relief and pensions. The relationship between master and journeymen and between journeyman and apprentice was also regulated by the guilds. These forms of security disappeared with the formal abolition of the guilds. Some continued to function in a reconstructed form as new voluntary associations. In Copenhagen, in particular, these associations developed and at times took on the role of functioning as an employer association. Some guilds dominated by journeymen evolved into sick- and funeral clubs. Some also functioned as an emergent form of a trade union, organizing strikes and forcefully compelling the employers to accept the need for increases in wages (Rerup 1989: 48). In other words, the combination of the right to form voluntary associations and the need to replace the guilds with new organizations influenced the development of a corporatist structure.

So far we have explained the reasons for voluntary associations assuming importance; but why did they become influential in the official political system? With the new liberal constitution in 1849, the old estate (stände) system broke down and interests were now thought to be represented by individuals in the parliament. This did not work. Although party formations took place, they were not sufficiently able to represent the interests of the market. Consequently, while political parties were in the process of developing, it did not take long for the organized interests in market and civil society to become visible. As time went by, a closer connection evolved between, on the one hand, the associational structure and the organized interests in the market and, on the other, the political parties in the parliament. 'Venstre' represented the farmers in the parliament and the labour movement was represented by the Social Democrats and so on. Moreover, since the Left (Venstre) – the farmers in particular – did not trust the Right and the conservative bureaucracy, they were already trying to include the voluntary associations in influencing public policy development before the turn of the century (Christiansen and Nørgaard 2003: 40). Another dimension is related to a specific state tradition in which various interest groups were included in some of the public administration agencies during the absolutist regime. Some commissions at the municipal level were also established in the years after the introduction of the liberal constitution of 1849 (Christiansen and Nørgaard 2003: 41). From the 1890s onwards, organized interest groups were gradually included in the political and administrative decision-making process (Christiansen and Nørgaard 2003: 42; Nørgaard 2000: 193-206). In other words, the development of the infrastructural power dimension of the Danish state has long historical roots.

Finally, an answer can be provided by pointing to the state-society relationship that developed during the post-1864 years, in which the state supported initiatives taken by actors in society as part of a help-to-self-help strategy. It was a form of compromise between a strategy of state intervention and non-intervention. It can be seen as an outcome of the compromise first between the Conservative and the Left (farmers) and later between the Center-Right and the Social Democrats. By recognizing the voluntary associations and, in particular, the prominent associations representing major interest groups in the market, the state reinforced the level and intensity of the organization of the interest groups. As an example we can point to the support given by the state to the unemployment system. The system was based upon a principle of voluntary participation. It operated separately from the trade unions, but was administered by them; thus there was strong encouragement for workers to organize and become members of a union (Knudsen 1999: 112-113).

The third critical juncture affecting the development of a corporatist structure in Danish society was World War One. Despite the fact that the country remained neutral throughout, it became clear that Denmark was constrained by the war as much as any other country. Exports were threatened due to problems of blockades and mines in the seas. Therefore, the importing of raw materials was also disrupted. The outcome was a shortage of supplies and price increases in goods. The low-income social groups, in particular, suffered. This could have led to more inequality and social tensions. Consequently, the state adopted a new strategy to solve the problems. Massive state intervention and regulation proved to be the answer. This strategy was, however, based upon a corporative structure in which the key societal organizations representing the major social groups and economic interests participated (Vigen 1950: 440-469). Immediately after the war broke out, the Danish government – with full support from the Parliament – established on August 7 1914 a Commission with the Minister of Interior Affairs, Ove Rode, in charge. The strong support of the Commission indicated a truce between the otherwise conflicting parties in the Parliament. The Minister appointed representatives from all major organizations, interest groups and social classes in Denmark. The farmers, the small-holders, industry, the trade unions, the ship owners, consumers, the social democrats, the liberals, and science were all represented (Vigen 1950: 444; Rasmussen 1965: 72). The Commission constructed an elaborate system of regulation which affected every economic and social area, including price policy, supply policy and rationing, and to a certain extent also income distribution policy. The Commission did this with considerable success. Denmark succeeded in coming through the war without major troubles, tensions or social conflicts.

The First World War is crucial to understanding corporatism in Denmark. Redistribution of income and welfare took place for the first time on a massive scale. Critical to this development is the means by which the state succeeded partly in getting support for these policies and partly in implementing them. The state increased its governing capacity, but so did all the major organizations representing the economic interest of the country. In 1899 the state had already recognized and accepted that the labour market was run by the employers and employees. The state also had some years before acknowledged the presence and importance of the other organizations, not least the farmers and industry. It was not until the First World War, however, that all these organizations were invited to take part in all sorts of commissions and committees set up by the government or a governmental institution. This gave them considerable influence and this process transformed these organizations into more stable and strongly institutionalized entities. They became indispensable and co-responsible for societal development in Denmark. It is hardly wrong to say that the First World War was a point of crystallization for the Danish model of 'effective corporatism'.

We will now move from a general discussion of the role of the state in the emergence of corporatism to focus on its role in labour market corporatism. By the end of the 19th century, the main organizations of the labour market had been established. Employers united into the Employers' Confederation of 1896, subsequently the Danish Employers' Confederation (Dansk Arbejdsgiverforening, DA). The trade union movement responded a little later by forming in 1898 the Co-operating National Trade Unions in Denmark (De samvirkende Fagforbund i Danmark, DsF) – known today as the National Organization in Denmark, LO (Landsorganisationen i Danmark), i.e. a confederation of trade unions (Due et al. 1994: 76-78).

Developing the Danish way of labour market corporatism

The development of the two main organizations, Dsf (LO) and DA, indicates a distinctive trait of the Danish labour market structure. Through the conflicts of the 1880s and 1890s, a tradition of negotiation emerged that was relatively free from state intervention. The state intervened only when the labour market parties were unable to resolve their disputes by themselves and when this resulted in comprehensive strikes or lockouts followed by a decrease in production (Mikkelsen 1992: 34; Due et al. 1994: 70). Following Nordlinger's differentiation between various forms of autonomy, the governance of the labour market and industrial relations in Denmark is very much a 'give and take system' in which the state facilitates a specific architecture, but much of the content is developed by actual negotiations between the social partners. The organizations were allowed relative autonomy in setting the conditions of the labour market, with minimal interference from the state. The role of the state was to function as guarantor of the formal rights necessary for the institutional practices of the labour market to develop. The legal preconditions defining the institutional development of the labour market were the 1849 Constitution, the Act on Freedom of Trade (*Næringsloven*) in 1857 and – as we shall now discuss – the September Compromise of 1899 (Skovgaard-Petersen 1985; Rerup 1989). The events that led to the signing of the September Compromise began in the spring of 1899. Starting out as a minor strike, conflict escalated between the two labour market parties, DsF and DA, causing DA to initiate a nationwide lockout of certain trades. Following months of opposing demands and refusals to settle the dispute, an agreement was reached in September that year which granted extensive rights to both parties concerned. Most importantly, the September Compromise constituted recognition of the management prerogative, which was the main goal of the employers. Furthermore, it promoted the centralization of the labour market, especially the structure of negotiation, thus leaving the employers' confederation victorious (Mikkelsen 1991: 8). Nonetheless, the Compromise was also a victory for the trade union movement because it firmly established the workers' right to organize (Due et al. 1994: 83; Rerup 1989: 51-54).

From the turn of the century, the centralized bodies, DA and DsF, conducted most labour market negotiations. This meant a strengthening of these central organizations at the expense of branch organizations, i.e. the separate trade unions and their complementary employer associations (Mikkelsen 1992: 55). By accepting this arrangement, the state allowed the associations themselves to come to an agreement that secured a stable and well-functioning labour market, as strike and lockout activities were considerably limited or at least circumscribed by rules that prevented the development of more serious conflicts. In principle the 1899 Compromise and the following ten years bear witness to state recognition of the two organizations. The state recognizes the presence of a conflict between capital and labour. The state officially recognizes the right and legitimacy of the two organizations to negotiate and to control industrial relations.

Thus on one level labour market corporatism in Denmark presents itself as a decision-making system requiring little state regulation. It appears self-regulating with the organized interests playing the dominant roles. The government, however, only respects the autonomy of the parties as long as the parties are able to find a compromise. Given the centrality of the negotiations, a major breakdown will affect almost the entire labour market. In the case of a general strike the state, of course, has to react. Thus Danish labour market corporatism has been conditioned by active and continuous state regulation and intervention. In the following paragraphs we will discuss some aspects of Danish labour market corporatism which place the state firmly at the center of the corporatist decision-making process.

At the heart of labour market corporatism is the collective agreement system, which is mainly controlled by the labour market parties. The most distinctive characteristic of the Danish model of labour relations is regulation by collective agreements rather than through legislation. As our account has shown, the relationship to the authorities is nonetheless strong. Hence, throughout the 20th century, the state has played a decisive role in the shaping of the legal framework and conditions of opportunities which, again, is an example of exercising infrastructural power. In the aftermath of the September agreement, the procedures surrounding collective bargaining were unclear and needed legal specification. Only a little more than 10 years after the September Compromise – in 1910 – the state created the Conciliation Board as a third agent in order to facilitate the negotiation process between the parties. The Board was formed so that it could intervene in the case of a bargaining deadlock. In addition, the labour market parties were mutually obliged to maintain industrial peace between collective agreements. During the 1930s the Conciliation Board became a tangible and legally enshrined nucleus of the collective bargaining system. The chairman of the Conciliation Board is appointed by the government and via the »right of concatenation«,[6] established by

6. The "right of concatenation" involves linking the labour market's many and different agreements together to form an aggregate conciliation proposal, so that in the first instance all trade unions and employer organizations had to vote in favour of the proposal, which otherwise lapsed. At the second stage

the Conciliation Board Act of 1934, this state body played a major role in solving conflicts in the labour market in the 20th century in Denmark. Emphasizing the role of the Conciliation Board as a government controlled conflict solver must, however, not cloud the fact that the resolution of conflicts in the labour market in Denmark is still primarily the business of the labour market parties. The Conciliation Board has mainly operated on the premises of the collective bargaining system and thus, indirectly, of the two parties. It has been firmly aimed at reaching a compromise based on the balance of power between the parties. Finally, an Industrial Court was set up to deal with breaches in the collective agreements (Due et al. 1994: 85-89; Christiansen et al. 2000: 10).

In other words, even though the emerging Danish model denoted a considerable degree of self-governance for labour and management, the state and the changing governments were highly influential in setting the legal framework and possibilities for their actions. In addition to this institutionalized intervention, a practice was established of direct state intervention in cases where inability to reach collective agreements caused a major industrial dispute. Quite a large number of conflicts in the labour market have been solved with the help of the Conciliation Board or with direct state intervention. In order to uphold the system the state intervened 10 times between 1934 and 1991 and the Conciliation Board no less than 11 times (Due et al. 1993: 251).

So far we have shown how the state has been an active and crucial player in the development of a corporatist system, which on the surface is characterized by little state involvement. The special 'model' encompassing an influential state with social partners with a large degree of autonomy has led to a strong integration of these partners into the political system when it comes to consultation, law preparatory work and implementation policies. Thus the corporative system reinforced itself during the 20th century. In general it is fair to conclude that the state has upheld its autonomy but has also strategically exploited this autonomy to facili-

joint voting was established for all areas covered by agreements, so that an aggregate majority in favour of the proposal meant adoption for all, even though some separate areas might have a majority against the proposal (Due et al. 1993: 498f).

tate a system in which it 'invites interest groups into the decision-making process in return for a commitment to support the implementation of the final decisions (Nordlinger 1981: 74ff). We shall now examine whether the state has continued to play a crucial role in regulating Danish corporatism in recent years.

Recent Developments – Employment and Integration policy

In this section we examine how the Danish corporatist system has coped with socio-economic challenges in the last decades of the 20th century, and the role the state has played in the process. Our conclusions are based upon an analysis of two policy areas: employment and immigration integration.[7] These areas have been chosen because they are rooted in different historical and institutional settings and present different challenges to Danish politics. By employment policy we mean the efforts of the government and the social partners to reduce unemployment. Employment policy is usually regarded as a policy area where corporatist ties have been strong and dominating. During the 1970s and 1980s Denmark experienced growing unemployment,[8] which became the dominant political problem in the early 1990s. Integration policy covers questions of how to integrate immigrants in society. The number of immigrants has increased in Denmark since the 1970s and this policy area has moved considerably closer to the top of the political agenda.

Employment policy

On the surface, employment policy in Denmark manifests all the characteristics of a genuinely corporatist system. We have already discussed how the recurrent rounds of wage negotiations are handled by the social partners. If no solution can be reached, the state intervenes – a situation that has been far from rare in Denmark. The state, however, also holds

7. Our analysis and conclusions are based upon interviews with key persons within the two areas in 2003 and 2004 (see attached list of interviewed persons.
8. The level of unemployment actually continued to rise up through the 1980s. In 1973 the level was app. 1 percent, in 1975 app. 5 percent, in 1983 app. 10,5 percent and in 1993 app. 12 percent (Rasmussen, 2000)

important informal capacities through the civil servants' close relationships to the labour market parties. The informal contacts between the National Labour Market Authority (AMS), LO and DA are extensive, and prior to every meeting in the National Employment Council[9] the Secretary of the Council (a civil servant) contacts representatives of LO and DA to discuss any controversial subjects on the agenda. Helle Svendsen, Secretary of the Employment Council, says: »It is my job to ensure that the level of conflict in the Council does not become too high« One of her greatest assets in this process is her exhaustive knowledge of subjects and policy changes which may prove to be controversial for the social partners. In cases where either LO's or DA's interests are compromised, the civil servants will always afterwards try to repair the relationship with possible side payments. Helle Svendsen continues: »It is very much a system of give and take. It is very often the case that they (the interest organizations) say: 'All right, you (the Ministry) get this but then we want something in return'. You cannot use them to achieve political legitimacy without giving them something in return.« Also, LO and DA are well aware that taking part in the corporatist game sometimes means accepting suffering losses. Ole Krog, director in Danish Industry, says: »In some cases the Government can choose to run right over the interest organizations and pursue its own specific policy goals.« But both civil servants and representatives of the organized interests also know that the corporatist game of give and take only functions if all parties are able to accept defeats without jeopardizing the system.

A labour market reform initiated in 1993 is often singled out as the most important implemented policy resulting in the quite impressive drop in unemployment that Denmark has experienced since the early 1990s. The reform is also presented as a strong example of how the social partners were able to handle the socio-economic challenges posed by unemployment (Jørgensen 2002). However, here we argue that the process leading up to the implementation of the reform and later moderations of it cannot be fully understood without taking into account the active role played by the state. The reform was based on extensive research work undertaken by the Zeuthen Committee, which included all relevant

9. The National Employment Council is an advisory board to the Government.

labour market parties. However, if we dig deeper and analyze how the actual work within the Committee was carried out, we find the influence of the Government and the central administration in the Committee to be quite striking.[10] Formally, the Government was not part of the Committee and participated only as Secretariat. However, it exerted strong influence on the work of the Committee because it prepared the major part of the technical analyses. The government's main reason for establishing the Committee was to find a way to control the growing expense of employment benefits.[11] The Government knew it would have a hard time convincing LO of the need for this kind of reform, but without it the Government's power base in Parliament, which depended on the support of the small social liberal party – de Radikale – would be in jeopardy. The strategy of the leader of the Secretariat, Jørgen Rosted, was to convince LO of the need to restrict expenditure on employment benefits and in return establish generous activation schemes as compensation or side payments to LO, thereby securing their support for the reform even though it worsened the conditions for LO's own members.[12]

We argue that the case of the Zeuthen Committee is an example of how the state exercised its autonomy in the corporatist policy-making system and exerted considerable influence on the conclusions of the work of the Committee. The state was instrumental in producing and facilitating the compromises that needed to be found and it was able to sway LO, in particular, towards the outcome it preferred by using side payments in the form of the establishment of new activation schemes which benefited LO's members. Thus we argue that Nordlinger's second and third type of autonomy was used in the process leading up to the labour market re-

10. We conducted interviews with the chairman of the committee, the representative from the Government (who was also leader of the secretariat of the committee), the representatives from the major employer and employee organizations (DA and LO), representatives from two smaller organizations on both sides (The Danish Confederation of Professional Associations and The Danish Association of Managers and Executives) and one of the independent experts.
11. Prior to the Labour Market Reform the unemployed had the right to re-qualify for entitlement to unemployment benefits by participation in an activation offer. After the reform this right was abolished.
12. This description of the purpose of the Zeuthen Committee was given in an interview with the leader of the secretariat Jørgen Rosted.

form. Since around 1995 the state has been more reluctant to include the parties in modifications of the labour market reform. These modifications have to a large extent been determined during the yearly budget negotiations. Civil servant boards were assigned to design the policy proposals (Winther 2003: 298f). One could argue that the state's policy of autonomy has changed during the 1990s towards the first of Nordlinger's strategies.

Integration policy

Up until the late 1980s, integration policy was largely absent from the political agenda. During the 1990s, and as a consequence of a general change in the population's perception of immigrants towards a more critical stance, integration policy became »high politics« in Denmark. In early 1998 polls showed that 47 percent of the Danish population regarded immigration/integration policy as the biggest problem for the country. The political result was the presence in Parliament of the Danish People's Party (a protest party very critical towards immigration), who won 7.4 percent of the votes in the 1998 election.

The role of the state also changed quite dramatically during the 1990s. Before the 1998 integration law came into force, integration schemes were carried out by a non-governmental organization, the Danish Refugee Council (DRC), and the relatively small scope of the task combined with little political interest provided for an arena with very little political conflict. However, when problems regarding integration started to appear in the mid-1990s, the social democratic Minister of Domestic Affairs, Birthe Weiss, decided to set up an »integration committee« with the task of analyzing existing rules and regulations and of proposing a tentative formulation for a new integration law (Indenrigsministeriet, 1997). The members of the Committee were representatives from a number of relevant ministries and organizations (including the labour market parties, DRC, Local Government Denmark (LG)[13] and immigrant organizations). In that sense the formative period of policy-making in the area of integration

13. Local Government Denmark is the association of municipalities in Denmark. The municipalities have relative independence form the central government with regards to taxation and service production. The central government does, however, set the boundaries within which the municipalities can act independently.

followed the traditions of Danish corporatism. The Committee published its conclusions and recommendations in May 1997. In 1998 the first integration law in Danish history was passed.

The contents of the law, however, looked very different from the recommendations given by the Committee, central parts of which the Government had decided to ignore. The Committee recommended that the final responsibility for integration and, more importantly, for the distribution of immigrants among municipalities should remain with DRC. However, the Government needed to divert final responsibility away from DRC in order to implement a new distribution of refugees among municipalities in Denmark[14] (Clausen and Hovmand 2001: 53). This amendment was necessary to silence the growing criticism of the Government's integration policy coming even from the Government parties' own rank-and-file – especially among social democrats. DRC was not an authority and DRC could not and would not force any municipality to receive a larger number of refugees.

Also, the feeling in DRC was that the growing integration task was becoming too large for them to handle without jeopardizing their self-perception as a non-governmental organization. DRC Secretary General Andreas Kamm says: »At that time it seemed relevant to ask whether a task of this magnitude should be handled by the state or an NGO. And there were a number of good reasons to answer that it should be handled by the state because ultimately the citizens are the responsibility of the state.«

Prime Minister Poul Nyrup Rasmussen's decision to appoint a new Minister of Domestic Affairs in 1997 – Thorkil Simonsen, a former mayor and former president of Local Government Denmark, and regarded in public as more of a hard-liner on integration issues than his predecessor – was the first part of the strategy. The second, the decision to move final responsibility from DRC to the municipalities, resulted in a lot of criticism from concerned organizations, who didn't want immigrants to be forced to move to new places around the country. LG was also critical because

14. Refugees and immigrants mainly live in the large cities and municipalities around Copenhagen. Especially among mayors of these municipalities the discontent with the distribution of immigrants and refugees was widespread. These mayors were mainly social democrats.

they did not want to see any of their members being forced to accept a larger number of immigrants and refugees. In the negotiations leading up to the final passing of the new integration law, the feeling among representatives from LG was that they had been given little choice but to accept the Government's decision because it was supported by almost all the political parties in Parliament. Birgit Hedegård, chief of section in LG, says: »We thought that if the social democrats, the liberals and the conservatives all have this position (that the municipalities should take over responsibility), it would probably be better to play along and influence the process instead of insisting on a voluntary solution.«

Today decisions regarding integration policy are made through close cooperation between the state and LG. The municipalities are the sole responsible authority for implementing policies in the area and LG is therefore *the* central player.

This development has stripped the immigrant organizations[15] of any influence they had earlier on. When we discussed this issue with civil servants in the Ministry for Refugees, Immigration and Integration Affairs, they all regretted that no central immigrant organization has evolved that can carry the views of the immigrant groups forward. Permanent Under-Secretary Martin Isenbech says: »We try to include them (immigrant organizations), but it is hard to find out who to talk with. Sometimes I find it hard to know who is actually representing whom«. The problem is that no immigrant organization has developed that can deliver what the Ministry is demanding: legitimacy and help in implementing the Ministry's policies. In other words, the immigrant organizations are not able to »play the corporatist game«. And when the Ministry finds that these organizations cannot ultimately deliver the expected sup-

15. The immigrant organizations in Denmark are quite heterogeneous and the two attempts to make umbrella organizations have experienced a number of problems. The first organization IND-Sam was founded in 1981 but closed down in January 2003 because the organization's accounts were in a mess, which resulted in removal of all state subsidies. In 1993 POEM was founded after a number of immigrant organizations disagreed with the leadership of IND-Sam. POEM has also led a somewhat chaotic life, but it does, however, still exist after some turbulent years (Mikkelsen 2003: 113f; Hammer & Bruun 2000: 68ff)

port to a specific proposal, the corporatist »give and take« system breaks down. The (now former) Permanent Secretary, Niels Preisler, from the Ministry for Refugees, Immigration and Integration Affairs, says about the immigrant organizations: »It seems like they feel it is their function to say no and always be discontented. It is, of course, their right, but it doesn't get us anywhere.«

The case of the integration law and integration policy in general is illustrative in showing how the role of the state and the exercise of autonomous power of the state can change over time. From being almost absent in the arena until the early 1990s, the state has acted very autonomously from the mid-1990s onwards. Towards the immigrant organizations the state acted in a way consistent with Nordlinger's first autonomy strategy. In the case of LG it was a mix of the second and third strategies. The state certainly tried to sway LG to accept the reform, but it also applied rather generous side payments to the municipalities in the form of new and large state subsidies.

Conclusion

Traditional corporatist theory neglects the importance of the state in the establishment and development of effective corporatism. By analyzing the origin and development of the Danish effective corporatist system, we have demonstrated the crucial role the state is playing in the corporatist system – a role which goes beyond just being a shadow behind the scenes of the social partners.

In this article we have argued that several actors have been and still are active in the development of the 'Danish model', but that these actors are often orchestrated by the state; indeed, at key moments the direction of these different actors is even determined by the state. Thus, it is crucial to understand the role of the state-as-an-actor if we want to comprehend fully the historical development and the dynamics of the Danish model. Theoretically, our analysis is underpinned by the work by Michael Mann and his conceptualization of the state as an autonomous actor resulting from the necessity of the state, the multiplicity of the functions of the state, and the territorial centralization of the state. These three properties are the defining dimension of the autonomous state and no other type of organization carries them. In order to specify the specific character of the autonomy of the state, we have been inspired by Nordlinger's work.

The historical analysis shows how the state has been an active player both in terms of providing a legal framework for corporate arrangements and by creating institutions like the Conciliation Board and the Industrial Court in the labour market. Moreover, we see that the state has not hesitated to intervene when agreements between the parties could not be reached. We see how the capacity of using infrastructural power is increasing over the years, but how elements of despotic power are still applied when need be, e.g. when major general strikes have been threatened. The two policy cases do to a large extent support the conclusions from the historical analysis. In the cases of employment and integration policy, the state has been very active in regulating the corporatist system. The evidence from integration policy even shows how the state's regulation efforts can result in a disintegration of corporatist relations. Whereas the integration policy area can mainly be seen as an example of Nordlinger's first type of autonomy (more despotic power), we see all three types of autonomy at play in the labour market arena. However, maybe slightly surprisingly, we see a tendency towards a shift from the second and the third type to the first type after the introduction of the reform. Although we have only studied two policy areas, both of them indicate a strengthening of the despotic power of the state.

One could argue that our state-centered approach has determined the way we have told the story of »the Danish model«. As indicated in the introduction, other scholars have also related the tale without using the state as a crucial actor (Due et al. 1993; Jørgensen 2002). Each story emphasizes a different facet of the more comprehensive narrative. Our intention in this article has been to highlight an aspect which has been somewhat neglected in earlier research.

References

Bernild, O. 2003, 'On the development of the Welfare State: the case of Denmark', Paper delivered at the *1. International Conference on Health, Humanity and Culture*. Los Angeles, October 2003.

Campbell, J.L., J.A. Hall and Pedersen, O.K. Pedersen (eds.) 2006, *National Identity and Varieties of Capitalism: The State of Denmark,* McGill University Press, Montreal.

Christiansen, P.M. and A.S. Nørgaard 2003, *Faste forhold – flygtige forbindelser,* Aarhus Universitetsforlag, Aarhus.

Clausen, M.C.L. and M. Hovmand 2001, *Integrationsansvar i brud. Analyse af beslutningsprocessen, der gik forud for Integrationslovens vedtagelse,* MA-thesis at the Institute of Political Science, University of Copenhagen.

Due, J., J.S. Madsen and N. Lubanski 2000, 'Nordic labour relations: – between national autonomy and EU integration', in R. Hoffmann, O. Jacobi, B. Keller, M. Weiss (eds.), *Transnational Industrial Relations in Europe,* Hans Böckler Foundation, ETUI.

Due, J., J.S. Madsen, C.S. Jensen 1993, *Den danske model. En historisk sociologisk analyse af det kollektive aftalesystem,* Jurist og Økonomforbundets Forlag, Copenhagen.

Due, J., J.S. Madsen, C.S. Jensen and L.K. Petersen 1994, *The survival of the Danish Model – A historical sociological analysis of the Danish system of collective bargaining,* DJØF Publishing, Copenhagen.

Folketingsbeslutning om bedre integration og sikring af udlændinges retsstilling i Danmark, nr. B 65, Passed on the 18 June 1992.

Forslag til Folketingsbeslutning om en samlet indsats for bedre integration af flygtninge og indvanderere, nr. B 71, fremsat den 19 November 1997.

Hammer, O. and I. Bruun 2000, *Etniske minoriteters indflydelseskanaler,* Magtudredningen, Århus.

Hvidt, K. 1990, *Det folkelige gennembrud og dets mænd. Gyldendal og Politikens Danmarkshistorie.* Gyldendal and Politiken, Copenhagen.

Indenrigsministeriet 1997, *Betænkning 1337: Integration. Betænkning afgivet af det af indenrigsministeren nedsatte Integrationsudvalg,* Indenrigsministeriet, Copenhagen.

Jørgensen, H. 2002, *Consensus, Cooperation and Conflict – The Policy Making Process in Denmark,* Edward Elgar, Cheltenham.

Kaspersen, L.B. and L. Ottesen 2001, 'Associationalism for 150 Years and Still Alive and Kicking: Some Reflections on Danish Civil Society', in *Critical Review of International Social and Political Philosophy,* 4 (1), Spring 2001.

Kaspersen, L.B. 2003, 'Denmark During the Eras of Internationalisation and Europeanisation 1801-2001', in *Sociologisk Rapportserie,* 2, Department of Sociology, University of Copenhagen, Copenhagen.

Kaspersen, L.B. 2004, 'How Denmark Became Democratic. The Impact of Warfare and Military Reforms', in *Acta Sociologica,* 47 (1), March, pp.. 71-89.

Kaspersen, L.B. 2006, 'The Formation of the Danish Welfare State: Decisions in the State of Exception', in J.L. Campell , J.A. Hall and O.K. Pedersen (eds.), *National*

Identity and the Varieties of Capitalism, McGill University Press, Montreal, pp. 99-132.

Katzenstein, P.J. 1985, *Small States in World Markets, Industrial Policy in Europe*, Cornell University Press, Ithaca and London.

Knudsen, K., H. Caspersen and V.O. Nielsen 1991, *Kampen for en bedre tilværelse – arbejdernes historie i Danmark fra 1800-tallet til 1990*, SFAH skriftserie, 26, SFAH, Copenhagen.

Knudsen, K. 1999, *Arbejdskonflikternes historie i Danmark – arbejdskampe og arbejderbevægelse 1870-1940*, SFAH skriftserie, 41, Copenhagen

Lembruch, G. 1984, 'Concertation and the Structure of Corporatist Networks', in J. Goldthorpe (ed.), *Order and Conflict in Contemporary Capitalism*, Oxford University Press, New York, pp. 60-80.

Lijphart, A. and M. Crepaz 1991, 'Corporatism and Consensus Democracy in Eighteen Countries', in *British Journal of Political Science*, 21, pp. 235-256.

Mann, M. 1977, 'States, ancient and Modern', in *Archives europennes de sociologie*, 18.

Mann, M. 1984, 'The autonomous power of the state: its origins, mechanism and results', in *Archives europennes de sociologie*, XXV, pp. 185-213.

Mann, M. 1986, *The Sources of Social Power, vol. 1. A History of Power from the Beginning to AD 1760*, Cambridge University Press, Cambridge.

Mann, M. 1988, *States, War and Capitalism*, Blackwell, Oxford.

Mann, M. 1993, *The Sources of Social Power vol. 2*, Cambridge University Press, Cambridge.

Mikkelsen, F. 1991, *Institutional Conflict in Scandinavia 1848-1990*, Papers in Organization, 8, CBS, Copenhagen.

Mikkelsen, F. 1992, *Arbejdskonflikter i Skandinavien 1848-1990*, Odense University Studies in History and Social Sciences, 143, Odense Universitets Forlag.

Mikkelsen, F. (ed.) 2003, *Invandrerorganizationer i* Norden, Nordisk Ministerråd and Akademiet for Migrationsstudier i Danmark Nord.

Nørgaard, A.S. 2000, 'Party Politics and the Organization of the Danish Welfare State 1890-1920: The Bourgois Roots of the Modern Welfare State', in *Scandinavian Political Studies*, 23 (3), pp. 183-215.

Nørgaard, A.S. 1999, 'Arbejdsmarkedspolitik: Korporatisme til alle tider og alle sider', in J. Blom-Hansen and C. Daugbjerg, *Magtens organisering. Stat og interesseorganizationer i Danmark*, Systime, Aarhus.

Rasmussen, E. 1965, *Danmarks Historie. Velfærdsstaten på Vej 1913-1939*, 13, Politikens Forlag, Copenhagen.

Rasmussen, S.H. 2000, 'Danmark efter 1973', in S. Busck and H. Poulsen (eds), *Danmarks historie – i grundtræk*, Aarhus Universitetsforlag, Aarhus.

Rerup, L. 1989, *Danmarks historie. Bd. 6. Tiden 1864*-1914, Gyldendal, Copenhagen.

Schmitter, P.C. 1981, 'Interest Intermediation and Regime Governability in Contemporary Western Europe and North America', in S. Berger (ed.), *Organizing Interests in Western Europe*, Cambridge University Press, Cambridge.

Schmitter, P.C. 1974, 'Still the Century of Corporatism?', in *Review of Politics*, 36 (1), pp. 85-131.

Skovgaard-Petersen, V. 1985, *Danmarks historie. Bd. 5. Tiden 1814*-1864, Gyldendal, Copenhagen.

Vigen, A. 1950, 'Rigsdagen og erhversorganisationerne', in *Den Danske Rigsdag, bd. III* (Rigsdagen og folket), Published by Statsministeriet and Rigsdagens Præsidium, J.H. Schultz, Copenhagen.

Zeuthenudvalget 1992, *Rapport fra udredningsudvalget om arbejdsmarkedets strukturproblemer*.

List of Interviews

Hedegaard, B., Head of Department, Local Government Denmark (integration policy).

Kamm, A., Secretary General, Danish Refugee Council (integration policy).

Kjær, K.U., Senior Research Fellow, The Danish Institute for Human Rights (integration policy) (interview conducted via e-mail).

Krog, O., Head of Departement, DA (The Danish Employers' Confederation) (employment policy).

Kyvsgaard, H., Afdelingsleder (assistant secretary), The Ministry for Refugee, Immigration and Integration Affairs (integration policy).

Larsen, F., Consultant in LO (The Danish Confederation of Trade Unions) (employment policy).

Lassen, M., Associate Professor Ålborg University (employment policy).

Mailand, M., Assistant Professer, FAOS, Department of Sociology, University of Copenhagen (employment policy).

Mikkelsen, F., Associate Professor, The Academy for Migration Studies in Denmark (integration policy).

Mølbach, J., AC (The Danish Confederation of Professional Associations) (employment policy).

Olsen, I., President of Ledernes Hovedorganisation (The Danish Association of Managers

and Executives) (employment policy).

Rosted, J., Leader of the Secretariat of the Zeuthen Committee, Financial director in the Ministery of Finance (employment policy).

Zeuthen, H.E., Professor Chairman Director of the Danish Statistical Agency and chairman of the Zeuthen Committee (employment policy).

Curriculum Vitae for Ove K. Pedersen

Personal Curriculum
Born 1948-02-06

Education
M.Sc. 1978 University of Copenhagen (Political Science).
Maitrise 1973 Universitè de Paris, VIII (Philosophy of Language).
Licence 1972 Universitè de Paris, VIII (Philosophy of Language).
1970 Danish School of Journalism, Århus (Journalism).

Academic specializations
Comparative Political Economy, Business and Politics, Institutional Analysis, Institutional History, Public Administration, Political Theory, State Theory, Philosophy of Science.

Professional employment
Director of International Center for Business and Politics, Copenhagen Business School, Copenhagen, 2004-2008.

Professor of Comparative Political Economy, Copenhagen Business School, Copenhagen, 2004-.

Adjunct Professor of Public Administration, Aalborg University, 2002-

Professor of Comparative Politics, Department of Political Science, Copenhagen University, 1997-2004.

Before 1997: Associate professor, Roskilde University and Copenhagen Business School.

A selected Bibliography of research published in English

Edited volumes

Pedersen, Ove K., (with Campbell, John L., Hall A. John), (eds.), 2006, *National Identity and Varieties of Capitalism: The Danish Experience.* Montreal: McGill-Queen´s University Press.

Pedersen, Ove K., (with Jacobsson, Bengt, Lægreid, Per), 2004, *Europeanization and Transnational States, Comparing Central Nordic Governments*, London: Routledge Press.

Pedersen, Ove K. (with Campbell, John L.), (eds.), 2001, *The Rise of Neoliberalism and Institutional Analysis*, New Jersey: Princeton University Press.

Pedersen, Ove K. (with Campbell, John L.), (eds.), 1996, *Legacies of Change. Transformations of Post Communist European Economies*, Aldine de Gruyter, New York.

Pedersen, Ove K. and Ronit, Karsten, (eds.), 1995 The Building of Interest Representation in Eastern Europe, Journal of Transforming Economies and Societies, vol. 1, no. 2, autumn 1994.

Pedersen, Ove K., Hausner, Jerzy and Ronit, Karsten, (eds.), 1995, *Evolution of Interest Representation and Development of the Labour Market in Post-Socialist Countries*, Cracow: Cracow Academy of Economies and Friedrich Ebert Stiftung.

Pedersen, Ove K., (with Jessop, Bob and Kastendiek, Hans, Nielsen Klaus), (eds.), 1991, *The Politics of Flexibility. Restructuring State and Industry in Britain, Germany and Scandinavia*, (eds.), Edward Elgar, London, England.

Papers and Chapters

Pedersen, Ove K. and Dorthe Pedersen, 2000, »The Europeanization of Local Interests in Denmark: The Strategic Choice – to Go Through vs. By-pass National Institutions«, in Janerik Gidlund and Magnus Jerneck (eds.), *Local and Regional Governance in Europe*, Aldershot: Edward Elgar, pp. 51-76.

Pedersen, Ove K and Peter Kjær, 2001, »Translating Liberalization: Neo-liberalism in the Danish Negotiated Economy«, in Campbell, John L. and Ove K. Pedersen, *The Rise of Neoliberalism and Institutional Analysis*, New Jersey: Princeton University Press, pp. 219-248.

Pedersen, Ove K. and John L. Campbell, 2001, »The Rise of Neoliberalism and Institutional Analysis«, in Campbell, John L. and Ove K. Pedersen, *The Rise of Neoliberalism and Institutional Analysis*, New Jersey: Princeton University Press, p. 1-24.

Pedersen, Ove K. and John L. Campbell, 2001, »The Second Movement in Institutional Analysis«, in Campbell, John L. and Ove K. Pedersen, *The Rise of Neoliberalism and Institutional Analysis*, New Jersey: Princeton University Press, pp. 249-282.

Jacobsson, Bengt, Per Lægreid and Ove K. Pedersen, 2004, »The Transnationalisation of Nordic Central Administration«, in *Zeitschrift für Staats- und Europawissenschaften*, hft 1/2004, pp. 32-55.

Pedersen, Ove K., 2006, »Negotiated Economy: Corporatism and beyond«, in John L. Campbell, John A. Hall and Ove K. Pedersen, (eds.), *National Identity and Varieties of Capitalism. The Danish Experience*, Montreal: McGill University Press, 245-270.

Pedersen, Ove K., 2006, »Denmark – An Ongoing Experiment«, in John L. Campbell, John A. Hall and Ove K. Pedersen, (eds.), *National Identity and Varieties of Capitalism. The Danish Experience*, Montreal: McGill University Press, 453-470.

Pedersen, Ove K. and John L. Campbell, 2007, »The Varieties of Capitalism and Hybrid Success. Denmark in the Global Economy«, *Comparative Political Studies*, vol. 40, no. 3, March 2007, pp. 307-332.

Pedersen, Ove K., 2007, »Interest Organizations and European Integration«, in Ron Holzhäcker and Erik Albæk, *Dialogue on Democracy*, London: Palgrave Macmillan.

Pedersen, Ove K. and Campbell John L., 2007, »Institutional Competitiveness in the Global Economy: Denmark, United States and the Varieties of Capitalism, *Regulation and Governance*, September.

Pedersen Ove K. and Campbell John L., 2007, »Knowledge Regimes and Comparative Political Economy«, in Daniel Bèland and Robert H. Cox, (eds.), *Ideas and Politics in Social Science Research*, Princeton: Princeton University Press.

Index